China's Low Fertility and the Impacts of the Two-Child Policy

This book examines China's fertility transition over the past seven decades and explores the socioeconomic impacts of the two-child policy.

The first half of this book highlights the characteristics of China's low fertility and the risk of falling to an ultra-low state, aiming to answer the question: *How China's fertility is changing and evolving? How low is China's fertility? What are the demographic structure, driving forces and institutional characteristics of China's low fertility?* The second half models the impacts of the two-child policy on China's population trends and demands for women, infant and child health services, and education resources for preschool, compulsive education, addressing the questions of *how the two-child policy affects fertility behaviours of Chinese women, particularly the second-child fertility? How would the two-child policy impact China's future population trends, particularly labour supply and population aging? What are the consequences for obstetrics and gynaecological services, paediatrics and childcare services; and for school capacity and demand for teachers over compulsory education?*

The book will be an essential read for students and scholars of Chinese studies, population and demography studies, and those interested in contemporary China.

Professor Wei Chen is a Professor of Demography at the Center for Population and Development Studies, the Renmin University of China. His areas of research interests include fertility and fertility policy. He publishes widely in the field of population and development, particularly on fertility and aging.

China's Low Fertility and the Impacts of the Two-Child Policy

Wei Chen

LONDON AND NEW YORK

This research is supported by a grant from China Social Sciences Foundation (No.15ZDC036).

First published 2024
by Routledge
4 Park Square, Milton Park, Abingdon, Oxon OX14 4RN

and by Routledge
605 Third Avenue, New York, NY 10158

Routledge is an imprint of the Taylor & Francis Group, an informa business

© 2024 Wei Chen

The right of Wei Chen to be identified as author of this work has been asserted in accordance with sections 77 and 78 of the Copyright, Designs and Patents Act 1988.

All rights reserved. No part of this book may be reprinted or reproduced or utilised in any form or by any electronic, mechanical, or other means, now known or hereafter invented, including photocopying and recording, or in any information storage or retrieval system, without permission in writing from the publishers.

Trademark notice: Product or corporate names may be trademarks or registered trademarks, and are used only for identification and explanation without intent to infringe.

English Version by permission of Tsinghua University Press.

British Library Cataloguing-in-Publication Data
A catalogue record for this book is available from the British Library

Library of Congress Cataloging-in-Publication Data
Names: Chen, Wei, 1964- author.
Title: China's low fertility and the impacts of the two-child policy / Wei Chen.
Description: Abingdon, Oxon ; New York, NY : Routledge, 2024. | Includes bibliographical references and index. |
Identifiers: LCCN 2023010557 (print) | LCCN 2023010558 (ebook) | ISBN 9781032552316 (hardback) | ISBN 9781032552354 (paperback) | ISBN 9781003429661 (ebook)
Subjects: LCSH: Fertility, Human—China. | China—Population policy. | Family policy—China.
Classification: LCC HB1064.A3 C34 2024 (print) | LCC HB1064.A3 (ebook) | DDC 362.82/5610951—dc23/eng/20230602
LC record available at https://lccn.loc.gov/2023010557
LC ebook record available at https://lccn.loc.gov/2023010558

ISBN: 978-1-032-55231-6 (hbk)
ISBN: 978-1-032-55235-4 (pbk)
ISBN: 978-1-003-42966-1 (ebk)

DOI: 10.4324/9781003429661

Typeset in Times New Roman
by codeMantra

Contents

1 Introduction 1

2 Trends in Fertility Transition 9

3 Estimation of China's Low Fertility Rates in 2000–2010 21

4 China's Fertility Trends in the Period from 2006 to 2017 57

5 How Low Is China's Fertility Rate 69

6 Structural Shifts in Fertility Rate 86

7 Quantum Effect and Tempo Effect of Fertility 93

8 Intermediate Fertility Variables 111

9 Counterfactual Fertility Trends 127

10 The Two-Child Policy and Fertility 141

11 Demographic Trends under the Two-Child Policy 159

12 Labor Supply 177

13	Aging Population	192
14	The Impact of the Two-Child Policy on Demand for Maternal and Child Health Services	217
15	The Impact of the Two-Child Policy on Preschool- and School-Age Populations and the Demand for Teachers	233
16	Pro-Natalist Policies in Developed Countries and Their Effects	274
17	Summary and Conclusion	290
	Index	*311*

1 Introduction

China's miracle of rapid demographic and economic change has received worldwide attention. From the perspective of China's development stage and population scale, China's demographic transition is a milestone event in human history, which has challenged the conventional theory of demographic transition and opened up a fast and successful path for the developing countries. China's demographic transition and its continuous low fertility have exerted a profound influence not only on China's population and development but also on the world's population trend and development pattern. At a time when China's population, economy and society are undergoing great transformations, China's fertility policy has also undergone a major shift, with the universal two-child policy implemented in 2016.

The end of the era of the one-child policy and the beginning of the era of the two-child policy are a critical turning point in the development history of China's population and family planning. In terms of demographic theory, the one-child policy (and the one-and-half-child policy) is a policy aiming at population reduction, while the two-child policy is a policy oriented to population stabilization and balanced development. A policy aiming at stable and balanced development is of great significance not only for intergenerational balance and family well-being but also for social harmony and economic development. The purpose of this study is to systematically sort out the process of China's fertility transition and low fertility, analyze the characteristics of the evolution of the low fertility and investigate the impact of the two-child policy on fertility. In addition, the social and economic effects of the two-child policy are also evaluated through the long-term impact of fertility changes on population size and structure. The influence of the two-child policy will be extensive and far-reaching, and the prospective research on its effect is full of challenges.

Research Objectives and Significance

Before the 1970s, fertility in China was similar to that of other developing countries, at a very high level of total fertility rate (TFR), around six births per woman. In the 1970s, China's fertility saw its first transition, falling by more than half in a short period of time, creating the so-called "Chinese Model" of demographic transition. Since the 1990s, China's fertility has experienced the second transition,

DOI: 10.4324/9781003429661-1

falling below the replacement level (2.1) and continuing to decline. As fertility continues to shift, China's fertility pattern has undergone profound changes. At the same time, sex selection at birth remains strong. China's fertility pattern at a low level is strikingly different from that of other low-fertility countries. Although numerous studies have been conducted on the transition of fertility and low fertility in China, there is still a lack of systematic review and comprehensive investigation on the transition process of fertility since the founding of the People's Republic and the continuous low fertility after entering this century. In particular, the process and level of China's low fertility have been debated for nearly 20 years. Meanwhile, the latest national fertility survey provides excellent data to examine the recent trend of low fertility in China, especially the impact of the two-child policy. One of the purposes of this study is to systematically investigate and analyze the transition and process of low fertility in China over the past 70 years and to estimate and analyze the low fertility level and evolution characteristics of low fertility in China by using data from a variety of sources and different methods and models. At the same time, fertility decline and low fertility in China are jointly determined by the family planning policy and economic and social development. The early stage of fertility decline is dominated by the family planning policy, while low fertility in the late stage is determined by the economic and social development. What would be the trend of China's fertility rate if the family planning policy were not implemented? This study also analyzes the long-term effects of China's family planning policy by using the human development index (HDI) data and counterfactual prediction of TFR assuming without the family planning policy based on the World Model and the East Model, respectively.

The study of the fertility transition and the pattern of low fertility in China not only has direct relevance for the strategic choice of national population development in the future but also provides insights into understanding the world population and development trend. According to the United Nations population data, during 1975–2000, the TFR of developing regions excluding China was 0.6–0.7 births higher than that of developing regions as a whole, and the population growth rate was 0.27–0.33 percentage points higher. Clearly, China's declining fertility rate has important implications for demographic trends in the developing world and the whole world. A recent study suggests that without China's family planning policy, the world's population would have increased by 1 billion by 2060 (Goodkind, 2017). Therefore, it's no exaggeration to say that China's impact on the global population is staggering.

The decline and evolution of China's fertility are similar to those of other low-fertility countries, but there are also big differences. Investigating the pattern of low fertility and analyzing the evolution characteristics of low fertility in China has important implications for understanding the future trend of fertility changes in China, and for the existing theories of fertility transition and low fertility. At the same time, it could shed light on the low fertility trap theory and its applicability to China.

From the selective to the universal two-child policy, the effect of the policy and the related fertility and population development trends have been widely concerned and discussed. What appears most frequently in various publications is the general opinion that the policy is largely ineffective, which often lacks clear and unified concept definition and method application. The implementation effect of the two-child policy involves all aspects of population and social economy. How to explore the policy effect comprehensively, objectively and scientifically and avoid biased understanding is of great academic and practical significance.

Therefore, another main purpose of this study is to explore the impact of the two-child policy on fertility and the future fertility trend, as well as its long-term impact on population size and structure based on the investigation of the evolution characteristics of China's low fertility. Through the change in population size and structure, the possible influence on social and economic development is further assessed. Finally, this study discusses policy implications and proposes a supporting policy system for fertility and family development for further adjusting and improving fertility policy and coping with the risk of falling into an extremely low fertility range.

Research Contents and Methods

The purpose of this study is to systematically review the process of fertility transition and the evolution of low fertility in China in the past 70 years, analyze the characteristics of low fertility pattern in China, investigate the recent levels and trends in fertility under the two-child policy and the population impact of the two-child policy, further explore the impact on social and economic development and provide some policy suggestions. According to this general purpose, the contents of this study are divided into 17 chapters.

Chapter 1 is the introduction, which clarifies the purpose and significance of this study, explains the data and methods used in this study and discusses the innovations and limitations of this study.

Chapter 2 reviews the trends in fertility in China, analyzing the changing pattern of fertility and evolution characteristics of fertility transition in different stages based on the economic, social and political changes and the family planning policies. The data used in this chapter come from China statistical yearbooks, population censuses, fertility surveys and world population datasets from the United Nations Population Division and the Population Reference Bureau. The research methods used in this study include a variety of demographic indicators and models for descriptive and comparative analysis.

In Chapter 3, we estimate the low fertility level in China, using various data and methods to analyze China's low fertility level since the beginning of this century. Using census data, education statistics and household registration statistics, we first estimate the fertility rate for over 2000–2009 by cohort analysis, regression analysis and backward survival method. Then, the fertility level in 2010 is estimated by using the Brass indirect fertility estimation method using two types of fertility data from the 2010 census. Finally, the average fertility rate from 2000 to 2010 is estimated as a verification of the results in the above two sections. Using 2000 and 2010 census data, generalized stable population models, including the variable-r method and integration method, are used for estimation.

4 Introduction

Chapter 4 evaluates the fertility levels and trends in China in the past decade using the 2017 National Fertility Survey data. The 2017 National Fertility Survey is the latest fertility survey organized by the former National Health and Family Planning Commission. It aims to assess and understand the current fertility behavior, fertility intention and childbearing and rearing services available in China, using mainly the pregnancy and birth history data of women in the survey to systematically estimate and analyze the recent fertility trend and the impact of the two-child policy through a variety of indicators measuring period and cohort fertility, progression-ratio-based fertility and intrinsic fertility.

Chapter 5 compares and analyzes the process of low fertility in China with different data sources, in order to better understand the evolution and characteristics of low fertility. The data that can be used to reflect the process and level of China's low fertility include the population survey data of the National Bureau of Statistics and the fertility survey data of the former National Health and Family Planning Commission, from which fertility levels and trends can be directly obtained. There are household statistics from the Ministry of Public Security, which can be used to estimate fertility levels and trends from the age data. These data from different sources have their own strengths and weaknesses and can reflect common trends of fertility. Where it is impossible to evaluate and confirm which data is the most reliable, comparative analysis of these data can also be used to judge the characteristics, levels and evolution of low fertility in China and reveal the differences in the trends of low fertility reflected by these data. The methods involve using fertility rate, first marriage rate and age at first marriage for descriptive analysis and comparative analysis.

Chapter 6 examines the changes in fertility structure, including parity, age, interval and sex structure, and analyzes the structural characteristics of low fertility in China through international comparison. The data used in this chapter come from China's population censuses and sample surveys, fertility surveys, as well as the European Union population database and human fertility database. In order to reveal the demographic characteristics of fertility change and low fertility pattern in China, descriptive analysis and comparative analysis are conducted using various fertility index, including average age at marriage and childbearing and sex ratio at birth.

Chapter 7 explores the structural changes of the "quantum effect" and "tempo effect", two driving forces of fertility change in the process of fertility transition and low fertility in China. Any change in fertility is determined by these two drivers, so a rise or a fall in fertility can be broken down into a rise or a fall caused by one or both of the two drivers. The period TFR is influenced by these two driving forces and often fails to reflect the actual fertility level. In view of the defects caused by the assumptions contained in the tempo-adjusted TFR, we use the intrinsic fertility rate to reflect fertility level. Data used in this chapter include fertility surveys, population censuses and sample surveys.

Chapter 8 discusses the intermediate variables of fertility, which are the factors that directly influence fertility, namely marriage, contraception, induced abortion and breastfeeding, and their impacts on the recent fertility trends in China. In 1978, Bongaarts proposed the intermediate variable fertility model to estimate the fertility level or decompose the intermediate variables influencing fertility. In 2015, Bongaarts made revisions based on the original model. This chapter uses the revised intermediate variable fertility model to estimate and analyze the fertility level and trend in China in recent years and examines the influence of the intermediate variables through a decomposition analysis.

Chapter 9 performs a counterfactual fertility analysis, which aims to estimate what levels and trends of China's fertility would have been if the family planning policy had not been implemented. Fertility decline and low fertility in China are jointly determined by the family planning policy and economic and social development. China's fertility decline in the early stage is dominated by the family planning policy, while low fertility in the late stage is determined by the economic and social development. This chapter uses HDI and fertility rate to construct regression models and makes counterfactual predictions on the TFR based on the World Model and the East Model, respectively, to explore the long-term effects of China's family planning policy.

Chapter 10 on the two-child policy and second-child fertility examines the trends in the second-child fertility and population characteristics of second births in China in the context of implementing the two-child policy. China's fertility policy is the most important institutional determinant of the low fertility pattern in China. The 2017 fertility survey data of the former National Health and Family Planning Commission provide the latest data to examine this institutional feature, namely the impact of the two-child policy on China's fertility. In Chapter 3, this survey data was used to analyze the recent fertility changes in China, and this chapter focuses on the investigation of the second-child fertility rate. In addition to the overall analysis of the impact of the two-child policy on the trend and level of the second-child fertility rate, the characteristics of women having a second birth are investigated, and the factors affecting the second-child fertility rate under the two-child policy are discussed using the discrete-time Logit model.

Chapter 11 looks at the long-term impacts of the two-child policy on China's population change. According to the two-child policy and the impact of future economic and social development on fertility, different fertility scenarios, high, medium and low, are prepared when conducting population projections to examine the trend of population size and structure in China. The low-fertility scenario is the one that maintains the original policy unchanged, while the medium and high scenarios are the assumptions of fertility trend under the two-child policy. The population effects of the two-child policy can be estimated by comparing the results of the medium and high scenarios with the low scenario.

Chapter 12 on labor supply provides further estimates of the effective labor supply based on the prediction of labor supply in the previous chapter and the impact of labor participation rate and human capital changes. By creating an effective labor supply model incorporating human capital, combining the quantity, structure and quality of labor force, the future labor supply in China can be more accurately estimated.

Chapter 13 on population aging examines trends and characteristics of the aging population in China, particularly the impacts of the two-child policy. The pace of

6 *Introduction*

aging is determined by the pace of fertility transition, and demographic simulations are prepared to reveal the relationship between fertility decline and aging, as well as the family structure, number and structure of relatives in different life stages of the elderly population at different fertility levels. The increasing heterogeneity of older people is also discussed.

Chapter 14 assesses the impacts of the two-child policy on maternal and child health service demand. The impacts of the two-child policy on the demand for medical and health services in pediatrics, obstetrics and gynecology are calculated based on the current medical and health resources, the number and age structure of pregnant and lying women, the proportion, type and standard of prenatal care and maternal health care, and the matching degree of beds, doctors and nurses according to the trends in births and child population under the two-child policy.

Chapter 15 discusses the impact of the two-child policy on preschool and school-age population and the demand for teachers. The two-child policy has brought about an increase in the number of births, and the accumulation of births will lead to an increase in the demand for child care, preschool and primary education in recent years, which will be mainly reflected in the demand for school facilities and teachers. Based on the demographic changes brought about by the two-child policy, this chapter measures the impact on education-related demand through indicators such as enrollment rate, teacher–student ratio and education expenditure index.

Chapter 16 reviews family policies in the developed countries and their effects on encouraging fertility. Explicit and implicit policies can be identified, represented by Sweden, France, Germany and Japan, and the fertility effects and the mechanisms are analyzed in the child cost-utility framework proposed by Leibenstein.

The final chapter, Chapter 17, summarizes the content of this research, draws conclusions and discusses policy implications.

Innovations and Limitations

This research is innovative in the following aspects:

1 In the estimation of fertility level, we use multiple sources of data and multiple methods for a comparative analysis and assessment. Previous studies generally relied on a single source of data or method to estimate fertility levels and relied on certain assumptions for data evaluation and adjustment. As there are many data sources that can be used to estimate fertility level, each type of data has its own advantages and disadvantages. Although the overall trend of fertility implied in these sources of data is broadly similar, there are great differences in the fertility level. In the past, scholars also had different assessments on the quality of various data, and there were debates about the quantity of reliable data. In fact, we still can't reach a consensus on which data is the most reliable and most useful. If only one kind of data is relied on to estimate fertility, the reliability of the estimate cannot be fully judged. Therefore, it is a scientific analysis perspective to use various data, seek common ground while reserving differences and use various methods to achieve the same goal. At the same time,

for a variety of data, the use of a variety of methods is also appropriate in the scientific research that could be adopted to check each other.
2 When analyzing the low fertility pattern, it is also a novel perspective to combine the demographic structure characteristics of fertility with the structural characteristics of driving force. The structural characteristics of fertility, such as number of children, age, interval and gender, are actually the static characteristics of fertility. The structural characteristics of the driving forces that divide fertility change into "quantity effect" and "tempo effect" can be said to be the dynamic characteristics of fertility, that is, how these two driving forces act independently or/and jointly to cause fertility change. In addition, the decomposition analysis of these two forces has been rare in previous fertility studies. Some studies have estimated the tempo effect of fertility decline in China in the 1990s, but it may be overestimated or underestimated due to the defects of tempo-adjusted fertility indicators. In this study, we estimate the two forces of fertility transition and low fertility process over the past several decades and use intrinsic fertility index, which can predict fertility level more accurately. The changing patterns and characteristics of these two forces are revealed, which shed new insights into understanding the low fertility pattern in China.
3 Based on the latest data from the 2017 National Fertility Survey, the levels and trends of fertility in China in the past decade are fully analyzed, and the influence of the two-child policy on fertility rate is discussed. The characteristics of women who have two children under the two-child policy and the influencing factors of the second-child fertility are investigated. In particular, the author discriminates the difference between the current population having a second child and the population having a second child before the implementation of the two-child policy, having noted the short-term effect in the increase of the second-child fertility from the perspective of the population characteristics having a second child. Having seen the dramatic decline in the rate of first marriage and first childbearing of women, it is proposed that China may have entered a marriage revolution, which will weaken the basis for the two-child policy to play a role in the long term. China is at great risk of falling into very low fertility.
4 When discussing the impact of population change brought by the two-child policy on labor supply, the effective labor supply is proposed and estimated. When discussing the impact of the two-child policy on labor force, we should not only examine the changing trend of working-age population but also need to consider the impact of labor force participation rate and labor quality (human capital). Censuses since 1990 have shown a steady decline in labor force participation rates for both sexes in China, especially among the young population. However, with the expansion of college and higher education, the education level of both sexes has been greatly improved, which can to a large extent compensate for the decline in labor force participation rate. In this study, an effective labor supply model incorporating human capital is established to more accurately estimate the future labor supply by combining the quantity, structure and quality of labor.
5 In terms of policy suggestions, this study proposes the construction of policy system, focusing on a strong family development support policy system to

promote marriage and fertility. It is not only systematic but also specific and directional, providing useful reference for decision-making and policy making.

There are also limitations in this study:

1 In the estimation of fertility, different sources of data are used recognizing their own advantages and disadvantages, but the data quality is not further evaluated. Part of the reason is that some studies have done evaluation on the registration process and characteristics of household registration statistics and education statistics through field investigations and interviews, but further and updated understanding of whether the situation has changed in recent years is needed, which can provide a more solid foundation to accurately estimate fertility in recent years.
2 The data of the 2017 National Fertility Survey are used to analyze the recent fertility changes, especially to investigate the impact of the two-child policy on fertility. By the year when the survey was conducted, it was only one and a half years after the implementation of the two-child policy, and the long-accumulated fertility potential had not been fully released. Thus, women's fertility intention and its relationship with fertility behavior cannot be fully investigated. In addition, the substantial decline in women's first marriage rate and first child birth rate reflected in the 2017 fertility survey is a significant change that deserves special attention. It is necessary to conduct more in-depth and detailed analysis, including population characteristics and influencing factors, and understand the marriage and childbearing behavior of different generations, as well as the impact of social environment and changing lifestyle through interviews and surveys, in order to explain this major shift and assess the future trend.

References

Goodkind D M. 2017. The Astonishing Population Averted by China's Birth Restrictions: Estimates, Nightmares, and Reprogrammed Ambitions. *Demography* 54:1375–1400.

2 Trends in Fertility Transition

Based on comparative historical analysis, China's family planning and economic reform are two great initiatives in human history, respectively, creating a "Chinese model" in economic takeoff and demographic transition. Western scholars take fertility transition in China as one of the most significant events in human history (Harrell et al., 2011). The reason why China's fertility transition can be seen as a revolution is that it is in the world's most populous and economically backward country that the most rapid fertility transition took place, and the transition also had a greater impact on global population development than other countries (Feeney, 1994). Fertility transition in China and low fertility have radically changed the development and scale of China's population, and the demographic dividend brought by them has contributed significantly to China's rapid economic growth over the past decades.

From the founding of the People's Republic to the early 1970s, fertility in China was similar to that of other developing countries, with a total fertility rate (TFR) of around six births per woman, while the current rate is far below the replacement level. According to the data provided by the United Nations, Figure 2.1 shows the change of TFR in China and developing regions. In the 1950s and 1960s, China and those regions had a high TFR. However, since the 1970s, China has witnessed a rapid decline in fertility, with the rate falling from 6 in 1965–1970 to 2.5 in 1980–1985 and below 2 in 1990–1995. During that period, fertility declined in other developing regions as well, but very slowly. At present, Africa records the highest TFR at 4.72 and Latin America has the lowest at 2.14, which are much higher than China's. Since the late 1990s, China's fertility has been on a downward trend. This chapter describes and analyzes the process and trend in fertility transition in China.

High Fertility Regime

Historical demographers believe that the high fertility before the founding of People's Republic was not uncontrolled, and even the marital fertility of Chinese women at that time was even lower than that of European women before the transition (Zhao, 1997a, 1997b). However, due to the differences in marriage patterns, the TFR in China was similar to Europe's, or even higher. According to some surveys conducted in the early 20th century, the average fertility of married women

DOI: 10.4324/9781003429661-2

10 *Trends in Fertility Transition*

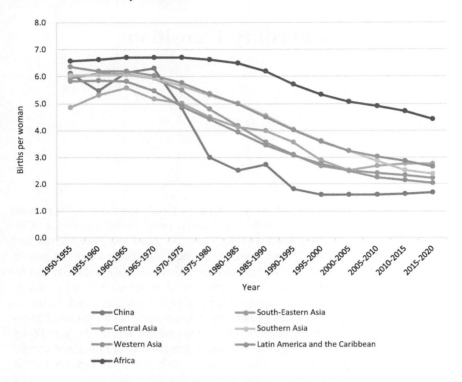

Figure 2.1 TFR in China and developing regions, 1950–2020
Source: United Nations. World Population Prospects: The 2019 Revision.

in China was 6–7 births. China's one-per-thousand fertility survey in 1982 shows that the average TFR in 1945–1949 was 5.1 (possibly underestimated due to older women being excluded due to backcasting). The population reproduction before 1949 is obvious, a pattern of high fertility and high mortality. The high fertility regime continued into the early period of the People's Republic.

Figures 2.2 and 2.3 show the demographic and fertility trends in China since 1949. In 1949, the birth rate for China was as high as 36 per thousand and the TFR was 6.14. By 1969, the birth rate was still as high as 34.11 per thousand and the TFR was 5.67. From 1949 to 1969, except for the significant decline due to three-year natural disasters, the birth rate was as high as 35–38 per thousand in most years, and TFR was as high as 5.5–6.5. In fact, there was no obvious change in birth rates or fertility levels in China during that period, which were actually stable and high. However, due to the dramatic decline in the death rate, China's population grew rapidly. The death rate dropped from 20 per thousand in 1949 to 9.5 per thousand in 1965, and the average life expectancy increased by 20 years. From 1962 to 1969, the natural population growth rate, the annual number of births and the annual population growth were over 26 per thousand, 25–30 million and 18–21 million, respectively.

Figure 2.2 Birth rate, death rate and natural growth rate in China from 1949 to 2019
Source: National Bureau of Statistics. https://data.stats.gov.cn/easyquery.htm?cn=C01.

In the early 1950s, China had a stable social environment after the founding of the People's Republic. Its industrial and agricultural production developed rapidly, and living standards and medical conditions improved significantly. During that period, the first baby boom occurred (Figure 2.4), and the population began to grow rapidly. At that time, China also copied Soviet planned economy model and population policy. In order to protect the health of women and children, Chinese government issued documents and decrees banning abortion in 1950 and 1952. This actually encouraged fertility. But the national population was 594 million in 1953 as reported in China's first census, much higher than expectations. The government started to realize the impact of rapid population growth on economic development and living standards, and some people wanted to have birth control because they had too many children. China carried out its first family planning between 1954 and 1958, during which the government issued related documents and took measures to encourage birth control and relax the restrictions on induced abortion. However, due to later unfavorable political environment, China failed to make substantive achievements.

The Great Leap Forward and three-year natural disasters were followed by a second, much larger-scale baby boom that lasted more than a decade (Figure 2.4). The Chinese government reconsidered population control in 1962 and introduced family planning in urban areas. The second family planning program from 1962

12   *Trends in Fertility Transition*

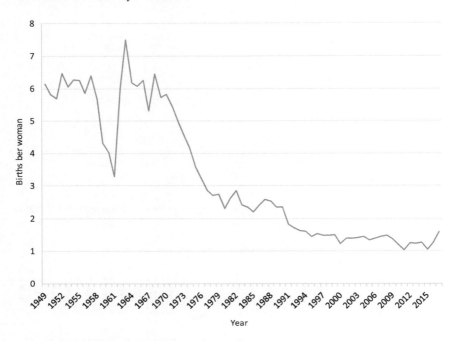

Figure 2.3 Total fertility rate in China from 1949 to 2017

Source: Data for 1949–1988 from the 1988 two-per-thousand fertility survey; Data for 1989 and later years from population censuses and population sample surveys.

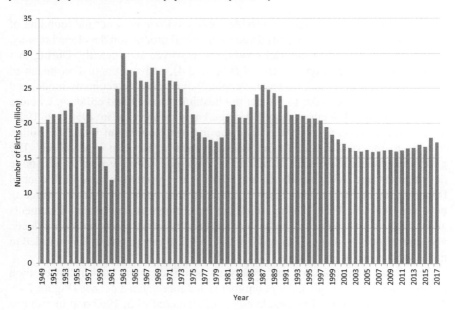

Figure 2.4 Number of births in China from 1949 to 2017

Source: National Bureau of Statistics. https://data.stats.gov.cn/easyquery.htm?cn=C01.

to 1966 had a significant impact on fertility in urban areas and even in some more developed rural coastal areas. The TFR in urban areas fell to 4.4 in 1964 and below 4 in 1965 and continued to decline. However, during the "Cultural Revolution", which is a political movement, family planning and other social and economic activities were suspended. In the late 1960s, the fertility of the whole country was at about 6. The average annual number of births was 27 million, and population increased by 20 million annually. The "Cultural Revolution" seriously damaged industrial and agricultural production and brought the national economy to the brink of collapse. By the early 1970s, many economic indicators, including per capita share of grain, were lower than those in the mid-1960s or even the mid-1950s (Zhai Zhenwu, 1999), while the population was growing rapidly. So in the early 1970s, the Chinese government decided to resume the family planning program, and the third round started. Unlike the previous two rounds, the third round was carried out nationwide with sustainability and strength.

First Fertility Transition

Despite the brief period of carrying out family planning in the 1950s and 1960s, its idea and plan were yet to be improved, requiring to be discussed and perfected. Finally, in the early 1970s, the government restarted the program in a large scale with strong determination to reduce fertility and control the population growth. In fact, the fertility control by women themselves and the continuous publicity since the 1950s and 1960s laid a foundation for the large-scale nationwide family planning in the 1970s. In 1971, the State Council issued a document first calling for nationwide family planning in both urban and rural areas. In 1973, the government released related policy called "later-longer-fewer" (later marriage, longer birth intervals and fewer children). The State Council and governments at all levels set up leading organizations for family planning, providing information and services about family planning, contraception and birth control. In the 1970s, China achieved one of the most rapid fertility transitions in human history. Its TFR fell by more than half just within a few years.

In 1970, the birth rate for China was 33.43 per thousand and the TFR was 5.75. By 1979, they had decreased to 17.82 per thousand and 2.80, respectively (Figures 2.2 and 2.3). The birth rate fell by almost half, while the TFR fell by more than half, resulting in a baby bust (Figure 2.4). The natural growth rate decreased from 25.83 per thousand in 1970 to 11.61 per thousand in 1979. The annual number of births dropped from nearly 28 million in 1970 to nearly 17 million in 1979, a decrease of more than 10 million. Annual population growth dropped from about 21 million to about 11 million. Throughout the 1970s, China's fertility continued to plummet. Western scholars described China's fertility transition in the 1970s as follows: except the periods of famine, plague and war, there has never been such a rapid decline in fertility as in China in human history (Freedman, 1995).

China's fertility transition not only conforms to the general law but also has distinct Chinese characteristics. The shift in fertility was preceded by a rapid change in mortality, a decline that affected people's decision on reproduction. Besides, the social change and economic development over the past 20 years after 1949 have laid a foundation for the fertility transition. Prior to the introduction of family planning in the cities in 1960s and the rural areas in 1970s, women who received higher education have already had birth control, and a spontaneous shift in fertility had begun among these groups (Lavely and Freedman, 1990). The function of China's family planning lies in reducing fertility as early as possible or greatly accelerating the transition under certain social conditions. Therefore, the rapid decline is due to a favorable social environment for population transition. When families and individuals wanted to have birth control, the government can take the advantage and greatly accelerate the decline of fertility by introducing family planning policy (Wu Cangping, 1986).

Social system and organizations are the keys of a favorable environment for fertility transition. The social transformation after 1949 has weakened or even eliminated many institutions and cultural mechanisms conducive to high fertility. Besides, the socialist ideological revolution and support for the Communist Party made collectivism and the support to national policy a common trend. In the 1970s, the family planning policy of "later-longer-fewer" was basically in line with the will of the people. Therefore, the policy received widespread support.

In the 1980s, China carried out the economic reform and opening up, greatly changing economic model and social life. China's family planning policy has become a basic national policy and has improved. The fertility has stopped declining and started to fluctuate at around the replacement level.

Fluctuation in Fertility

In 1980, the TFR for China reached 2.32, close to the replacement level. In the 1980s, China's average TFR was 2.44, fluctuating between 2.1 and 2.8 without a trend of decline (Figure 2.3). Compared with the 1970s, although the central government and governments at all levels paid more attention to family planning, made stricter rules and implemented the policy on a larger scale, fertility started to hover and fluctuate, instead of declining as before.

In fact, the fluctuation in fertility in China in the 1980s was the result of changes in family planning policy, economic reform, age structure and the tempo effects of marriage and childbirth. In September 1980, at the third session of the National People's Congress, the State Council proposed that effective measures should be taken to implement the one-child policy throughout the country (except in marginal and minority areas with sparse population) in order to achieve the goal of controlling the population at 1.2 billion by the year 2000. The CPC Central Committee issued an open letter asking communists, Communist Youth League members and state cadres to take the lead in implementing the policy. In the early 1980s, the government implemented this policy through administrative measures and a series of other powerful measures. In rural areas, people obviously wanted to have more than one child. In addition, the economic reform has weakened the collectivism and administrative mechanism and strengthened the role of family economic production. Thus, the family planning work suffered setbacks. In 1984, the CPC Central Committee proposed that one-child policy should be improved based on "logical, widely supported family planning policy which is easy for the officials to promote". Thus, adjusting the one-child policy, the so-called one-and-a-half-child policy was introduced.

Demographically speaking, the promulgation and implementation of the new Marriage Law in 1980 let the age for late marriage required by administrative regulations in the past lose its binding force, resulting in younger marriage and childbearing age and accumulation of marriages and births. In years when women delay childbearing, fertility is depressed; in years with earlier births, fertility tends to increase (Bongaarts and Feeney, 1998). The increasing delay in the age of first marriage in the 1970s contributed significantly to the decline in TFR, while the accumulation of marriages and births in the 1980s led to a rebound in TFR. In addition, the age structure inertia (the baby boomers in the 1960s were entering marriage and childbearing) also contributed to the rebound and fluctuation of births and fertility in the 1980s. In the late 1980s, the birth rate rose to 22–23 per thousand (Figure 2.2), the TFR was 2.4–2.5 (Figure 2.3), and the third baby boom occurred, with the annual average population growth rising to 24–25 million (Figure 2.4).

The fluctuation of fertility in China in the 1980s was economically, demographically and policy determined, but it also conformed to the general laws of demographic transition. The experiences of fertility transition in Japan, South Korea and Singapore suggest that they all experienced a period of wandering fertility when penetrating the replacement level zone. Fertility falls further below the replacement level after several years or even decade-long fluctuation around the replacement level, which is relatively stable. There are similar experiences in Western countries, but the time is shorter than that in the Eastern countries. China achieved its second fertility transition in the 1990s, with fertility falling below the replacement level.

Second Fertility Transition

Due to the concern about fluctuating and rising fertility, the Chinese government in the early 1990s reaffirmed the importance of family planning and called for stronger enforcement while guaranteeing the existing policy implementation. The 1990 census revealed a total population of 1.13 billion, 10 million more than expected, and showed that 1 million births were underreported each year between 1982 and 1990 (Feng Litian and Ma Yingtong, 1999). Faced with the grim population situation, the CPC Central Committee and the State Council issued the Decision on Strengthening Family Planning Program and Strictly Controlling Population Growth in May 1991, requiring that the leaders of the governments at all levels personally handle family planning program and assume the overall responsibility. In addition, the family planning work and the completion of the population plan would be taken as an important indicator to evaluate the performance of Party committees and governments at all levels and their leaders. Based on the decision made by the central government and their reality, all provinces formulated or improved the corresponding regulations on family planning. Since 1991, the central government has held annual Symposium on Population and Family Planning (renamed Symposium on Population, Resources and Environment work in 1997) to make plans for population and family planning work. Due to the strengthened implementation of the family planning policy, fertility in China declined sharply in the early 1990s and finally fell below the replacement level, achieving a qualitative leap in fertility transition.

In the 1990s, China kept its family planning policy sustainable and stable, but the related work had reforms, which can be seen in "Three Priorities" and "Three Combinations" in the early 1990s and later high-quality family planning service. "Three Priorities" refer to publicity, contraception and ideological work. "Three Combinations" means that family planning should be combined with the development of the socialist market economy, with the people's effort for a well-off life and with the goal of building civilized and happy family. Fertility quota has been gradually removed, and people changed their willingness to bear children significantly. And in the 1990s, China's rapid economic development and great changes in lifestyle made the low fertility sustainable and stable. Exogenous low fertility gradually changed to endogenous low fertility (Li Jianmin, 2004).

In 1990, the birth rate was 21.06 per thousand and the TFR was 2.31. By the year 2000, the birth rate had fallen by 14.03 per thousand, and the TFR had fallen to 1.5 (TFR was 1.22 in the 2000 census) (Figures 2.2 and 2.3). The natural population growth rate dropped below 10 per thousand in 1998, which is a historic breakthrough. Accordingly, the annual number of births dropped from 24 million to 18 million. By the end of the 1990s, China had achieved a historic shift in population reproduction to a pattern of low birth rate, low death rate and low growth rate.

Looking at the change in birth rate, China's fertility continued to decline in the 1990s. The various fertility surveys, population sample surveys and censuses conducted by the former National Population and Family Planning Commission and the National Bureau of Statistics show a consistent decline in fertility, and the TFR calculated from these surveys is getting increasingly lower. This result shows that China's fertility has indeed declined significantly, which is below the replacement level. But at the same time, there are worries that fertility may be underestimated due to data quality, such as under-reporting and concealing of births. Therefore, the second fertility transition in China lacks the support of accurate data, and scholars could not agree on how low the fertility was while emphasizing that China's fertility was well below the replacement level. Research into the second fertility transition has actually been focused on the estimate of the true fertility level.

According to the 1990 census, TFR in China was 2.31, while the rate revealed by 2000 census was as low as 1.22. Although the 1990s saw a further dramatic decline in fertility, it seems unlikely that TFR could fall well below the policy fertility. Therefore, different scholars re-estimated the fertility in 2000 based on the data of 2000 census, under-reporting and other data, and the estimated result shows that China's TFR was 1.6–1.8 (Yu Xuejun, 2002).

Based on the number of births reported over the years, the National Bureau of Statistics has calculated the TFR since the 1990s. The results showed that the TFR dropped steadily from about 2.2 in the early 1990s to about 1.7 in the late 1990s (Cui Hongyan, 2008). Other studies reconstructed the age and sex structure of the lower age group in the 2000 census and estimated the TFR in the 1990s based on the number of primary school students in China over the years, with cohort analysis, backward survival and curve fitting and regression analysis (Zhai Zhenwu and Chen Wei, 2007; Chen Wei, 2009). The results show that China's fertility has been at or below replacement level since 1992 and continued to decline, with the TFR between 1.7 and 1.8 in 2000.

Fertility below the replacement level will result in a radical change in population growth. With fading population inertia in the age structure, population growth will gradually become zero and then negative. Therefore, the government at that time emphasized that the center of population and family planning work would be stabilizing the low fertility and arriving an appropriate level of low fertility.

Persistent Low Fertility

Since 2000, China's fertility has continued the downward trend of the 1990s. The TFR in the 2010 census was lower than in the 2000 census, at 1.18. Fertility from the 2015 one-percent population sample survey dropped further to 1.05. The birth rate published by the National Bureau of Statistics also fell from 14.03 per thousand in 2000 to 11.90 in 2010, but rose slightly to 12.07 in 2015 (the birth rate published by the National Bureau of Statistics implies a significantly higher birth rate than the census results). The natural population growth rate dropped below 5 per thousand in 2009, another 2.5 million fewer than in the late 1990s. In fact, these data show that fertility has been persistently low since 2000. According to the Population Reference Bureau's World Population Data Sheets for 2010 and 2015, the average TFR in developed countries was 1.7, while the average in Europe fell from 1.6 to 1.4. Estimates for China's TFR are 1.5 and 1.7, respectively.

Since 2000, while continuing to stabilize the current family planning policy, the Chinese government has actively transformed its working philosophy and methods. In March 2000, the CPC Central Committee and the State Council issued the Decision on Strengthening Population and Family Planning Work to Stabilize the Low Fertility, stressing that overpopulation is still a prominent problem in China and that it would be a long-lasting major problem in the primary stage of socialism. After realizing the historic transition in the pattern of population reproduction, the main task will be maintaining low fertility and raising population quality. In December 2001, the Twenty-fifth Session of the Standing Committee of the Ninth National People's Congress adopted the Law on Population and Family Planning, which came into force in September 2002. Therefore, family planning as a basic national policy can be protected by laws, and the population and family planning work can be carried out based on laws and deliver quality service. In March 2003, the name of the State Family Planning Commission was changed to the National Population and Family Planning Commission, with more functions such as exploring the strategies of population development, making related plans and promoting the development of reproductive health industry. Population and family planning departments at all levels have also changed their names to improve their coordination. From the 16th to the 17th CPC National Congress in particular, the CPC Central Committee put forward a series of major strategic thinking, such as establishing and implementing the Scientific Outlook on Development, building new socialist villages and building a socialist harmonious society, providing new ideas and perspectives for understanding and solving the population problem. In December 2006, the CPC Central Committee and the State Council adopted the Decision on Comprehensively Strengthening the Population and Family Planning Work to Solve the Population Problem, pointing out that China's population and family planning work has entered a new stage of stabilizing the low fertility, solving the population problem in a holistic way and promoting all-round human development. Since then, maintaining a moderately low fertility and gradually adjusting the population structure have become an important part of population and family planning.

Since the 21st century, China's population trend has undergone a major change, and the internal driving force and external conditions for population development have undergone fundamental changes. The government constantly improved the policy and implemented a selective two-child policy in 2013 and then a universal two-child policy in 2015 in order to better follow the law of population development and meet the need of having children, optimizing the population structure, promote the population long-term balanced development and the sustainable and harmonious development of social economy. In December 2015, the central government issued the Decision on Implementing the Universal Two-Child Policy to Reform and Improve the Family Planning. As a historic move, the decision marks the end of the restrictive family planning policy dominated by the one-child policy and will have a profound impact on China's fertility and population development trend. However, according to international experience, China's fertility will continue to be low in the long run. The long-term trend of China's population growth will not change. In fact, the fertility required in policy will gradually increase, with the change of population structure, the gradual relaxation of birth interval and the continuous adjustment and improvement of the policy. At the same time, the low fertility will be greatly changed by fertility potential accumulated since the 1990s due to fewer and delayed births and the birth peak brought by age structure. A survey about fertility in some areas of China shows that both the number of births conform to the policy or not are rising, though the sex preference remains strong.

Throughout the progress of China's population development, China has completed a historic transition in population reproduction in less than 30 years under underdeveloped social productive forces, making it one of the countries with low fertility. From the analysis of the population changes in different stages above, China has experienced a transition from quantity to quality, which follows the general law of human fertility change and manifests distinct Chinese characteristics. China's family planning policy is an initiative in human history. To solve China's population problem, Chinese people should rely on their own wisdom and adhere to the socialism with Chinese characteristics (Yu Xuejun, 2008). However, as the former strictly restrictive policy becomes more spontaneous, the major challenge for China to achieve long-term balanced population development is to gradually increase the fertility to 1.8 and make it close to the replacement level.

Concluding Remarks

Western scholars believe that a spontaneous shift in fertility had already occurred among highly educated women in China before the huge decline in fertility in the 1970s. In fact, studies by historical demographers show that China's high fertility in the pre-transition period was not uncontrolled, and the marital fertility was even lower than that of European women before the transition.

The process of fertility transition in China can be divided into two parts. The first occurred in the 1970s, when fertility fell by more than half, from nearly 6 to less than 3. This rapid change is known as "Chinese model" of demographic transition, a miracle of human birth control. The second part occurred in the 1990s, when China's fertility fluctuated above replacement level throughout the 1980s, then fell below replacement level in the early 1990s and then continued to decline.

Against the backdrop of rapid economic development, urbanization and ever-changing employment and lifestyles, China's fertility will remain low. The implementation of the two-child policy, or even no birth restrictions, will not change the trend of low fertility. According to the experiences of countries with low fertility, the rate tends to fluctuate or become even lower when it falls below the replacement level, instead of being stable. Different levels of low fertility will make the trend of future population different. In view of the complexity of China's population development in the new era and the long-term nature of population issues, the target of 1.8 TFR set by the National Population Development Strategy and National Population Development Planning (2016–2030) is a proper choice for China to guarantee long-term, stable and sustainable development.

China has experienced a rapid, significant shift in fertility that is unprecedented in human history. Great practices create a great model. Family planning with Chinese characteristics has made important contributions to the theory and practice of global demographic transition. Thus, China's demographic transition has attracted world-wide attention and is certainly a remarkable achievement in the history of human development.

References

Bongaarts, J. and Feeney, G. 1998. On the Quantum and Tempo of Fertility. *Population and Development Review* 24(2): 271–291. doi:10.2307/2807974.

Chen Wei. 2009. Re-examining Fertility Level in China. *Population Research* (4): 38–42.

Cui Hongyan. 2008. Assessment of the Quality of Data from the 2005 National 1% Population Sample Survey. Paper presented at 2008 Annual meeting of China Population Association, Xi 'an, China.

Feeney, G. 1994. *Fertility in China: Past, Present, Prospects*. East-West Center Reprints. Population Studies, No. 313.

Feng Litian and Ma Yingtong. 1999. Evolution of China's Fertility Policy in the Past 50 Years. Pp. 247–267 in Zha Ruichuan (ed.), *A Century of Population Studies in China*. Beijing: Beijing Press.

Freedman, R. 1995. *Asia's Recent Fertility Decline and Prospects for Future Demographic Change*. Asia-Pacific Population Research Reports, No. 1. Program on Population, East-West Center.

Harrell, S., Wang, Y., Hua, H., Santos, G. D., and Zhou, Y. 2011. Fertility Decline in Rural China: A Comparative Analysis. *Journal of Family History* 36(1): 15–36.

Lavely, W. and Freedman, R. 1990. The Origins of Chinese Fertility Decline. *Demography* 27(3): 357–367.

Li Jianmin. 2004. Childbearing Rationality, Fertility Decision and the Transformation of Stabilizing Mechanism of Low Fertility in China. *Population Research* (6): 2–18.

Wu Cangping. 1986. Theoretical Explanation of Fertility Decline in China. *Population Research* 1: 10–16.

Yu Xuejun. 2002. Estimates of the Size and Structure of China's Population from the Fifth National Census Data. *Population Research* (3): 9–15.

Yu Xuejun. 2008. Review of 30 Years Family Planning Policy in China. *China Population Today* (5): 31–34.

Zhai Zhenwu. 1999. The Practice of Family Planning Called for Population Theory. Pp. 161–183 in Zha Ruichuan (ed.), *A Century of Population Studies in China* (in Chinese). Beijing: Beijing Press.

Zhai Zhenwu and Chen Wei. 2007. Fertility Levels in China in the 1990s. *Population Research* (1): 19–32.

Zhao Zhongwei. 1997a. Deliberate Birth Control under a High-fertility Regiem: Reproductive Behavior in China before 1970. *Population and Development Review* 23(4): 729–767.

Zhao Zhongwei. 1997b. Demographic Systems in Historical China: Some New Findings from Recent Research. *Journal of the Australian Population Association* 14(2): 201–232.

3 Estimation of China's Low Fertility Rates in 2000–2010

After reaching the replacement level in the early 1990s, China's total fertility rate (TFR) fell further and has remained low ever since. According to the results of the 1992 Fertility Survey and the annual population sample surveys in the 1990s, China's TFR dropped to 1.7 in the first half of the 1990s and then dipped further to 1.5 or even lower in the late 1990s. Record-low TFRs of 1.22 and 1.18 were reported in 2000 and 2010 censuses, respectively. Since the TFR fell below the replacement level in the early 1990s, scholars have begun to estimate and debate how low China's fertility is; yet, the debate has never ended and no consensus has been reached. Under the long-time influence of China's family planning policy, coupled with the tremendous changes marking China's booming socioeconomic development, Chinese people's fertility desire has also undergone seismic shifts. However, it's beyond doubt that the data quality of China's population censuses, population sample surveys and fertility surveys has all deteriorated to varying degrees since the 1990s due to the widespread underreporting or concealing of births and young children. China's population censuses and fertility surveys used to be highly applauded by Western scholars in the 1980s by dint of their unrivaled data quality across the globe (Coale, 1989). However, social changes, especially the growth of migrant population, have thwarted China's efforts to obtain accurate information from population censuses and sample surveys. Alongside the underreporting of young children, China is also no stranger to the underreporting or overreporting of population in other age groups, making it a daunting challenge for China to get a clear picture of its population.

Except for a handful of countries that lack demographic data, China might be the only country whose fertility level is constantly under debate. Although it is widely accepted that China's TFR has been lingering below replacement level for a long time, behind this consensus lies a substantial divergence of estimates on China's TFR. There are extreme opinions holding that China's current TFR is as low as the census suggests, or it's as high as 1.8. Others argue that it is between 1.5 and 1.6 or between 1.6 and 1.7. Of course, there are also scholars holding to the opinion that China's TFR is below 1.5 or slightly higher than the results of censuses. These divided estimates are not only linked to the use of different data and methods but also stem from different understanding and thinking logic.

DOI: 10.4324/9781003429661-3

It is extremely important to estimate China's current fertility rate as accurately as possible. Whilst the fertility rate provides a factual foundation that the government can build upon to adjust its fertility policy (that is, the adjustment of fertility policy and the formulation of population development strategy must be grounded in the judgment of fertility level and demographic trend), against the backdrop of China's roll-out of the two-child policy, it also provides a basis for estimating and judging the effect and impact of the policy. On the premise of stable fertility desire, a still-relatively-high fertility rate suggests a weaker impact of the two-child policy. Otherwise, the impact is deemed strong.

The level and trend of fertility are also crucial to the debate on whether China has fallen into the "low fertility trap". Judging from the results of the population censuses and sample surveys conducted by the National Bureau of Statistics, China's TFR has been lingering below 1.5 for two decades since the mid-1990s, which obviously meets the criteria for "low fertility trap". Still, it is also unscientific to presume that China has already fallen deeply into the "low fertility trap" by turning a blind eye to the widespread underreporting in population censuses and sample surveys. Has China's TFR been below 1.5 for a long time? Finding the right answer to this question entails meticulous and rigorous analysis. Although determining the fertility rate is never a daunting task, the problem of data quality casts a dark cloud over this "easy" task. In this chapter, we will first review the existing studies and then build upon the data from 2000 and 2010 censuses and methods such as cohort analysis, regression analysis, survival estimation and demographic models to determine China's fertility rates from 2000 to 2010.

Estimated Fertility Rates in the Period from 2000 to 2010

With regard to the estimation of and debate on China's low fertility rates, scholars have come to different or even divergent conclusions due to the use of different data and methods. To summarize, there are three different types of studies. The first type of studies directly used census data for estimation, tacitly acquiescing that the census data are credible and accurate, and they tended to obtain the lowest TFRs – often lower than 1.5. For example, Guo Zhigang (2011) estimated China's fertility rates from 1990 to 2010 through the "shooting method" using data from the censuses, concluding that China's TFR plunged from the early 1990s to 1.4 in the period 1996–2003, followed by a sluggish rebound to around 1.5 in recent years. Building their calculations upon the data from population censuses and sample surveys, Hao Juan and Qiu Changrong (2011) opined that China's TFRs during 2000–2010 fluctuated between 1.22 and 1.47, never surpassing the policy fertility rate of 1.47 and staying below the very low fertility level of 1.5. Taking China's 0- to 9-year-old population in 2010 as the target, Zhu Qin (2012) reconstructed China's fertility rates in the period 2000–2010 through repeated simulations, arriving at a conclusion that China's TFR fluctuated between 1.3 and 1.5 in this period, with average TFR standing at 1.48. He also argued that the underreporting of the 2000 Census did not lead to an underestimation of China's fertility rate and that China's very low fertility (less than 1.5) has been going on for at least a decade.

The second type of studies would question the quality of census data and make necessary adjustments when using census data to estimate the fertility rate. Among such studies, scholars are substantially divided in their approaches to adjustment and estimation. Cui Hongyan et al. (2013) conducted a comprehensive assessment of the data quality of the 2010 Census and also estimated China's fertility rates in the period from 2000 to 2010. By comparing the births and sampling ratio between the long form and short form, they came to the conclusion that the registered births were lower than the actual births and therefore China's TFR in 2010 should be 1.42. They further calculated the underreported births based on the births reported by the sample surveys on population changes and the births reported in the 2010 Census to obtain an adjusted TFR of 1.5 for 2010 and opined that China's TFRs in the period 2000–2010 might fall within the range of 1.50–1.64 based on the data from the sample surveys on population changes. Through the comparison of data from various censuses, Wang Jinying and Ge Yanxia (2013) carried out underreporting correction of the data for children and adolescents obtained through the 2010 Census and adjusted the data after taking into account the repeated reporting of women of childbearing age and sampling bias, concluding that China's TFRs in the period 2001–2010 might fall within the range of 1.5–1.6. They further argued that should the higher underreporting effect of the 2010 Census be taken into account, China's TFRs in the period 2001–2010 might fall within the range of 1.75 (highest) to 1.45 (lowest). Taking the demographic data (disaggregated by urban/rural area, gender and age) of the 2000 Census as the base period data and the discrete population dynamics model of Leslie matrix as the basic model, Li Handong and Li Liu (2012) adjusted the respective parameters of the model to estimate China's TFRs in the period 2000–2010, finding that officially published data were internally inconsistent and contradictory, thus arguing that China's average TFR in the first decade of the 21st century should be around 1.57.

In regard to the various problems with the data from population censuses and sample surveys, the third type of studies harnessed the data collected by other systems (such as education system, *Hukou* system, etc.) to correct and adjust the census data before estimating the fertility rates. Yang Fan and Zhao Menghan (2013) analyzed the characteristics of the data from censuses, education system and *Hukou* system, respectively, opining that the problems with the data from the Sixth Census can be foreseen from the flaws in the data from the Fifth Census. This is because the causes of concealing and underreporting in the census were left unaddressed over the ten years, and therefore, the same problems were likely to occur in the younger age groups in the Sixth Census in 2010. Analyses have found that the data from education system are of stable quality and high accuracy; yet, there might be some limitations in timeliness when such data are used for estimating the fertility rate. Although data quality varies in individual age groups, data from the *Hukou* system are deemed of satisfactory quality in recent years. Therefore, they estimated that the lowest range of China's TFR since 2000 was roughly 1.5–1.63 through the consolidation of data from education system and *Hukou* system, direct calculations based on the data from the *Hukou* system and calculations based on the population registration rate of the *Hukou* system. Based on the incomplete registered number of 5-year-old children in the data from the *Hukou* system, they estimated that China's fertility rate already reached 1.55 in 2007. Arguing that China's fertility rate couldn't go any lower, they arrived at a conclusion that China's TFR has fallen within the range of 1.6–1.7 since 2000.

Some scholars have raised doubts about the fact that the fertility rates estimated based on the census data adjusted for other sources are often significantly higher than the census results. Zhang Guangyu and Yuan Xin (2004) held the opinion that there is insufficient evidence suggesting the large-scale underreporting of births in China's population censuses and sample surveys, arguing that birth underreporting might be exaggerated and that the low fertility rates obtained might result from the already-low actual fertility rates. Guo Zhigang (2010a) also pointed out that birth underreporting and low fertility rates are excessively overestimated in China and that researchers should place more trust in data from field surveys, such as censuses, rather than relying too heavily on subjective judgments. He believed that there were serious flaws in previous population estimates and projections, which overestimated fertility rate and population growth and thus underestimated the level of population aging (Guo Zhigang, 2011). Cai Yong (2009) and Guo Zhigang (2010b) also questioned the quality of data from the education system, arguing that the policy of "two exemptions and one subsidy" might have prompted certain stakeholders to overreport the number of students in order to receive more subsidies. Since education statistics themselves are no longer pure, they cannot be used as a "gold" standard for estimating fertility rates.

In the context of low fertility, Chinese demographers' attempts to estimate China's fertility rate are reflective of the application of varying demographic analysis techniques. Tempo-adjusted TFR and intrinsic TFR aim to overcome the tempo effects of delayed childbearing and prolonged birth interval on TFR to reflect a more realistic fertility level. The mother–children match or reconstruction of fertility history aims to match the mother's information (number of children born, age at the time of childbirth) and the child's information (age, parity) in the censuses, in an effort to obtain a more accurate number of total births, the number of births by parity and the age of women giving birth. The data obtained can be used to calculate the overall TFR, TFR by parity and average age of women giving birth. Demographic simulation and projection ("shooting method") differs from general population forecasting methods in estimating past fertility rates. Instead of estimating the future population, it utilizes population forecasting methods to estimate parameters such as TFR and deaths based on the known numbers of farther past population and nearer past population, a process like "shooting a target". For example, what fertility rate would it take in the ten years between the Fifth and Sixth Censuses to allow the population to climb from the number in the Fifth Census to the number in the Sixth Census? There are also methods such as regression analysis and backward survival, which follows the general steps for TFR calculation – that is, TFR can only be obtained under the premise of having the number of births, the number of women of childbearing age and the fertility pattern by age. Such methods are mainly used in fertility estimations using data from multiple sources, aiming to adjust for underreporting in the current data or to estimate hard-to-obtain data.

Estimation of China's Low Fertility Rates 25

Building on numerous previous studies, this chapter will utilize data from different statistical systems to further estimate, compare and comprehensively judge China's fertility rates and trends in the period from 2000 to 2010.

Data and Methodology

The premise of estimating fertility rate is to first estimate the numbers of births and women of childbearing age. Although it is relatively simple and easy to estimate the number of women of childbearing age, and there has been little debate over the quality of the corresponding data, the number of births is the linchpin, especially when there are varied kinds of data available for evaluation, not to mention the ongoing debate over the quality of such data. We built our estimation on the data from 2000 Census, data from 2010 Census, data for 2000–2010 from education system, data for 2010 from *Hukou* system and data from 2001–2009 annual population surveys. The births from 2000 to 2010 were estimated using data from censuses, education system and *Hukou* system; the numbers of women of childbearing age were estimated using census data; and the age distribution of births was calculated using the data from annual population surveys. The age-specific fertility rate and the TFR can be obtained from the number of births by age and the number of women of childbearing age by age and by the age of giving birth.

The methods we used included cohort analysis, regression analysis, Brass logit transformation and survival-based estimation. Cohort analysis was used to compare data from different sources to assess underreporting in census data. Regression analysis was used to estimate and derive the lower-age populations in the census data. Brass logit transformation was used to obtain life tables for the years between the censuses so that the life table survival ratios could be used to extrapolate the various populations needed in estimating fertility rate, including women of childbearing age, lower-age populations and the corresponding births in each year. The specific application of these methods will be further explained in this chapter. The research design was: (1) to compare the census data and the data from different sources to access the underreporting of census data in the lower-age populations; (2) to adjust and estimate the lower-age populations in 2010 using data from different sources and based on the assumption that the 2010 Census and 2000 Census shared the same degree of underreporting in the lower-age populations; and (3) to extrapolate births from the estimated lower-age populations in 2010 and then calculate age-specific births and age-specific women of childbearing age, thus deriving the age-specific fertility rates and the TFR.

Estimation of Fertility Rates Since 2000

The estimation of fertility rates was broken down into three steps: (1) estimation of births, which were further disaggregated by the age of women of childbearing age; (2) estimation of age-specific women of childbearing age; and (3) calculation of the age-specific fertility rate and TFR. The first step is not only pivotal but also relatively complex. We compared the populations aged 0–10 years obtained from the 2000 Census with those of same cohorts obtained from other sources and calculated the populations of the same age groups as the 0–10 age groups in the 2000 Census by uniformly adjusting the survey time point and using the life table survival ratios, followed by the regression fits for census data and data from other sources. Building upon these regression equations and the populations aged 0–10 years in the 2010 Census, we extrapolated various estimates of populations aged 0–10 years in 2010 and finally obtained different estimates of births.

1 Estimation of populations aged 0–10 years in the 2010 Census

Estimation of populations aged 0–10 years in the 2010 Census is based on the populations aged 0–10 years in the 2000 Census and the assumption that the underreporting rate remains unchanged. Table 3.1 shows the populations aged 0–10 years in the 2000 Census and the same-cohort populations obtained from different data sources. Populations aged 0–10 years in the 2000 Census (Column 2) were compared with populations aged 10–20 years in the 2010 Census (Column 4), population aged 10 years in the data for 2000–2010 from the education system (Column 5) and populations aged 10–20 years in the data for 2010 from the *Hukou* system (Column 6). With the exception of the last cohort, figures from different sources for the same cohort are generally larger than those obtained in the 2000 Census, suggesting substantial underreporting of populations in the lower-age groups in the 2000 Census. Figure 3.1 shows the survival ratios for populations of different cohorts, suggesting that the underreporting rates of lower-age populations are greater than those of higher-age populations.

Due to the different survey or statistical time reference of data from different sources, in order to facilitate further calculations, it is necessary to unify the time reference. The 2000 and 2010 censuses were both conducted on November

Table 3.1 Same-Cohort Populations from Different Data Sources (Million)

Age	2000 Census Data	Age	2010 Census Data	Education Data	Hukou Data
(1)	(2)	(3)	(4)	(5)	(6)
0	13.79	10	14.45	16.36	14.79
1	11.50	11	13.94	16.14	14.43
2	14.01	12	15.40	16.92	15.46
3	14.45	13	15.23	17.37	15.62
4	15.22	14	15.89	17.91	16.35
5	16.93	15	18.02	18.49	17.44
6	16.47	16	18.79	18.78	17.43
7	17.91	17	20.78	19.68	18.50
8	18.75	18	20.76	20.49	19.24
9	20.08	19	21.54	22.04	20.57
10	26.21	20	28.03	24.79	25.49

Source: National Bureau of Statistics. Tabulation on the 2000 Population Census of China. China Statistics Press, 2002; Tabulation on the 2010 Population Census of China. China Statistics Press, 2012; education data for 2000–2010 comes from the China Education Statistical Yearbooks for 2000–2010; *Hukou* data for 2010 comes from the Ministry of Public Security.

Estimation of China's Low Fertility Rates 27

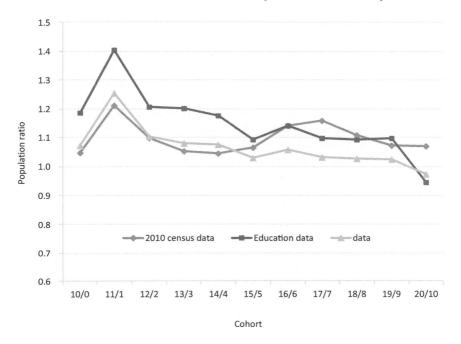

Figure 3.1 Survival ratios by cohort
Source: Same as Table 3.1.

1; the statistics of education data were conducted on September 1; and the statistics of *Hukou* data were conducted on December 31. Both education data and *Hukou* data must be adjusted for the time reference point of the censuses. In previous studies, scholars generally built their calculations on the assumption that the births were evenly distributed among months. By observing the monthly distribution of births in the 2000 and 2010 censuses, it's found that births were not evenly distributed among months, which can be observed from the marked differences between November/December and other months. Births in November/December accounted for more than 10% of yearly births, while births in other months only accounted for 6–9% of yearly births. According to the 2010 Census, births in September and October combined accounted for 13% of yearly births, while births in November and December combined accounted for 24% of yearly births. Therefore, when adjusting the education data for the time reference point of censuses, the following equation was used:

$P_x^{'} = P_x - 0.13P_x + 0.13P_{x-1}$, where $P_x^{'}$ is the adjusted population aged x years and P_x is the unadjusted population aged x years.

When adjusting the *Hukou* data for the time reference point of censuses, the following equation was used:

$P_x^{'} = P_x - 0.24P_x + 0.24P_{x+1}$, where $P_x^{'}$ is the adjusted population aged x years and P_x is the unadjusted population aged x years.

28 *Estimation of China's Low Fertility Rates*

After unifying the time reference points of different data, we could then extrapolate back to the population of the same age. In Table 3.2, populations aged 10–20 years in the 2010 Census, populations aged ten years in the education data for 2000–2010 and populations aged 10–20 years in the *Hukou* data for 2010 were all rolled back to populations aged 0–10 years through the life-table survival ratios shown in Figure 3.2. According to Table 3.2, the highest levels of underreporting (with underreporting rate reaching as high as 15.8%) were found in populations extrapolated from the education data; the lowest levels of underreporting (with underreporting rate reaching as low as 7.4%) were found in populations extrapolated from the *Hukou* data; and moderate levels of underreporting (with underreporting rate averaging at 10.0%) were found in populations extrapolated from the 10- to 20-year-old populations in the 2010 Census.

We assumed that the underreporting rate in populations aged 0–10 years in the 2010 Census is the same as the underreporting rate in the same cohorts in the 2000 Census, which means that the three different underreporting rates mentioned above were used to estimate the populations aged 0–10 years in the 2010 Census, and then, the life table survival ratios were used to extrapolate the births. Assuming the 2010 Census and the 2000 Census share the same age pattern in terms of the underreporting of populations aged 0–10 years, yet considering the different age structures in populations aged 0–10 years in the two censuses, we did not directly use the underreporting rates in the 0- to 10-year-old populations in 2000 to adjust the same cohorts in 2010. Instead, we first established the linear regression equations for the data from various sources in Table 3.2 and data from the 2000 Census and then substituted the 0- to 10-year-old populations in 2010 into these regression equations to derive the 0- to 10-year-old populations in 2010 adjusted for data from different sources.

Figures 3.3–3.5 show the regression fit graph of the 2010 census data and the 2000 census data, the regression fit graph of the education data and the 2000 census data and the regression fit graph of the *Hukou* data and the 2000 census

Table 3.2 Population at Ages 0–10 in 2000: Estimated from Various Sources of Data (Million)

	2000 Census Data	2010 Census Data	Education Data	Hukou Data
0	13.79	14.66	16.58	15.12
1	11.50	14.02	16.27	14.44
2	14.01	15.48	16.90	15.79
3	14.45	15.29	17.38	15.73
4	15.22	15.95	17.91	16.59
5	16.93	18.09	18.48	17.77
6	16.47	18.86	18.81	17.49
7	17.91	20.85	19.63	18.83
8	18.75	20.83	20.46	19.49
9	20.08	21.63	21.92	20.98
10	26.21	28.14	24.53	26.78

Source: Calculations by author.

Estimation of China's Low Fertility Rates 29

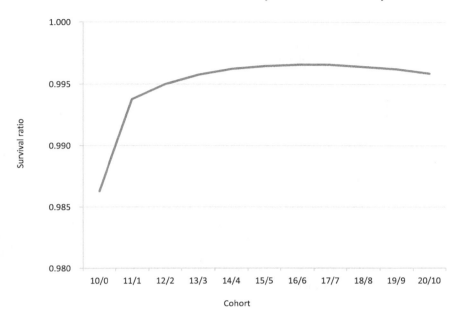

Figure 3.2 Life table survival ratios for different cohorts

Source: Estimated by Brass logit transformation from the life tables for 2000 and 2010 published by the National Bureau of Statistics.

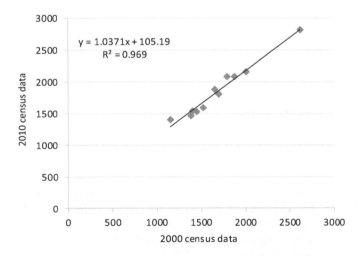

Figure 3.3 Regression analysis of 2010 census data and 2000 census data

Source: Table 3.2 and calculations by author.

30 *Estimation of China's Low Fertility Rates*

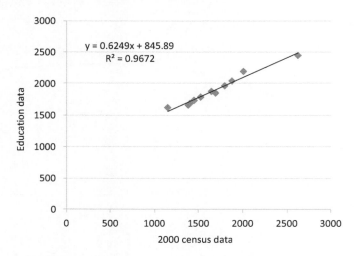

Figure 3.4 Regression analysis of education data and 2000 census data
Source: Table 3.2 and calculations by author.

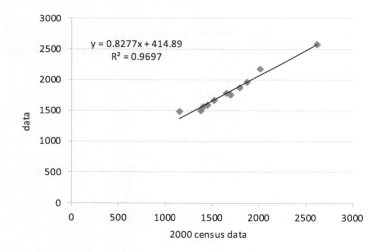

Figure 3.5 Regression analysis of *Hukou* data and 2000 census data
Source: Table 3.2 and calculations by author.

data. The coefficients of determination (R^2) of the regression equations are all above 0.96. We substituted the 0- to 10-year-old populations in 2010 Census into the regression equations shown in the figures to derive the 0- to 10-year-old populations in 2010 adjusted for data from different sources. Then, we used the life table survival ratios (see Figure 3.6) to extrapolate births from the population of each age, as shown in Table 3.3, which also shows the births directly extrapolated from the 0- to 10-year-old populations in the 2010 Census and the births for 2000–2010 as published by the National Bureau of Statistics.

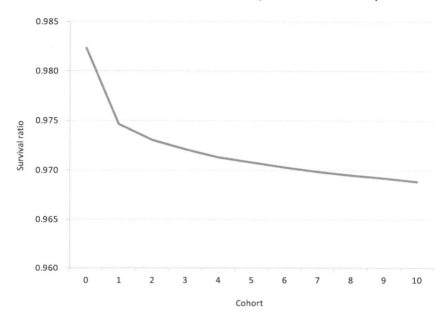

Figure 3.6 Life table survival ratios from birth to each age

Source: Estimated by Brass logit transformation from the life tables for 2000 and 2010 published by the National Bureau of Statistics.

2 Births

According to Table 3.3, the lowest births were extrapolated from populations aged 0–10 years in the 2010 Census, while the highest births were derived from the education data. The births extrapolated from *Hukou* data are very close to the births extrapolated from populations aged 10–20 years in the 2010 Census, and the two curves almost overlap in Figure 3.7. Except for the births published by the National Bureau of Statistics, the births estimated by other different sources are consistent in their changing trends. China's births tumbled in the period 2000–2003 and then rebounded after 2003. Except for an obvious increase in 2004 compared with 2003, the births remained rather stable after 2004 with a minor upturn. It is worth noting that the births published by the National Bureau of Statistics in the early years were significantly higher than the births calculated based on the 0- to 10-year-old populations in the 2010 Census, though the two were almost identical in the later years. This means the National Bureau of Statistics may have over-adjusted the births in the early years but then corrected the adjustment in later years. The births published by the National Bureau of Statistics were close to the births adjusted for education data in the early years, but much lower than the births adjusted for education data in later years, and also lower than the births adjusted for *Hukou* data and populations aged 10–20 years in the 2010 Census.

It should be pointed out that the surge in births in recent years mirrors the fourth baby boom China is undergoing, though the baby boom this time is

Table 3.3 Estimates of Annual Number of Births, 2000–2010: Derived from Various Sources of Data (Million)

	2000	2001	2002	2003	2004	2005	2006	2007	2008	2009	2010
Derived from 2010 census data at ages 0–10	14.92	14.70	14.10	13.85	15.26	15.18	15.67	15.69	16.05	16.07	14.03
Derived from 2010 census data at ages 10–20	16.56	16.33	15.70	15.44	16.91	16.82	17.33	17.35	17.73	17.74	15.63
Derived from education data	18.05	17.92	17.53	17.37	18.25	18.20	18.50	18.51	18.72	18.72	17.38
Derived from *Hukou* data	16.63	16.45	15.95	15.74	16.91	16.84	17.24	17.25	17.55	17.56	15.84
NBS published birth numbers	17.71	17.02	16.47	15.99	15.93	16.17	15.85	15.95	16.08	15.91	15.92

Source: Calculations by author.

palpably weaker than the previous baby booms. However, the baby boom would not end early in 2010, and the sudden drop in births in 2010 is not a manifestation of the actual trend. Since this study uses a linear regression fitting method to estimate births, the results are bound to be consistent with the changes in the lower-age populations in the 2010 Census. That is, because the 0-year-old population in the 2010 census showed a sudden decline compared to the populations aged 1–4 years, the births estimated through linear regression fitting will also replicate the same decline. Therefore, the estimated births in 2010 are unreliable. According to data released by the National Bureau of Statistics, China's births did not go down in 2010 but continued the trend of recent years.

3 Women of childbearing age

The number of women of childbearing age is also a requisite for the estimation of fertility rate. Our estimation was based on one scenario only. On the one hand, we extrapolated the age-specific number of women of childbearing age for each year in 2001–2010 from the 2000 census data. Before the extrapolation, we used education data to adjust the lower-age populations in the 2000 Census, and then based on the adjusted age structure for 2000, we used the life table survival ratios to estimate the age-specific number of women of childbearing age for each future year. On the other hand, building upon the 2010 census data,

Estimation of China's Low Fertility Rates 33

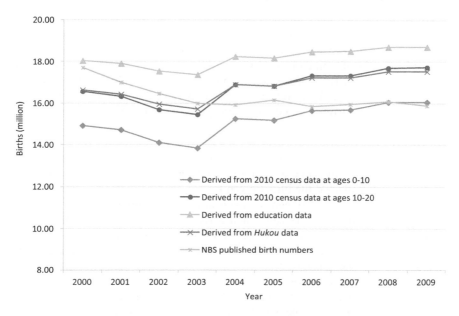

Figure 3.7 Estimates of annual number of births, 2000–2009: derived from various sources of data (million)

Source: Table 3.3.

we used the life table survival ratios to extrapolate the age-specific number of women of childbearing age for each year in 2000–2009. Lastly, we calculated the average of the numbers of women of childbearing age derived through the above two methods and took the average as the final estimate of the number of women of childbearing age.

The yearly life tables between two censuses used to estimate the number of women of childbearing age was calculated through Brass logit transformation. Although the National Bureau of Statistics has published the life expectancies for 2000 and 2010, it has not published the life tables. Therefore, we calculated the life tables for each year using the Brass logit transformation. Brass developed a linear equation between two survival probabilities l_x obtained from two different life tables using logit transformation; thus, we can derive a new life table from a standard life table because of the approximately linear relationship between the two. By applying logit transformation to the survival probabilities of the life tables for 1982, 1990 and 2000 and fitting them with linear regression, we found that the mortality rate was decreasing, but the mortality pattern remained basically stable. Therefore, we assumed that the mortality pattern remained unchanged but the mortality rate kept dropping in the period 2000–2010. The mortality rates for 2000 and 2010 were both extrapolated from the average life expectancies published by the National Bureau of Statistics. That is, with the known life expectancy and through Brass logit transformation, we can calculate the life tables for the years from 2000 to 2010. The total population and life tables for both males and females were all calculated this way.

Based on the life tables calculated for each year, we obtained the age-specific survival ratios of women in each year and then used the age structure obtained in the 2000 and 2010 censuses to extrapolate the age-specific number of women of childbearing age for each year, as shown in Table 3.4. It can be seen that the total number of women of childbearing age kept going up, but their age structure underwent changes.

4 Fertility rate

To obtain age-specific fertility rates and TFR, it is also necessary to break down the yearly births into the births given by age-specific women of childbearing age. We collected the births given by age-specific women of childbearing age in the 2000 and 2010 censuses and in the annual population surveys conducted between the two censuses and derived the age distribution of births as shown in Table 3.5. To obtain stable results, we used the age distribution for the 5-year-age group. The age distribution of births also exhibited an "aging" trend in these ten years, as can be seen from the growing proportion of births given by women aged 30 and above.

Based on the age distribution of births in each year in Table 3.5 and the total births in each year in Table 3.3, we can derive the births given by age-specific women of childbearing age in each year. With further reference to the numbers of age-specific women of childbearing age in Table 3.4, we can derive the age-specific fertility rates and TFR for each year.

Table 3.6 shows the estimated age-specific fertility rates and TFRs for the calendar years from 2000 through 2010 based on data from different sources. Figure 3.8 shows the changes in fertility rate over the period 2000–2009. China's fertility rate tumbled in the period 2000–2003 and then saw a marked increase in 2004, after which it began to level off. Although there are noticeable differences in fertility rate between different data sources, the trends of fertility rate are basically consistent among data sources (except for the fertility rates estimated using the births published by the National Bureau of Statistics). The highest fertility rates are derived from the education data, reaching 1.7 in 2000, falling below 1.7 in the period 2001–2003 and then lingering below 1.8 in the

Table 3.4 Age-Specific Number of Women of Childbearing Age: 2000–2010 (Million)

	2000	2001	2002	2003	2004	2005	2006	2007	2008	2009	2010
15–19	50.33	52.05	53.58	55.81	58.56	61.75	60.87	57.93	55.55	51.83	47.28
20–24	47.31	46.69	48.99	49.25	49.50	50.17	51.89	53.43	55.66	58.41	61.60
25–29	57.76	55.53	52.25	50.03	48.33	47.12	46.51	48.81	49.08	49.33	50.00
30–34	61.90	62.15	63.60	61.78	60.70	57.50	55.29	52.03	49.83	48.14	46.95
35–39	52.82	59.08	59.55	59.47	59.98	61.56	61.82	63.27	61.47	60.42	57.25
40–44	39.18	36.28	37.15	42.32	47.65	52.44	58.67	59.15	59.10	59.62	61.20
45–49	41.71	42.96	43.62	43.49	40.69	38.76	35.91	36.79	41.94	47.24	52.00
Total	351.00	354.75	358.74	362.15	365.42	369.31	370.97	371.42	372.62	374.99	376.28

Source: Extrapolated from age-specific populations obtained in 2000 and 2010 censuses.

Table 3.5 Age Distribution of Births in 2000–2010

	2000	2001	2002	2003	2004	2005	2006	2007	2008	2009	2010
15–19	0.0225	0.0084	0.0091	0.0188	0.0207	0.0261	0.0197	0.0147	0.0185	0.0212	0.0231
20–24	0.4077	0.3171	0.3431	0.3801	0.3694	0.3843	0.3430	0.3098	0.3135	0.3304	0.3306
25–29	0.3964	0.4528	0.4009	0.3732	0.3682	0.3314	0.3313	0.3383	0.3201	0.3192	0.3279
30–34	0.1404	0.1774	0.1963	0.1804	0.1874	0.1895	0.1943	0.1906	0.1807	0.1755	0.1741
35–39	0.0257	0.0373	0.0439	0.0400	0.0460	0.0569	0.0817	0.0981	0.0983	0.0927	0.0887
40–44	0.0049	0.0052	0.0054	0.0056	0.0068	0.0090	0.0225	0.0322	0.0459	0.0374	0.0367
45–49	0.0023	0.0019	0.0012	0.0020	0.0014	0.0028	0.0075	0.0163	0.0230	0.0236	0.0189
Total	1.0000	1.0000	1.0000	1.0000	1.0000	1.0000	1.0000	1.0000	1.0000	1.0000	1.0000

Source: National Bureau of Statistics. Tabulation on the 2000 Population Census of China. China Statistics Press, 2002; Tabulation on the 2010 Population Census of China. China Statistics Press, 2012; survey data on population changes in 2001–2009 came from the China Population and Employment Statistical Yearbooks for 2001 through 2009.

period 2004–2009. Fertility rates derived from populations aged 10–20 years in the 2010 Census are very close to those from *Hukou* data, both reaching 1.56 in 2000, then falling below 1.5 and subsequently lingering between 1.64 and 1.69. Fertility rates derived from the births published by the National Bureau of Statistics are: (1) close to the fertility rates extrapolated from the education data in 2000; (2) much lower than the fertility rates extrapolated from the education data in the period 2004–2009; (3) lower than the fertility rates extrapolated from *Hukou* data and the 10–20-year-old populations in the 2010 Census; and (4) close to the fertility rates extrapolated from the 0- to 10-year-old populations in the 2010 Census (i.e., 1.5–1.55). Judging from these estimates combined, China's fertility rate might be close to 1.7 in the late 2000s.

Nonetheless, an important assumption of this study is that the lower-age populations in the 2010 Census share the same underreporting rate with the same cohorts in the 2000 Census. However, the underreporting rates of the two censuses reported by the National Bureau of Statistics are distinctly different, with the net underreporting rate of the 2010 Census being only 0.12%. If the underreporting rate of lower-age populations in the 2010 Census is also lower than that in the 2000 Census, the estimated fertility rate would also go lower. This is possibly true because if the net underreporting rate of 0.12% in the 2010 Census is accurate, and if the underreporting rate of lower-age populations in the 2010 Census is the same as that in the 2000 Census, it means that the rate of repeated reporting could be very high in the higher-age populations in the 2010 Census. However, if the problem of duplicate reporting has been well resolved in the 2010 Census, as said by Mr. Ma Jiantang (former director of the National Bureau of Statistics), then the underreporting rate of the lower-age populations in the 2010 Census must be much lower than that in the 2000 Census. If this assumption holds, then it's possible for China's fertility rate to stand at 1.6 or 1.5 in the late 2000s. In regard to the measures taken in the 2010 Census to ensure data quality, building upon the "registration of permanent residence" as used in the 2000 Census, the 2010 Census followed the practice of "registration at first

Table 3.6 Age-specific Fertility Rates and Total Fertility Rates in the Period 2000–2010

	2000	2001	2002	2003	2004	2005	2006	2007	2008	2009	2010
Derived from 2010 census data at ages 0–10											
15–19	0.007	0.002	0.002	0.005	0.005	0.006	0.005	0.004	0.005	0.007	0.007
20–24	0.129	0.100	0.099	0.107	0.114	0.116	0.104	0.091	0.090	0.091	0.075
25–29	0.102	0.120	0.108	0.103	0.116	0.107	0.112	0.109	0.105	0.104	0.092
30–34	0.034	0.042	0.044	0.040	0.047	0.050	0.055	0.057	0.058	0.059	0.052
35–39	0.007	0.009	0.010	0.009	0.012	0.014	0.021	0.024	0.026	0.025	0.022
40–44	0.002	0.002	0.002	0.002	0.002	0.003	0.006	0.009	0.012	0.010	0.008
45–49	0.001	0.001	0.000	0.001	0.001	0.001	0.003	0.007	0.009	0.008	0.005
TFR	1.407	1.380	1.328	1.335	1.485	1.486	1.527	1.505	1.528	1.514	1.308
Derived from 2010 census data at ages 10–20											
15–19	0.007	0.003	0.003	0.005	0.006	0.007	0.006	0.004	0.006	0.007	0.008
20–24	0.143	0.111	0.110	0.119	0.126	0.129	0.115	0.101	0.100	0.100	0.084
25–29	0.114	0.133	0.121	0.115	0.129	0.118	0.123	0.120	0.116	0.115	0.102
30–34	0.038	0.047	0.048	0.045	0.052	0.055	0.061	0.064	0.064	0.065	0.058
35–39	0.008	0.010	0.012	0.010	0.013	0.016	0.023	0.027	0.028	0.027	0.024
40–44	0.002	0.002	0.002	0.002	0.002	0.003	0.007	0.009	0.014	0.011	0.009
45–49	0.001	0.001	0.000	0.001	0.001	0.001	0.004	0.008	0.010	0.009	0.006
TFR	1.562	1.534	1.480	1.489	1.646	1.647	1.689	1.665	1.687	1.671	1.456
Derived from education data											
15–19	0.008	0.003	0.003	0.006	0.006	0.008	0.006	0.005	0.006	0.008	0.008
20–24	0.156	0.122	0.123	0.134	0.136	0.139	0.122	0.107	0.105	0.106	0.093
25–29	0.124	0.146	0.135	0.130	0.139	0.128	0.132	0.128	0.122	0.121	0.114
30–34	0.041	0.051	0.054	0.051	0.056	0.060	0.065	0.068	0.068	0.068	0.064
35–39	0.009	0.011	0.013	0.012	0.014	0.017	0.024	0.029	0.030	0.029	0.027
40–44	0.002	0.003	0.003	0.002	0.003	0.003	0.007	0.010	0.015	0.012	0.010
45–49	0.001	0.001	0.000	0.001	0.001	0.001	0.004	0.008	0.010	0.009	0.006
TFR	1.703	1.682	1.652	1.675	1.777	1.781	1.802	1.775	1.782	1.764	1.620
Derived from *Hukou* data											
15–19	0.007	0.003	0.003	0.005	0.006	0.007	0.006	0.004	0.006	0.007	0.008
20–24	0.143	0.112	0.112	0.121	0.126	0.129	0.114	0.100	0.099	0.099	0.085
25–29	0.114	0.134	0.122	0.117	0.129	0.118	0.123	0.120	0.114	0.114	0.104
30–34	0.038	0.047	0.049	0.046	0.052	0.055	0.061	0.063	0.064	0.064	0.059
35–39	0.008	0.010	0.012	0.011	0.013	0.016	0.023	0.027	0.028	0.027	0.025
40–44	0.002	0.002	0.002	0.002	0.002	0.003	0.007	0.009	0.014	0.011	0.009
45–49	0.001	0.001	0.000	0.001	0.001	0.001	0.004	0.008	0.010	0.009	0.006
TFR	1.569	1.545	1.503	1.517	1.646	1.648	1.680	1.655	1.670	1.654	1.476
Derived from NBS published birth numbers											
15–19	0.008	0.003	0.003	0.005	0.006	0.007	0.005	0.004	0.005	0.006	0.008
20–24	0.153	0.116	0.115	0.123	0.119	0.124	0.105	0.092	0.091	0.090	0.085
25–29	0.122	0.139	0.126	0.119	0.121	0.114	0.113	0.111	0.105	0.103	0.104
30–34	0.040	0.049	0.051	0.047	0.049	0.053	0.056	0.058	0.058	0.058	0.059
35–39	0.009	0.011	0.012	0.011	0.012	0.015	0.021	0.025	0.026	0.024	0.025
40–44	0.002	0.002	0.002	0.002	0.002	0.003	0.006	0.009	0.012	0.010	0.010
45–49	0.001	0.001	0.000	0.001	0.001	0.001	0.003	0.007	0.009	0.008	0.006
TFR	1.671	1.598	1.551	1.542	1.550	1.583	1.544	1.530	1.531	1.499	1.483

Source: Calculations by the authors.

Estimation of China's Low Fertility Rates 37

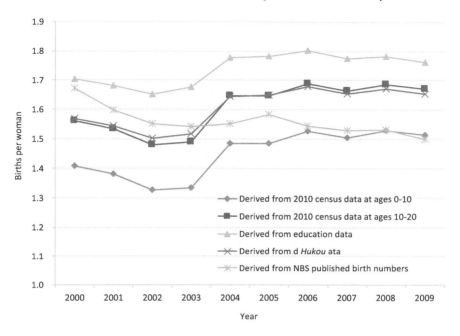

Figure 3.8 Total fertility rates derived from different sources of data, 2000–2009
Source: Table 3.6.

sight", which means the registration was carried out at both the registered residence and the current residence of respondents to avoid underreporting as best as possible. Therefore, even if we are skeptical about whether the overall data quality of the 2010 Census might literally outcompete that of the 2000 Census, we can still be assured that the underreporting rate of the lower-age populations in the 2010 Census should be lower than that in the 2000 Census.

Lastly, it is worth mentioning that, except for the fertility rates extrapolated from the births published by the National Bureau of Statistics, all other estimates have shown a sudden dip in the fertility rate in 2010. Of course, this is caused by the sudden drop in births in 2010. As mentioned earlier, because the estimated births are calculated by regression fitting, this sudden drop is directly linked to the age structure of the lower-age populations in the 2010 Census. In the 2010 Census, the 0-year-old population suddenly dropped by 1.87 million compared to the 1-year-old population, which will also lead to an inevitable plunge in the estimated births. According to the 2010 Census, the 1- to 4-year-old populations went up slowly but steadily; yet, a sudden dip was found in the 0-year-old population. In the absence of drastic fluctuations in China's economic development, social environment and fertility policy, even if we rule out a potential baby boom brought about by population inertia, a plunge in births is highly unlikely to take place. Therefore, the sudden drop in fertility in 2010 is largely unlikely. Instead, it should continue the trend of steady change in previous years.

Estimation of Fertility Rate in 2010

The previous section did not give a good estimation of the fertility rate in 2010. As a matter of fact, after the release of data from the "Sixth Census", the academia's estimates and debates on the fertility level focus mainly on China's fertility rates since 2000, and there is little attention paid to the estimation of China's fertility rate in 2010. Due to the lack of data, it's extremely difficult to estimate the fertility rate in 2010. In this section, we will use a relatively simple but classic method to indirectly estimate China's fertility rate in 2010.

Data and Methodology

As mentioned earlier, the data used in previous studies to estimate fertility rate tend to fall into two categories. Census data pertain to the first category, i.e., the census data are used to estimate the fertility rates between censuses – be they the data on lower-age groups or the same data adjusted for higher-age groups in the next census. The other category encompasses data from other sources, mainly education data and *Hukou* data. Scholars who use these data hold the opinion that whether it is the census data and sample survey data from the National Bureau of Statistics, or the fertility survey data or fertility statistics from the National Population and Family Planning Commission, they are all "intra-system" data that are deemed to have consistency error. Neither comparison nor adjustment between these data can overcome the challenge of "intra-system" data error. In spite of strong internal consistency, it's difficult to derive convincing estimates with such data. Therefore, in pursuit of data from other sources, scholars began to jump out of the "system" and embrace other systems, such as the education system or the *Hukou* system, in an attempt to adjust the "intra-system" results through the comparison with data from different systems.

Should the demographic data registered by each system be complete and accurate, the results obtained by each system ought to be consistent, and yet, that's not what happened. For example, the census data on lower-age cohorts are supposed to be the most complete and the largest in numbers, while the number of primary school students registered in the education system or the number of residents registered in the *Hukou* system is supposed to be slightly smaller. The census is also supposed to obtain the largest numbers of older-age populations, and yet, the largest numbers are found in *Hukou* data. Therefore, it seems that data from different systems have their respective flaws. In theory, it is logical to compare and adjust the data of the census system with the data from other systems. However, since data from other systems are also flawed, such comparisons and adjustments are deemed unscientific. Against that backdrop, some studies have attempted to prove that data from other sources are more accurate and less flawed. Their theoretical analysis, as well as evidence from local surveys, point to greater accuracy in education data or *Hukou* data, which can thus be used to adjust data from the census system.

Let's go back to "intra-system" and use only census data to estimate the fertility rate in 2010. Previous studies built on census data tended to use the data on lower-age populations. In this study, we used the fertility-related data obtained from the census, including number of children born to each woman and the period fertility rate in 2010. Although the number of children born to each woman is useful for estimating the period fertility rate, it is rarely used in demographic studies.

Both types of data are available in China's four censuses from 1982 to 2010, and they are actually what we call cohort fertility rate and period fertility rate. The cohort fertility rate is the number of children born to each woman. The tabulations on censuses published by the National Bureau of Statistics contain the number of children born and the mean number of children born per woman at different ages. The period fertility rate refers to the fertility occurred in the last 12 months prior to the census, and the number of children born to each woman by age and the age-specific fertility rate are also provided in the tabulations on censuses. The mean number of children born per women by age represents the reproductive experience of women in each age cohort from the outset of their reproductive years to the time of the census. For women whose reproductive years have ended, this number represents their lifetime fertility rate. As for the period fertility rate, if we add up the period fertility rates from younger to older ages, we will get the cumulative fertility rate at each age, and eventually the TFR. The TFR represents the lifetime fertility rate of a hypothetical cohort – that is, the lifetime fertility rate that this hypothetical cohort would have achieved if the women in this cohort had lived their lives according to the age-specific fertility rates in the year preceding the census. The mean number of children born and the cumulative fertility rate for each age are very similar in form and can be tested for consistency by comparing the two.

If the fertility rate (including fertility level and fertility pattern) remains stable over a long period of time, then the mean number of children born per woman at each age and the cumulative fertility rate for the corresponding age (or the lifetime fertility rate and the TFR, respectively) should be exactly equal. Even with a decline in fertility, these two indicators should be relatively consistent across younger age groups. Under normal circumstances, the number of children born will be more accurate in the younger age groups, while it may be underreported in the older age groups due to reasons such as the child(ren) being deceased or having left home. The fertility data for the year preceding the census may be subject to errors or underreporting due to reporting interval, or, as in China, widespread underreporting. The period fertility rate can be tested by comparing it with the number of children born per woman. Generally speaking, comparing the mean number of children born per woman aged below 35 or 30 and the period fertility rate can help test and then adjust the period fertility rate.

In the 1960s, William Brass proposed a method of adjusting and estimating the period fertility rate using the P/F ratio – that is, using the fertility rate as reflected in the number of children born per woman to adjust the period fertility rate (Brass and Coale, 1968). Simple in design and clear in logic, this method is easy to understand and apply. In a nutshell, the method is to calculate the ratio of the mean number of children born per woman at each age ($P(i)$) to corresponding cumulative fertility rate for each age ($F(i)$) and then to calculate the average of such ratios for women in younger age groups, followed by multiplying this average by the period fertility rate to obtain the adjusted TFR. Although only the ratios for women in younger age groups are used for adjustment, calculating the ratios for women in different age groups and observing how this ratio changes with age can help uncover flaws in the data or reveal a certain fertility trend. For example, a noticeable dip in P/F ratio in the older age groups would indicate a possible underreporting of the number of children born per woman in the older age groups, which happens frequently, while a decrease in the consistency of P/F ratio in parallel with the increase in age would suggest a continued decline in fertility rate over the past decade or two.

$P(i)$ refers to the mean number of children born per woman at each age (i = 1, 2, ..., 7, corresponding to age groups 15–19, 20–24, ..., 45–49, respectively), while $F(i)$ refers to the age-specific cumulative fertility rate matched to $P(i)$. We usually add up the fertility rates from younger to the older age groups to obtain the cumulative fertility rate for each age, which does not match $P(i)$. This is because the cumulative fertility rate for each age group corresponds to the value at the end of the age group, but the mean number of children born per woman for each age group does not. Therefore, we need to adjust the cumulative fertility rate for each age group in order to match $P(i)$. Brass has proposed the following adjustment methods: if $\phi(i)$ represents the cumulative fertility rate for each age group, then $\phi(i)$ can be adjusted to $F(i)$ using the equation of $F(i) = \phi(i-1) + a(i)f(i) + b(i)f(i+1) + c(i)\phi(7)$, where $f(i)$ refers to the age-specific fertility rate, and a, b and c refer to the adjustment coefficients obtained through linear regression fitting using Coale–Trussell fertility model for the fertility interpolation between adjacent age groups, thereby adjusting $\phi(i)$ to $F(i)$. Table 3.7 shows the a, b and c coefficient values for each age group.

Estimation of China's TFR in 2010

China's previous population censuses and 1% population sample surveys (mini-censuses) since 1982 all provided data on the number of children born to women and the number of births in the year preceding the census. For example, Table 3.8 shows these two figures obtained from the two censuses and one mini-census conducted since 2000. Examining and comparing these two types of figures has led to certain findings. For example, for any age group, the number of children born to women should be greater than the number of births, because the number of births is only the births in the year preceding the census, while the number of children born is actually the cumulative number of births over the years prior to the census. Theoretically, the two may be equal, but in fact, the number of children born to women should be greater than the number of births, and it is absolutely impossible for the number of children born to women to be less than the number of births. However, in the 2000 census, the number of children born to women aged 15–19 years was less than the number of births. In the 2005 mini-census, the two were almost equal. Obviously, the former result doesn't make sense, while the latter is not necessarily reasonable, suggesting that there is a flaw in the number of children born to women aged 15–19 years. In the previous censuses and mini-censuses conducted

Table 3.7 Coefficients Used to Adjust $\phi(i)$ to $F(i)$

i	Age Group	a	b	c
1	15–19	2.147	−0.244	0.0034
2	20–24	2.838	−0.758	0.0162
3	25–29	2.760	−0.594	0.0133
4	30–34	2.949	−0.566	0.0025
5	35–39	3.029	−0.823	0.0006
6	40–44	3.419	−2.966	−0.0001
7	45–49	3.535	−0.007	−0.0002

Note: This set of coefficients applies to the age-specific fertility rates calculated from the births given by women disaggregated by the age at childbirth, which are exactly the age-specific fertility rates provided in the Tabulation on the Sixth Census. A further set of coefficients applies to the age-specific fertility rates calculated from the births given by women disaggregated by the age as of the end of year preceding the census (United Nations, 1983, p. 34).

Source: United Nations. 1983. *Manual X: Indirect Techniques for Demographic Estimation*. Pp. 27–64. New York, NY: United Nations, Department of Economic and Social Affairs, ST/ESA/SER.A/81.

Table 3.8 Number of Children Born to Women at Different Ages and Number of Births in the Period 2000–2010

Age Group	2000 Number of Children Born	2000 Number of Births	2005 Number of Children Born	2005 Number of Births	2010 Number of Children Born	2010 Number of Births
15–19	24,321	26,626	4,271	4,209	54,942	27,474
20–24	1,266,045	481,919	164,787	61,889	1,514,471	393,426
25–29	5,399,789	468,568	529,128	53,367	3,938,366	390,225
30–34	8,927,373	165,965	1,007,643	30,521	5,775,399	207,233
35–39	9,475,226	30,407	1,396,376	9,157	8,358,273	105,550
40–44	7,829,280	5,749	1,415,364	1,447	9,930,802	43,617
45–49	9,675,351	2,720	1,192,174	451	9,258,278	22,535

Source: National Bureau of Statistics. Tabulation on the 2000 Population Census of China. China Statistics Press, 2002; Tabulation on the 2005 1% Population Sample Survey of China. China Statistics Press, 2007; Tabulation on the 2010 Population Census of China. China Statistics Press, 2012.

since 1982, except for the 1982 and 2010 censuses, other censuses and mini-censuses all had the same problem. However, such problem is hard to discern in other age groups. We could generally run simulations with the use of the model fertility tables to check the differences between actual numbers and those generated by model simulation, and then, we would analyze and discern any potential problems.

By comparing the mean number of children born per woman in different age groups (as shown in Table 3.9), it can be seen that except for the increase in all three years in the 15–19 age group and in two years in the 20–24 age group, the mean number of children born per woman declines in all other age groups. Through longitudinal comparison (i.e., intra-cohort comparison), it can be seen that except for the decline in 2005 in the 40–44 age group and in 2010 in the 45–49 age group, or the decline in 2000 in the 35–39 age group and in 2010 in the 45–49 age group, the mean number of children born per woman increases with age within all other cohorts. This is logically reasonable and inevitable, and a decline is unreasonable and impossible. The above analysis has pointed to some data inaccuracies or errors at both ends of the age groups (i.e., the lowest age group and the highest age group). In the indirect estimation of fertility rates, data at both ends of the age groups are often excluded to make sure the estimates are more consistent and reasonable.

Using the figures in Tables 3.8 and 3.9 and Brass P/F ratio estimation method, we obtained the results shown in Table 3.10. Table 3.10 actually shows the key calculation steps for the P/F ratio. The P/F ratio shows improbable anomaly in the 15–19 age group and a marked increase in the highest age group; yet, the results for other age groups are comparatively stable and consistent.

As shown above, the P/F ratios were remarkably consistent from the 20–24 age group through the 35–39 age group, with marked increases in the last two age groups, which are reflective of China's decline in fertility rate in the 1990s. As mentioned earlier, if the P/F ratio increases from low to high age groups, it suggests that the fertility rate has undergone a continued decline in the past decade or two, making $P(i)$ and $F(i)$ embark on different trends. In such a circumstance, using the fertility rate reflected by the $P(i)$ value to adjust the period fertility rate would be risky or even obtain an opposing result. However, the consistent P/F ratios from the 20–24 age group through the 35–39 age group in Table 3.10 suggest that

Table 3.9 Mean Number of Children Born per Woman at Different Ages in the Period 2000–2010

Age Group	2000	2005	2010
15–19	0.0054	0.0062	0.0125
20–24	0.3061	0.3070	0.2596
25–29	1.0246	0.9266	0.8440
30–34	1.5245	1.3712	1.2928
35–39	1.8493	1.6656	1.5235
40–44	2.0470	1.9052	1.6871
45–49	2.3563	2.0852	1.8366

Source: Same as Table 3.2.

Table 3.10 Calculation of the P/F Ratio

i	Age Group	$P(i)$	$f(i)$	$\phi(i)$	$F(i)$	P/F ratio
1	15–19	0.0125	0.0059	0.0296	−0.0002	
2	20–24	0.2596	0.0695	0.3770	0.1822	1.4252
3	25–29	0.8440	0.0841	0.7973	0.5975	1.4126
4	30–34	1.2928	0.0458	1.0265	0.9249	1.3978
5	35–39	1.5235	0.0187	1.1201	1.0777	1.4136
6	40–44	1.6871	0.0075	1.1576	1.1318	1.4907
7	45–49	1.8366	0.0047	1.1810	1.1739	1.5645

Source: Calculated from the data in Tables 3.2 and 3.3.

China's fertility rate has not changed much and has remained relatively stable over the past 15 years. This also complies with the assumptions used by this method. Then, the average of the P/F ratios for the 20–24 through 35–39 age groups (i.e. 1.4123) can be used as the adjustment coefficient for China's fertility rate in 2010. This value shows that the underreporting rate associated with the period fertility rate in 2010 was as high as 40% or more. Therefore, multiplying this coefficient by the TFR of 1.18 obtained from the 2010 Census gives the adjusted TFR in 2010, which is 1.66. This estimate coincides with the fertility estimates since 2000 obtained by adjusting the census data for the *Hukou* data. Because the data and methods used to derive the two estimates differ significantly, whether such consistent results are just a coincidence deserves further study and discussion.

Estimation of Average Fertility Rate Between Censuses

In both sections above, fertility data were used to estimate the fertility rate. First, we estimated the underreporting rate associated with the fertility data, and then, we adjusted the fertility data to arrive at an estimate of fertility rate. In this section, we will use another indirect estimation method – the generalized stable population model – to estimate the average fertility rates between censuses. Bypassing fertility data, this method estimates the fertility rates between two censuses using only the age distribution data from the two censuses.

Data and Methodology

In this section, we will use two fertility estimation methods developed based on the generalized stable population model, which can be collectively referred to as the variable-r method. In the early 1980s, Preston and Coale (1982) and Preston (1983) extended the stable population theory to develop a generalized stable population model, thereby expanding the application of the population estimation method underlain by the stable population model from stable, closed populations to unstable, open (in any state) populations. Some application cases of them and other scholars have derived good and satisfactory results. There are few studies applying these methods to Chinese data, and thus, it is worth our exploration. Next, we will first expound on these methods and then use them to estimate China's fertility rates between censuses conducted from 1982 to 2010. Although details about these methods can be found in the original articles, for ease of understanding, we will briefly introduce them here.

According to Preston and Coale and Preston and Preston et al., for any population, if $x > y$, the relationship between populations at different ages ($N(a)$) can be represented by the following equation:

$$N(x,t) = N(y,t)\, e^{-\int_y^x r(a,t)\,da} \frac{l_x}{l_y} \tag{1}$$

where x and y refer to age; t refers to the time stamp; $r(a)$ refers to the growth rate of population at each age; and $\dfrac{l_x}{l_y}$ refers to the survival probabilities from age y to age x. For simplicity, the time stamp t is excluded from the equation. Meanwhile, if y is 0 year old, then $N(0) = B$ (i.e., the number of births) and Equation (1) is transformed into:

$$N(x) = B\, e^{-\int_0^x r(a)\,da}\, p(x) \tag{2}$$

where $p(x)$ refers to the survival probabilities from birth to age x. If both sides of equation (2) are divided by the total population N:

$$\frac{N(x)}{N} = \frac{B}{N}\, e^{-\int_0^x r(a)\,da}\, p(x) \tag{3}$$

$\dfrac{N(x)}{N}$ is actually the age structure, represented by $c(a)$, while $\dfrac{B}{N}$ is the birth rate, represented by b; then:

$$c(a) = b\, e^{-\int_0^a r(x)\,dx}\, p(a) \tag{4}$$

In fact, Equation (4) is an extension of the stable population age structure equation – that is, if the growth rate remains the same for populations at all ages, Equation (4) will become $c(a) = b e^{-ra} p(a)$. This is the well-known stable population characteristic equation. Other stable population characteristic equations can also be extended in a similar way, so that the estimation method based on stable population model can be generalized to populations of any state.

Based on Equations (2) and (4), Preston and Coale and Preston derived two methods for estimating fertility. The first method is to use the age distribution data from the two censuses and Brass logit transformation to estimate births and age-specific mortality probabilities between two censuses, i.e., b and $p(a)$ in Equation (4). Although they did not further convert the estimated birth rate into the estimated TFR, we can easily convert the birth rate into the number of births and then extrapolate the age-specific fertility rates and TFRs from the reproductive age structure and age distribution of women of reproductive age in the two censuses. Another method is to directly estimate the net reproductive rate and TFR from the data on age distribution and women's reproductive age structure in the two censuses. This study will use these two methods separately to estimate China's fertility rates between censuses. Although both methods are based on the growth rates of populations at different ages – thus, they can be collectively referred to as variable-r method – according to Preston, we call the former method the "Integrated System for Demographic Estimation" and the latter the "variable-r method".

According to the integrated approach, Equation (4) can be reorganized as follows:

$$\frac{1}{p(a)} = \frac{be^{-\int_0^a r(x)dx}}{c(a)} \qquad (5)$$

According to the logit transformation proposed by Brass, the logit transformation of mortality/survival probabilities in any two life tables will arrive at a kind of approximate linear relationship, as shown below:

$$\ln\frac{q(a)}{p(a)} = \alpha + \beta \ln\frac{q_s(a)}{p_s(a)} \qquad (6)$$

where $q_s(a)$ and $p_s(a)$ refer to the mortality and survival probability functions from the "standard" life table; α refers to the mortality rate parameter; and β refers to the mortality pattern parameter. For "standard" life tables, we tend to choose model life tables with similar mortality patterns, so that β can be ignored, i.e., assuming $\beta = 1$. Therefore, Equation (6) can be transformed into:

$$\frac{1}{p(a)} = e^\alpha \frac{q_s(a)}{p_s(a)} + 1 \qquad (7)$$

By combining Equations (5) and (7), we have:

$$\frac{be^{-\int_0^a r(x)dx}}{c(a)} = e^\alpha \frac{q_s(a)}{p_s(a)} + 1 \qquad (8)$$

If k is represented by e^α, then Equation (8) can be transformed into:

$$\frac{e^{-\int_0^a r(x)dx}}{c(a)} = \frac{1}{b} + \frac{k}{b}\frac{q_s(a)}{p_s(a)} \qquad (9)$$

Equation (9) is the one used to estimate births and mortality rate from the data on age structure and "standard" life tables. By performing linear regression with $\frac{e^{-\int_0^a r(x)dx}}{c(a)}$ as the dependent variable (Y) and $\frac{q_s(a)}{p_s(a)}$ as the independent variable (X), the reciprocal of the intercept of the regression line is the birth rate, and the slope of the regression line multiplied by the birth rate would derive the estimated mortality rate. Using the birth rate estimated by this method, we can further obtain the TFR. The life tables estimated by this method will also be used to calculate the survival probabilities needed by the latter method (i.e., variable-r method) in estimating the TFR.

46   Estimation of China's Low Fertility Rates

So, how does the variable-r method estimate the fertility rate? The variable-r method can first estimate the net reproductive rate and then estimate the TFR. The calculation equation defined with the net reproduction rate (*NRR*) is as follows:

$$NRR = \int_{\alpha}^{\beta} m(a)p(a)\,da \tag{10}$$

where $m(a)$ refers to the age-specific fertility rate. Since $m(a) = \dfrac{B(a)}{N(a)}$, by replacing its denominator $N(a)$ with Equation (2) and then substituting it into Equation (10), we have $NRR = \int_{\alpha}^{\beta} \dfrac{B(a)}{B} e^{\int_{0}^{a} r(x)dx}\,da$. If $v(a)$ is used to represent the age structure $\dfrac{B(a)}{B}$ of women of childbearing age, then:

$$NRR = \int_{\alpha}^{\beta} v(a) e^{\int_{0}^{a} r(x)dx}\,da \tag{11}$$

From Equation (11), we can see that unlike the traditional method for calculating *NRR*, the new method here no longer needs age-specific fertility rate and age-specific mortality rate, but only needs the growth rates of populations at different ages and the age structure of births.

After *NRR* is obtained, the gross reproductive rate (GRR) and TFR can then be calculated using the following equations: $GRR = NRR / p(\bar{m})$ and $TFR = GRR\,(1 + SRB)$, where $p(\bar{m})$ refers to the probability of surviving to average reproductive age, and *SRB* refers to sex ratio at birth. Taken altogether, the equation for estimating TFR is as follows:

$$TFR = \frac{NRR\,(1 + SRB)}{p(\bar{m})} \tag{12}$$

According to this equation, in addition to NRR, both SRB and survival probability would have an effect on TFR. China's high SRB will push up the TFR.

Estimation of Fertility Rates Between Censuses

Fertility estimation based on the generalized stable population model uses age–sex distribution data from two censuses. When using the age–sex distribution data from the four censuses from 1982 to 2010, we included age–sex distribution data for the military population. However, the calculation results show that whether the military population is included or not has a minor or even negligible effect on the estimates.

Using the integrated approach, Table 3.11 shows China's estimated fertility rates between the 2000 Census and the 2010 Census. This method requires us to do separate calculations for men and women. Table 3.11 presents the estimated birth rates and mortality rates of male populations between the two censuses based on the age distribution data from the 2000 Census and the 2010 Census. The steps for estimating the birth rates and mortality rates of female populations between the two censuses are completely the same and thus will not be repeated here.

First, calculate the age-specific population growth rates between the two censuses:

$$r(x) = \frac{\ln \dfrac{N_{t+h}(x)}{N_t(x)}}{h} \tag{13}$$

Where h refers to the number of years between the two censuses. The values of $r(x)$ are listed in column 5 of the table and added up from age 0 to age a to get the values listed in column 6. Then, the number of person-years lived at each age between the two censuses is obtained:

$$N(a) = \frac{N_{t+h}(a) - N_t(a)}{r(a)\,h} \tag{14}$$

The values of $N(a)$ are listed in column 4 of the table and are used to calculate the annualized proportion of age-specific populations $c(a)$:

$$c(a) = \frac{N(a) + N(a-5)}{10 \sum_{0}^{\infty} N(a)} \tag{15}$$

The values of $c(a)$ are listed in column 7 of the table. We can then obtain dependent variable $\dfrac{e^{-\int_0^a r(x)\,dx}}{c(a)}$, the values of which are listed in column 8. Next, by calculating $\dfrac{q_s(a)}{p_s(a)}$ from the selected "standard" life table, we get the independent variable, the values of which are listed in column 9. This study did not choose the model life table as the "standard" life table, but chose the life table calculated based on the 1982 census data as the "standard" life table (Information Processing Office, Population Research Institute, Renmin University of China, 1987). This is because the data quality of the 1982 Census is particularly high, and the use of the life table calculated from the 1982 census data can give considerably better representation for China's mortality pattern and make the estimation results more accurate.

We employed robust regression to perform linear regression fitting on the dependent and independent variables calculated through the above steps, using the values for the 10–14 through 75–79 age groups (data at both ends of the age groups are prone to be underreported or misreported). Then, we can estimate the birth rate between two censuses from the reciprocal of the intercept of regression line. The regression equation for the male population fitted to the data in Table 3.11 is: $Y = 75.3653 + 45.9398X$, i.e., $b = \dfrac{1}{75.3653} = 0.013269$. Applying the same method, the regression equation for the female population is: $Y = 76.4149 + 44.2032X$, i.e., $b = \dfrac{1}{76.4149} = 0.013086$. By multiplying the male and female birth rates by their respective total populations (the total male population is the sum of column 4 in Table 3.11), we can get the male and female births. The total number of births was 16.88 million, and the estimated average birth rate between the 2000 and 2010 censuses was 13.18 per thousand population.

What is the fertility level will the birth rate or the number of births estimated by us reflect? To estimate the TFR, we need to break down the total number of births into the numbers of births given by women of different childbearing ages and then divide the age-specific number of births by the age-specific number of women of childbearing age to get the age-specific fertility rate and TFR. We can first break down the estimated total number of births according to the average age-specific numbers of births given by women of childbearing age in the two censuses, and with the average age-specific numbers of women of childbearing age in the two censuses, we can eventually obtain the age-specific fertility rates and TFRs between the two censuses. The results showed that the average TFR was 1.56 in the period 2000–2010. We employed the same method to estimate the birth rates, number of births, and TFRs in the periods 1982–1990 and 1990–2000, and the corresponding results are shown in Table 3.12. According to our estimates, the TFR between the 1982 and 1990 censuses and between the 1990–2000 censuses was 2.63 and 1.68, respectively.

By comparing our estimates with the birth rates and births published by the National Bureau of Statistics (see Table 3.12), it can be seen that our estimates for the periods 1982–1990 and 2000–2010 are relatively close to those published by the National Bureau of Statistics, while our estimates for the period 1990–2000 are significantly different from those published by the National Bureau of Statistics. Specifically, the birth rates estimated for the periods 1982–1990 and 2000–2010 were only 0.07 percentage points higher than those published by the National Bureau of Statistics, while the birth rate estimated for the period 1990–2000 was 0.2 percentage points lower than that published by the National Bureau of Statistics. When converted into births, the average number of births estimated was about 800,000 greater than the number published for the period 1982–1990, 600,000 greater than the number published for the period 2000–2010, and 2.87 million fewer than the number published for the period 1990–2000.

The above estimates of China's fertility rate, obtained through the integrated approach, are not only consistent with many existing studies but also coincide with our judgment about China's fertility level. Next, we will use the variable-r method to estimate fertility rates between censuses to test whether the results of the two methods are consistent. Table 3.13 shows the calculation steps of the variable-r method.

First, Equation (13) is used to calculate the age-specific population growth rate for women in the period 2000–2010, the values of which are shown in column 6 of Table 3.13. Then, the population growth rates are added up from age 0 to age a (column 7), and the corresponding exponents are calculated (column 8). Next, the age distribution of births in the period 2000–2010 is calculated (column 2), followed by the calculation of net reproduction rate NRR (column 9). Lastly, Equation (12) can be used to estimate the TFR from the net reproductive rate. The results show that the average TFR in the period 2000–2010 was 1.68. This estimate is

Estimation of China's Low Fertility Rates   49

Table 3.11 Male Populations in the Period 2000–2010

Age	Population by Age in 2000	Population by Age in 2010	Number of Person-years Lived by Age	Population Growth Rate by Age	Cumulative Growth Rate	Annualized Proportion of Population by Age	Ratio of Negative Exponent of Cumulative Growth Rate to Age Structure	Ratio of Death Probability to Survival Probability
	$N(a)_{2000}$	$N(a)_{2010}$	$N(a)$	$r(a)$	$\int_0^a r(x)dx$	$c(a)$	$\dfrac{e^{-\int_0^a r(x)dx}}{c(a)}$	$\dfrac{q_s(a)}{p_s(a)}$
(1)	(2)	(3)	(4)	(5)	(6)	(7)	(8)	(9)
0	37,648,694	41,062,566	39,330,940	0.0087	0.0000	0.0125	76.4525	0.0542
5	48,303,208	38,464,665	43,197,364	−0.0228	0.0087	0.0144	74.4300	0.0611
10	65,344,739	40,267,277	51,798,193	−0.0484	−0.0141	0.0159	86.0156	0.0653
15	53,686,859	52,151,487	52,915,461	−0.0029	−0.0625	0.0166	83.5715	0.0711
20	48,659,026	64,999,573	56,435,575	0.0290	−0.0654	0.0170	70.4173	0.0787
25	60,657,818	51,305,390	55,851,157	−0.0167	−0.0365	0.0172	75.9816	0.0866
30	65,539,595	49,782,658	57,300,500	−0.0275	−0.0532	0.0176	85.2844	0.0963
35	56,271,164	60,515,080	58,367,410	0.0073	−0.0807	0.0168	85.9955	0.1097
40	42,288,791	63,661,239	52,248,499	0.0409	−0.0734	0.0168	85.9955	0.1097
45	43,967,965	53,812,914	48,724,786	0.0202	−0.0325	0.0153	76.7825	0.1294
50	32,818,233	40,376,977	36,467,137	0.0207	−0.0123	0.0129	82.2612	0.1601
55	24,068,942	41,090,065	31,824,459	0.0535	0.0084	0.0104	92.5160	0.2122
60	21,676,235	29,835,670	25,539,084	0.0319	0.0619	0.0087	84.2963	0.3032
65	17,549,348	20,748,471	19,104,288	0.0167	0.0938	0.0068	92.3233	0.4748
70	12,436,154	16,403,453	14,328,380	0.0277	0.1106	0.0051	113.3796	0.7919
75	7,175,811	11,278,859	90,732,38	0.0452	0.1383	0.0036	141.0377	1.4776
80	3,203,868	5,917,502	4,422,801	0.0614	0.1835	0.0020	195.0643	3.0640
85+	1,342,707	2,857,250	2,005,561	0.0755	0.2449	0.0010	301.3367	

Source: National Bureau of Statistics. Tabulation on the 2000 Population Census of China. China Statistics Press, 2002; Tabulation on the 2010 Population Census of China. China Statistics Press, 2012.

Table 3.12 Fertility Estimates Between Censuses from 1982 Through 2010 Versus the Results Published by the National Bureau of Statistics

Indicator	1982–1990	1990–2000	2000–2010
Birth rate estimated (per 1,000)	22.33	15.08	13.18
Birth rate published per 1,000)	21.58	17.25	12.50
Births estimated (million)	23.78	17.80	16.88
Births published (million)	23.09	20.67	16.27
TFR estimated	2.63	1.68	1.56

Source: Calculations by author.

0.12 higher than that obtained by the integrated approach. Against the backdrop of low fertility, 0.12 is no small difference. We further estimated the TFRs in the periods 1982–1990 and 1990–2000 using the variable-r method (results are shown in Table 3.14), which stood at 2.60 and 1.61, respectively. The TFR for the period 1982–1990 obtained by the variable-r method is almost identical with that obtained by the integrated approach (with a difference of only 0.03); yet, the TFR for the period 1990–2000 obtained by the variable-r method is only slightly lower than that obtained by the integrated approach (with a difference of 0.07). By comparing the results obtained by these two methods, it can be seen that the difference is gradually increasing.

Calculating the net reproductive rate with traditional methods would need the age-specific fertility rates and mortality rates, while the variable-r method sidesteps these data, using the age distribution of population and the age structure of births instead to estimate the net reproductive rate. Against the backdrop of deteriorating quality of fertility and mortality data from China's population censuses, variable-r method is without doubt a simple and effective method for estimating fertility rate. This is because not only are the age distribution of population and the age structure of births easy to collect, but such data are also significantly more accurate than the data on levels of fertility and mortality. Of course, its effectiveness hinges largely on the accuracy of the age distribution data from the two censuses. However, because the estimates are based on the age-specific population growth rates between the censuses, the relative accuracy of the age distribution data from the two censuses is deemed of paramount importance. In other words, even if the age distribution data from the two censuses are underreported or repeatedly reported, but if the level of underreporting or repeated reporting remains consistent, the accuracy of estimation results won't be compromised. This is especially conducive to estimations based on China's census data. Moreover, the data on age structure of births needed in this method are actually the age pattern of fertility, which also has little effect on the accuracy of estimation.

Cai Yong (2008) and Zhao Menghan (2015) both used the variable-r method to estimate the fertility rates in the periods 1990–2000 and 2000–2010, respectively, and the fertility rates in these two periods as obtained by this study are basically identical with their results. In his study, Cai Yong confirmed that compared to the 1990 Census, the 2000 Census saw no change to the underreporting pattern and no

Estimation of China's Low Fertility Rates   51

Table 3.13 Estimated Net Reproduction Rate in the period 2000–2010

Age	Age Distribution of Births in the Period 2000–2010 $v(a)$	Population by Age in 2000 $N(a)_{2000}$	Population by Age in 2010 $N(a)_{2010}$	Population Growth Rate by Age $r(a)$	Cumulative Growth Rate $\int_0^a r(x)\,dx$	Exponent of Cumulative Growth Rate $e^{\int_0^a r(x)\,dx}$	Net Reproductive Rate $v(a)e^{\int_0^a r(x)\,dx}$
(1)	(2)	(4)	(5)	(6)	(7)	(8)	(9)
0–4		31,329,680	34,470,044	0.0096			
5–9		41,849,379	32416884	−0.0255	−0.0161	0.9840	
10–14		60,051,894	34,641,185	−0.0550	−0.2175	0.8045	
15–19	0.0184	50,170,752	47,987,193	−0.0044	−0.3661	0.6934	0.0128
20–24	0.3481	46,666,004	63,426,563	0.0307	−0.3006	0.7404	0.2577
25–29	0.3600	57,404,984	50,195,097	−0.0134	−0.2574	0.7731	0.2783
30–34	0.1806	61,972,390	47,637,178	−0.0263	−0.3567	0.7000	0.1264
35–39	0.0645	53,021,514	57,650,515	0.0084	−0.4016	0.6693	0.0432
40–44	0.0192	39,007,731	61,153,229	0.0450	−0.2682	0.7647	0.0147
45–49	0.0092	41,588,890	51,824,489	0.0220	−0.1008	0.9041	0.0083
Total	1.0000						0.7414

Source: National Bureau of Statistics. Tabulation on the 2000 Population Census of China. China Statistics Press, 2002; Tabulation on the 2010 Population Census of China. China Statistics Press, 2012.

52 Estimation of China's Low Fertility Rates

Table 3.14 Estimated Fertility Rates Between Censuses from 1982 Through 2010

Indicator	1982–1990	1990–2000	2000–2010
Net reproduction rate (NRR)	1.1515	0.7085	0.7414
Sex ratio at birth (SRB)	1.0988	1.1408	1.1740
Survival probability ($p(\bar{m})$)	0.9286	0.9444	0.9582
Total fertility rate (TFR)	2.6027	1.6060	1.6821

Note: The SRB between censuses is the average of SRBs in the two censuses; the survival probabilities come from the $p(25)$ values for female population in the life tables estimated by the integrated approach.
Source: Calculations by author.

decline in data quality. He pointed out that the variable-r method provides a simple but stable approach to estimation, and thus, it's confirmed that China's average fertility rate was around 1.6 in the 1990s. Zhao Mengzheng made three estimations of fertility rate using the unadjusted and adjusted census data, all showing that the average fertility rate in the 2000s is higher than the average fertility rate in the 1990s estimated by Cai Yong. Making estimations using the census data with military population included, this study has also arrived at the same conclusion.

The fertility rates in the three periods between censuses estimated by this study show that China's fertility rate did drop significantly below the replacement level in the 1990s. However, the average fertility rate estimated with the variable-r method went up in the 2000s, which was inconsistent with the actual case. In regard to populations aged under 20 in the 2010 Census, the average population aged 10–19 years was 17.48 million, and the average population aged 1–9 years was 14.74 million. According to the *Hukou* data for 2015, the average population aged 15–24 years (born in the period 1991–2000) was 17.1 million, and the average population aged 5–14 years (born in the period 2001–2010) was 15.6 million. Despite the discrepancies between *Hukou* data and census data, they all point to the fact that the average births in the 1990s significantly outnumbered those in the 2000s. However, the estimates obtained by variable-r method show that the average fertility rate in the 2000s is higher than that in the 1990s. The changes in fertility pattern are inadequate to account for such reversed difference, and it is likely caused by different integrity levels of the census data. The underreporting rates in 1990, 2000 and 2010, as released by the National Bureau of Statistics, were 0.06%, 1.81% and 0.12%, respectively. Obviously, the data integrity levels of the three censuses are inconsistent, with the underreporting rate of 2000 Census significantly higher than that of previous and next censuses. This may lead to the underestimation of fertility rate in the 1990s and the overestimation of fertility rate in the 2000s, because the population growth rate in the period 1990–2000 will be underestimated, while that in the period 2000–2010 will be overestimated. Of course, theoretically, excessive repeated reporting in the 2010 Census could also lead to the same consequences;

yet, it should be absolutely impossible for the repeatedly reported population to exceed the underreported population.

Therefore, leaving aside the differences between the estimated fertility rates, as far as how the fertility rate changes across the three periods, the estimates obtained by the integrated approach are obviously more reasonable and reliable. In regard to the fluctuations in populations of different ages, as shown in the census data and *Hukou* data, the number of births fell first and then rebounded in the period 1990–2010. Specifically, the births kept going down in the period 1990–2010 and then kept going up in the period 2003–2010. However, the yearly average number of births in the 1990s still significantly outnumbered that in the 2000s. Obviously, the average fertility rate in the 1990s was higher than that in the 2000s. Anyhow, China's average fertility rate in the period 2000–2010 should be around 1.6.

Concluding Remarks

China's TFR stood at around 1.2 in both the 2000 and 2010 censuses, the lowest one in the world. However, the underreporting rate of the two censuses differed significantly, with the underreporting rate in the 2010 Census being only one-fifteenth of that in the 2000 Census. Has China fallen into the "low fertility trap"? According to this study, the answer is "No". First, we used data from different statistical systems to estimate and compare different fertility rates and their trends in the period 2000–2010, and then, we estimated the fertility rate in 2010 and the average fertility rate between the censuses using the indirect demographic estimation methods to help with the comprehensive judgment on China's recent fertility rate and trend.

Through the comparison and adjustment of census data, education data and *Hukou* data, as well as the application of methods such as regression analysis, backward survival estimation, etc., we managed to estimate different sets of populations aged 0–10 years in 2010 and then extrapolated the number of births in the corresponding year and finally the different fertility rates and fertility trends. Taken together, these estimates reveal China's fertility rate first tumbled to as low as 1.5 and then rebounded to approximately 1.7 in the 10 years from 2000 to 2010. The fertility rate in 2010 was not estimated in a reasonable manner due to data and methodological reasons. We estimated the fertility rate in 2010 using the indirect demographic estimation method and the fertility data from the 2010 census.

We estimated that China's TFR was 1.66 in 2010 using the number of children born per woman obtained through the census and the fertility data for the year preceding the census and applying P/F ratio method proposed by Brass. The P/F ratio was 1.4, suggesting that the period fertility rate of 1.18, as obtained through the 2010 Census, points to an underreporting rate of 40%. Meanwhile, the P/F ratio remained stable and consistent in the 20–24 through 35–39 age groups, suggesting that over the past 15 years, China's fertility rate remained relatively stable and saw no further decline. Although the P/F ratio method proposed by Brass is mainly used in African countries and countries with high fertility rates, it is also fit for China, as the fertility rate has remained relatively stable over the past few years.

The two estimates above are both adjusted for the estimated underreporting rate of the fertility in the censuses. To further test the reasonableness of the above estimates, we used another indirect estimation method – the generalized stable population model – to estimate the average fertility rate between censuses. Circumventing the fertility data, this method simply uses the age distribution data from the two censuses to estimate the fertility rate between censuses. Two fertility estimation methods based on the generalized stable population model was used in this study. Although the results vary, both estimates for the average TFR in the period 2000–2010 are around 1.6.

Taken together, the three estimates of fertility rate obtained through this study can help make a reasonable judgment on China's fertility rates and trends in the period 2000–2010. Over these ten years, China's fertility rate steadily hovered around 1.6 (but no less than 1.5) with a minor uplift, with TFR standing at no less than 1.6 in 2010. The fertility estimates and judgments obtained through this study are in high agreement with the fertility estimates obtained through a study of Zhai Zhenwu et al. (2015), which were based on *Hukou* data. According to their study, the TFRs in the period 2006–2010, as extrapolated from age-specific populations in *Hukou* data, were all above 1.6. In particular, the yearly births in the period 2008–2010 were all above 17 million and the corresponding TFRs all stood at 1.66. Therefore, the general conclusion is that China's TFR in the late 2000s was neither lower than 1.5 nor higher than 1.7.

In testing and adjusting census data using data from different sources, this study might have implied that data from other sources are more accurate. The different characteristics, pros and cons of these varying data have been examined in detail in certain studies, and thus, they will not be repeated here. Furthermore, in fertility estimation, we also assumed that the 2010 Census and the 2000 Census shared the same level of underreporting in the lower-age population, and such assumption may have skewed fertility rate toward higher estimates.

As for the models for indirect demographic estimation, in estimating China's fertility rate in 2010 with the P/F ratio method, there are two possibilities that may compromise the accuracy of estimates. One possibility is about the quality of data. Since this method builds its estimation upon the matching between the number of children born per woman and the fertility data for the year preceding the census, the accuracy of the estimates is directly linked to the accuracy of the number of children born per woman and the fertility data in the year preceding the census. By comparing the data from 1990 and 2000 censuses, it's found that the number of children born per woman in the 2010 Census is more accurate than the fertility data for the year preceding the census. Another possibility is about the a, b and c adjustment coefficients used in the P/F ratio method. These coefficients are fitted from the Coale–Trussell fertility model. If China has a different fertility pattern, then these coefficients may not be appropriate for China.

The generalized stable population model extends a demographic estimation method based on the assumption of stable population to a method that can be used under any conditions. Fertility estimation methods developed using the generalized stable population model do not require fertility data, but only the age distribution data obtained through the census. As long as the age distribution data are accurate – or, even if the data inaccurate, as long as there are consistent flaws in the age distribution data from the two censuses – the estimates will not be affected. Therefore, the generalized stable population model boasts tremendous potential and value for application in demographic estimation or data quality assessment. We have good reason to believe that the demographic estimates based on the generalized stable population model might be more robust and accurate than those obtained by other methods that require more restrictive conditions.

Many studies have linked China's low fertility to socioeconomic development and pointed to an ever-fading role played by the family planning policy, and some scholars even opined that the fertility policy has no effect at all. According to the general correlation between fertility rate and economic development in different countries worldwide, even at China's current level of economic development, a fertility rate of approximately 1.6 is still too low. If China's current TFR is not lower than 1.6, it is likely that most couples have a second child, and a universal two-child policy implemented in such a context may cut no ice. Although China's fertility rate may undergo certain fluctuations, the general trend of low fertility is inevitable.

Moreover, the data quality of China's censuses and sample surveys is also likely to turn better upon implementation of the universal two-child policy. According to the data from the 2005 National 1% Population Sample Survey, the proportion of women aged 35 and over who illegally gave births (mostly second births) has been hovering above 19% since 1990. After the roll-out of the universal two-child policy, any second children who are illegal under the former policy will be legalized and there is no need to conceal the birth of such second children. We are optimistic that the data quality of future censuses and sample surveys will improve tremendously and that we will then be able to obtain accurate estimates of China's fertility level.

References

Brass, W. and Coale, A. J. 1968. Chapter 3 Methods of Analysis and Estimation. Pp. 88–139 in W. Brass and others (eds.), *The Demography of Tropical Africa.* Princeton: Princeton University Press.

Cai Yong. 2008. An Assessment of China's Fertility Level Using the Variable-r Method. *Demography* 2: 271–281.

Cai Yong. 2009. Does Enrollment Statistics Provide a Gold Standard for Chinese Fertility Estimates? *Population Research* 4: 22–33.

Coale, A. J. 1989. Marriage and Childbearing in China Since 1940. *Social Forces* 67(4): 833–850.

Cui Hongyan, Xu Lan, and Li Rui. 2013. An Evaluation of Data Accuracy of the 2010 Population Census of China. *Population Research* 1: 10–21.

Guo Zhigang. 2010a. China's Low Fertility and the Neglected Demographic Risks. *International Economic Review* 10: 112–126.

Guo Zhigang. 2010b. Low Fertility Level and Other Related Population Issues in China. *Academia Bimestris* 1: 5–25.

Guo Zhigang. 2011. The Sixth Census Data Indicates Serious Biases in Past Population Estimations and Projections. *Chinese Journal of Population Science* 6: 2–13.

Hao Juan and Qiu Changrong. 2011. A Comparative Analysis of Urban and Rural Fertility in China Since 2000. *South China Population* 5: 27–33.

Information Processing Office, Population Research Institute, Renmin University of China. 1987. 1981 National and Provincial Life Tables of China. *Population Research* 1: 59–64.

Li Handong and Li Liu. 2012. Estimating China's Fertility Level Since 2000: Based on the 6th Population Census. *Chinese Journal of Population Science* 5: 75–83.

Preston, S. H. 1983. An Integrated System for Demographic Estimation from Two Age Distributions. *Demography* 20(2): 213–226.

Preston, S. H. and Coale, A. J. 1982. Age Structure, Growth, Attrition, and Accession: A New Synthesis. *Population Index* 48: 217–259.

United Nations. 1983. Chapter 2 Estimation of Fertility Based on Information about Children Ever Born. Pp. 27–64 in *Manual X: Indirect Techniques for Demographic Estimation*. New York, NY: United Nations, Department of Economic and Social Affairs, ST/ESA/SER.A/81.

Wang Jinying and Ge Yanxia. 2013. Assessment of 2010 Census Data Quality and Past Population Changes. *Population Research* 1: 22–33.

Yang Fan and Zhao Menghan. 2013. China's Fertility Level since 2000: A Reestimation. *Population Research* 2: 54–65.

Zhai Zhenwu, Chen Jiaju, and Li Long. 2015. China's Recent Total Fertility Rate: New Evidence from the Household Registration Statistics. *Population Research* 6: 22–34.

Zhang Guangyu and Yuan Xin. 2004. Considerations on Birth Underreporting and Fertility Estimation in the 1990s. *Population Research* 2: 29–36.

Zhao Menghan. 2015. An Estimation of Fertility Level in China, 2000–2010. *Population Research* 6: 49–58.

Zhu Qin. 2012. Estimation of Fertility Level in China 2000–2010: A Preliminary Study Based on the 6th Population Census Data. *Chinese Journal of Population Science* 4: 68–77.

4 China's Fertility Trends in the Period from 2006 to 2017

In Chapter 3, we estimated China's fertility rates since 2000 using a variety of data and methods, and the results reveal that China's fertility rate lingered around 1.6. There is no gainsaying the fact that China's ongoing low fertility is palpably linked to China's burgeoning socioeconomic development, while the continuous adjustment of fertility policy and the population inertia also steer the evolution of China's low fertility. In 2017, the former National Health and Family Planning Commission conducted a national fertility survey, which provided the much-needed data for our probe into China's fertility rates in recent years. The estimation of China's low fertility in Chapter 3 mainly built on indirect approaches, because the data used are not the fertility data from censuses and the methods used are also linked to models for indirect estimation. The 2017 Fertility Survey provides the most direct data on women's reproductive behaviors for extrapolating and analyzing fertility rate, making it possible for us to analyze China's fertility rates and trends without relying on indirect estimation methods. Meanwhile, the data from 2017 Fertility Survey can also be cross-checked against the indirect estimates obtained in Chapter 3 to check for consistency and mutual data support.

Launched by the former National Health and Family Planning Commission, the 2017 Fertility Survey covered 31 provinces (autonomous regions and municipalities) and the Xinjiang Production and Construction Corps, involving 6,078 townships (towns, sub-districts) of 2,737 counties (cities, districts) and a total of 12,500 village-level (neighborhood-level) sample points. The survey adopted a three-stage hierarchical probability proportionate to size sampling method to obtain an effective sample of 249,946 women. After the survey, 64 sample points (5 per 1,000) were singled out from 12,500 sample points nationwide for post-enumeration survey, and 2,833 respondents were also randomly selected for telephone follow-up. The results of post-enumeration survey showed that the proportions of consistency in birth date, marital status and number of births were 96.6%, 98.0% and 96.3%, respectively. The comparison between the results of telephone follow-up and the survey results showed that the proportion of consistency in the number of children was 98.9%, indicating that the birth information obtained from the survey has high accuracy. During the post-weighting of sample structure, the age, marital status and registered permanent residence of respondents in the sample were weighted according to the residence registration information registered by the Ministry of

DOI: 10.4324/9781003429661-4

Public Security, data from 2015 1% population sample survey, and data from the 2000 and 2010 censuses, so as to ensure that high-quality data were used to estimate and extrapolate the national fertility rate.

This survey targeted Chinese females aged 15–60 living in Mainland China at the time of 0:00 on July 1, 2017. The age range of samples was so designed to allow full reflection of the changes in China's fertility rate over the past ten years. This survey covered fertility behaviors, fertility intentions, contraceptive methods and childcare services. This study mainly uses data from the part of fertility behaviors, i.e., the "pregnancy history" information of every woman, including the ending year and month of each pregnancy, the pregnancy outcome and so on.

This part of the study uses four fertility indicators (i.e., total fertility rate, progression-based fertility rate, intrinsic fertility rate and cohort fertility rate) to estimate and compare China's fertility rates and trends in recent years. Due to merits such as less data required and simple calculations, total fertility rate has become the most commonly used indicator for measuring fertility level. When the patterns of marriage and childbirth remain constantly stable, the total fertility rate can best reflect the cohort fertility. The interference of varied period factors could lead to the result of parity-specific TFR exceeding 1, in which case it would be inappropriate to take TFR as the lifetime fertility rate. Even if the true cohort fertility is constant, TFR tends to fluctuate widely – sometimes dragged down, sometimes pushed up. The changes in China's fertility rate over the past few decades can well illustrate this point – as reflected in a debate in around 1983 of Chinese demographers over China's total fertility rate (TFR) (Guo Zhigang, 2002). In the wake of China's burgeoning socioeconomic development, especially the continuous adjustment of China's fertility policy in recent years, the marriage and childbearing patterns of Chinese women of childbearing age have undergone a seismic shift in a short period of time, thus putting a dent in the effectiveness of period TFR.

Given the drawbacks of TFR, scholars have put forward alternative fertility indicators in a bid to measure the fertility level more accurately. Bongaarts and Feeney (1998) proposed the tempo-adjusted TFR (TFR') indicator to eliminate the effect of changes in the age at childbirth on period TFR. This indicator has been widely used in research on China's fertility level (Guo Zhigang, 2000a, 2000b, 2004; Hao Juan and Qiu Changrong, 2012). However, as these researchers themselves have noted, an important premise of establishing TFR' is that subsequent cohorts all delay or advance childbirth to the same extent, which is almost impossible in reality. Moreover, the high sensitivity of TFR' to the changes in average age at childbirth can lead to highly variable estimates. Before TFR' was proposed, Feeney (1983), Feeney and Yu (1987) and Ma Yingtong et al. (1986) had put forward the "Parity Progression-based Fertility Rate" which controls for the parity structure in women of childbearing age on the basis of harnessing conventional fertility indicators to control for the age structure in women of childbearing age. Rallu and Toulemon (1994) proposed parity-age-interval-specific TFRs, on the basis of which McDonald and Kippen (2007) developed the indicator of "Intrinsic Fertility Rate". Both the progression-based fertility rate and the intrinsic fertility rate apply the progression ratio and the probability theory to calculate the parity-specific fertility rates. Since the parity progression ratio for each parity cannot be greater than 1, these two indicators well avoid the accumulation of age-specific period fertility. Meanwhile, since the progression-based fertility rate can control for the age and parity structures in women of childbearing age, and the intrinsic fertility rate can control for age structure, parity structure and parity interval in women of childbearing age, they are significantly better than the conventional fertility rate indicators for measuring and analyzing period TFR. However, due to demanding data requirements and complicated calculation steps, progression-based fertility rate and intrinsic fertility rate are seldom applied in the research on China's fertility rate. As a matter of fact, all the above-mentioned period fertility indicators are aimed at estimating the actual fertility level, while the cohort lifetime fertility rate is meant to directly reflect the actual fertility rate of a cohort. Although the cohort fertility rate is more meaningful when calculations are conducted after a certain cohort has aged beyond their reproductive years – suggesting that this indicator is "lagged" to a certain extent – it provides a basic reference for testing the fertility rate at that time.

In contrary to the simple steps for calculating total fertility rate and cohort fertility rate, the steps for calculating progression-based fertility rate and intrinsic fertility rate are much more complicated, involving the use of parity progression ratios and life tables. Please refer to the relevant articles for the specific calculation steps (Feeney, 1983; Feeney and Yu, 1987; Rallu and Toulemon, 1994; McDonald and Kippen, 2007).

Trends in Period Fertility Rate

Total Fertility Rate

Calculations based on the data from 2017 Fertility Survey signal an upward trend – despite the fluctuations – of the total fertility rate in China over the past ten years under the influence of China's burgeoning socioeconomic development, continuous adjustment of fertility policy and population inertia combined. The calculation results show that China's TFRs fell within the range of 1.41–1.78 in the past ten years, with average TFR standing at 1.65 (Table 4.1). Due to China's holding of the Olympic Games, zodiac preferences and fertility policy adjustments, China's TFR topped 1.7 in 2008 (the year of the Olympics), 2012 (the year of the Dragon) and 2016–2017 (years immediately following the roll-out of the universal two-child policy), but tumbled to a record low of 1.41 in 2015 (the year of the Sheep). The effects of the selective two-child policy and the universal two-child policy are manifested in the pronounced uplift in fertility rate in 2014 and 2016, respectively, compared with the previous years.

Parity-specific fertility rate can further reveal the characteristics of China's fertility rate changes over the years. First, the TFR for first births has dropped significantly since 2012 (Table 4.1). As a matter of fact, the decline began long before 2012, though the year of the Dragon in 2012 temporarily held back the slide. The TFR for first births has fallen dramatically to a record low as never before in history, and it was largely due to the significant delay in the age at which women marry or have children. In the period from 2006 to 2017, women's average age at first marriage increased from 23.6 to 26.5 years, and their average age at first childbirth rose from 24.3 to 27.3 years, both delayed by three years. Moreover, the delayed since 2012 have been significantly longer than in previous years. Second, the TFR for second births ran counter to the trend in the TFR for first births. In particular, the TFR for second births saw an upsurge in the past few years, surpassing the TFR for first births in 2015 and topping 1 in 2017, a reflection of the accumulation of second births driven obviously by fertility policy adjustments. According to Figure 4.1, the average age of women at second birth was declining prior to 2012 and then started to rebound after 2012, especially after 2015. The previous trend is linked to the successive abolition of birth spacing restriction, while the trend in recent years mirrors the cumulative effect of the two-child policy on older women rushing to have a second child. Despite the low fertility rate for first births in 2016 and 2017, TFR still rebounded by a large margin because the pickup in the TFR for second births helped push up the overall TFR, a reflection of the marked effect of the universal two-child policy.

Progression-Based TFR

China's TFR has fluctuated greatly over the past ten years due to the impact of period factors, which could even impair our judgment on China's fertility rates and trends. Progression-based fertility rate, which controls for both age and parity, can diminish the impact of period factors to a large extent. This is because childbirth is in fact a strictly progressive event – that is, only women who have never given birth can have a first child and only women who have had a first birth but haven't had a second birth can have a second child. The parity progression ratio is defined

Table 4.1 China's Parity-Specific TFRs in the Period 2006–2017

Year	TFR	TFR for First Births	TFR for Second Births	TFR for Multiple Births
2006	1.625	0.899	0.581	0.144
2007	1.691	0.924	0.619	0.148
2008	1.714	0.939	0.617	0.158
2009	1.677	0.904	0.614	0.159
2010	1.637	0.892	0.591	0.154
2011	1.613	0.882	0.574	0.157
2012	1.781	0.955	0.658	0.167
2013	1.554	0.807	0.593	0.154
2014	1.670	0.809	0.697	0.163
2015	1.410	0.616	0.642	0.152
2016	1.770	0.668	0.943	0.159
2017	1.719	0.540	1.013	0.166

Note: Since the survey date was July 1, 2017, it is assumed that the births occurred before the survey date accounted for 1/2 of the total births in 2017. All the Tables and Figures contained in this chapter are calculated from the original data of the 2017 Fertility Survey, and the source of the data won't be further specified.

as the proportion of women of a given parity who go on to have another child. Progression-based TFR for a given parity can largely eliminate the tempo effect or accumulation effect. Table 4.2 shows China's parity-specific progression-based TFR in each year.

It can be seen that progression-based TFRs differ from conventional TFRs after controlling for the parity structure – progression-based TFRs are all higher than TFRs except in 2008, 2012, 2016 and 2017. This is because there were first-child baby boom in 2008 and 2012 and second-child baby boom in 2016 and 2017. Progression-based calculations have smoothed the accumulation of period fertility

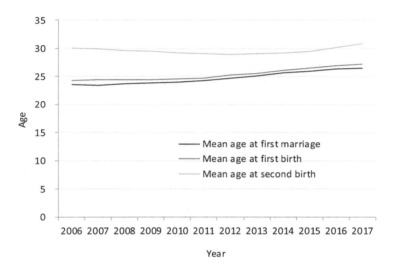

Figure 4.1 Average ages of Chinese women at marriage and childbirth in the period 2006–2017

Table 4.2 China's Parity-Specific Progression-based TFR in the Period 2006–2017

Year	Progression-based TFR	Progression-based TFR for First Births	Progression-based TFR for Second Births	Progression-based TFR for Multiple Births
2006	1.645	0.965	0.554	0.127
2007	1.689	0.967	0.576	0.146
2008	1.701	0.967	0.574	0.160
2009	1.687	0.969	0.563	0.155
2010	1.662	0.964	0.547	0.151
2011	1.632	0.951	0.532	0.149
2012	1.745	0.970	0.590	0.185
2013	1.612	0.956	0.523	0.134
2014	1.688	0.958	0.580	0.150
2015	1.525	0.926	0.495	0.103
2016	1.726	0.932	0.658	0.137
2017	1.690	0.902	0.667	0.121

to a certain extent. In all years, the progression-based TFRs for first births are all higher than the TFRs for first births, and the variation in progression-based TFR for first births over the years is also the smallest among all births – all staying above 0.9 in all years, suggesting that even if the postponed age of women at first birth has led to lower TFR for first births in certain years, the vast majority of women of childbearing age will still have at least one child (Figure 4.2). The progression-based TFRs for second births are lower than the TFRs for second births, especially in those most-favored zodiac years and years following policy adjustments, suggesting that birth accumulation should account for the higher TFR for second births in these years (Figure 4.3). This is also true for TFRs for third-plus births – except in 2008 and 2012, the progression-based TFRs for third-plus births are also lower than the TFRs for third-plus births (Figure 4.4).

Looking at the trend of progression-based fertility rates, China's TFR for first births has not declined much, as more than 90% of Chinese women will have one child anyway. The declining TFR for first births in recent years is largely a manifestation of the tempo effect, rather than the fact that the TFR for first births literally tumbled by such a large margin. According to the progression-based TFRs for second births, although the number of women who have had a second birth is not as many as the conventional fertility rate reflects, basically 60% of women will have a second child. According to the progression-based TFRs for third plus births, women who have had third and more births only take up a minor share of 15%, and yet, this figure has been further shrinking in the past few years. That is to say, the pickup in TFRs for second and third births in recent years is largely a manifestation of the accumulation effect of second and third births, rather than the fact that the fertility rates for second and third births have climbed to levels as high as reflected in the TFRs for second and third births.

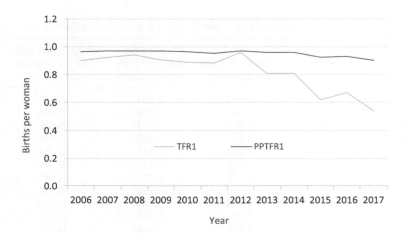

Figure 4.2 China's TFRs and progression-based TFRs for first births in the period 2006–2017

China's Fertility Trends from 2006 to 2017 63

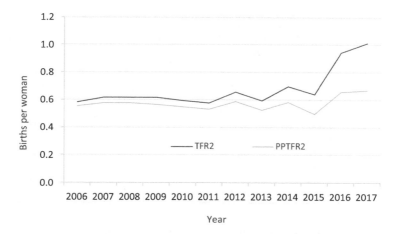

Figure 4.3 China's TFRs and progression-based TFRs for second births in the period 2006–2017

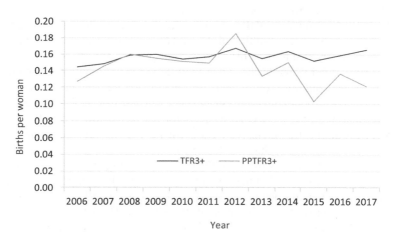

Figure 4.4 China's TFRs and progression-based TFRs for third-plus births in the period 2006–2017

Intrinsic TFR

The "tempo effect" on total fertility rate, in addition to the above-mentioned age structure and parity structure, also encompasses parity interval. By further controlling for the parity interval on the basis of parity progression-based fertility rate, we can obtain the age-parity-interval-specific total fertility rate, which is also known as the intrinsic total fertility rate. Intrinsic TFR is a period fertility rate indicator which can best reflect the real fertility level that is not affected by population structure. Table 4.3 shows the parity-specific intrinsic TFR for each year.

Table 4.3 China's Parity-Specific Intrinsic TFR in the Period 2007–2016

Year	Intrinsic TFR	Intrinsic TFR for First Births	Intrinsic TFR for Second Births	Intrinsic TFR for Multiple Births
2007	1.760	0.967	0.627	0.165
2008	1.784	0.967	0.640	0.177
2009	1.771	0.969	0.624	0.179
2010	1.744	0.964	0.608	0.172
2011	1.697	0.951	0.582	0.163
2012	1.824	0.970	0.656	0.198
2013	1.657	0.956	0.564	0.137
2014	1.743	0.958	0.631	0.154
2015	1.582	0.926	0.547	0.109
2016	1.806	0.932	0.732	0.142

After controlling for age structure, parity structure and interval structure, the intrinsic TFR is higher than either TFR or progression-based TFR in all years, suggesting that the real fertility rates in the past decade are higher than that reflected by TFRs. Since the progression interval of first births is the age of woman at first childbirth, the age and interval distribution of progressive births is equivalent to the progressive age distribution of first births, and the age- or interval-specific progression-based fertility rate for first births is also equal to the age-specific progression-based fertility rate for first births. After controlling for parity interval, the intrinsic TFRs for second and third (or higher) births are greater than the progression-based TFRs for the corresponding parities in all years. The intrinsic TFR for second births is greater than the TFR for second births before 2012 but lower than the TFR for second births after 2012 (inclusive). The intrinsic TFR for third (or higher) births is greater than the TFR of third (or higher) births before 2013 but lower than the TFR for third (or higher) births after 2013 (inclusive) (Figures 4.5 and 4.6). These differences arise from the fact that the intrinsic TFR further controls for the parity interval. If the parity interval is narrowed, TFR will be pushed up. Therefore, after further controlling for the parity interval, the intrinsic TFRs for second and third (or higher) births all fall below the TFR for the corresponding births after 2012 and 2013.

By comparing the TFRs, progression-based TFRs and intrinsic TFRs for second births, it is self-evident that due to the changes in the birth interval in the past decade, the progression-based TFRs for second births have underestimated the fertility rates for second births to a certain extent, while the TFRs for second births underestimated the fertility rates for second births before 2012 and then overestimated the fertility rates for second births thereafter. The same is true for the fertility rates for third-plus births and is largely linked to the changes in parity interval and the accumulation of births against the backdrop of China's continued adjustments to its fertility policy in the past ten years. In conclusion, similar to the case of progression-based TFR for second births, the changes in the intrinsic TFR for second births further prove that the upsurge in the TFR for second births in recent years is largely a manifestation of birth accumulation, only its estimate

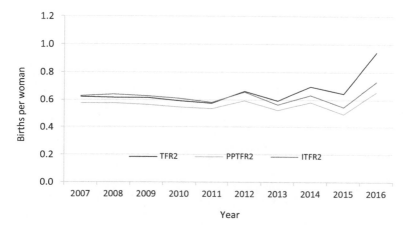

Figure 4.5 China's TFRs, progression-based TFRs and intrinsic TFRs for second births in the period 2007–2016

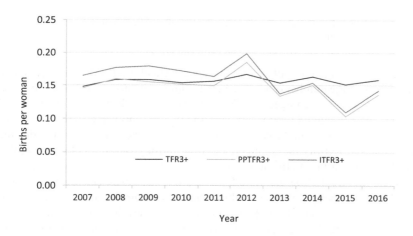

Figure 4.6 China's TFRs, progression-based TFRs and intrinsic TFRs for third-plus births in the period 2007–2016

of the actual fertility rate for second births is way higher than that made by the progression-based TFR for second births. The same is also true for the fertility rate for third plus births.

Changes in Cohort Fertility Rates

The 2017 Fertility Survey also asked the number of children ever born to women of different ages, which can be used to examine the lifetime fertility rate for women in different cohorts (Figure 4.7). Immune to the tempo effect, the cohort fertility rate changes steadily and can provide a basic reference for evaluating period fertility

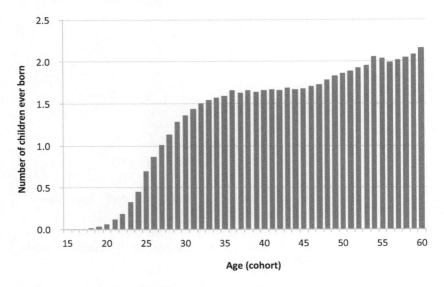

Figure 4.7 Average cumulative or lifetime number of children ever born to women in each cohort in China

rate. In women aged 45–49 years who have basically passed their reproductive years, the average number of children ever born per woman is 1.7–1.8. This figure is around 1.9 in women aged 50–53 years and greater than 2 in women over 54. In 2017, women aged 45–49 years were the cohort who came to the age of marriage and childbearing in the early 1990s. Under the strict birth control policy then, China's period fertility rate plunged and total fertility rate fell below the replacement level. According to the annual surveys conducted by the National Bureau of Statistics, China's TFR at that time fell to 1.5 or even lower. However, the number of children ever born to women in this cohort over their lifetime was significantly higher than what would be reflected in the period fertility rate. Even in women aged 35–44 years, the average number of children ever born per woman is as high as 1.6–1.7, and they all came to the age of marriage and childbearing in the late 1990s and early 2000s, during which the annual surveys by the National Bureau of Statistics got lower TFRs. In certain years, TFR was even lower than 1.3; yet, the actual fertility rate was way higher.

Concluding Remarks

Based on the data from 2017 Fertility Survey, we estimated in this chapter China's fertility rates and trends over the past ten years. From either the period fertility rate over the years or the cohort fertility rate of women over 35 years old, China's TFRs in recent years all stayed above 1.6, signaling that the universal two-child policy has further and significantly pushed up China's fertility rate.

In this chapter, we examined China's fertility rates over the past decade using TFR, progression-based TFR and intrinsic TFR. Although all these three indicators pertain to period fertility measures, they are all aimed at progressively eliminating the tempo effect on fertility rate to yield at a result as close as possible to the actual fertility rate. TFRs over these ten years average out at 1.65, progression-based TFRs at 1.67 and intrinsic TFRs at 1.74. Compared with TFR and progressive TFR, intrinsic TFR is obviously a better period fertility measure for measuring fertility level. It can also be seen that if the current reproductive patterns (age, parity and interval patterns) of women remain unchanged for a long time (at least 35 years), TFR will eventually be equal to the intrinsic TFR. Therefore, the difference between intrinsic TFR and TFR is a measure of the tempo effect hidden in the existing demographic structure of women.

The plunge in the TFR for first births in recent years does not necessarily mirror the sharp decline in the fertility rate for first births, but largely reflects the tempo effect caused by women's postponement of marriage and childbirth. This is because although the TFR for first births has tumbled to about 0.6, the intrinsic TFR for first births still stays above 0.9. The salient trend toward postponed marriage and childbearing had a lot to do with the burgeoning advancement of urbanization, especially with the substantial uplift in women's education level as a result of the higher education expansion policy since the late 1990s. Furthermore, the upsurge in the TFR for second births in recent years does not necessarily mirrors the rapid increase in the fertility rate for second births, but largely reflects the birth accumulation brought about by the universal two-child policy. This is because although the TFR for second births has surpassed 0.9, the intrinsic TFR for second births still lingers around 0.7. The intrinsic TFR for third and higher births is also lower than the TFR for third and higher births.

It is worth mentioning that the fertility rate estimated using the data from 2017 Fertility Survey surprisingly coincides with the estimates based on *Hukou* data and indirect estimation – that is, same results are obtained using data from different sources and through different techniques. Whether or not this is a coincidence deserves further examination. Moreover, both period and cohort fertility rates suggest that in the years of China's implementation of the "one-child policy", most couples actually had given birth to two children. This study also shows that the period analysis and cohort analysis combined can best shed light on China's fertility trends.

References

Bongaarts, J. and Feeney, G. 1998. On the Quantum and Tempo of Fertility. *Population and Development Review* 24(2): 271–291. doi:10.2307/2807974

Feeney, G. 1983. Population Dynamics Based on Birth Intervals and Parity Progression. *Population Studies* 37(1): 75–89.

Feeney, G. and Yu, J. 1987. Period Parity Progression Measures of Fertility in China. *Population Studies* 41(1): 77–102.

Guo Zhigang. 2000a. Fertility Level of China in the 1990s: An Analysis Based on Multiple Indexes. *Chinese Journal of Population Science* 4: 11–18.

Guo Zhigang. 2000b. Lifetime Fertility of Chinese Women: A Look at the Recent Period Fertility Behavior. *Population Research* 1: 7–18.

Guo Zhigang. 2002. The Inner Imperfection and Improvement of Total Fertility Rate. *Population Research* 5: 24–28.

Guo Zhigang. 2004. An Study and Discussion on Fertility Level of China in 1990s. *Population Research* 2: 10–19.

Hao Juan and Qiu Changrong. 2012. Revisiting the Tempo Adjusted Total Fertility Rate. *Population Research* 3: 81–88.

Ma Yingtong, Wang Yanzu, and Yang Shuzhang. 1986. The Proposal of Progression Model of Population Development and the Establishment of Index of Parity Progression Total Fertility Rate. *Population & Economics* 2: 40–43.

McDonald, P. and Kippen, R. 2007. *The Intrinsic Total Fertility Rate: A New Approach to the Measurement of Fertility*. New York, NY: Population Association of America.

Rallu, J. L. and Toulemon, L. 1994. Period Fertility Measures: The Construction of Different Indices and Their Application to France, 1946–89. *Population: An English Selection* 6: 59–93.

5 How Low Is China's Fertility Rate

As mentioned in the preceding studies, since China entered the ranks of low-fertility countries, especially since the Sixth Census, there have been a great number of studies probing into the trends, evolution and characteristics of China's low fertility, with some keen on debating or estimating how low China's fertility rate is. According to the data from population censuses and 1% population sample surveys conducted by the National Bureau of Statistics since 2000, China's fertility rate has not only tumbled to an extremely low level but is also continuing its downward slide. Among countries with a vast population across the globe, China has become the one with the lowest fertility rate. What's worse, the universal two-child policy, introduced in 2016, has produced little effect. These conclusions and viewpoints are widely accepted and embraced by an overwhelmingly majority of scholars. So, how was China's low fertility trending and evolving in the past few years? Has it been edging down continuously over the past two decades? What kind of future trend do the evolutionary characteristics of China's low fertility herald? It is very important but also difficult to find answers to these questions. The purpose of this chapter is to provide some useful observations and insights to help answer these questions through the comparative analysis of data from different systems. The data used here come from the population censuses and sample surveys conducted by the National Bureau of Statistics since 2000, the 2017 Fertility Survey conducted by the former National Health and Family Planning Commission, and the 2017 *Hukou* statistics published by the Ministry of Public Security. Data from different systems collectively unfold the important characteristics and laws of the evolution of China's low fertility, though there also exist some palpable discrepancies. The comparative analysis of data from different systems can provide meaningful insights into answering these questions. In practice, however, even with such abundant data, it seems impossible to accurately answer these research questions due to the discrepancies among data.

Trends and Evolution of China's Low Fertility

Figure 5.1 provides the total fertility rates (TFRs) calculated using the data from the population censuses and sample surveys conducted by the National Bureau of Statistics since 2000, and the TFRs calculated using the data from 2017 Fertility

DOI: 10.4324/9781003429661-5

Survey conducted by the former National Health and Family Planning Commission. The TFRs derived from the data source of the National Bureau of Statistics are not TFRs directly published by the National Bureau of Statistics, but are obtained by adding up the age-specific fertility rates published by the National Bureau of Statistics after population censuses and sample surveys. The TFRs derived from the data source of the former National Health and Family Planning Commission are extrapolated using the data on the pregnancy and fertility history of women from the 2017 Fertility Survey. The 2017 Fertility Survey collected detailed data on the pregnancy and fertility history of women aged 15–60 years, which can be used to extrapolate China's fertility rates over the years since 2006. Considering that the fertility rate among Chinese women over 40 is extremely low, it is basically all right to extrapolate further back to 2000.

The dramatic drop in China's fertility rate in the 1990s is an indisputable fact that does not require further discussion. However, from the births in the 1990s published by the National Bureau of Statistics, China's average TFR is estimated to be around 1.8. With the exception of the early 1990s, the TFRs estimated using the data from either the population censuses or the sample surveys conducted by the National Bureau of Statistics are all substantially lower than 1.8. Apparently, the fertility rates implied by the births published by the National Bureau of Statistics are significantly higher than those obtained through the surveys. Many studies have attempted to adjust fertility rate estimates by estimating the underreporting rate of births or lower-age populations in the census data (Cui Hongyan et al., 2013; Wang Jinying and Ge Yanxia, 2013; Yang Fan and Zhao Menghan, 2013; Zhao Menghan, 2015). Since the estimation of underreporting rate entails a lot of assumptions and data from other sources, we deliberately avoided this controversial issue in the previous chapter, using only the age distribution data from two censuses and the generalized stable population model to estimate the average fertility rate between two censuses. In this way, we didn't need to estimate the underreporting rate in the census data, or use any fertility data from censuses, or assume that the census data are complete and accurate. Instead, we only needed to assume that the levels and patterns of underreporting, repeated reporting or misreporting are similar between the two censuses. What's more, some scholars opined that in spite of the possibility of underreporting, the census data are basically credible (Guo Zhigang, 2013; Guo Zhigang, 2017; Guo Zhigang and Tian Siyu, 2017). In this case, it is even less problematic to use a generalized stable population model.

Estimates show that the average TFR in the 1990s was 1.68, with the average number of births being nearly 3 million less than the figure published by the National Bureau of Statistics. Estimates also suggest an average TFR of 2.63 for the period 1982–1990, which is markedly consistent with the survey result, while the average number of births also coincides with the result published. The censuses and fertility surveys launched by China in the 1980s were lauded by Western scholars as surveys of exceptionally high data quality (Coale, 1989). This also mirrors the considerable reliability of estimates derived through the generalized stable population model. Furthermore, based on the data from 2017 Fertility Survey, China's average TFR in the 1990s estimated to be 1.62, which is also comparatively close

How Low Is China's Fertility Rate 71

to the estimate derived through the generalized stable population model. Based on this, we can conclude that government and scholars have overestimated the fertility rates in the late 1990s. Using the generalized stable population model and the data from 2017 Fertility Survey, it can be extrapolated that the fertility rates in the late 1990s should hover around 1.5. This once again proves that in the 1990s, China's fertility rate fell from above the replacement level to significantly below the replacement level, and such a sharp dip arose from the combined effect of the tightening of family planning policy in the 1990s, the postponement of women's age at first marriage and the cohort of baby bust generation born in the 1970s reaching their marriage and childbearing ages.

China's fertility rate continued its downward slide in the first few years of this century but gradually rebounded from 2003 with the cohort of baby boomers born in the 1980s reaching their ages of marriage and childbearing. From either the age-specific population data from the 2010 Census and the 2015 mini-census or the data from 2017 Fertility Survey, it can be seen that China's fertility ascended markedly. However, the fertility rates obtained through the censuses and sample surveys do not show such a clear upward trend. According to Figure 5.1, sample surveys found China's fertility rates hovered around 1.4 in the period 2001–2009 and then 1.2 after 2010 (except 2017). In the period 2005–2016, there was a significant difference of 0.25 to 0.52 between the two curves. Likewise, we also estimated the average fertility rate in the period 2000–2010 using a generalized stable population

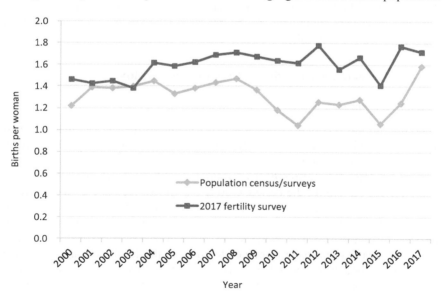

Figure 5.1 Trends in the TFR from 2000 to 2017

Source: Census data and sample survey data come from the China Population and Employment Statistical Yearbook (2001–2018) published by the National Bureau of Statistics. Beijing: China Statistics Press (2002–2019). The data relating to 2017 Fertility Survey are calculated from computer record data file of the survey.

model, and it came out to be 1.56. The estimated average number of births is also very close to the figure published by the National Bureau of Statistics. We further obtained an average fertility rate of 1.57 for the period 2000–2010 by extrapolating from the data from 2017 Fertility Survey, and another average fertility rate of 1.58 by extrapolating from the *Hukou* data for 2017. These three figures happen to be highly consistent.

However, the uplift in fertility rate did not last long. China's fertility rate embarked on its downward spiral after peaking in 2008, edging down slowly in the period 2008–2012 but then undergoing seismic fluctuations due to fertility policy adjustments and zodiac preferences after 2012. China's fertility rate climbed up sharply in 2014 and 2016 as a result of fertility policy adjustments. Due to zodiac preferences, China's fertility rate went up in 2012 (the year of the dragon) but descended in 2015 (the year of the sheep). Both the sample survey on population changes and the 2017 Fertility Survey revealed the same characteristics of demographic fluctuations.

China's low fertility has exhibited a wave-like evolution. Although China's low fertility is consequent on determinants such as socioeconomic development, higher education expansion and accelerating urbanization, its trends mirror the regularities in demography, which are manifested in the changes brought by the fertility policy adjustments and population inertia. China's fertility rate plummeted to record lows in the 1990s, leveled off at an extremely low level in the period 1997–2003 and then started to climb up in seismic fluctuations, following which China's fertility rate is anticipated to continue its downward slide and there is a high risk of China sliding into very low fertility.

Characteristics of the Evolution of China's Low Fertility

TFR for First Births

According to the experiences in low-fertility countries, changes in marriage pattern play a decisive role in the fluctuations in fertility rate (Jones, 2007; Frejka et al., 2010; Yoo and Sobotka, 2018). The evolution of China's low fertility over the past two decades is also reflective of the impact from the changes in women's first-marriage pattern. In the period 1990–2017, the average age at first marriage among Chinese women went up by 3.5 years according to the data from population censuses and sample surveys, or four years according to the data from 2017 Fertility Survey (Figure 5.2). The changes took place in phases. Specifically, women's average age at first marriage continued to climb in the 1990s, but dropped in the early 2000s, though it rebounded slowly in the late 2000s and embarked on an upward trajectory after 2010. The pace of the postponement of women's age at first marriage after 2010 has been the most rapid since the founding of the People's Republic of China, and it has had a major impact on China's fertility trends.

The postponement of women's age at first marriage has directly led to a dip in the fertility rate for first births. Although the average age of women at first marriage rose by roughly 1.3 years in the 1990s, the fertility rates for first births extrapolated

How Low Is China's Fertility Rate 73

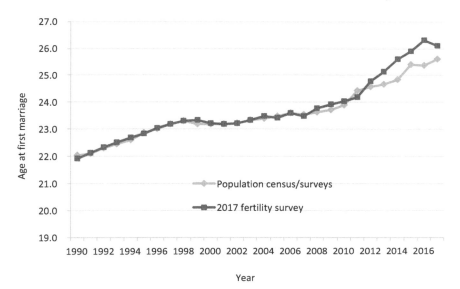

Figure 5.2 Average age at first marriage among Chinese women in the period 1990–2017

Source: Census data and sample survey data come from the China Population and Employment Statistical Yearbook (1991–2018) published by the National Bureau of Statistics. Beijing: China Statistics Press (1992–2019). The data relating to 2017 Fertility Survey are calculated computer record data file of the survey.

from the sample survey data for the 1990s are found to be unusually high, surpassing 1 in many years, while those calculated using the data from 2017 Fertility Survey drop significantly to below 0.9. The average age of women at first marriage leveled off in the 2000s, and accordingly, the fertility rate for first births remained basically stable. As can be seen from Figure 5.3, data from both the sample surveys and the 2017 Fertility Survey produce comparatively stable fertility rates for first births, though the fertility rates calculated using the data from the 2017 Fertility Survey are markedly lower than those calculated using the data from the sample surveys. After 2010, however, the fertility rates calculated using the data from the 2017 Fertility Survey began to surpass those calculated using the data from the censuses and sample surveys, and the differences were particularly noticeable in the period 2000–2012. However, the differences in the average age of women at first marriage, as shown in Figure 5.2, do not seem to support such a huge difference in the fertility rate for first births.

After 2012, both the sample surveys and the 2017 Fertility Survey point to a substantial decline in the fertility rate for first births. In the period 2013–2017, the fertility rates for first births extrapolated using data from the two types of surveys are very close, with sample surveys producing slightly lower fertility rates than the 2017 Fertility Survey. The plunge in the fertility rate for first births can also be evidenced by the substantial increase in women's average age at first marriage from 2010, as shown in Figure 5.2. What is puzzling is that the increase in women's

74 How Low Is China's Fertility Rate

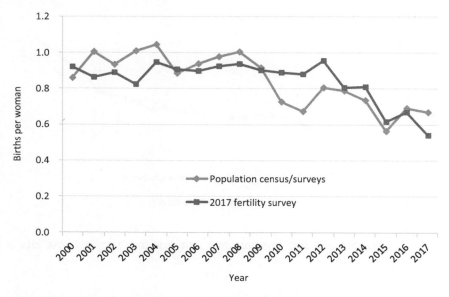

Figure 5.3 Trends in the TFR for first births from 2000 to 2017
Source: Same as Figure 5.1.

average age at first marriage reported by the 2017 Fertility Survey outrivals the result obtained through the sample surveys, and yet, the fertility rate for first births reported by the 2017 Fertility Survey also exceeds the result obtained through the sample surveys. However, if we rule out the baby boom in 2012, the data from 2017 Fertility Survey are indeed reflective of a continued decline in the fertility rate for first births since 2008, which accords closely with the continued rise in women's average age at first marriage. Such consistent trends, however, are not found in the data from censuses and sample surveys. In Figure 5.3, although the two curves tend to resemble each other in general, the curve representing census and sample surveys fluctuates more markedly from staying above the curve representing the 2017 Fertility Survey before 2009 to falling below the later curve after 2009.

TFR for Second and Multiple Births

Some scholars argued that an important reason for the continued decline in China's fertility rate is that women are postponing their age at first marriage. The evolution of China's low fertility since 2000 has been marked by the fall in the fertility rate for first births (Guo Zhigang, 2013; Guo Zhigang, 2017; Guo Zhigang and Tian Siyu, 2017). As discussed in the previous chapter, this argument holds up from either the results of sample surveys or the data from 2017 Fertility Survey. However, the comparison of results obtained through these two types of surveys points to a finding that the fertility rates obtained through the sample surveys are lower in terms of the fertility rates for second births rather than for first births. As can be

How Low Is China's Fertility Rate 75

seen from Figure 5.4, the two curves gradually diverge over time, with difference expanding from 0.1 in the first few years to 0.2–0.3, and even to 0.45 in 2016. Such differences in fertility rate are undoubtedly huge. Since almost all couples will have one child, and the first birth is not subject to any policy restrictions, it is only natural for the two data sources to produce basically consistent fertility rates. This is because birth concealing or underreporting due to the policy restrictions barely existed in first births, and the fertility rate for first births would only be affected by the postponement of women's age at first marriage. The fertility rate for second births, however, is completely different. Due to policy restrictions, gender preferences and other reasons, concealing and underreporting of second births occurred from time to time, and this is especially true for third and further births. Although the third and further births are smaller in number, the two data sources have produced larger differences. In almost all years, the fertility rate for third and further births reported by the 2017 Fertility Survey was more than twice that reported by the censuses and sample surveys (Figure 5.5). Quite by chance, in 2002, the two data sources produced exactly equal fertility rates for third and further births. Moreover, it can also be observed that in the census years, the fertility rate for third and further births ran counter to the fertility rates for first births and for second births, which did not happen in the 2017 Fertility Survey.

Since the fertility rate differences between these two data sources are mainly manifested in the difference in the fertility rate for second births, we calculated how each difference has contributed to the total difference, and it turned out the difference in the fertility rate for second births contributes more than two-thirds,

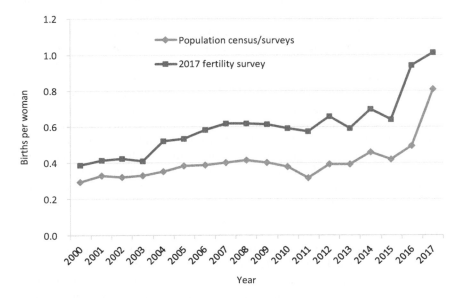

Figure 5.4 Trends in the TFR for second births from 2000 to 2017
Source: Same as Figure 5.1.

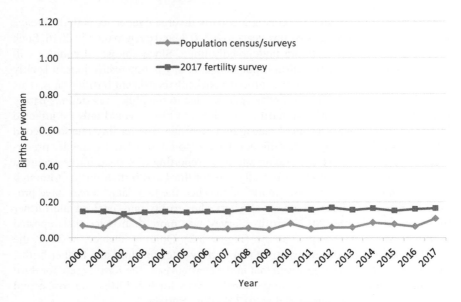

Figure 5.5 Trends in the TFR for third-plus births from 2000 to 2017
Source: Same as Figure 5.1.

while the difference in the fertility rate for third and further births also contributes more than 30%. Since the differences between censuses, sample surveys and Fertility Survey are not manifested in the fertility rate for first births, but in the fertility rates for second births and for third and further births, it is untenable to conclude that China's low fertility isn't, or is, consequent on birth underreporting. So far, we have no way of verifying which data source is more reliable.

Therefore, if the data from 2017 Fertility Survey data are deemed accurate, then the dip in the fertility rate for first births, as caused by marriage postponement, shouldn't be seen as the main contributor to China's low fertility. Instead, the concealing and underreporting of second births (or third and further births) should be regarded as the key contributor to China's low fertility. If the data from censuses and sample surveys are deemed accurate, then the overestimation of fertility rate is by no means consequent on our neglect of marriage postponement, but the overreporting of second births (or third and further births). Although no one knows which type of survey data is of better quality and greater reliability, as mentioned earlier, data from *Hukou* statistics reveal that China's fertility rates since 2000 as implied by the age structure data from *Hukou* system are highly consistent with the results extrapolated using the data from the 2017 Fertility Survey. Although we have no way of verifying whether the *Hukou* data are accurate and reliable, compared with other survey systems, we have good reasons to believe that the *Hukou* data on young women are more accurate and reliable. This is because, on the one hand, they are minimally affected by mortality, and on the other hand, they are less likely to be underreported or over-reported in the *Hukou* system due to migration or school enrollment.

Other Observations

A closer look at and comparison of the data from censuses and sample surveys with the data from the 2017 Fertility Survey have pointed to certain facts. The first fact is that the trends in women's age at first marriage do not accord with the trends in women's average age at first childbirth (Figure 5.6). As revealed by the data from the 2017 Fertility Survey, women's average age at first marriage increased by 0.8 years in the period 2000–2010, while women's average age at first childbirth only went up by 0.1 year. In the period 2000–2005, women's average age at first marriage edged up slightly, while women's average age at first childbirth also edged down slightly. The seemingly divided trends were caused by the shift in the interval between first marriage and first childbirth. In the period 2000–2010, the narrowing interval between first marriage and first childbirth offset the effect of rising age at first marriage on the postponed age at first childbirth. The period 2010–2015 witnessed the marked ascent in both women's average age at first marriage and women's average age at first childbirth, with women's average age at first marriage going up by 1.86 years and women's average age at first childbirth by 1.96 years. During this period, the interval between first marriage and first childbirth was continuously extended. As a result, woman's average age at first childbirth increased more than women's average age at first marriage.

Data from censuses and mini-censuses resemble the data from the 2017 Fertility Survey in the period 2000–2005. The postponement of women's average age at first marriage did not lead to the corresponding postponement of women's average age at first childbirth, suggesting that the interval between first marriage and first childbirth was narrowing. However, the latter two periods exhibited trends opposite to the results of the 2017 Fertility Survey. In the period 2005–2010, women's average age at first marriage increased by 1.12 years, while women's average age at first childbirth increased by 2.06 years, suggesting that the interval between first marriage and first childbirth was prolonged. In the period 2010–2015, however, women's average age at first marriage increased by 0.72 years, while women's average age at first childbirth saw no increase at all or even edged down slightly, suggesting once again that the interval between first marriage and first childbirth was narrowing. For the opposite trends exhibited by data from the two different sources, further verification studies would be needed to discern which one is more plausible or accurate. Judging from experience alone, the results of the 2017 Fertility Survey seem more plausible. Perhaps we can use the raw data from censuses or mini-census for further calculations and tests.

The second fact is that the effects of zodiac preferences are not entirely consistent. The zodiac preferences are self-evident in the data from the 2017 Fertility Survey – fertility rate ascended in the years of the dragon (2000 and 2012) but descended in the years of the sheep (2003 and 2015). As shown in Figure 5.1, the highest fertility rates are found in 2012 (1.78) and 2016 (1.77), while the lowest

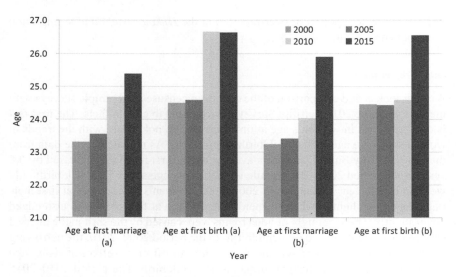

Figure 5.6 Women's average ages at first marriage and first childbirth from the two data sources

Note: The average age at first marriage (a) and the average age at first childbirth (a) are calculated using the data from censuses and mini-censuses, while the average age at first marriage (b) and the average age at first childbirth (b) are calculated using data from the 2017 Fertility Survey.

Source: Same as Figure 5.1.

ones are found in 2003 (1.38) and 2015 (1.41). According to the data from censuses and sample surveys, we can see that in the first few years, the actual results ran counter to the zodiac preferences – the fertility rate decreased in the year of the dragon (2000), and it didn't dip in the year of the sheep (2003). In 2012 (year of the dragon) and 2015 (year of the sheep), however, the fertility rates calculated using both data resources all accord with the zodiac preferences, only the fertility rate in 2012 falling markedly lower than the fertility rates prior to 2010. Furthermore, the lowest fertility rate is found in 2011 and the second lowest in 2015. This doesn't make any sense and requires further examination and analysis.

Zodiac preferences have long existed in Singapore and Taiwan Province of China (Goodkind, 1991, 1996). Since the 1970s, fertility has often peaked in the years of the dragon and troughed in the years of the tiger (Figure 5.7). Cultural similarities have led to the accumulation of birth in the years of the dragon, yet the zodiac years evaded by couples vary from country to country – in China, couples dislike the years of the sheep, while in Singapore and Taiwan Province of China, couples loathe the years of the tiger). Although Japanese couples are also evading certain zodiac years, they tend to combine the 12 zodiac signs with the five elements, and therefore, the fertility troughed in 1966 (the year of fire horse). The next fertility trough is expected to take place in 2026. In China, Singapore and Taiwan Province of China, the effect of zodiac preferences on fertility arises every 12 years, while in Japan, it arises every 60 years. Moreover, it can be observed that the effect of zodiac preferences is only seen after the fertility rate has tumbled to a low level, but not in times of high fertility rate. Perhaps the zodiac preference has always existed, but it was infeasible to make reproductive choices in times of high fertility rate. When the fertility rate has fallen to or below the replacement level, people would have only 1–2 children, Burgeoning economic development, technology advances, seismic shift in lifestyles and the pursuit of children's wellbeing and future success will prompt couples to satisfy their zodiac preferences.

The third fact is linked to the inconsistent effects of the two-child policy. As shown in Figure 5.1, data from the 2017 Fertility Survey point to the pronounced effect of the two-child policy – the fertility rate kicked off its ascent in 2014, ushered in a greater increase in 2016 and only edged down slightly in 2017 while still staying at a high level. Data from sample surveys also reveal the same positive effect of the two-child policy, and yet not only is the effect much weaker than that shown by the data from 2017 Fertility Survey but also puzzling phenomena are observed. The first phenomenon is that the fertility rate in 2016 (1.25) was close to that in 2014 (1.28). Due to the zodiac preferences, births in 2015 may be partially postponed to 2016, indicating that in the first year following the roll-out of the universal two-child policy, the fertility rate rebounded less than that in the first year following the roll-out of the selective two-child policy. In 2017, the second

Figure 5.7 TFRs of Mainland China, Singapore and Taiwan Province of China in the period 1974–2016

Source: Data for China come from the National Two-Per-Thousand Fertility Survey in 1988 (National Family Planning Commission, Tabulation on National Fertility Survey, Beijing: China Population Publishing House, 1990) and the 2017 Fertility Survey (calculated from computer record data file). Data for Singapore and Taiwan Province of China come from the World Bank database (https://data.worldbank.org).

year following the roll-out of the universal two-child policy, the fertility rate soared to 1.58, the highest ever recorded by the National Bureau of Statistics since 1994. However, while the number of births in 2017 (17.23 million) published by the National Bureau of Statistics was lower than that in 2016 (17.86 million), the fertility rate in 2017 was surprisingly higher than that in 2016. This is impossible and incomprehensible. The apparent contradiction between births and fertility rate suggests that one of them must be absolutely problematic.

The Risk of Ultra-Low Fertility in China

The previous analysis of fertility trends arrived at a conclusion that China's fertility rate began its ascent in 2003 and continued the upward trend until 2008, after which it embarked on a downward slide. The continued decline in China's fertility rate was temporarily stalled by the seismic fluctuations consequent on zodiac preferences and fertility policy adjustments. Still, China's fertility rate will soon continue its downward trend and there is a huge risk for China to slide into ultra-low fertility. This is because the first marriage rate in women has plummeted continuously since 2012, leading to the corresponding plunge in the first birth rate (Figure 5.8). In the 1970s, China also underwent a substantial decline in both first marriage rate and first birth rate, which was spurred by interventions of the "late, thin and less" fertility policy. The amendment to the minimum age of marriage prescribed in the Marriage Law in 1980 led to a decrease in women's age at first marriage in the 1980s. Coupled with the accumulation of first marriages and first births, first marriage rate and first birth rate surged at the same time, with TFR and TFR for first births

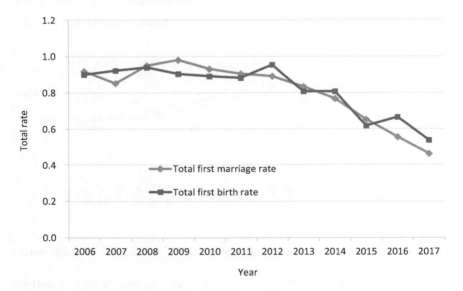

Figure 5.8 Total first marriage rate and total first birth rate in the period 2006–2017

Source: Calculated from computer record data file of the 2017 Fertility Survey.

both staying higher than 1 for many years. The big difference is that the dip in first marriage rate and first birth rate in recent years took place against the backdrop of China's persistent push to adjust and relax the family planning policy. That is to say, the decline in both first marriage rate and first birth rate among Chinese women in the 2010s should be seen as an entirely endogenous trend, while the drop in both rates in the 1970s should be mainly perceived as an exogenous shift. Meanwhile, women's first marriage rate and first birth rate in these days have fallen below the lowest levels in the 1970s.

As mentioned earlier, some scholars argued that the evolution of China's low fertility has been marked by the fall in the fertility rate for first births caused by women's postponement of marriage and childbirth. As a matter of fact, since the founding of the People's Republic of China, the age of Chinese women at first marriage has been edging up slowly but continuously (Coale, 1989; Wei Yan et al., 2013), only the shift taking pace in 2010s was way more noticeable than ever before. In 2007, Gavin Jones (2007), an esteemed demographer who has long been engaged in the research on Asian marriage patterns, said:

> China provides the greatest challenge to theories of marriage change. If we compare percentages of women remaining single at age 30 around the year 2000, the figures for Thailand, Taiwan, and the Chinese populations of Singapore and Malaysia are in the 20-30 percent range; in China, the figure is less than 2 percent. The figure for Bangkok is 33 percent; for Shanghai, 3 percent. These are extraordinarily wide differences.

Ten years into his arrival at that conclusion, the pattern of first marriages among Chinese women has undergone a seismic shift, which was stepping up in recent years. According to the 2017 Fertility Survey, in the past decade, the average age at first marriage among Chinese women has increased by three years to nearly 27 years, and the total first marriage rate has plunged from over 0.9 to an astonishing low of less than 0.6. Whilst such a revolutionary shift does not necessarily suggest that Chinese women are giving up on marriage, it at least points to the widespread postponement of marriage by Chinese women, and perhaps many women may eventually give up on marriage.

The universal two-child policy has missed policymakers' expectations due to the inhibitory effect of declining first marriage rate and first birth rate on the TFR. However, if we look only at the fertility rate for second births, data from the 2017 Fertility Survey reveals that the fertility rate for second births embarked on an upward course in the wake of the roll-out of the selective two-child policy and surged rapidly following the launch of the universal two-child policy, thus leading to considerable accumulation of births. In 2016 and 2017, the fertility rate for second births attained a level corresponding to the fertility rate for second births in 1950s and 1960s when every Chinese women gave birth to an average of six children. In this sense, the two-child policy was very successful. However, a stark fact is that China's fertility rate for first births has fallen sharply since 2012, tumbling to a record low these days. The decline in the fertility rate for first births has chipped away at the upsurge in the fertility rate for second births driven by the two-child policy, making the two-child policy less successful.

The key point is the diverging trends in the fertility rates for first births and for second births will soon fall out of balance. The increase in the fertility rate for second births driven by the two-child policy results mainly from the unleashing of fertility potential that had been long suppressed in the past years, and it's only a flash in the pan. To ensure long-lasting effects of the two-child policy, we will need to rely on young people who are about to reach their marriage and childbearing ages, because the plunge in first marriage rate and first birth rate is exactly a manifestation of the marriage and childbearing behaviors of these young people. Meanwhile, we must be aware that in the next 15 years or so, the young people reaching their marriage and childbearing ages are exactly the cohort born during the baby bust in the period 1995–2005, not to mention their shrinking size.

It took roughly 20–30 years for Western countries and Japan to witness their women's age at first marriage climb to China's current level and their total first marriage rate fall to China's present low level (Sardon, 1993). Therefore, the ongoing shift in China is way faster. In developed countries, the average age of women at first marriage keeps going up, surpassing 30 years already in most countries, and the total first marriage rate has also remained at a low level. On that account, there is still plenty of room for the average age of Chinese women at first marriage to go further up, and the total first marriage rate is likely to linger at a low level. What's worse, young people who will reach their marriage and childbearing ages in the forthcoming ten years will continue to shrink in size. All these combined will prompt an inevitable decline in the first marriage rate and first birth rate, which will in turn lead to a further slump in the fertility rate for second births. It is foreseeable that China will face a huge risk of sliding into ultra-low fertility in the next ten years or so.

Concluding Remarks

Through comparative analysis of data from difference sources, this chapter has attempted to shed light on the trends, evolution and characteristics of China's low fertility over the past two decades and to warn of the impending risk of China sliding into ultra-low fertility. China's fertility rate has undergone a wave-like evolution, plummeting sharply in the 1990s, remaining sluggish for about a decade around 2000 and then rebounding from 2003. Data from the 2017 Fertility Survey show that China's fertility ascended markedly in the past ten years, yet the data from censuses and sample surveys only point to a minor or even subtle uplift. This upward trend turned into a downward trend in the 2010s, yet the continued decline in China's fertility rate was temporarily stalled by the seismic fluctuations consequent on zodiac preferences and fertility policy adjustments in the 2010s. Still, China's fertility rate will soon carry on with its downward trend. Although China's fertility trends are largely shaped by China's burgeoning socioeconomic development, the evolution of China's low fertility over the past 20 years also mirrors the cyclical fluctuations driven by population inertia.

By comparing the data from censuses and sample surveys conducted by the National Bureau of Statistics with the data from the 2017 Fertility Survey launched by the former National Health and Family Planning Commission, it's found that although the decline in the fertility rate for first births due to marriage and childbirth postponement is generally viewed as a prominent characteristics of China's low fertility, the differences in the fertility rates for second births and for third and further births extrapolated from the two data sources should be counted as another important characteristics of China's low fertility. Since 2000, the differences in the fertility rates for second births and for third and further births have contributed 98% to the total difference in the fertility rates extrapolated from the two data sources. As a matter of fact, in the period 1990–2003, data from both sources produced fertility rates that were highly consistent in both trend and level. After 2003, the fertility trends and rates extrapolated from the two data sources began to diverge, with the difference in TFR widening from 0.2 to 0.5 and lingering in the range of 0.2–0.4 in most years. We cannot tell which data source is more accurate and reliable, but the differences and facts we have observed can provide surely some insight.

First, the generalized stable population model we used only needs the age structure data from the censuses to derive more accurate estimate of the average fertility rate between censuses. The generalized stable population model is independent of complete and accurate census data – it does not matter if the census data are underreported, over-reported or misreported or not, as long as the degree or pattern of underreporting, over-reporting or misreporting remains consistent or close. Estimate of the fertility rate between 1982 and 1990 censuses is almost identical to the result of fertility survey conducted in the 1980s. However, the estimates of the fertility rates in the period 1990–2000 point to a stark fact that China's fertility rates in the 1990s were significantly lower than what the government and scholars believed at that time, while estimates of the fertility rates in the period 2000–2010 basically accord with the births published by the National Bureau of Statistics and are significantly higher than those directly obtained through the censuses and sample surveys. The estimate is almost exactly the same as the average fertility rate for 2000–2010 calculated using the data from the 2017 Fertility Survey. Second, we also referred to the *Hukou* data for 2017 from the Ministry of Public Security and used the age-specific population data therefrom to extrapolate China's fertility rates since 2000, discovering that the estimates obtained are highly consistent with those obtained using the data from the 2017 Fertility Survey. Although we are uncertain about the completeness and reliability of *Hukou* data, due to the uniqueness of ID number over one's lifetime, the possibility of underreporting and over-reporting of the young people in *Hukou* data due to factors such as death, migration or school enrollment should be minimal. Furthermore, it's also found that women's average age at first marriage and their average age at first childbirth are inconsistent in how they changed over time; zodiac preferences posed weak or even contradictory impact on fertility; and the first two years into China's roll-out of the universal two-child policy witnessed an unusual divergence between the number of births and the fertility rate. All these phenomena are reflective of the potential problems in the data from censuses and sample surveys.

Still, it should be noted that the data from the National Bureau of Statistics accord well with the data from the former National Health and Family Planning Commission in terms of the sharp decline in China's fertility rate for first births since 2012. Judging from the trends of women postponing the age at first marriage and the total first marriage rate maintaining its slide, China is probably experiencing a marriage transition as never before in history, which can be called a marriage revolution. So far, China is still deemed a society of universal marriage, and Western scholars used to see China as the greatest challenge to the theory of marriage transition. However, judging from some seismic shifts taking place in recent years, although China's marriage revolution started late, it is likely to advance at a faster pace. This marriage revolution is likely to determine where China's low fertility goes. According to the experiences of developed countries and Japan, there is still plenty of room for the average age of Chinese women at first marriage to go further up, and the total first marriage rate is likely to linger at a low level. Moreover, young people who will reach their marriage and childbearing ages in the forthcoming ten years will continue to shrink in size. All these combined will prompt an even steeper drop in fertility. Even if the fertility policy is further relaxed, the protracted downturn in the fertility rate for first births will eventually weaken the effects of the fertility policy. It is foreseeable that China will face a huge risk of sliding into ultra-low fertility. In devising the fertility and family support policies, it is imperative to take marriage promotion into consideration, and the need for us to build and implement strong policies for promoting marriage and fertility is pressing.

References

Coale, A. J. 1989. Marriage and Childbearing in China Since 1940. *Social Forces* 67(4): 833–850.
Cui Hongyan, Xu Lan, and Li Rui. 2013. An Evaluation of Data Accuracy of the 2010 Population Census of China. *Population Research* 1: 10–21.
Frejka, T., Jones, G. W., and Sardon, J. P. 2010. East Asian Childbearing Patterns and Policy Developments. *Population and Development Review* 36(3): 579–606.
Goodkind, D. M. 1991. Creating New Traditions in Modern Chinese Populations: Aiming for Birth in the Year of the Dragon. *Population and Development Review* 17(4): 663–686.
Goodkind, D. M. 1996. Chinese Lunar Birth Timing in Singapore: New Concerns for Child Quality Amidst Multicultural Modernity. *Journal of Marriage and Family* 58(3): 784–795.
Guo Zhigang 2013. Where Is the Fertility Level Low in China — Analysis Based on Six Data. *Chinese Journal of Population Science* 2: 2–10.
Guo Zhigang 2017. Main Characteristics of the Low Fertility Process in China: Implications from the Results of the 1% Population Sample Survey in 2015. *Chinese Journal of Population Science* 4: 2–14.
Guo Zhigang and Tian Siyu. 2017. The Influence of Late Marriage on Low Fertility of Contemporary Young Women. *Youth Studies* 6: 16–25.
Jones, G. W. 2007. Delayed Marriage and Very Low Fertility in Pacific Asia. *Population and Development Review* 33(3): 453–478.

Sardon, J. P. 1993. Women's First Marriage Rates in Europe: Elements for a Typology. *Population: An English Selection* 5: 120–152.

Wang Jinying and Ge Yanxia. 2013. Assessment of 2010 Census Data Quality and Past Population Changes. *Population Research* 1: 22–33.

Wei Yan, Dong Shuo, Jiang Quanbao B. 2013. Changes of First Marriage Patterns in China: An Analysis Based on Marriage Table. *Population and Economics* 2: 21–28.

Yang Fan and Zhao Menghan. 2013. Estimation of the Fertility Level in China Since 2000. *Population Research* 2: 54–65.

Yoo, S. H. and Sobotka, T. 2018. Ultra-low Fertility in South Korea: The Role of the Tempo Effect. *Demographic Research* 38: 549–576.

Zhao Menghan. 2015. An Estimation of Fertility Level in China, 2000–2010. *Population Research* 5: 49–58.

6 Structural Shifts in Fertility Rate

The changes in fertility rate are bound to be accompanied by the structural shifts in fertility rate. In tandem with the continued changes in fertility rate, China has also witnessed a seismic shift in fertility pattern – both in terms of the parity structure and the age structure of its fertility – with births increasingly concentrated in certain age group and parity. In this chapter, we will examine the structural shift of China's fertility from aspects such as parity, age, birth interval and sex.

Parity Structure of Fertility

The plunge in China's fertility is marked by the decline in the fertility rate for high-order births. Figure 6.1 shows how parity-specific fertility rates trended over the years. During the first fertility transition, the proportion of third and further births in the total fertility rate (TFR) dropped from two-thirds to one-fourth, and the proportion of first births rose from less than one-fifth to almost one-half. During the second fertility transition, the proportion of third and further births in the TFR continued to tumble sharply to only 6.6% in 2010, while the proportion of first births climbed all the way up to 61.3%. After 2000, although the overall fertility rate did not change much, the fertility rate for first births embarked on a downward slide, while fertility rates for second births and for third and further births began to go up.

It is worth noting that the roll-out of the two-child policy in recent years has had a major impact on China's fertility trends. Overall, the slight pick-up in TFR has masked the divided shifts in the fertility rate for first births, which descended continuously, and the fertility rate for second births, which ascended sharply. Since 2010, the proportion of first births in TFR has continued to edge down; the proportion of second births has been going all the way up; and the proportion of third and further births has remained constantly low. Meanwhile, the fertility rate for second births has outrivaled that for first births. According to the data from 2017 sample survey, China's TFR stood at 1.58, of which the TFR for first births fell below 0.7, and the TFR for second births rose to over 0.8, which accords with the TFR for second births in 1974 when China's TFR was as high as 4.2. It can be seen that the two-child policy has played a pivotal role in pushing up the fertility rate for second births.

DOI: 10.4324/9781003429661-6

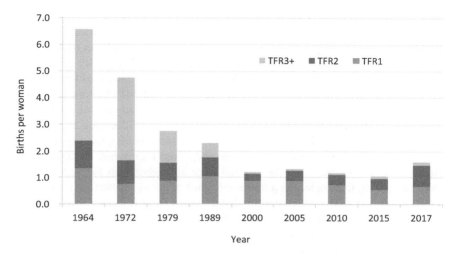

Figure 6.1 Changes in China's parity-specific fertility rates from 1964 to 2017

Source: Data for years preceding 1989 come from the National One-Per-Thousand Fertility Survey conducted in 1982, while data for years succeeding 1989 come from population censuses and sample surveys.

Compared with developed countries, China outrivals developed countries in terms of the proportion of first births in TFR but falls behind developed countries in terms of the proportions of childlessness, second births and further births in TFR (Zhongwei Zhao et al., 2017). According to the Human Fertility Database (https://www.humanfertility.org), among women born in 1970, the lifetime rate of childlessness reached 10–20% in major developed countries, with the highest rate of 27% found in Japan. Even in Taiwan Province of China, this rate is as high as 15.7%. According to the data from 2015 mini-census, the rate of childlessness among Chinese women aged 40 years was only 4.6%. Although there has been a tremendous uplift compared with previous years, this rate in China is still significantly lower than those in developed countries. From the 1990s to the mid-2000s, first births accounted for 60–70% and second births for 23–32% in China's TFR, compared with less than 50% and around 35%, respectively, in developed countries. However, in the past ten years, the parity structure of China's fertility rate has undergone a seismic shift, with TFR for first births gradually falling down and TFR for second births progressively climbing up, a parity structure that is increasingly similar to that in developed countries. However, with the gradual dissipation of second birth accumulation brought about by the two-child policy, it is important for us to keep a close eye on how the parity structure of China's fertility rate will evolve in the years to come.

Age Pattern of Fertility

The shift in the parity structure of China's fertility rate is also manifested in the changes in the age pattern of fertility rate. Specifically, fertility rate among older women plunged in the 1970s, followed by the drop in fertility rate among younger women. In the 1990s, the age pattern of fertility rate ushered in a further shift, with fertility rate also coming down in the youngest women, especially in those at peak childbearing age. The age pattern of "early, wide and high" gradually gave way to the age pattern of "late, thin and low". After 2000, the age pattern of fertility rates saw little change. Compared with 2000, the age pattern in 2010 became apparently "lower". In 2000, the peak childbearing age was 24 years old, and the fertility rate for women at this age was 145.7‰. In 2010, the peak childbearing age was still 24 years old; yet, the fertility rate dived to 99.1‰. Nonetheless, fertility rate made its way up among older women. As can be seen from Figure 6.2, the age-specific fertility rates for women over 28 in 2010 were all higher than the same rates in 2000, suggesting that there was a noticeable shift in the age pattern of fertility rate in the period 2000–2010 in spite of the barely changed TFR in the same period. In recent years, due the continued postponement of women's childbearing age and the roll-out of the two-child policy, the peak childbearing age has continued to go up, in addition to an evident uplift in the fertility rate among older women. In 2017, the peak childbearing age was postponed to 27 years old, and the fertility rate for women at this age reached 114.5‰. The fertility rate for women aged 30–40 years in 2017 was 1.5–2.0 times higher than in 2010.

Still, childbearing postponement in China is not as severe as in developed countries. In China, peak childbearing ages were 20–24 years prior to 2006, after which the peak childbearing ages gradually turned into 25–29 years. In developed countries, peak childbearing ages fall within the range of 30–34 years, which are way closer to the normal distribution of peak childbearing ages.

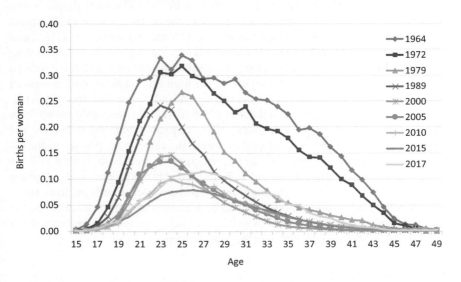

Figure 6.2 Changes in the age pattern of China's fertility from 1964 to 2017
Source: Same as Figure 6.1.

Age at Marriage/Childbirth and Birth Interval

The shift in China's fertility pattern is also marked by the postponement of women's age at marriage and childbirth and the lengthening of birth interval. Since the founding of the People's Republic of China, women's average age at first marriage has been edging up gradually. In the 1970s, under the influence of the "later, longer and less" fertility policy, Chinese women tended to marry and give birth late, thus pushing up women's average age at first marriage from 21 to 23. In the 1980s, women's average age at first marriage dropped by one year and stabilized at 22. Since the 1990s, women's average age at first marriage has followed a trend of continued postponement. Results of the Sixth Census showed that women's average age at first marriage rose from 23.17 in 2000 to 23.89 in 2010. According to the data from 2017 Fertility Survey, women's average age at first marriage climbed from 23.6 years in 2006 to 26.3 years in 2016, an increase of nearly three years in the past ten years (He Dan et al., 2018).

Women's average age at first childbirth trended in a similar way to women's average age at first marriage. Prior to the launch of the family planning policy, Chinese women's average age at first childbirth was generally 22–23 years old. Under the influence of the family planning policy launched in the 1970s, Chinese women gradually postponed their first marriage and first childbirth. From 1970 to 1980, women's average age at first childbirth was postponed by 2.5 years from 22.8 to 25.3 years. In the 1980s, however, policy adjustment pushed back the average age at first childbirth by 1.7 years. Since the 1990s, women's average age at first childbirth has followed a trend of continued postponement, increasing by almost one year in the period 1990–2000, evening out in the period 2000–2005 and reaching 24.6 years in 2005 and further to 25.7 years in 2010. According to the data from 2017 sample survey, women's average at first childbirth reached 26.77 years in 2017, an increase of more than one year compared with 2010. The postponement of women's average age at first childbirth in China, albeit very noticeable, is less significant compared with developed countries. Chinese women's average age at first childbirth is close to that in North American and Eastern European countries (25–27 years old), but far lower than that in Western European and Northern European countries (28–31 years old).

The trends of Chinese women's average age at second childbirth basically accord with the trends of their average age at first childbirth. From 1970 to 2010, women's average age at second childbirth was postponed by five years from 25.3 to 30.37, an increase outrunning the increase of almost three years in woman's average age at first childbirth in the same period. Chinese women's average age at second childbirth maintained basically stable as from 2010 until reaching 30.77 years in 2017. Although Chinese women have a lower average age at first childbirth than their counterparts in Western European and Northern European countries, women's average age at second childbirth in China is close to that (30–33 years) in these countries, suggesting that Chinese women have a longer inter-birth interval than women in these countries. The average inter-birth interval in Chinese women was more than four years in 2000 and more than five years in 2005. With

90 *Structural Shifts in Fertility Rate*

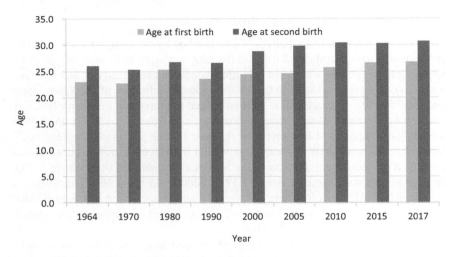

Figure 6.3 Changes in Chinese women's average age at childbirth from 1964 to 2017
Source: Same as Figure 6.1.

the family planning policy gradually lifting restrictions on birth spacing, the average inter-birth interval narrowed accordingly to 4.6 years in 2010 and further to 4.0 years in 2017 (Figure 6.3). In Western European and Northern European countries, however, the average inter-birth interval is only 2–3 years.

Sex Ratio at Birth

The change in the sex structure of fertility is another characteristic drawing extensive attention to the shift in China's fertility pattern. China's SRB continued to edge up and became increasingly skewed as from the mid-1980s, which is never seen in the development history of any populous country. The rising SRB was another important characteristics marking China's second fertility transition, and it occurred as China's fertility fell below the replacement level and dived further downward.

The normal range for SRB is 103 to 107 (Chahnazarian, 1988; Waldron, 1998). In the mid-1980s, China's SRB rose from 107.6 in 1982 to 111.3 in 1990, 116.9 in 2000, 120.5 in 2005 and 121.2 in 2010, far beyond the upper limit of the normal range (Figure 6.4). In the early years, skewed SRB was mainly found in rural areas, and it gradually seeped into urban areas as from the 1990s. SRB is universally skewed toward either rural residents, urban residents or migrants. In 2010, SRBs in cities, townships and villages stood at 118.3, 122.8 and 122.1, respectively.

Another characteristics of China's skewed SRB is that there are large differences in SRB among birth orders and SRB is severely skewed among second and higher-order births. In other words, the higher the birth order, the higher the SRB. According to the Sixth Census, the SRB was 113.7, 130.3 and 161.6, respectively,

Structural Shifts in Fertility Rate 91

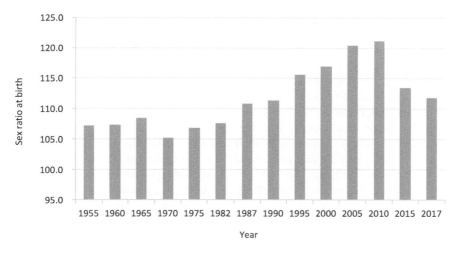

Figure 6.4 Changes in China's SRB from 1955 to 2017
Source: Same as Figure 6.1.

in 2010 for first births, second births and third births. In parallel with the surprisingly high SRBs for second and third births, the SRB for first births was also noticeably high. Sex selection among first births has further driven up China's SRB and dragged down China's fertility rate. The "son preference" deeply rooted in traditional Chinese culture is the underlying cause of sex selection, while the availability of sex selection techniques is deemed the direct cause of sex selection. Furthermore, the underreporting of baby girls is also an important contributor to China's high SRB. Studies have shown that the underreporting of baby girls contributed to nearly half of the skewed portion of China's SRB in the 1990s (Chen Wei and Zhai Zhenwu, 2007).

However, the upward curve of China's SRB bent in 2010 and kept going down for years until China's SRB dropped to 113.5 in 2015 and further to 111.9 in 2017. Amid the fertility transition taking place in countries across the globe, only Asian countries have undergone and are undergoing changes in their SRBs. According to the experiences of South Korea and Taiwan Province of China, in the wake of booming economic development and comprehensive social modernization, the cultural and economic determinants underlying high SRB will eventually wane and disappear over time. This is best illustrated by the continuous decline of China's SRB over the past few years.

Concluding Remarks

Fertility pattern refers to the structural characteristics of fertility in terms of parity, age, birth interval and sex, and it always goes hand in hand with fertility rate. In parallel with the rapid change and the continued decline in China's fertility rate, the fertility pattern among Chinese women has also undergone a seismic shift. From the 1960s to the 2000s, women's childbearing ages became increasingly concentrated. The interquartile range of childbearing age decreased from ten years to six years. The proportion of third and further births in the TFR tumbled from two-thirds to less than 5%, while the proportion of first births soared from one-fifth to nearly 70%. The interval between first and second births lengthened from 2 to 3 years to more than five years. Meanwhile, gender-biased sex selection had become an increasingly common practice since the mid-1980s.

In the 2010s, in sympathy with the slight rebound in fertility due to cyclical factors, especially with the substantial increase in the fertility rate for second birth since the roll-out of the two-child policy, the age pattern of China's fertility also underwent a marked shift. In 2017, the interquartile range of childbearing age increased to eight years, and the fertility rate among women aged 30–40 years was 1.6–2.2 times higher than that in 2010. The dip in the fertility rate for first births and the ascent in the fertility rate for second births in recent years prompted a major shift in the parity structure of China's fertility, with the fertility rate for second births overtaking the fertility rate for first births. In addition to the shortened inter-birth interval, there was also a noticeable change in the sex structure of fertility, with SRB edging down continuously for years.

In terms of the characteristics of low fertility, China is vastly different from other low-fertility countries. In short, despite the largely identical fertility level, the fertility structures are varied. China falls behind European countries and the United States in terms of the proportions of childlessness, second births and further births in TFR. Furthermore, out-of-wedlock births take up a considerable share in the TFR in European countries and the United States and even surpass one-half in certain countries. China, however, doesn't have the figure in this regard. The peak childbearing age and average age at first childbirth in European countries and the United States are significantly higher than those in China; yet, China has a longer inter-birth interval to even out the difference and thereby get an average age at second childbirth close to that in European countries and the United States. Needless to say, the change in SRB is a unique characteristics of the fertility pattern of China (or some Asian countries).

References

Chahnazarian, A. 1988. Determinants of the Sex Ratio at Birth: Review of Recent Literature. *Social Biology* 35(3–4): 214–235.
Chen Wei and Zhai Zhenwu. 2007. Sex Ratio at Birth in China in the 1990s: How High Did It Really Climb? *Population Research* 5: 1–8.
He Dan, Zhang Xuying, Zhuang Yar, Wang Zhili, and Yang Shenghui. 2018. A Report of Fertility Status in China, 2006–2016. *Population Research* 6: 35–45.
Waldron, I. 1998. Factors Determining the Sex Ratio at Birth. Pp. 53–63 in *Too Young To Die: Genes or Gender?* New York, NY: United Nations.
Zhongwei Zhao, Qinzi Xu, and Xin Yuan. 2017. Far Below Replacement Fertility in Urban China. *Journal Biosocial Science* 49(S1): S4–S19.

7 Quantum Effect and Tempo Effect of Fertility

Fertility level is indeed the result of the interplay between fertility behaviors and demographic structure. Any change in either or both factors could lead to a consequential shift in fertility rate over time. According to Bongaarts and Feeney (1998), the fertility rate is composed of two components: quantum and tempo. Even if the quantum of fertility remains invariant, the total fertility rate (TFR) will descend or ascend in sympathy with the tempo changes. To address the flaws in TFR, they proposed the tempo-adjusted TFR (TFR'), which can restore the advanced or deferred births that were not reflected in the TFR by adjusting TFR for tempo effect, thereby obtaining a period fertility rate that is closer to the lifetime fertility rate. Guo Zhigang (2000a, 2000b, 2002, 2004) used TFR' to analyze the changes in China's fertility rate since the 1990s and found that this measure could literally produce estimates closer to the actual cohort-specific lifetime fertility rates than the TFR measure. In the mid-to-late 1990s, the TFRs obtained through fertility surveys fell within the range of 1.3–1.4, while the TFR's stood at 1.7. Guo Zhigang opined that TFR' can substitute for TFR in estimating lifetime fertility rate, while TFR can still be used to estimate the period fertility rate. The difference between TFR' and TFR can be used to estimate the impact of fertility postponement on the current fertility level.

According to the TFR' calculated by Guo Zhigang, it can be seen that China's ultra-low fertility is largely a reflection of the tempo effect of fertility. Some scholars have suggested that TFR' is also flawed in obtaining accurate estimates of fertility level and that the fertility rate can only be accurately estimated by controlling for age, parity and birth interval at the same time (McDonald and Kippen, 2007; Ni Bhrolchain, 2011). French scholars Rallu and Tolemon proposed in 1994 the parity-age-duration total fertility rate, which simultaneously decomposes and controls for the components of "tempo effect", i.e., age structure, parity structure and inter-birth interval. Since 2007, Australian scholars McDonald and Kippen (2007, 2009) have written a number of articles to further probe into the connotations of this measure. They put forward the intrinsic total fertility rate (ITFR) and used this measure to analyze the fertility transition in Australia. In this chapter, we will use this measure to examine China's fertility transition and low fertility and will decompose the quantum and tempo effects of China's fertility transition in different periods.

DOI: 10.4324/9781003429661-7

The data used herein are from the National Two-per Thousand Fertility Survey in 1988, One-per thousand sample of the Fifth Census in 2000, National One-per Thousand Sample Survey on Population Changes in 2008 and the 2017 Fertility Survey. In the data from 1988 Fertility Survey, the sample size of women over the age of 15 was 657,250. In the data from the sample of the Fifth Census in 2000, the sample size of women over 15 was 425,839. In the data from the National One-per Thousand Sample Survey on Population Changes in 2008, the sample size of women over 15 was 404,827. In the data from the 2017 Fertility Survey, the sample size of women over 15 was 249,946. These data sets are basically sufficient for calculating the intrinsic TFR. In this chapter, the figures presented in all charts are calculated or extrapolated from these data sets, and we won't further specify the data source one by one.

Our approach is to calculate TFR and ITFR. As introduced in Chapter 3, ITFR, like TFR, is a hypothetical cohort measure harnessing the period life table method to obtain the intrinsic births proportional to the actual fertility behaviors in the period by applying age-specific, parity-specific and interval-specific progression probabilities to the cohort population, thereby arriving at better estimates of period fertility. Please refer to the corresponding literature for a detailed introduction to this method (Rallu and Toulemon, 1994; McDonald and Kippen, 2007).

Changes in Period Fertility Rate

Figure 7.1 shows the TFR and ITFR for each year from 1970 to 2016, while Tables 7.1a and 7.1b show the total and parity-specific differences between TFR and ITFR for each year. It should be noted that the fertility rates after 2007 in Figure 7.1 were calculated using the data from the 2017 Fertility Survey, which are significantly higher than those calculated using the data from the sample surveys. Such a jump in fertility rate is caused by data discrepancies, not a reflection of the actual fertility rate. Although the fertility rates did go up in this period, it's unlikely for such a noticeable jump to happen.

Judging from the trends of China's TFR over the past four decades, the transition of China's fertility can be divided into three stages. China's fertility plummeted in Stage I (1970–1979), fluctuated in Stage II (1980–1989), fell below the replacement level and dived further downward in Stage III (1990–2003) and finally rebounded in Stage IV (from 2004 onwards).

All in all, if the transition of China's fertility since the 1970s is divided into different stages based on the trends of ITFR, the results will basically coincide with the results of TFR. Judging from the figures of ITFR, the fertility rate among Chinese women of childbearing age had remained below the replacement level since 1990, plunging dramatically in the early 1990s and lingering at a very low level of less than 1.5 since 1994. These results are highly consistent with the results obtained by Guo Zhigang (2000a) through the multi-indicator analysis of different data. In recent years, the fertility rate has increased markedly, albeit in noticeable fluctuations.

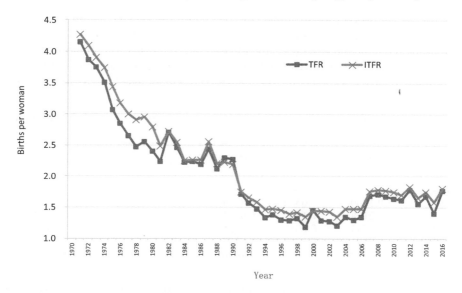

Figure 7.1 Changes in TFR and ITFR from 1970 to 2016

Specifically, in Stage I, the difference between ITFR and TFR was noticeable and expanding year by year, with ITFR remaining higher than TFR. From the parity perspective, in the period 1970–1979, ITFRs for first, second and third births were substantially higher than the TFRs for first, second and third births. The difference between ITFR and TFR for first births was the greatest in the period 1973–1978, while the difference between ITFR and TFR for second births began to grow significantly after 1977. This suggests that amid the fertility decline in the 1970s, the shift in the fertility pattern for first births was the most obvious in the mid-1970s, but gradually waned in the mid-to-late stage of fertility transition, in which time the postponement of second births became increasingly pronounced. It can be seen that the birth postponement by parity in the 1970s was neither consistent in timing nor identical in the years postponed.

In Stage II, both ITFR and TFR show marked fluctuations. In spite of the generally insignificant difference between the two, the differences among birth orders are particularly significant. For example, the difference between ITFR and TFR was only 0.0785 in 1983, yet the ITFR for first births was 0.2374 lower than the TFR for first births and the ITFR for second births was 0.2427 than the TFR for second births, suggesting that there was evident accumulation of first births in 1982, which was accompanied by the postponement of second births. After 1984, ITFR–TFR differences for first births and second births both underwent fluctuations. As a matter of fact, throughout the first half of the 1980s, there existed noticeable accumulation of first births and evident postponement of second births. Many studies have confirmed the significant contribution of rural reforms and the new Marriage Law to the accumulation of first births. However, since the average age of women at second birth did not drop significantly in this period, the probability for women in prime reproductive years (i.e., 20–30 years old) to have a second birth after an interval of less than three years fell significantly. On the contrary, the probability for them to have a second child after an interval of more than three years went up

Table 7.1a Total Difference and Parity-Specific Differences between TFR and ITFR from 1971 to 2008

Year	Total Difference	Parity-Specific Difference				
		1	2	3	4	5+
1971	0.1200	0.0522	0.0779	0.0242	−0.0591	0.0275
1972	0.2198	0.1562	0.0432	0.0626	−0.0117	−0.0283
1973	0.1534	0.2018	−0.0165	0.0270	−0.0114	−0.0464
1974	0.2391	0.1903	0.0553	0.0408	0.0234	−0.0696
1975	0.3642	0.2279	0.1808	0.0292	0.0335	−0.1065
1976	0.3349	0.2399	0.1696	0.0328	−0.0166	−0.0900
1977	0.3564	0.2305	0.1986	0.0514	−0.0211	−0.1030
1978	0.4286	0.2259	0.2629	0.0545	−0.0224	−0.0922
1979	0.3967	0.1341	0.2369	0.0586	0.0008	−0.0336
1980	0.3844	0.0725	0.2662	0.0817	0.0292	−0.0653
1981	0.2431	−0.0084	0.2752	0.0641	−0.0193	−0.0685
1982	0.0187	−0.3118	0.2315	0.1091	0.0258	−0.0358
1983	0.0785	−0.2374	0.2417	0.0786	0.0273	−0.0317
1984	0.0178	−0.1151	0.1348	0.0261	0.0034	−0.0314
1985	0.0188	−0.0646	0.0629	0.0207	0.0189	−0.0190
1986	0.0771	−0.0323	0.0733	0.0292	0.0226	−0.0157
1987	0.1132	−0.1178	0.0987	0.0462	0.0751	0.0111
1988	0.0891	−0.0359	0.1112	0.0071	0.0112	−0.0045
1989	−0.0706	−0.1527	−0.0559	0.0447	0.0575	0.0358
1990	−0.0812	−0.1396	−0.0435	0.0334	0.0446	0.0238
1991	0.0355	0.0463	0.0233	−0.0247	−0.0090	−0.0005
1992	0.0773	0.0574	0.0638	−0.0273	−0.0139	−0.0027
1993	0.1113	0.0599	0.0732	0.0027	−0.0166	−0.0078
1994	0.1251	0.1112	0.0594	−0.0245	−0.0159	−0.0052
1995	0.0950	0.0559	0.0687	−0.0136	−0.0102	−0.0058
1996	0.1545	0.0891	0.0850	−0.0028	−0.0110	−0.0057
1997	0.1114	0.0650	0.0727	−0.0110	−0.0108	−0.0044
1998	0.0896	0.0198	0.0868	−0.0050	−0.0084	−0.0035
1999	0.1600	0.0927	0.0854	−0.0087	−0.0066	−0.0028
2000	−0.0160	−0.0916	0.0842	−0.0015	−0.0051	−0.0019
2001	0.1465	0.0489	0.0985	−0.0112	0.0076	0.0027
2002	0.1514	0.0463	0.1026	0.0002	0.0020	0.0003
2003	0.1398	0.0773	0.0562	−0.0006	0.0068	0.0001
2004	0.1335	0.0338	0.0802	0.0106	0.0071	0.0017
2005	0.1855	0.0550	0.1151	0.0108	0.0040	0.0005
2006	0.1316	0.0342	0.0643	0.0275	0.0050	0.0006
2007	0.0616	0.0138	0.0319	0.0129	0.0031	−0.0001
2008	0.0637	0.0198	0.0243	0.0207	−0.0001	−0.0009

Note: Differences were obtained by subtracting TFR from ITFR.

noticeably. As a result, instead of the accumulation, second births were put off. We believe this phenomenon may be largely a consequence of the "one-child" policy.

In Stage III, both TFR and TFR fell below the replacement level in 1990 and the downturn continued until 1999. TFR approached 1.5 in 2000 and had since fluctuated around 1.3. Except in 2000, the ITFR curve has been hovering above the TFR curve. From the parity perspective, ITFRs for both first and second births remained slightly higher than TFRs for first and second births in each year, suggesting that there was slight postponement of both first and second births during this period. Whilst Guo Zhigang (2000a) argued that the decline in China's fertility in the 1990s was mainly driven by the marked postponement of marriage and childbearing, our calculations using data from the 1‰ sample data of the 2000 Census also point to the marked postponement of childbearing age for all birth orders, and hence, the estimated TFR' was much higher than TFR but the ITFR was lower than TFR'. This shows that the decline in fertility rate in the 1990s was due to the fact that, on the one hand, births were also "postponed" due to the postponement of marriage and childbearing, and on the other hand, some postponed births vanished in the aftermath of a shift in marriage and childbearing patterns. It should be noted that the fertility trends in the early 2000s basically accord with the fertility trends in the mid-to-late 1990s, and there is basically no significant difference between ITFR and TFR for third and further births. Since the late 1990s, however, the ITFR–TFR differences for first and second births had been largely consistent.

In Stage IV, both ITFR and TFR ascended in fluctuations. This stage is somewhat similar to Stage II (1980s), only it's subject to greater fluctuations caused by temporal disturbances. Overall, ITFR slightly outrivaled TFR; yet, the differences between the two were significant. The ITFR–TFR difference for first births was subtle prior to 2012, after which the difference continued to widen, a reflection of how the increasing tempo effect constantly dragged down the TFR for first births.

Table 7.1b Total Difference and Parity-Specific Differences between TFR and ITFR from 2007 to 2016

Year	Total Difference	Parity-Specific Difference		
		1	2	3+
2007	0.0690	0.0436	0.0082	0.0172
2008	0.0702	0.0279	0.0236	0.0186
2009	0.0948	0.0648	0.0103	0.0198
2010	0.1075	0.0724	0.0174	0.0177
2011	0.0840	0.0691	0.0082	0.0067
2012	0.0427	0.0144	−0.0028	0.0310
2013	0.1030	0.1489	−0.0286	−0.0173
2014	0.0731	0.1482	−0.0657	−0.0094
2015	0.1725	0.3096	−0.0946	−0.0425
2016	0.0362	0.2637	−0.2109	−0.0166

Note: Differences were obtained by subtracting TFR from TFR. Due to the small sample size of higher-order births and thus the poor stability of calculation results, the third and further births were combined for calculation.

The ITFR–TFR difference for second births, however, was quite the opposite. The TFR for second births surged in the wake of the roll-out of selective two-child policy and the universal two-child policy, respectively; yet, the ITFRs for second births point to an overestimation of the TFRs for second births. Likewise, the TFRs for third and further births were also overestimated, only the impact is minor due to their extremely low figures.

Structural Shift in Fertility Behaviors

ITFR is capable of providing more structural details on fertility transition. We selected one year from each of the three stages of fertility transition – i.e., 1975, 1983 and 1994 – to take a deep dive into how age-, parity- and interval-specific fertility rates had changed. There are two reasons for us to pick these three years for comparative analysis. First, these three years are all in the earlier phase of the three transition stages, thus retaining the early characteristics of each stage of fertility transition. Second, while differing significantly in the structure of fertility behaviors, the three years also retain the characteristics marking the corresponding transition stages, and thus, they can give a comprehensive picture of how fertility rate trended amid the fertility transition. Fertility rates in Stage IV were subject to greater fluctuations caused by temporal disturbances. In particular, the fertility rate for second births was significantly influenced by the roll-out of the two-child policy. Therefore, we purposely selected 2007, 2012 and 2016 to analyze the changes in age-, parity- and interval-specific fertility rates. In this section, we will focus our analysis on the changes in the fertility rate for second births. The intrinsic fertility rate for first births encompasses only the age dimension, and thus, there is relatively little information for in-depth analysis. Third and further births are small in number, and there might be occasional fluctuations that would compromise our trend analysis.

Figures 7.2–7.4 show the age- and interval-specific probabilities for women of childbearing age to have a second birth in 1975, 1983 and 1994, respectively. The graphs clearly illustrate how the fertility pattern shifted in these years. In 1975, the probability of having a second birth peaked at 0.26 among 26-year-old women. Women aged 17–26 years would generally have a second birth after an interval of two years, while women aged 27 and over were more likely to do so after an interval of three or more years. In 1982/1983, the peak age for having a second birth was advanced to 23 years old, but the peak probability dropped to 0.20. However, women in the 17–28 age group had a higher probability of having a second birth after an interval of one year than their counterparts in 1975. In 1994, women aged 22–24 years were most likely to have a second birth, yet the probability dropped significantly.

On the whole, from the 1970s to the 1990s, the age-specific and interval-specific patterns of second births underwent the following transitions: (1) The probability of second birth dropped significantly among women of all ages and tumbled to near zero among woman over 35 after the 1980s; (2) The peak age for having a second birth was continuously postponed from around 23 to roughly 26 during the 1970s,

Quantum Effect and Tempo Effect of Fertility 99

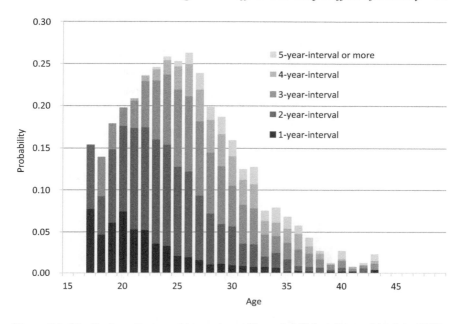

Figure 7.2 Distribution of age- and interval-specific probabilities of second birth in 1975

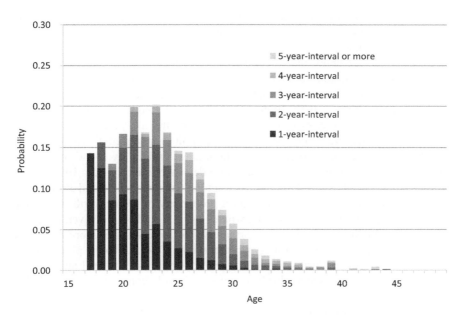

Figure 7.3 Distribution of age- and interval-specific probabilities of second birth in 1983

100 Quantum Effect and Tempo Effect of Fertility

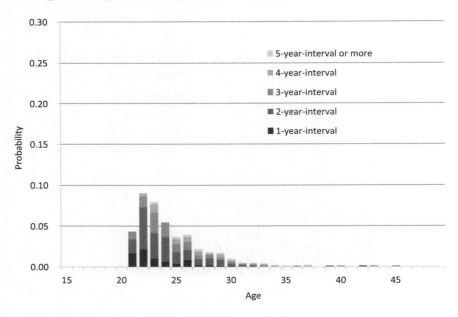

Figure 7.4 Distribution of age- and interval-specific probabilities of second birth in 1994

then rolled back to around 23 in 1986 and once again postponed beyond 30 in the period from 1987 to the late 1990s; and (3) The probability of having a second birth after an interval of more than three years fell markedly among women of all ages, earlier and faster than the probability of having a second birth after an interval of less than two years.

Figures 7.5–7.7 show the interval-specific probabilities of second birth for women aged 23, 26 and 30, respectively, in 1975, 1983 and 1994. In 1975, for women of all three ages, the interval had a significant impact on their probability of having a second birth, only the highest probability is found for the interval of three years and the probability of having a second birth after a 1-year interval remains basically the same. Women of all three ages exhibit pronounced differences in the interval-specific fertility structure, with the highest probability found for the age of 23. In 1983, the probability of second birth decreased slightly from 1975 among women aged 23, but dropped dramatically among women aged 26 and 30. Furthermore, among women aged 23, the highest probability of second birth was found for the interval of three years. Among women aged 26 and 30, however, the probability of having a second birth after an interval of three years or more is slightly lower than the probability after a 2-year interval. In 1994, due to the plunge in the fertility rate for second births, the influence of age and birth interval on women's probability of having a second birth waned significantly compared with the 1970s and 1980s.

By probing into women's age- and interval-specific probabilities of second birth or higher-order birth, as a component of the ITFR measure, we have obtained the

Quantum Effect and Tempo Effect of Fertility 101

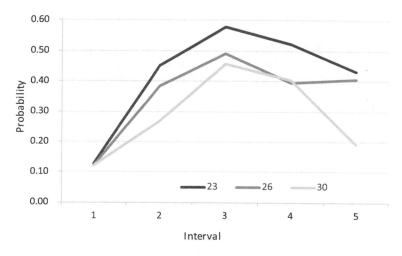

Figure 7.5 Distribution of interval-specific probabilities of second birth for women aged 23, 26 and 30 in 1975

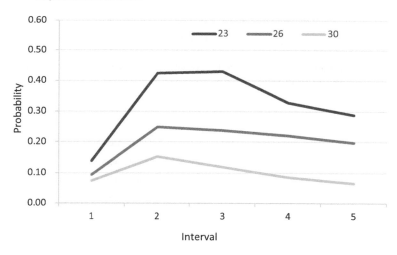

Figure 7.6 Distribution of interval-specific probabilities of second birth for women aged 23, 26 and 30 in 1983

detailed distribution of age- and interval-specific births from 1971 to 2008, which gives an intuitive picture of how these two elements changed amid the fertility transition. Generally speaking, age had a significant impact on women's probability of having a second birth and this probability varied greatly in different periods. The differences among different ages were noticeable when fertility declined rapidly, but became less significant after the fertility rate had reached a lower level. Furthermore, birth interval also had a significant impact on women's probability of having a second birth, and this probability varied greatly among women of different ages.

102 Quantum Effect and Tempo Effect of Fertility

Moreover, such structural differences also varied distinctly in different periods of the fertility transition.

Figures 7.8–7.10 show women's age- and interval-specific probabilities of having a second birth in 2007, 2012 and 2016, respectively. It can be seen that in 2007, the probabilities of second birth averaged 0.08 with subtle differences for women

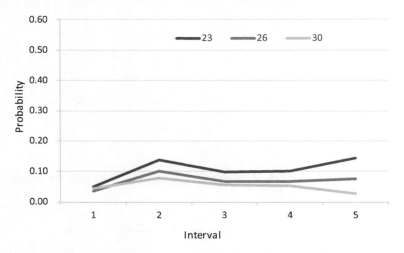

Figure 7.7 Distribution of interval-specific probabilities of second birth for women aged 23, 26 and 30 in 1994

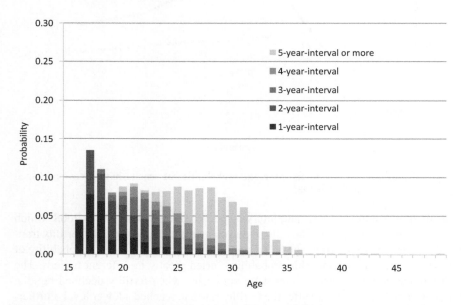

Figure 7.8 Distribution of age- and interval-specific probabilities of second births in 2007

Quantum Effect and Tempo Effect of Fertility 103

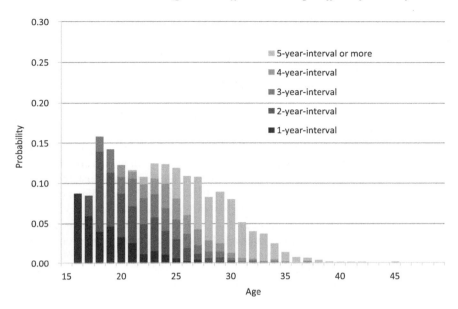

Figure 7.9 Distribution of age- and interval-specific probabilities of second births in 2012

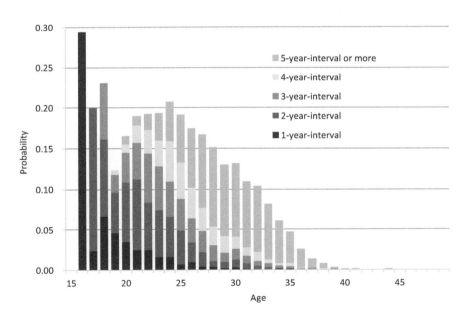

Figure 7.10 Distribution of age- and interval-specific probabilities of second births in 2016

Note: The probability of second births for younger-age women is highly unstable due to a small base of younger-age women having had a first birth, and the value could be unreasonably high.

aged 19–30. The probability diminished gradually after the age of 30, averaging only 0.03 for women aged 31–35 and decreasing to almost zero for women over 35. In 2012, the probabilities averaged 0.11 for women aged 19–30, and the uptick was particularly noticeable for women aged 19–25, yet the probabilities for women over 30 changed little compared with 2007. In 2016, the probabilities averaged 0.17 for women aged 19–30 and picked up significantly for women over 30 compared with 2007 and 2012, averaging 0.08 for women aged 31–35 and remaining above zero for women over 35. In short, the probability of second birth edged up year by year. Compared with 2006, women's probability of having a second birth increased slightly in 2012, and the pickup was the most pronounced among women aged 19–25. The launch of the universal two-child policy greatly pushed up women's probability of having a second birth in 2016, especially for women over 30.

In all three years, there are significant differences in birth interval among women of different ages. Women aged 19–24 years generally had a second birth after a 2-year interval, whereas women aged 25 and over were more prone to have a second birth after a 3-year interval or more. In all three years, the probability of women having a second birth after an interval of 3 years or more increased significantly earlier and faster than the probability of women having a second birth after an interval of two years or less.

Figures 7.11–7.13 show the distribution of interval-specific probabilities of second birth for women aged 23, 26, 30 and 35, respectively, in 2007, 2012 and 2016. In short, among these 4 ages, the younger a woman is, the greater the probability of her having a second birth after an interval of three years or less. The probability of having a second birth after a 4-year interval was the highest at the ages of 26 and 23, and the probability of having a second birth after an interval of five years or more was the highest at the ages of 30 and 26. 35-year-old women were less likely

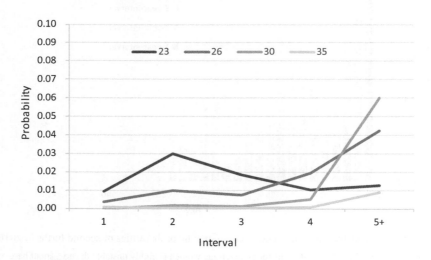

Figure 7.11 Distribution of interval-specific probabilities of second birth for women aged 23, 26, 30 and 35 in 2007

Quantum Effect and Tempo Effect of Fertility 105

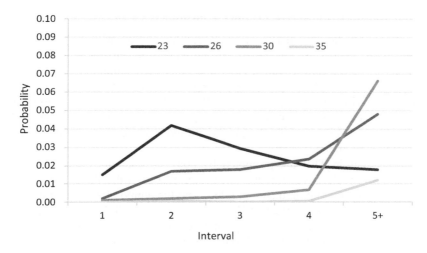

Figure 7.12 Distribution of interval-specific probabilities of second birth for women aged 23, 26, 30 and 35 in 2012

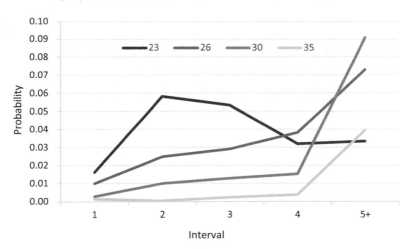

Figure 7.13 Distribution of interval-specific probabilities of second birth for women aged 23, 26, 30 and 35 in 2016

to have a second birth after an interval of five years or more than the other three ages in 2007 and 2012 but were more likely to do so than 23-year-old women in year 2016, a reflection of the pivotal role played by the universal two-child policy in boosting the probability of older mothers having a second birth after a long birth interval. Of course, the policy also significantly pushed up the probability of women of other ages having a second birth after a long birth interval. Due to the substantial increase in the fertility rate for second births, woman's age and birth interval began to exert an increasing impact on the probability of second birth.

A Decomposition Analysis of Fertility Transition

As mentioned earlier, the changes in period fertility rate are driven by tempo effect and quantum effect. The TFR' measure proposed by Bongaarts or any other adjustments to the period fertility rate all aim to capture the quantum effect underlying the changes in period fertility, thereby getting a more accurate picture of the actual changes in fertility level that is free from the disturbance caused by tempo effect, which could lead to inaccurate estimates of quantitative changes when the fertility rate fluctuates. ITFR is artfully designed to provide an effective way of accurately measuring both effects.

The changes in TFR are prompted by both the quantum effect and tempo effect of fertility. Since ITFR represents the number of births, the change in ITFR amounts to the variation in quantum effect, and the tempo effect is manifested in the difference between ITFR and TFR. By calculating the difference in ITFR from year t to year $t+1$, it represents the quantum effect of fertility change from year t to year $t+1$. By calculating the difference between TFR and ITFR in year $t+1$, it represents the tempo effect of fertility change from year t to year $t+1$. The results are shown in Figure 7.14.

Over the past four decades, except in a few years, the tempo effect of fertility has been driving down the period fertility rate. According to the calculated yearly averages, in the 1970s, 1980s and 1990s, both the quantum effect and tempo effect of fertility contributed to the descent in fertility. In the 2000s and 2010s, the quantum effect started to drive up the fertility rate, while the tempo effect was still driving down the fertility rate, only the tempo effect driving down the fertility rate outweighed the quantum effect driving up the fertility rate. In the 1970s, China's fertility rate plummeted as never before in history, with quantum effect driving

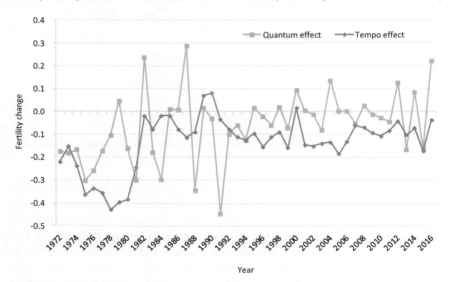

Figure 7.14 Quantum effect and tempo effect of China's fertility transition and low fertility

down fertility by an average of 0.165 (or 34.6%) per year and tempo effect by 0.312 (or 65.4%) per year. In the 1980s, China's fertility rate fluctuated but saw little decline, with quantum effect driving down fertility by an average of 0.073 (or 42.8%) per year and tempo effect by 0.097 (or 57.2%) per year. In the 1990s, both quantum effect and tempo effect dragged down fertility by 0.088 per year, with quantum effect contributing 50.1% and tempo effect contributing 49.9%, almost on par with each other. It can be seen that amid China's fertility decline from the 1970s to the 1990s, the quantum effect grew stronger over time in contrast to the weakening tempo effect. Still, both effects played a pivotal role in driving down China's fertility rate. Since 2000, there had been certain changes to these two effects underlying China's fertility transition, with tempo effect continuing to drive down fertility but quantum effect starting to drive up fertility. During this period, however, the quantum effect was relatively weak and the change in fertility rate was dominated by the tempo effect. In the 2000s, the quantum effect pushed up fertility by an average of 0.0098 per year, yet the tempo effect drove down fertility by an average of 0.11 per year. In the 2010s, the quantum effect pushed up fertility by an average of 0.0049 per year, yet the tempo effect drove down fertility by an average of 0.088 per year.

The fertility trends in these periods sometimes concealed the marked fertility fluctuations between years. In the 1970s, prior to 1979, both the quantum effect and the tempo effect contributed to the decline in fertility, with tempo effect outweighing quantum effect. During this period, interventions of the "late, thin and less" fertility policy significantly postponed women's average age at first marriage and drove down the total first marriage rate, a reflection of the strong tempo effect underlying the fertility decline. In the 1980s, the amendment to Marriage Law and the economic reforms in rural areas gradually ate away at the tempo effect underlying the fertility decline, while the quantum effect was driving up fertility in half of the years. In the 1990s, with the further tightening of family planning policy, the quantum effect played a dominant role in early years in driving down fertility, yet in later years, it gave way to the tempo effect. Since 2000, tempo effect had been the main contributor to the persistent downturn in fertility, and quantum effect only plays a marginal role. Due to varied temporal disturbances, while the tempo effect had been driving down fertility all the time, the quantum effect fluctuated significantly as in the 1980s. In years when the fertility rate soared due to zodiac preferences and the two-child policy, quantum effect was indeed the linchpin of fertility uptick. As a matter of fact, marriage postponement among Chinese women had further intensified since 2000. In particular, in addition to the plunge in total first marriage rate, women's average age at first marriage was postponed by three years in the past ten years, a reflection of the strong tempo effect underlying fertility decline. However, under the influence of certain major events, the overall fertility rate rebounded instead of declining. All in all, since the 1970s, except for a few years, the tempo effect has always been an important contributor to China's fertility decline and persistently low fertility, while the quantum effect behaved differently in different periods and under the influence of different factors, sometimes dragging down fertility and sometimes pushing up fertility.

Concluding Remarks

From the perspective of ITFR, this chapter probes into the quantum effect and tempo effect underlying China's fertility transition and low fertility trends since the 1970s and arrives at the following conclusions:

First, changes in overall fertility rate and parity-specific fertility rates.

In the early 1970s, women generally had three or more children. Subsequently, the fertility rate plunged for each age and each birth order, especially for third and further births. In terms of age distribution, fertility rates for first and second births dropped most markedly among younger women aged below 25. During this period, ages at lower-order births were postponed and the inter-birth interval was lengthened, in addition to the universal decline in the fertility rates for higher-order births among women of all ages. In the 1980s, the structure of fertility decline underwent a pronounced shift. Compared with the 1970s, the declining fertility rate for first births began to level off among younger women aged below 25 and even rebounded slightly in the early 1980s. The stabilized fertility rate for first births was even higher than the average fertility rate for women in the same age group in the 1970s. During this period, the fertility decline was predominantly driven by the decreasing fertility rates for all birth orders among women aged over 25, though the fertility rates for third and further births remained the dominant contributor to the fertility decline. The early 1990s witnessed the sharp decline in fertility rates for all birth orders. Compared with the first and second stages of fertility transition, age-, parity- and interval-specific fertility rates had maintained stable and seen little fluctuations over the years since the 1990s. In the past ten years, under the influence of a string of major events, especially the two-child policy, age-, parity- and interval-specific fertility rates underwent noticeable changes, with fertility rate for second births surging among older women, and fertility rate for first births plummeting among younger women.

Second, impact of birth interval.

In the 1970s when China's fertility rate was still high, women would generally have a second child, and the birth interval had a significant impact on the probability of second birth. Specifically, the probability of second birth varied from interval to interval, and the impact wasn't linear. With the increase in birth interval, the age-specific probabilities of second birth would go up initially. However, if the birth interval went beyond a specific value (usually three years), the fertility rate would go down instantly. In the wake of the fertility decline, especially with the universal decline in the fertility rate for second births after the 1990s, the birth interval no longer had a significant impact on the probability of second birth among women of all ages. In recent years, the two-child policy has prompted older women to give birth to a second child, thereby pushing up the probability of women having a second birth after a long birth interval.

Third, deviation of period TFR from actual births.

Studies found that during the fertility plunge in the 1970s, TFR was flawed in estimating the intrinsic fertility behaviors, i.e., it underestimated the fertility rates for first, second and third births. In the 1980s, although TFR was not much different from ITFR in terms of absolute value, there was in fact a significant change in the parity structure. Throughout the 1980s, TFR overestimated the fertility rate for first births, but underestimated the fertility rates for second and third births to varying degrees. In the 1990s, although the fertility rate leveled off at a low level, it still edged down slightly, and the pronounced shift in fertility behaviors also led to the minor underestimation of the fertility rates for first and second births by TFR throughout the period. In the past ten years, due to an array of temporal disturbances, TFR significantly underestimated the fertility rate for first births, but overestimated the fertility rate for second births.

Fourth, quantum effect underlying the fluctuations in period fertility rate.

In the 1970s, in parallel with the continued fall in ITFR, the quantum effect was also driving down the fertility rate over the years, especially in 1975 and 1976. In the 1980s, the magnitude and role of quantum effect showed strong volatility, and its fluctuations were extremely sharp in individual years such as 1986 and 1987. The number of births plunged markedly in the early 1990s, followed by a subtle decline in the late 1990s, and the changes in fertility behaviors between adjacent periods were relatively gentle. In spite of an upward trend of the fertility rate, there were strong fluctuations in the quantum effect, such as in 2015 and 2016.

In terms of methodology, ITFR builds its calculations of tempo effect on the actual fertility behaviors in the period, and thus, it trumps TFR' in that it can adjust for the tempo effect to obtain a more accurate number of births. Moreover, it has also been proven to be a better measure in the analysis of China's fertility transition.

Fifth, tempo effect underlying the fluctuations in period fertility rate.

ITFR encompasses two different senses of "tempo effect". First, by subtracting the ITFR difference between two adjacent periods from the TFR difference between the same periods, we will get the change in the number of births, which is the number of births that are deferred or advanced when comparing the two periods. Second, the difference between period ITFR and TFR amounts to the tempo effect of TFR in estimating lifetime fertility rate. We hold the opinion that the "tempo effect" in the second sense is of greater realistic significance for comprehending the processes of fertility transition.

In the 1970s, both marriage and childbirth were significantly postponed, with tempo effect ranging from 0.2 to 0.4, suggesting that marriage and childbirth postponement literally dragged down fertility rather than temporarily postponing the number of births. In the 1980s, TFR-based estimates of period fertility were less susceptible to the tempo effect due to its minor magnitude. Since the 1990s, due to the relatively small changes in the tempo structure of fertility, the tempo effect has basically remained in the range of 0.1–0.2. In the past ten years, the tempo effect underlying the changes in the fertility roughly stood at 0.1.

To conclude, it should be pointed out that we can further explore ITFR's control for women's demographic structure and other demographic structures, even the control for socioeconomic structures. For example, since sex selection remains a pivotal contributor to China's low fertility, we can consider controlling for the gender structure. We can also consider controlling for socioeconomic structures such as place of residence, educational attainment, etc. Although it's of important theoretical significance for doing so, it will be extremely hard to implement in practice.

References

Bongaarts, J. and Feeney, G. 1998. On the Quantum and Tempo of Fertility. *Population and Development Review* 24(2): 271–291. doi:10.2307/2807974

Guo Zhigang. 2000a. Fertility Level of China in the 1990s: An Analysis Based on Multiple Indexes. *Chinese Journal of Population Science* 4: 11–18.

Guo Zhigang. 2000b. Lifetime Fertility of Chinese Women: A Look at the Recent Period Fertility Behavior. *Population Research* 1: 7–18.

Guo Zhigang. 2002. The Inner Imperfection and Improvement of Total Fertility Rate. *Population Research* 5: 24–28.

Guo Zhigang. 2004. An Study and Discussion on Fertility Level of China in 1990s. *Population Research* 2: 10–19.

McDonald, P. and Kippen, R. 2007. The Intrinsic Total Fertility Rate: A New Approach to the Measurement of Fertility. New York, NY: Population Association of America.

McDonald, P. and Kippen, R. 2009. Measuring the Quantum of Fertility during a Long-term Shift from Early to Late Childbearing: Australia 1946–2007. Paper presented to the 2009 IUSSP International Population Conference, Marrakech.

Ni Bhrolchain, M. 2011. Tempo and the TFR. *Demography* 48: 841–861.

Rallu, J. L. and Toulemon, L. 1994. Period Fertility Measures: The Construction of Different Indices and their Application to France, 1946–89. *Population: An English Selection* 6: 59–93.

8 Intermediate Fertility Variables

The changes in fertility rate are mainly driven by socioeconomic factors and fertility policies, which however did not directly affect fertility behaviors but steered the fertility trends through a string of "intermediate variables". These intermediate variables bridge the gap between the two – seeping from distal determinants into proximate determinants, and further into the fertility behaviors – to construct a logical and full-fledged theoretical framework for fertility analysis. This intermediate variable analysis framework was first proposed by demographers Davis and Blake in 1956 and then simplified by Bongaarts in 1978. Davis and Blake (1956) proposed 11 intermediate variables directly influencing fertility, while Bongaarts condensed them into only four intermediate variables, arguing that proportion married, contraception, induced abortion and postpartum infecundability are the four proximate determinants of fertility, while other social, economic, cultural and environmental factors exert indirect influence through these four proximate determinants. Bongaarts (1978) also constructed the far-famed model of intermediate fertility variables, which is widely used to estimate fertility rate, fertility difference and fertility trends and to analyze the effects of different intermediate variables on fertility.

In this chapter, we will use data from the 2017 Fertility Survey and the Bongaarts' fertility model to re-estimate the fertility rates over the five years preceding the survey and to examine the effects of intermediate variables on fertility. With the passage of time, the intermediate fertility variables model proposed by Bongaarts is no longer fit for the fertility context and fertility trends in these days. In 2015, Bongaarts made several revisions to the model to make it more robust (Bongaarts, 2015). In this chapter, we will use Bongaarts' new fertility model to estimate China's fertility rates in the period 2012–2016, thereby probing into the effect of each intermediate fertility variable.

In previous studies, some scholars also attempted to employ Bongaarts' intermediate fertility variables model to estimate China's fertility rate (Gao Ersheng et al., 1989; Kang Xiaoping and Wang Shaoxian, 1989; Qin Fangfang, 1989; Liu Longjian, 1990; Hu Ying et al., 1991), or to probe into the influencing factors (Yang Chenggang and Zhang Xiaoqiu, 2011). However, most of these studies were conducted in the 1980s and 1990s, and they tended to build their fertility analyses on the data from surveys. So far, most of studies have focused on the old Bongaarts' model. In 2015, Bongaarts proposed an improved new model and confirmed the stability of the new model by using data from Demographic and Health Surveys (DHS) to estimate the fertility rates in 36 developing countries (Bongaarts, 2015). Furthermore, Krishna and Akash (2019) used this new model to probe into factors influencing fertility transition in respective regions of India in the period 1997–2011. Seifadin (2020) also applied this new model and used the cross-sectional data from DHS for 2005, 2011 and 2016, respectively, to estimate the fertility rates in Ethiopia. To date, no Chinese scholar has ever used Bongaarts' new model to estimate China's fertility rate. On the one hand, the new model has just been proposed, and thus, it has drawn little attention; on the other hand, Bongaarts' new model has extremely high requirements on data, and not much data is available to meet such demanding requirements. This study marks the first-ever application of Bongaarts' new model in China. Using the data from the 2017 Fertility Survey, we estimated the total fertility rates (TFRs) over the five years preceding the survey (i.e., from 2012 to 2016) and examined the effects of intermediate variables on TFR.

Intermediate Fertility Variables Model and Its Revisions

The intermediate fertility variables model proposed by Bongaarts in 1978 mainly measures fertility levels through the index of marriage, index of contraception, index of abortion and index of postpartum infecundability. If the fertility-inhibiting effect of celibacy is removed, fertility will increase to a level TM, the total marital fertility rate. If all practice of contraception and induced abortion is also eliminated, fertility will rise further to a level TN, the total natural marital fertility rate. Removing the practice of lactation and postpartum abstinence further increases fertility to the total fecundity rate, TF. Through the use of this model, the combined effect of the above-mentioned four determinants will lead to an estimate close to the actual TFR. Each index can only take a value between 0 and 1. The smaller the index, the greater the inhibiting effect on fertility; the larger the index, the less the inhibiting effect on fertility.

In the wake of burgeoning economic development and profound social changes over the past four decades, fertility behaviors have seen substantial shifts in countries across the globe. While the effects of these four intermediate variables on fertility varied dynamically in tandem with the development of the times, many assumptions in Bongaarts' old model are no longer fit for the current fertility situations. Furthermore, Bongaarts' old model was less demanding on the indicators, and therefore, the assumptions and parameter settings in the model can hardly stand a thorough statistical test (Zeng Yi et al., 2011). In 2015, Bongaarts made several adjustments to the original model and used the DHS data for 36 developing countries to test the validity of the new model, confirming that the new model is more robust than the previous model. Below, we will give a brief introduction to the specific revisions that Bongaarts made to the model (Bongaarts, 2015).

Revisions to the marriage index: In the original model, Bongaarts assumed that sexual intercourse and reproductive behavior only take place within stable marriages, and marriage index in the original model mainly measured the effect of the proportion of women married on fertility. Today, against the backdrop of the second demographic transition, marriage is increasingly giving way to long-term cohabitation in some low-fertility countries. Even in China, the social tolerance for extramarital sex such as cohabitation before marriage is much higher than in the old days. In particular, for the younger age groups, although the average age at first marriage has been postponed, the proportion of cohabitation before marriage is edging up, and ignoring extramarital sexual behavior will surely lead to inaccurate estimates of the model. Therefore, Bongaarts sees unmarried women of childbearing age who have used contraception, gotten pregnant or experienced postpartum infecundability as the same group at risk of pregnancy as those married women of childbearing age, regardless of their marital status. Therefore, in calculating the marriage index, the new model not only retains the proportion of married women of childbearing age $m(a)$ but also incorporates the proportion of women experiencing extramarital sex $ex(a)$. Accordingly, the marriage index is also renamed as sexual exposure index $C_m^*(a)$.

$$C_m^*(a) = m(a) + ex(a)$$

Revisions to the contraception: Among the four intermediate variables, the new model has made the greatest revisions to the contraception index. Bongaarts made new assumptions for each variable included in the contraception index, adjusted the fecundity adjustment factor r, the contraceptive prevalence rate u and the effectiveness of contraception e and included a new variable of the overlap between contraceptive use and postpartum infecundability. The final equation for calculating contraception index with the new model is as follows:

$$C_c^*(a) = 1 - r^*(a)\left(u^*(a) - o(a)\right)e^*(a)$$

1. Fecundity adjustment factor $r^*(a)$. Women of childbearing age are not always fecund, and therefore, the impact from infecund women must be taken into account. In the original model, Bongaarts arrived at an empirical value of 1.08 for parameter r after making estimates using data for different countries on the natural fertility rate of married women by age and the proportion of fecund women by age. In the new model, Bongaarts used a new method to estimate r. He introduced a new variable $f_{nc}(a)$, which is defined as the fertility rate of exposed women that would be observed in the absence of abortion and postpartum infecundability. This variable can be calculated with the following equation from the revised marriage index, postpartum infecundability index and abortion index (Bongaarts, 2015):

$$f_{nc}(a) = \frac{f(a)}{C_m^*(a)C_i^*(a)C_a^*(a)} = f_f^*(a)C_c^*(a) = f_f^*(a)\left[1 - r^*(a)\left(u^*(a) - o(a)\right)e^*(a)\right]$$

$f_{nc}(a)$ can be calculated through the first equation. Then, $f_{nc}(a)$ can be used as the dependent variable and $\left(u^*(a) - o(a)\right)e^*(a)$ as the independent variable to perform OLS regressions. These regressions yield estimates of the intercept (which estimates $\overline{f_f}(a)$, the average of $f_f^*(a)$ for all countries) and the slope (which estimates the average impact $S(a)$ of a unit increase in $\left(u^*(a) - o(a)\right)e^*(a)$ for all countries. $r^*(a)$ can be obtained through the following equation:

$$r^*(a) = S(a) / \overline{f_f}(a)$$

After performing OLS regressions using DHS data for all 36 countries, Bongaarts calculated $f_f^*(a)$ and $r^*(a)$ through five-year-old age group, and the results are shown in Table 8.1:

2 Contraceptive prevalence $u^*(a)$. Women of different ages have different preferences for contraceptives and frequencies of contraceptive use. In the original model, the contraception index was calculated from the prevalence of contraception among all married women aged 15–49 and did not take into account the effect of the age structure of women of childbearing age. The contraception index, however, is closely related to the age structure of women of childbearing age. Therefore, in the new model, Bongaarts proposed that in calculating the contraception index, it's necessary to calculate the age-specific proportion of women using contraception to all women at risk of childbearing. This revision has well enhanced the accuracy of the calculation of contraceptive prevalence.

3 Contraceptive effectiveness $e^*(a)$. The e in the original model refers to the average effectiveness of various contraceptive methods among married women. While it did take into account the effects of a set of different contraceptive methods on average contraceptive effectiveness, it did not make allowance for the age differences in average contraceptive effectiveness. The revised model takes

Table 8.1 Bongaarts' Estimates of $r^*(a)$ and $f_f^*(a)$

	15–19	20–24	25–29	30–34	35–39	40–44	45–49
$\overline{f_f}(a)$		679	631	588	514	380	192	60
$S(a)$	–416	–516	–586	–546	–409	–224	–88
$r^*(a) = S(a)/\overline{f_f}(a)$		0.62	0.81	0.99	1.08	1.14	1.26	1.62

Source: Bongaarts, J. 2015. Modeling the Fertility Impact of the Proximate Determinants: Time for a Tune-up. *Demographic Research* 33: 535–560.

into consideration both the effects of age structure and contraceptive method on the average contraceptive effectiveness. Therefore, in the new model, the age-specific proportions of women using different contraceptive methods to the total number of women using contraception are used as a weight to further calculate the weighted average of the effectiveness of different contraceptive methods.

4 The new model includes the overlap $o(a)$ between contraceptive use and postpartum infecundability. Every woman will experience a period of postpartum infecundability after giving birth, which is mainly due to physiological factors such as lactational amenorrhea or cultural factors such as postpartum abstinence in certain places. With the passage of time, the culture of postpartum abstinence gradually fades, and the duration of postpartum infecundability is now mainly determined by the length of breastfeeding. In particular, in countries that vigorously promote breastfeeding or contraceptive use, women tend to use contraception during the period of postpartum lactation. Ignoring this overlap between contraceptive use and postpartum infecundability would bias the model results. Therefore, the new model needs to exclude such overlap in calculating the contraception index.

Revision to the abortion index: In the original model, the abortion index was estimated based on contraceptive prevalence and assumed that each abortion would avert 0.4 birth. In a later study, Bongaarts and Westoff (2000) re-examined this measure, arguing that the number of births averted per abortion should be calculated as the ratio of average birth interval associated with abortion to the average birth interval associated with live births, with estimates of the former being roughly 14 months and the latter being roughly 18.5 months plus the average duration of postpartum infecundability i. Therefore, the revised equation for calculating the number of births averted per abortion is:

$$b^* = \frac{14}{18.5 + i(a)}$$

In practice, the calculation of the abortion index is often hampered by the lack or poor quality of abortion statistics. A relevant study of abortion by Sedgh et al. pointed to the fact that abortion rates by age have an inverted U graph-shape, with peak rates between ages 20 and 29 (Sedgh et al., 2012). In his study, Bongaarts assumed that abortion rates in all countries have this inverted U graph-shape and further assumed that this shape is the same as that of age-specific fertility rates. With this simplifying assumption, the ratio of age-specific abortion rates to age-specific fertility rates is equal to the ratio of total abortion rate to TFR. As a result, the equation can be simplified as:

$$C_a^* \approx \frac{TFR}{TFR + b^* TAR}$$

5 Assumption on the postpartum infecundability index. A fecund woman does not necessarily become pregnant through sexual intercourse all the time. For example, a woman cannot conceive during pregnancy or for a period of time

after childbirth. The duration of postpartum infecundability depends not only on the time a woman takes to resume ovulation and sex after childbirth but also the duration of postpartum breastfeeding. Bongaarts (1982) proposed an empirical equation for calculating the duration of postpartum infecundability based on the duration of breastfeeding:

$$i = 1.753 \exp\left(0.1396L - 0.001872L^2\right)$$

where *i* refers to the duration of postpartum infecundability caused by postpartum lactation or abstinence and *L* refers to the average length of breastfeeding (both are in months). Due to the differences in the cultural environment and breastfeeding habits in different countries and regions, the length of breastfeeding determines the average duration of postpartum infecundability in a specific country or region and also indirectly determines the magnitude of the postpartum infecundability index. Theoretically, the duration of postpartum infecundability should be affected by age structure, but in practice, this duration increases only slightly with age. In its study, Bongaarts assumed that the duration of postpartum infecundability is the same for all ages (Bongaarts, 2015).

Revision to total fecundity rate TF^*: In the original model, Bongaarts uniformly set TF to 15.3, which means the maximum number of children born to each woman in her lifetime in the absence of birth control and can be regarded as the upper limit of a woman's fecundity. After revision, the uniform value of 15.3 gives way to the age-specific fecundity rates $f_f^*(a)$, the sum of which can be used to extrapolate the total fecundity rate TF^* of women of childbearing age in a specific country for that year. This also means that the total fecundity rate of different countries and regions is no longer fixed for different years.

Bongaarts' revised proximate determinants model is divided into age-specific and aggregate models. In the age-specific model, each variable takes into account the impact of age structure, while the aggregate model is weighted on the basis of the age-specific model. Both models lead to consistent estimates. The calculation methods of the two models are shown in the following tables (Table 8.2 for the age-specific model and Table 8.3 for the aggregate model).

Fertility Estimates and Effects of Intermediate Variables

Data and Methodology

The data used in this chapter are derived from the 2017 Fertility Survey conducted by the former National Health and Family Planning Commission. Opting for a stratified, three-stage PPS sampling method and with survey day being July 1, 2017, the 2017 Fertility Survey had a sample size of 249,946 women aged 15–60 years living in mainland China. This study mainly used the data on fertility behaviors.

Since Bongaarts' revised intermediate fertility variables model involves a variety of complex variables and has demanding requirements on data, even the data from the 2017 Fertility Survey could not fully meet all the requirements of the

Table 8.2 Bongaarts' Revised Age-Specific Intermediate Fertility Variables Model and Explanation of Variables

	Equations	Variables
Marriage index	$f(a) = C_m^*(a) C_c^*(a) C_i^*(a) C_a^*(a) f_f^*(a)$ $C_m^*(a) = m(a) + ex(a)$	*: represents revised measures $m(a)$: age-specific proportion married $ex(a)$: age-specific proportion of extramarital exposure
Contraception index	$C_c^*(a) = 1 - r^*(a)\left(u^*(a) - o(a)\right) e^*(a)$	$u^*(a)$: age-specific contraceptive prevalence (exposed women) $o(a)$: overlap between contraceptive use and postpartum infecundability $e^*(a)$: age-specific average contraceptive effectiveness $r^*(a)$: age-specific fecundity adjustment
Postpartum infecundability index	$C_i^*(a) = \dfrac{20}{18.5 + i(a)}$	$i(a)$: age-specific average duration of postpartum infecundability (months)
Abortion index	$C_a^*(a) = \dfrac{f(a)}{f(a) + b^* ab(a)}$ $b^* = \dfrac{14}{18.5 + i(a)}$	$ab(a)$: age-specific abortion rate b^*: number of births averted per abortion

Source: Bongaarts, J. 2015. Modeling the Fertility Impact of the Proximate Determinants: Time for a Tune-up. *Demographic Research* 33: 535–560.

new model. For example, although the 2017 Fertility Survey collected the detailed pregnancy history of respondents, it did not collect their marital history and contraceptive history, making it impossible to estimate the fertility rates over a longer period with Bongaarts' new model. Therefore, we can only estimate the fertility rate at the time of the survey. In this chapter, we assumed that the marital status and

118 Intermediate Fertility Variables

Table 8.3 Bongaarts' Revised Aggregate Intermediate Fertility Variables Model and Explanation of Variables

	Equation	Variable
	$TFR = \sum C_m^*(a) C_c^*(a) C_i^*(a) C_a^*(a)$	TF^*: revised total fecundity rate
	$f_f^*(a) = C_m^* C_c^* C_i^* C_a^* TF^*$	$f_f^*(a)$: revised age-specific fecundity rate
Marriage index	$C_m^* = \sum C_m^*(a) w_m(a)$	$f_m^*(a)$: age-specific fertility rate, exposed women
	$w_m(a) = \dfrac{f_m^*(a)}{\sum f_m^*(a)}$	
	$f_m^*(a) = C_c^*(a) C_i^*(a) C_a^*(a) f_f^*(a)$	
Contraception index	$C_c^* = \sum C_c^*(a) w_c(a)$	$f_n^*(a)$: natural exposed fertility
	$w_c(a) = \dfrac{f_n^*(a)}{\sum f_n^*(a)} \approx \dfrac{f_f^*(a)}{\sum f_f^*(a)}$	
	$f_n^*(a) = C_i^*(a) C_a^*(a) f_f^*(a)$	
Postpartum infecundability index	$C_i^* = \sum C_i^*(a) w_i(a) \approx C_i$	
Abortion index	$C_a^* = \sum C_a^*(a) w_a(a) \approx \dfrac{TFR}{TFR + b^* TAR}$	

Source: Bongaarts, J. 2015. Modeling the Fertility Impact of the Proximate Determinants: Time for a Tune-up. *Demographic Research* 33: 535–560.

contraceptive use maintained stable among survey respondents over the past five years and then estimated China's fertility rates in the period 2012–2016 using data from the 2017 Fertility Survey. Furthermore, in using the survey data, we found that the age-specific fertility rate and abortion rate were prone to fluctuations in the younger age groups (especially in the 15–17 age group), and such fluctuations had an impact on the estimates. Therefore, we excluded the 15–17 age group from age-based calculations. In calculating other variables, we handled the data from the 2017 Fertility Survey as follows in accordance with the requirements of the new model.

1. In the new model, the proportion of married women of childbearing age and the proportion of in-union women of childbearing age are two important variables

under the marriage index. In the 2017 Fertility Survey, there were two questions about marriage, i.e., "What is your current marital/union status?" and "What was the time of your first marriage/union?" The answers to the first question are: single, first marriage, remarriage, divorced, widowed, unmarried cohabitation, cohabitation after divorce and cohabitation after widowhood. Due to the data constraints, we cannot obtain accurate data on the age-specific number of married women of childbearing age and the number of in-union women of childbearing age over the years, especially the latter. Since individuals can repeatedly enter or exit the cohabitation status in a relatively short period of time, the union status shown in the current data is only specific to the time of survey. However, we can get the age-specific number of first-married women of childbearing age over the years. Using the number of first-married women to represent the number of married women in that year would lead to an underestimation of the actual number of married women. In particular, the earlier the time, the more likely the number of first-married women will be underestimated, since it does not include women who were married that year but divorced or widowed later. In this chapter, we will use the two indicators of first marriage and unmarried cohabitation to measure marital status and extramarital sex status, respectively, thereby calculating the age-specific proportion of married women $m(a)$ and the age-specific proportion of women exposed to extramarital sex $ex(a)$, the sum of which is the proportion of women of childbearing age at risk of childbearing $C_m^*(a)$.

2 While the survey collected detailed information on the pregnancy history of respondents, we picked two questions about the "ending year of pregnancy" and "pregnancy outcome" for this study. Pregnancy outcomes include live birth of baby boy, live birth of baby girl, stillbirth, spontaneous abortion, induced abortion and others. In this chapter, we will combine live birth of baby boy and live birth of baby girl into live births and take them as the number of births in the year, and then, we will further use the number of women of childbearing age and the number of sexually exposed women in that year to obtain the age-specific fertility rate $f(a)$ and the age-specific fertility rate $f_m^*(a)$ among women at risk of childbearing. In the same way, we can get the age-specific abortion rate among women of childbearing age $ab(a)$ according to the age-specific number of abortions over the years. In calculating the abortion rate, we only need to calculate the abortion rate among women at risk of childbearing, rather than all women of childbearing age.

3 Calculation of the contraception index must be done in combination with the questions asked in the survey. The relevant questions include: (1) "How was your contraceptive use following your last childbirth/abortion?" (2) "What contraceptive method did you use?" (3) "How many months after childbirth/abortion did you start using this contraceptive method?" (4) "Has your contraceptive use changed since then?" (5) "Which contraceptive method are you currently using?" (6) "When did you start using your current contraceptive method?"

Calculation of contraceptive prevalence. First, we should distinguish between women with and without a history of pregnancy. For women with a history of pregnancy, we need to learn about the time of their last pregnancy and then determine the interval from their childbirth to the commencement of contraceptive use according to question 3, after which we will get the time of their first contraceptive use after the last childbirth/abortion. We can determine whether and when the contraceptive method has changed according to questions 4 and 6 and then learn about the contraceptive method used before and after such change according to questions 1, 2 and 5. For women without a history of pregnancy, we can learn about which contraceptive method they are currently using and when they started using the current contraceptive method through questions 5 and 6. Lastly, we can synthesize the timing of contraception initiation for all women using contraception. According to the data, we can only get the change in contraceptive method since the last childbirth/abortion, and the survey only asked about the last change. In practice, women using contraception may switch between contraceptive methods from time to time or use a mix of contraceptive methods. Due to data constraints, however, precise distinctions cannot be made here.

Calculation of contraceptive effectiveness. The survey categorized contraceptive methods into male sterilization, female sterilization, intrauterine device, subdermal implant, contraceptive injection, oral contraceptive, topical contraceptive, condom, other methods, rhythm method, withdrawal method, menopause/amenorrhea, hysterectomy and no contraception. Here, menopause/amenorrhea, hysterectomy and no contraception are excluded, and the rhythm method and withdrawal method are included into other methods. According to the contraceptive effectiveness of various contraceptive methods published by the World Health Organization (see Table 8.4), we calculated the total contraceptive effectiveness of women of childbearing age over the years by the weighting method. Although it is impossible to accurately estimate which contraceptive method women used at different times, the final estimates of contraceptive effectiveness were unlikely affected after weighting.

Calculation of the overlap between contraceptive use and postpartum infecundability. Question 3 "How many months after childbirth/abortion did you start using this contraceptive method?" can be used to estimate the overlap between contraceptive use and postpartum infecundability, a new measure introduced by Bongaarts' new model. According to the average breastfeeding duration in China and the empirical equation, we can then calculate the duration of postpartum infecundability in China, i.e., 5.93 months. There will be an overlap if contraceptive use is started less than six months after childbirth. Therefore, such overlap must be excluded from the estimation.

Handling of fecundity adjustment factor. Considering that this measure varies little between countries and regions, in this chapter, the fertility adjustment estimates from Bongaarts' study are used (see Table 8.1).

4 Calculation of the postpartum infecundability index. The average duration of postpartum infecundability is mainly determined by the average breastfeeding duration of women. According to a report published in 2013 by the World Breastfeeding Trends Initiative (WBTi),[1] the median breastfeeding duration in China was 10.1 months for 2013 (figures for other years are temporarily

Table 8.4 Effectiveness of Different Contraceptive Methods

Method	Male Sterilization	Female Sterilization	IUD	Subdermal Implant	Contraceptive Injection	Oral Contraceptive	Topical Contraceptive	Condom	Other Methods
Contraceptive effectiveness	0.97	0.99	0.99	0.99	0.97	0.92	0.93	0.85	0.80

Source: World Health Organization (https://www.who.int/zh/news-room/fact-sheets/detail/family-planning-contraception).

unavailable). This study assumes that the average breastfeeding duration in China for each year from 2012 to 2016 is equal to the median breastfeeding duration for 2013. It's calculated the duration of postpartum infecundability is 5.93 months for each year, on the basis of which we can then calculate the postpartum infecundability index. Since Bongaarts assumed that the postpartum infecundability index varies little at different ages and that the age-specific postpartum infecundability index is approximately equal to the total postpartum infecundability index, China's postpartum infecundability index should remain constant in the period 2012–2016.

5 Adjustment to total fecundity rate TF. In the new model, total fecundity rate is calculated by adding up the age-specific fecundity rates $f_f^*(a)$. During estimation, if the calculation is based on the raw data, the fluctuations in fertility rate and abortion rate in younger age groups would lead to abnormal age-specific fecundity rate $f_f^*(a)$ in younger age groups, which would in turn indirectly lead to a calculation error in total fecundity rate TF. According to the equation for calculating TF in the new model, TF is calculated based on four intermediate variables, making it a measure that is most likely to produce anomalies. In estimating the fertility level of Ethiopia with the new model, Seifadin (2020) kept the TF constant at 15.3 as suggested in the original model. In this chapter, the 15–17 age group is excluded to ensure relative stability of TF.

Results and Analysis

Based on the above assumptions, we then estimated China's TFRs from 2012 to 2016 using Bongaarts' revised model. Our study found that China's TFR fluctuated between 1.510 and 1.842 from 2012 to 2016, and the five-year average fertility rate was 1.688 (see Table 8.5).

The variations in TFR are reflective of the impact of zodiac preferences and fertility policy adjustments on China's TFR. China's TFR stood at 1.727 in 2012. Many scholars have attempted to estimate China's fertility rates in the period 2000–2010. Guo Zhigang (2011) opined that China's average fertility rate during the said decade should be 1.48, while other scholars believed that it should never be lower than 1.5 (Li Handong and Li Liu, 2012; Cui Hongyan et al., 2013; Chen Wei, 2016), but basically it's impossible to surpass 1.7. According to the estimate in this chapter, China's fertility rate in 2012 was significantly higher than the average fertility rate in the previous decade, and such an increase could be attributable to the strong influence from the traditional culture of "giving birth to auspicious offspring in the year of the dragon". In November 2013, the Third Plenary Session of the 18th CPC Central Committee adopted the "Decision of CPC Central Committee on Major Issues Concerning Comprehensively Deepening Reforms", which specifically called for "instituting a policy that allows couples to have two children if one parent is a single child" – a colossal adjustment to China's family planning policy that had been implemented for decades. China's TFR quickly rebounded in in 2014 as a result of the policy adjustment, but soon tumbled to a record low of 1.5 in 2015, the year of the sheep, which is perceived as an inauspicious year for giving birth to offspring.

Table 8.5 Estimates of China's TFRs from 2012 to 2016 Based on Bongaarts' New Model

Year	C_m^*	C_c^*	C_i^*	C_a^*	TF^*	TFR
2012	0.428	0.453	0.819	0.837	13.005	1.727
2013	0.398	0.402	0.819	0.828	14.109	1.531
2014	0.404	0.451	0.819	0.823	15.014	1.842
2015	0.388	0.375	0.819	0.793	15.990	1.510
2016	0.389	0.378	0.819	0.838	18.142	1.828

Source: Calculations by author using data from the 2017 Fertility Survey.

In October 2015, the Fifth Plenary Session of the 18th CPC Central Committee announced to implement the "Universal Two-Child Policy" to benefit more couples. The new policy was greeted by another rebound in China's TFR in 2016.

Not only can Bongaarts' model be used to estimate fertility rate, but it can also be used to uncover the effects of various determinants on fertility. In regard to these four indices that have direct impact on fertility, the marriage index lingers at a low level, meaning that marriage has the greatest impact on fertility. In particular, China is basically a country of universal marriage and universal childbirth, and childbirth often comes after the marriage, a culture largely different from the Western culture which doesn't discriminate against out-of-wedlock births. Therefore, marriage is deemed the primary inhibiting factor dragging down fertility. From the results shown in Table 8.5, China's marriage index exhibits a downward trend in the period from 2012 to 2016. In this chapter, the handling of the marriage index was based on the two indicators of first marriage and unmarried cohabitation, and it's assumed that the marital status remains relatively constant during the five years. In fact, the earlier the time, the more likely it is to underestimate the number of marriages measured by the number of first marriages. In practice, the marriage index ought to be higher in earlier years. Therefore, the postponement of first marriage among women has become a pivotal contributor to the continuous decline in fertility rate in recent years (Guo Zhigang, 2017; Guo Zhigang and Tian Siyu, 2017).

Aside from marriage, contraception also has an impact on fertility, albeit less significant. According to the estimates, the contraception index has been decreasing in these five years. The 2017 Fertility Survey did not ask about the contraception history of respondents, only their contraceptive use following the last childbirth/abortion and their latest change in contraceptive method. For women who have experienced multiple pregnancies and who have changed contraceptive methods several times, it's impossible to get the relevant details. This has resulted in an underestimation of contraceptive prevalence in early years, thus giving rise to high contraception index in early years.

The abortion index is the most accurate of the four indices because detailed abortion information was collected from respondents in the 2017 Fertility Survey. Overall, the abortion index changes little, basically remaining above 0.82, with a significant decline only in 2015. This is because 2015 is the year of the sheep, and zodiac preference might have prompted some pregnant women to have an abortion,

Table 8.6 China's Urban and Rural TFRs in 2016

	C_a^*	C_c^*	C_i^*	C_a^*	TF^*	TFR
Urban	0.331	0.382	0.819	0.818	17.696	1.498
Rural	0.426	0.363	0.819	0.849	17.645	1.899

Source: Calculations by author using data from the 2017 Fertility Survey.

thus pushing up the abortion rate. Meanwhile, the marriage index and contraception index are also the lowest in 2015, suggesting that women of childbearing age carried out birth control in various ways in that year.

There are a variety of factors influencing fertility. Davis and Blake (1956) proposed 11 most influential factors, while Bongaarts condensed them into four proximate determinants. However, there are also some distal determinants of fertility, only they are less important than proximate ones. Still, these relatively unimportant distal determinants will be manifested in TF (Seifadin, 2020). According to Table 8.5, the total fecundity rate of China in the five years ranges from 13.005 to 18.142, averaging 15.252, which is close to the empirical value of 15.3, and is even closer to the average of 15.22 estimated by Bongaarts (2015) based on data from multiple countries.

In order to test the validity of Bongaarts' new model, we estimated the TFRs for 2016 by urban and rural areas, respectively, obtaining a TFR of 1.498 for urban areas and a TFR of 1.899 for rural areas (see Table 8.6). In the "Report on China's Fertility Rates from 2006 to 2016 – Based on the Data from the 2017 China Fertility Survey", He Dan et al. (2018) estimated that China's urban TFR and rural TFR in 2016 were 1.54 and 2.05, respectively, which are close to our results estimated with Bongaarts' new model. Since 2016 is the closest year to the survey, the estimates ought to be more reliable. With regard to the various intermediate variables, marriage remains the key variable affecting fertility, and it is also the main contributor to the gap between urban TFR and rural TFR. The marriage index in urban areas is almost 0.1 lower than that in rural areas, meaning that the proportion of married women in urban areas is lower than that in rural areas. In 2016, the average age at first marriage was 26.9 years among urban women and 25.6 years among rural women. The impact of the declining proportion of women married and the rising average age at first marriage on fertility rate deserves our full attention (He Dan et al., 2018).

Concluding Remarks

Based on Bongaarts' revised model and the data from the 2017 Fertility Survey, this chapter probes into China's fertility rates and trends in the period from 2012 to 2016 and examines the effects of various intermediate variables on China's fertility. Estimated using the new model, China's average TFR in these five years stood at 1.688, and it's found that both cultural and policy factors contributed to the fertility changes. By analyzing the four intermediate variables of the model, it is further found that the changes in marriage index have contributed the most to China's low fertility in recent years, and it has a tendency to go further down. It can be seen that marriage postponement and the declining proportion of married women have become the key contributors to China's low fertility.

There exists the following limitations in applying Bongaarts' new model to examine China's fertility rates in recent years. First, due to the lack of marital history information in the survey data, the practice of using the number of first marriages and the number of unmarried cohabitants to substitute for the number of married women and the number of women exposed to extramarital sex might lead to an underestimation of marriage index in early years. Second, due to insufficient contraceptive information, the estimation of contraception index could only rely on information about the contraceptive use of women following their last childbirth/abortion. Furthermore, the survey only asked about the last change in contraceptive method. The two limitations combined would lead to the underestimation of contraceptive prevalence and in turn the overestimation of contraception index in early years. Third, due to the lack of breastfeeding statistics, only the data for 2013 were used, thus making the postpartum infecundability index constant for five years, which is completely untenable in reality.

TFRs estimated through Bongaarts' new model are slightly higher than those calculated directly using the same data set, though they are very close to each other, suggesting that Bongaarts' revised model is also applicable to Chinese data and the resulting estimates are highly reliable. Given the protracted debates over China's low fertility rate, it is imperative to build our estimations on different methods and different statistics. Different methods, especially those indirect estimation methods, involve certain assumptions, while different statistics also have their own pros and cons. Therefore, the estimates derived through different methods and different statistics can be tested against each other to paint a comprehensive and objective picture of China's fertility level.

Note

1 WBTi is a global data repository of information on breastfeeding and IYCF policies and programs.

References

Bongaarts, J. 1978. A Framework for Analyzing the Proximate Determinants of Fertility. *Population and Development Review* 4: 105–132.
Bongaarts, J. 1982. The Fertility-inhibiting Effects of the Intermediate Fertility Variables. *Studies in Family Planning* 13(6/7): 178–189.
Bongaarts, J. 2015. Modeling the Fertility Impact of the Proximate Determinants: Time for a Tune-up. *Demographic Research* 33: 535–560.
Bongaarts, J. and Westoff, C. 2000. The Potential Role of Contraception in Reducing Abortion. *Studies in Family Planning* 31(3): 193–202.
Chen Wei. 2016. A Reassessment of China's Recent Fertility. *Academia Bimestris* 1: 67–75.

Cui Hongyan, Xu Lan, and Li Rui. 2013. An Evaluation of Data Accuracy of the 2010 Population Census of China. *Population Research* 1: 10–21.

Davis, K. and Blake, J. 1956. Social Structure and Fertility: An Analytic Framework. *Economic Development and Cultural Change* 4: 211–235.

Gao Ersheng, Chen Changzhong, and Gu Xingyuan. 1989. An Analysis of Intermediate Fertility Variables in Shanghai, Hebei and Shaanxi. *Chinese Journal of Population Science* 1(3): 329–343.

Guo Zhigang. 2011. The Sixth Census Data Indicates Serious Biases in Past Population Estimations and Projections. *Chinese Journal of Population Science* 6: 2–13.

Guo Zhigang 2017. Main Characteristics of the Low Fertility Process in China: Implications from the Results of the 1% Population Sample Survey in 2015. *Chinese Journal of Population Science* 4: 2–14.

Guo Zhigang and Tian Siyu. 2017. The Influence of Late Marriage on Low Fertility of Contemporary Young Women. *Youth Studies* 6: 16–25.

He Dan, Zhang Xuying, Zhuang Yar, Wang Zhili, and Yang Shenghui. 2018. A Report of Fertility Status in China, 2006–2016. *Population Research* 6: 35–45.

Hu Ying, Meng Canwen, and Thomas K Burch. 1991. Analysis of Intermediate Variables of Fertility in Five Provinces and One City. *Population Research* 5: 13–17.

Kang Xiaoping and Wang Shaoxian. 1989. Factors that Directly Affect Fertility of Rural Women. *Chinese Journal of Population Science* 1(3): 345–355.

Krishna, M. P., and Akash, K. 2019. Regression Estimation of Bongaarts Indices from the Childbearing Indices: A Study of India/States/Districts. *Momoma Ethiopian Journal of Science* 1: 108–123.

Li Handong and Li Liu. 2012. Estimating China's Fertility Level Since 2000: Based on the 6th Population Census. *Chinese Journal of Population Science* 5: 75–83.

Liu Longjian. 1990. A Preliminary Study on the Direct Factors Affecting Fertility Rate of Women of Childbearing Age in Three Provinces of Southwest China. *Population Research* 1: 32–36.

Qin Fangfang. 1989. The Impact of Family Planning on Fertility in China: An Evaluation. *Chinese Journal of Population Science* 1(2): 139–153.

Sedgh, G., Bankole, A., Singh, S., and Eilers, M. 2012. Legal Abortion Levels and Trends by Woman's Age at Termination. *International Perspectives on Sexual and Reproductive Health* 38(3): 143–153.

Seifadin, A. S. 2020. Roles of Proximate Determinants of Fertility in Recent Fertility Decline in Ethiopia: Application of the Revised Bongaarts Model. *Open Access Journal of Contraception* 11: 33–41.

Yang Chenggang and Zhang Xiaoqiu. 2011. An Analysis of the Effect of Marriage Structure and Birth Control on Fertility Level in China: Based on the Simplified Bongaart Intermediate Variables Fertility Model. *Population Journal* 2: 14–20.

Zeng Yi, Zhang Zhen, Gu Danan, and Zheng Zhenzhen. 2011. *Methods and Applications of Demographic Analysis* (2nd Ed.). Beijing: Peking University Press.

9 Counterfactual Fertility Trends

China's fertility transition was driven by the family planning policy in the early stage and then steered by socioeconomic development in the later stage. Instituted nationwide in the early 1970s, China's family planning policy went through "torturous, heroic and glorious" moments (Lu Yu and Zhai Zhenwu, 2009). After decades of implementation, the family planning policy has had a long-lasting impact on the fertility pattern of the Chinese people.

According to the experiences of developed countries, driven by socioeconomic development, the fertility rate will decrease gradually to mark the spontaneous completion of demographic transition. The negative correlation between fertility and socioeconomic development has been widely accepted among social scientists. Many scholars opine that socioeconomic development is the fundamental driving force behind the fertility decline, and policy only plays an auxiliary role. This is especially true for China. With the advent of the new century, economic factors are now playing an increasingly prominent role, while policy is getting increasingly insignificant. This also makes a lot of people question the necessity of China's family planning policy and blame the policy for China's ongoing population aging, the looming risk of "low fertility trap"[1] and the early advent of negative population growth.

Recognizing that China's fertility decline is consequent on the combined effect of external factors such as the fertility policy and internal factors such as economic development and social changes, how would China's fertility rate be trending in the absence of the family planning policy? If we want to separate the two factors and only look at the impact of policy factor, we must not only avoid the shortcomings of trend extrapolation but also choose more scientific and reasonable indicators for our projections and analyses.

HDI-related Fertility Research

In this chapter, we will use the human development index (HDI) to estimate China's fertility rates and fertility trends in the absence of the family planning policy. In 1990, the UN Development Programme launched the first Human Development Report, which defines human development as "a process of enlarging people's choices ... the three essential ones are for people to lead a long and healthy life, to

DOI: 10.4324/9781003429661-9

acquire knowledge and to have access to resources needed for a decent standard of living" (United Nations Development Programme [UNDP], 1990). Based on this definition, the HDI came into being. HDI is a composite indicator explained by three groups of indicators, i.e., life expectancy, education and per capita income. It is used to measure a country's average achievement in key dimensions of human development and is reflective of a country's development level to a certain extent. Since the launch of the HDI, the United Nations has been calculating and ranking the HDI scores of all nations according to their development levels, thus drawing extensive attention from governments, organizations and people from countries across the globe. As a measure with colossal international influence, HDI is scientific and tenable for measuring the level of human development.

Although it's universally agreed that "development is the best contraceptive", the fact is a growing number of empirical studies confirm that fertility rate has rebounded after decline in some highly developed countries (Millo Myrskylä et al., 2009; Angela Luci and Olivier Thévenon, 2010; Angela Luci-Greulich and Olivier Thévenon, 2014). There are some Chinese and foreign researchers keen on studying the inverse J-shaped association between total fertility rate (TFR) and HDI (Millo Myrskylä et al., 2009; Fumitaka Furuoka, 2013; Kenneth Harttgen and Sebastian Vollmer, 2014; Zhou Changhong, 2015; Zhai Zhenwu and Chen Jiaju, 2016). They fit the relationship between TFR and HDI and found that when HDI is at medium-to-low levels, development will continue to drive down fertility, and when HDI is at a high level, further development will reverse the decline in fertility. That is, TFR will rebound with the further increase in HDI, and the correlation between the two will reverse from negative to positive at an HDI level of 0.86 (Millo Myrskylä et al., 2009). Zhou Changhong (2015) fit the quadratic functions of TFR and HDI to 2010 data for 109 countries with a population of more than 5 million, discovering that TFR in the absence of fertility policy dropped from 5.39 in 1980 to 2.39 in 2010. According to the latest method for HDI calculation, Hu Angang et al. (2013) calculated the HDI scores of respective Chinese provinces, on which basis Tao et al. (2017) further calculated the TFRs in respective Chinese provinces using data from the Fourth Census and data adjusted by certain scholars, only to discover that there is no inverse J-shaped association between the TFR and HDI of respective Chinese provinces in the corresponding years.

This chapter attempts to unfold the longer-term relationship between TFR and HDI and to probe into the counterfactual fertility trends in China.

Data and Methodology

TFR and HDI are widely used to measure a country's fertility and development levels. In this chapter, TFR will be used as a dependent variable and HDI as an independent variable. In scheme 1, we will model the relationship between TFR and HDI in all countries around the world, which is called the World Model. In scheme 2, we will model the relationship between TFR and HDI in eight Eastern countries and regions whose cultures are similar to China's, which is called the

East Model. We will harness these two models to make counterfactual projections of China's TFRs in the absence of the family planning policy in a bid to estimate China's TFR levels and trends over the years.

Since this study focuses on analyzing the effects of the family planning policy, the top priority is to determine when the family planning policy was first introduced. In the 1950s and 1960s, China attempted an advocacy-based fertility policy (Mao Zhuoyan et al., 2018), which relied largely on the voluntariness of married couples (Zhai Zhenwu, 2000). In the 1970s, China began to tighten its fertility policy. Specifically, in July 1971, the State Council circulated the "Report on Properly Carrying out the Work of Family Planning" and called for strengthening leadership over the family planning work. Shortly thereafter, CPC Central Committee and the State Council promulgated a flurry of family planning documents to steer the family planning work across the country and began to impose strict requirements on the number of births allowed. Therefore, in this chapter, we will take 1971 as the starting year of China's family planning policy and will probe into the long-term effects of the family planning policy over the years from 1971 to 2100,

The dependent variable TFR comes from World Development Indicators (World Bank, 2020), while the independent variable HDI comes from the Human Development Reports (UNDP) published by the United Nations from 1990 through 2019. HDI is a normalized value between 0–1. Since it was first proposed in 1990, HDI has undergone seven revisions of indicators, calculation method and data sources in 1990, 1991, 1994, 1995, 1999, 2010 and 2014, respectively. Nonetheless, HDI has always maintained the three dimensions of "Long and healthy life", "Knowledge" and "A decent standard of living", making adjustments to only the indicators and calculation method and insisting on addressing the profound and rich human development issues in simple, clear ways. The latest revision was made in 2014, and the specific components are shown in Table 9.1.

The Human Development Reports have published HDI statistics for 1970 through 2018. Prior to 1990, HDI statistics were published every five years (in 1975, 1980, 1985 and 1990, respectively); after 1990, HDI statistics were basically published every year (except for 1991 and 1996). Since there is no data available for analysis after 2018, it's necessary to make assumptions based on China's previous development trends and the development experience of other countries in order to make the projections.

Table 9.1 Components of Human Development Index (HDI)

Dimension	Indicator	Max.	Min.
Long and healthy life	Life expectancy at birth (years)	85	20
Knowledge	Means years of schooling (years)	15	0
	Expected years of schooling (years)	18	0
A decent standard of living	GNI per capita (PPP$)	75,000	100

130   Counterfactual Fertility Trends

Since HDI was first proposed in 1990, all nations have experienced the rises and falls of their HDI scores, which are generally edging up in fluctuations, albeit of different magnitudes. In 2010, the global average HDI stood at 0.624. Countries with high HDI scores ("high-HDI countries") had an average HDI of 0.717, while countries with very high HDI scores ("very-high-HDI countries") had an average HDI of 0.878 (UNDP, 2010). By 2018, the HDI averages for the world, high-HDI and very-high-HDI countries had grown to 0.731, 0.750 and 0.894, respectively (UNDP, 2019).[2] In the period from 2010 to 2018, the HDI scores of high-HDI countries increased at an average rate of 0.004 per year, while those of very-high-HDI countries only edged up at an average rate of 0.002 per year. With a HDI score of 0.758 in 2018, China is still considered as a high-HDI country. Assuming that China's HDI score will continue to grow at the average rate of 0.004 per year for high-HDI countries in the forthcoming years, by 2029, China's HDI score will rise to 0.802, allowing China to enter the ranks of very-high-HDI countries (HDI≥0.800). After that, assuming that China's HDI remains at a very high level and maintains a steady growth at the rate for very-high-HDI countries (i.e., 0.002 per year), by the end of the century, China's HDI will increase to 0.944.

Scatter plots of yearly TFRs and HDIs worldwide are drawn to observe how they changed over time from 1970 onwards, and it is found that the relationship between the two does not always follow the "inverse J-shaped" pattern. Prior to the 1980s, TFR and HDI showed an "inverted J-shaped" nonlinear relationship. In the early 1990s, with the increase of HDI, TFR continued to edge down, and there existed a linear negative correlation between the two. After the mid-1990s, the "inverse J-shaped" pattern of TFR began to emerge and the relationship between the two became nonlinear again (see Figure 9.1).

Before 1985 and after 1995, due to the nonlinear relationship between TFR and HDI, the quadratic term of the variables must be included. So the model is set as:

$$\text{TFR} = \beta_0 + \beta_1 \text{HDI} + \beta_2 \text{HDI}^2 + \varepsilon \tag{1}$$

Amid the shift from the "inverted J-shaped" pattern in early years to the "reverse J-shaped" pattern in later years, there inevitably exists a linear relationship for a period of time. After several attempts, it was found that the model failed the significance test after including the quadratic term of the variables in 1985, 1990, 1992, 1993 and 1994. Therefore, the model for these years is set as:

$$\text{TFR} = \beta_0 + \beta_1 \text{HDI} + \varepsilon \tag{2}$$

Through the model, OLS regression can be performed on the cross-sectional data for the existing years, and thus, we can estimate China's counterfactual fertility rates over the years from 1971 to 2018. Fertility rates were calculated by interpolation for data-missing years. Since there is no data available after 2019, it's necessary to estimate the fertility trends in future years based on the existing relevant research and our own judgment of China's fertility situations.

Counterfactual Fertility Trends 131

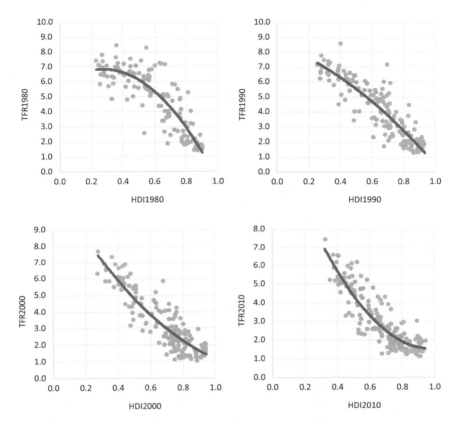

Figure 9.1 Curve fitting of TFR and HDI in different periods

Source: HDIs in 1980 and 1990 come from Human Development Report 2009 (UNDP), HDIs in 2000 and 2010 come from Human Development Report 2002 and Human Development Report 2018 (UNDP), respectively; TFRs come from World Development Indicators (World Bank, 2020).

On the basis of ensuring the same measurement method for HDI, the existing data can produce the panel data for three stages, i.e. 1992–1995, 1997–2007 and 2010–2018. Panel data can not only allow better observation of trends over time but also overcome the problem of data shortage after 2019. We selected the 2010–2018 panel data for countries with very high HDI scores (45 countries in total) and used a fixed effects model to model the relationship between TFR and HDI at very high levels. According to our assumption, China will enter the ranks of very-high-HDI countries by 2029. Therefore, we will predict China's TFRs following 2029 using the 2010–2018 model for very-high-HDI countries (Table 9.2 Model (6)). For TFRs in the period 2019–2028, we will build our estimation on the model for the 2018 world cross-sectional data (Table 9.2 Model (5)).

132 Counterfactual Fertility Trends

Table 9.2 Regression Models

	(1) TFR 1980	(2) TFR 1990	(3) TFR 2000	(4) TFR 2010	(5) TFR (2019–2028)	(6) TFR (2029–2100)
HDI	7.888***	−9.002***	−16.489***	−24.623***	−21.460***	29.983***
	(2.973)	(0.369)	(2.445)	(2.745)	(2.856)	(8.837)
HDI^2	−14.265***		6.160***	12.630***	10.434***	−18.228***
	(2.514)		(1.882)	(2.079)	(2.065)	(5.025)
constant	5.753***	9.936***	11.507***	13.542***	12.429***	−10.578***
	(0.809)	(0.252)	(0.753)	(0.870)	(0.955)	(3.884)
N	136	161	175	187	185	405
R^2	0.768	0.789	0.806	0.784	0.751	0.116

Note: *$p < 0.10$, **$p < 0.05$, ***$p < 0.01$.

Counterfactual Fertility Estimations and Projections

Results Based on the World Model

The TFRs projected by the model can be seen as the TFRs complying with the general development trends in countries across the world in the absence of the family planning policy, and the differences between them and the actual TFRs can be perceived as the net effect of the family planning policy on fertility. In fact, China's TFR dropped below the replacement level in the early 1990s due to the combined effect of policy factors and socioeconomic factors. In the counterfactual projections, however, policy factors are excluded and only socioeconomic factors are taken into consideration. The results show that China's TFR would only fall below the replacement level in 2021 in the absence of the family planning policy, meaning that the family planning policy has advanced China's entry into low fertility[3] by nearly three decades.

The difference between actual TFR and projected TFR stayed above two prior to the mid-1990s, after which the gap gradually narrowed to less than 1 in the early 2000s (Table 9.3). As an important measure of fertility level, TFR mirrors the strictness of the family planning policy. The changes in the gap between the two TFRs from large to small are also reflective of the gradual relaxing of the fertility policy with the passage of time. Even without the family planning policy, China's TFR will go down gradually. China's fertility decline was accelerated by the family planning policy.

Results Based on the East Model

Results based on the World Model are projected from the average fertility rates of nearly 200 countries around the world. However, the starting year and the pace of demographic transition vary from country to country. From a global perspective, although the fertility rates worldwide exhibit a universal downward trend, there are significant differences between countries.

Table 9.3 Projected Counterfactual Fertility Rates of China from 1971–2100 under the World Model

Year	HDI	TFR
1975	0.530	6.162
1980	0.533	5.905
1985	0.556	5.123
1990	0.608	4.463
1995	0.650	3.494
2000	0.726	2.783
2005	0.777	2.406
2010	0.706	2.453
2015	0.743	2.310
2020	0.766	2.113
2025	0.786	2.008
2030	0.804	1.745
2035	0.814	1.750
2040	0.824	1.752
2045	0.834	1.749
2050	0.844	1.743
2055	0.854	1.734
2060	0.864	1.720
2065	0.874	1.703
2070	0.884	1.683
2075	0.894	1.658
2080	0.904	1.630
2085	0.914	1.599
2090	0.924	1.564
2095	0.934	1.525
2100	0.944	1.482

In Northern and Western European countries, fertility rate has rebounded after falling below the replacement level or even to very low levels. Although the timing and magnitude of rebound vary from country to country, most countries have experienced a "reverse J-shaped" rebound in fertility rate since the early 2000s (see Figure 9.2). In Eastern countries, however, such "reverse J-shaped" rebound in fertility rate has not taken place. As the first country in East Asia to experience demographic transition, Japan saw its TFR fall below replacement level in the 1960s, which then dive further downwards to a very low level. For South Korea and Singapore which also boast a very high level of development, the changes in fertility rate coincided with the fertility trends of Japan. South Korea's TFR fell below 1 in 2018, a sign suggesting that it has completely fallen into the "low fertility trap" (see Figure 9.3).

Countries with similarly high HDI scores diverge from each other in fertility trends. Apparently, the conclusion from previous studies that higher levels of economic development tend to spur a rebound in fertility does not necessarily apply to all countries. Given the different institutional systems, cultural norms and policy environments in different countries, the fertility reversal mechanism must be

134 Counterfactual Fertility Trends

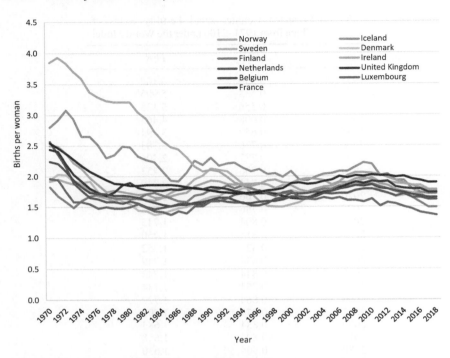

Figure 9.2 TFR trends in Northern and Western European countries from 1970 to 2018
Source: World Development Indicators (World Bank, 2020).

examined from other perspectives. Some studies probed into the differences in fertility rate between Eastern and Western countries from a cultural perspective (Wu Cangping and Jia Shan, 1991; Zhai Zhenwu and Chen Jiaju, 2016); some attempted to explain this disparity from the perspective of gender equality, arguing that gender equality is a prerequisite for reversing the association between development and fertility (Millo Myrskylä et al., 2011; Peter McDonald, 2013; Thomas Anderson and Hans-Peter Kohler, 2015; Wu Fan, 2016; Zhao Menghan, 2016); and others found that social policies such as employment support after childbirth, leave entitlements and public childcare services play a pivotal role in driving up fertility (Angela Luci-Greulich and Olivier Thévenon, 2013).

Although scholars have different perspectives, whether it is culture, gender, or policy, they are inextricably linked. The fertility rebound in five Nordic countries and English-speaking countries was largely due to their social policies to support work-life balance, a dividend from gender equality (Angela Luci and Olivier Thévenon, 2010; Peter McDonald, 2013; Thomas Anderson and Hans-Peter Kohler, 2015). The effect of policies on fertility could also be affected by social attitudes and traditional culture to a certain extent. A lack of orientation toward gender equality could hinder such policies from driving up fertility (Wu

Counterfactual Fertility Trends 135

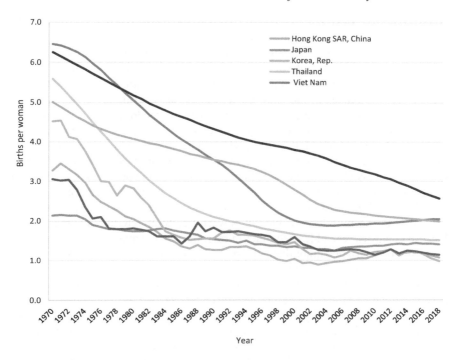

Figure 9.3 TFR trends in selected Eastern countries and regions from 1970 to 2018
Source: World Development Indicators (World Bank, 2020).

Fan, 2016). Japan, South Korea and Singapore have successively introduced policies to encourage childbirth, only to see little effect (Tang Mengjun, 2013; Ik Ki Kim, 2017). This is mainly because in East Asian societies, the traditional family pattern of husband as breadwinner and wife as housekeeper are making women stuck in a hard choice between work and childbearing (Shen Ke et al., 2012). Existing policies, however, fail to provide more benefits for women. It can be seen that the level of gender equality is the key contributor to the differences in fertility rate among developed countries, but the critical driving force behind gender equality comes from the deep-rooted cultural traditions.

Coale, a prominent demographer, opined in the 1970s that fertility transition is not entirely driven by economic development, arguing that culture also plays a pivotal role in fertility transition. He mentioned countries and regions in the "Chinese cultural circle", finding that countries and regions whose cultures are of Chinese origin have all experienced a rapid decline in fertility (Coale, 1973). Through comparative analysis, Wu Cangping and Jia Shan (1991) found that countries in the Chinese cultural circle tended to lead the fertility decline and be burdened by low fertility. In this chapter, we will select eight countries and regions with similar culture to China as representatives of Eastern countries and regions, i.e. Japan, South Korea, Thailand, Vietnam, Malaysia, Singapore, the Philippines and

Hong Kong SAR of China. Located in East and Southeast Asia and geographically proximate to China, these eight countries and regions all share a common Confucian culture and the long-standing patriarchal traditions and family values, and the prevalence of the family pattern of "husband as bread-winner and wife as housekeeper" has led to low levels of gender equality. By comparing the Global Gender Gap[4] ("GGG") indices of the eight Eastern countries with those of Northern and Western European countries, it is found that except for the Philippines, which ranks high in GGG, all other countries are outrivaled by Northern and Western European countries. Japan, which ranks 19th in HDI, and South Korea, which ranks 23rd in HDI, rank only 121st and 108th, respectively, in GGG (see Table 9.4). China's GGG ranking also lags behind its HDI ranking in the same period. While differing significantly from Western countries, these Eastern countries share strong commonalities within the cultural circle – similar and stable social consciousness and values. These seemingly invisible but powerful cultural determinants make these Eastern countries resemble each other in reproductive behaviors that exude strong Eastern characteristics quite distinct from those of the West. Therefore, from the cultural perspective, we will take these eight countries and regions as representative countries under the East Model. Compared with the World Model, projections based on the East Model can best reflect the counterfactual fertility trends in China.

According to the East Model, the projections prior to 1995 were obtained through the OLS regressions of the cross-sectional data for these eight Eastern countries and regions, and the panel data for periods 1997–2007 and 2010–2018 were used to project TFRs in the corresponding years using the fixed effects model. Projections after 2018 were obtained through a similar method to the World Model, and the TFRs for the period 2019–2028 were calculated using the same panel model for the period 2010–2018. Unlike the World Model, TFRs beyond 2029 were projected in two stages. In the first stage (2029–2075), the 1997–2007 panel data for Eastern countries and regions with very high HDI scores (including Japan,

Table 9.4 Comparison of GGG Index between Western and Northern European Countries and East and Southeast Asian Countries

NEU & WEU	GGG	Ranking	EA & SEA	GGG	Ranking
Iceland	0.877	1	The Philippines	0.781	16
Norway	0.842	2	Singapore	0.724	54
Finland	0.832	3	Thailand	0.708	75
Sweden	0.820	4	Vietnam	0.700	87
Ireland	0.798	7	Malaysia	0.677	104
Denmark	0.782	14	China	0.676	106
France	0.781	15	South Korea	0.672	108
U.K.	0.767	21	Japan	0.652	121
Belgium	0.750	27			
Netherlands	0.736	38			
Luxembourg	0.725	51			

Source: Global Gender Gap Report 2020, https://www.weforum.org/reports/gender-gap-2020-report-100-years-pay-equality/

South Korea, Singapore and Hong Kong SAR of China) were used. In the second stage (2076–2100), the 2010–2018 panel data for these countries were used. This is because according to our assumption, China will only reach an HDI of 0.895 in 2075, which is the average HDI of these four very-high-HDI countries and regions in 2010 (UNDP, 2018). Presently, the HDIs of Japan, South Korea, Singapore and Hong Kong SAR of China are all higher than this average. In the period 2010–2018, while the HDIs of these four countries and regions climbed higher, their TFRs went down lower. Therefore, this stage is definitely not suitable for estimating the fertility trends of China at a time when China just enters the ranks of very-high-HDI countries. In contrast, the period 1997–2007 is more suitable. When China makes further strides in HDI in 2075, the panel model for 2010–2018 can then be used for projection. Since the TFRs in these countries and regions falling within the Chinese cultural circle do not show a "reverse J-shaped" pattern, and their fertility rates are far lower than those of Western countries, the linear regression model was applied for the East Model.

Projections based on the East Model (Table 9.5) show that China's fertility rate would fall below 4 in the late 1980s, below 3 in the mid-1990s and below the replacement level in 2008, which is 13 years ahead of the projection based on the

Table 9.5 Projected Counterfactual Fertility Rates of China from 1971 through 2100 under the East Model

Year	HDI	TFR
1975	0.530	5.879
1980	0.533	4.896
1985	0.556	4.531
1990	0.608	3.863
1995	0.650	3.120
2000	0.726	2.412
2005	0.777	2.149
2010	0.706	1.907
2015	0.743	1.830
2020	0.766	1.782
2025	0.786	1.740
2030	0.804	1.569
2035	0.814	1.539
2040	0.824	1.509
2045	0.834	1.479
2050	0.844	1.449
2055	0.854	1.419
2060	0.864	1.389
2065	0.874	1.359
2070	0.884	1.329
2075	0.894	1.299
2080	0.904	1.247
2085	0.914	1.239
2090	0.924	1.230
2095	0.934	1.222
2100	0.944	1.213

World Model and about 15 years behind the actual year when China became a low-fertility country. Given the declining trend of TFR among Eastern countries, China's TFR would drop to a very low level in 2040, below the extremely low threshold of 1.3 in 2075, and further to 1.213 in 2100, which is equivalent to the TFR in Hong Kong SAR of China in the 1990s but slightly higher than the current TFR in South Korea.

Concluding Remarks

China's family planning policy came into existence against the historical background and in answer to the needs of socioeconomic development. As a legacy of a special time in history, China's family planning policy has been carried out against obstacles for more than half a century. In this chapter, through the measure of HDI, we have made counterfactual projections of China's TFRs from 1971 through 2100 in the absence of China's family planning policy based on the World Model and the East Model, respectively, in an attempt to shed light on the long-term effects of China's family planning policy.

Under the World Model, in the absence of the family planning policy, China's TFR would fall below the replacement level in 2021. The family planning policy has advanced China's slide into low fertility by about 30 years. Under the East Model, China's TFR would see a faster decline and fall below the replacement level in 2008, meaning that the fertility policy has advanced China's slide into low fertility by about 13 years.

Aside from economic development and social advances, factors influencing fertility also include historical and cultural traditions, level of gender equality, coordination among family support policies, etc. Building on the social norms and cultural traditions unique to Eastern countries, the East Model introduced in this chapter incorporates a gender equality perspective to differentiate it from the World Model. Given China's low level of gender equality and relatively weak family support policies, and taking into account the lessons from East Asian countries such as Japan and South Korea and our judgment of China's current realities, we believe that predictions based on the East Model are more representative of China than the World Model. Still, no projection method can perfectly and accurately estimate the counterfactual fertility rates and trends of China in the absence of the family planning policy. Either the World Model or the East Model is merely aimed at providing instructive information about China's fertility rates, not the iron law that China's fertility transition will follow anyhow. While taking the general trend into consideration, we must also pay close attention to our own characteristics. We should continue to observe how the fertility rate will change in the midst of social development and transition, so that we could devise reasonable population policies in a timely manner to ensure the healthy and sustainable development of Chinese population.

Notes

1 Low fertility trap: After total fertility rate has fallen below 1.5, the declining fertility tends to reinforce itself, as if falling into a trap, and it will be difficult or even impossible to reverse the declining trend.

2 Very high human development: HDI≥0.800; high human development: 0.700≤HDI≤0.799; medium human development: 0.550≤HDI≤0.699; low human development: HDI<0.550 (Human Development Report 2019, UNDP).
3 Internationally, low fertility is defined as having a TFR below 2.1; very low fertility is defined as having a TFR below 1.5; and ultra-low fertility is defined as having a TFR below 1.3.
4 Global Gender Gap: An index that examines the gap between men and women in Economic Participation and Opportunity, Educational Attainment, Health and Survival and Political Empowerment. The higher the index, the smaller the gender gap and the higher level of gender equality.

References

Angela Luci and Olivier Thévenon. 2010. Does Economic Development Drive the Fertility Rebound in OECD Countries? https://hal.science/hal-00520948
Angela Luci-Greulich and Olivier Thévenon. 2013. The Impact of Family Policies on Fertility Trends in Developed Countries. *European Journal of Population* 29: 387–416.
Angela Luci-Greulich, Olivier Thévenon. 2014. Does Economic Advancement 'Cause' a Re-increase in Fertility? An Empirical Analysis for OECD Countries (1960–2007). *European Journal of Population* 30: 187–221.
Coale, A. J. 1973. Demographic Transition. *Liege: Proceedings of the International Population Conference* 1: 53–72.
Fumitaka Furuoka. 2013. Is There a Reversal in Fertility Decline? An Economic Analysis of the "Fertility J-Curve". *Transformations in Business & Economics* 12(2): 44–57.
Hu Angang, Wang Hongchuan, and Wei Xing. 2013. Human Development in Different Regions of China: Great Progress and Great Convergence (1980–2010). *Journal of Tsinghua University (Philosophy and Social Sciences Edition)* 5: 55–68.
Ik Ki Kim. 2017. Rethinking China's New Population Policy: A Comparison with Low Fertility and Aging Populations in Japan and South Korea. *Academia Bimestris* 1: 134–143.
Kenneth Harttgen and Sebastian Vollmer. 2014. A Reversal in the Relationship of Human Development with Fertility. *Demography* 51(1): 173–184.
Lu Yu and Zhai Zhenwu. 2009. *60 Years Population of the People's Republic of China*. Beijing: China Population Press.
Mao Zhuoyan, Shen Xiaoju, and Zhang Wenlei. 2018. Population Inertia and Choice of Fertility Policy: International Comparison and Implications. *Southern Population* 2: 15–28.
Millo Myrskylä, Hans-Peter Kohler, and Francesco Billari. 2009. Advances in Development Reverse Fertility Declines. *Nature* 460: 1–24.
Millo Myrskylä, Hans-Peter Kohler, and Francesco Billari. 2011. High Development and Fertility: Fertility at Older Reproductive Ages and Gender Equality Explain the Positive Link. Population Studies Center, University of Pennsylvania, PSC Working Paper Series, PSC 11-06. http://repository.upenn.edu/psc_working_papers/30
Peter McDonald. 2013. Societal Foundations for Explaining Low Fertility Gender Equity. *Demographic Research* 28: 981–994.
Shen Ke, Wang Feng, and Cai Yong. 2012. The Implications for China of the Shift of International Population Policy. *International Economic Review* 1: 112–131.
Tang Mengjun. 2013. The Choice of China's Birth Policy: Based on the Experience of East Asia and Southeast Asia. *Population Research* 6: 77–90.
Tao Tao, Jin Guangzhao, and Yang Fan. 2017. Reexamining the Relationship between Socio-economic Development and Fertility in China. *Population Research* (6): 33–44.
Thomas Anderson and Hans-Peter Kohler. 2015. Low Fertility, Socioeconomic Development, and Gender Equity. *Population and Development Review* 41(3): 381–407.

United Nations Development Programme. 1990. *Human Development Report 1990*.
United Nations Development Programme. 2010. *Human Development Report 2010*.
United Nations Development Programme. 2018. *Human Development Report 2018*.
World Bank. 2020. World Development Indicators. http://wdi.worldbank.org/table/2.14
Wu Cangping and Jia Shan. 1991. Chinese Culture and Fertility Decline. *Chinese Journal of Population Science* 5: 7–12.
Wu Fan. 2016. Family Policy and Fertility Change in Europe: Implications for the Risk of Low Fertility Trap in China. *Sociological Research* 1: 49–72.
Zhai Zhenwu. 2000. Review and Re-evaluation of China's Population Policy in the 1950s. *Chinese Journal of Population Science* 1: 17–26.
Zhai Zhenwu and Chen Jiaju. 2016. The Evolution of International Fertility Level and its Influencing Mechanism since the 20th Century. *Chinese Journal of Population Science* 2: 12–25.
Zhao Menghan. 2016. Re-examining the Missing Concept of Gender Equality in Public Policy under the Universal Two-child Policy. *Population Research* 6: 38–48.
Zhou Changhong. 2015. Quantitative Analysis of the Relationship between Economic and Social Development and Fertility Change. *Population Research* 2: 40–47.

10 The Two-Child Policy and Fertility

China's transition to a Two-Child Fertility Policy in 2015, its implementation effects and the associated fertility and population trends have drawn extensive attention and sparked broad discussions. The most frequent comments appearing in the media reports are typically about how this policy turns out to be ineffective, depending on births and birth rates published by China's National Bureau of Statistics (NBS) which show rises in 2016 and then declines in 2017. Surprisingly, however, the annual population surveys conducted by the NBS, which provide basis for the NBS to estimate and publish births and birth rates, reported a dramatic increase in fertility rates in 2017 compared with that in 2016. These results contradict themselves and are unable to shed light on assessing the policy effects.

Evidence from a recent national fertility survey conducted in 2017 by the former National Health and Family Planning Commission of China challenges the views that the policy loosening had little impact on parent's fertility decisions. Second-child fertility rates soared by about 50% in 2016/2017 compared to the average of 2010–2015. However, the overall fertility increased only slightly because of the dramatic drop in the first birth rates since 2012. However, it is important to be aware that the two-child policy targets the second child and has nothing to do with other parities. Thus, evaluation of the implementation effects of the two-child policy must focus on the second-child fertility. In fact, the number and proportion of second births in the national newborn population from the NBS data had increased rapidly, surpassing those of the first births in 2017. Using the 2017 Fertility Survey data, this chapter will examine the initial effects of the two-child policy based on the developments in the second-child fertility over the past decade.

The changes in national fertility rate and the impact of the two-child policy often conceal huge regional and population-group differences. This chapter will also examine socio-demographic differentials in the impact of the two-child policy on the second-child fertility and identify the factors affecting the second-child fertility from both macro and micro perspectives.

This study uses total fertility rate (TFR) to indicate the fertility level and calculates the parity-specific TFR in the period from 2006 to 2017. To facilitate analysis, total first marriage rate is also calculated over the period. In order to examine the differences in fertility rate, we also calculate the second-child fertility in different population groups in the same period. The discrete-time logit model is used

DOI: 10.4324/9781003429661-10

to examine the influencing factors of the second-child fertility. This approach, by converting the data on individual women into the data in women's person-years, avoids the assumption of proportional hazards (Allison, 2010). All the tables and figures presented in this chapter are produced from 2017 China National Fertility Survey and, thus, their data sources are no longer further noted.

Recent Trends and Patterns of Fertility in China

Annual fertility rates derived from the 2017 National Fertility Survey data are presented in Figure 10.1, which shows the overall TFR and TFR by parity. In Chapter 4, we discussed recent trends and changes in China's fertility rate over 2006–2017. The fertility rate saw great fluctuations, reaching the lowest 1.41 in 2015 and the highest 1.78 and 1.77 in 2012 and 2016, respectively, with average value being 1.65 over the decade. This result is largely consistent with the fertility rates obtained in some recent studies using either data of registered permanent residence from the Ministry of Public Security or population census data by indirect estimation methods (Yang Fan and Zhao Menghan, 2013; Chen Wei and Yang Shenghui, 2014; Zhai Zhenwu et al., 2015; Zhao, 2015), but much higher than the results reported by China's 2010 population census, 2015 1% population sample survey and the annual population surveys over the last decade.

The considerable fluctuations in China's fertility rate over the past decade have a lot to do with the important events taking place during this period and the preference for certain zodiac animals for childbearing. The 2008 Olympic Games, the Selective two-child policy promulgated in 2013 and the Universal Two-Child Policy launched in 2015 all contributed to the rise or peaking of fertility rate in the corresponding years. China's TFR exceeded 1.7 in the 2008 Olympic Year and during the two years immediately after the promulgation of the Universal Two-Child Policy. The preference for certain zodiac animals led to the highest TFR in 2012 (the Year of Dragon) and the lowest TFR in 2015 (the Year of Sheep). After the adjustment of fertility policy, the TFR increased as predicted, indicating that the fertility policy still has a certain impact on the fertility rate, but such impact is highly group specific and has been greatly weakened as compared to the previous fertility policies.

Figure 10.1 demonstrates that with the successive adjustments of the birth policy, the second-child fertility has been rising persistently. The second-child fertility stood at around 0.6 before 2011 and began to rise from 2011 onward and then soared after 2015. In 2015, the second-child fertility exceeded the first-child fertility, reached 0.94 in 2016 and even exceeded 1 in 2017. After the founding of the People's Republic, the second-child fertility once exceeded 1 in the 1950s and 1960s. Shortly after the establishment of the People's Republic in the early 1950s, the economy restored gradually and people's lives got stable and better, and there came the first birth peak. The total second-child fertility exceeded 1 during 1953–1955. In the 1960s, after the three years of famine disasters finally came to an end, the compensatory births led to the second birth peak, with the second-child fertility exceeding 1 in 1963–1966. Unlike the 1950s and 1960s,

The Two-Child Policy and Fertility 143

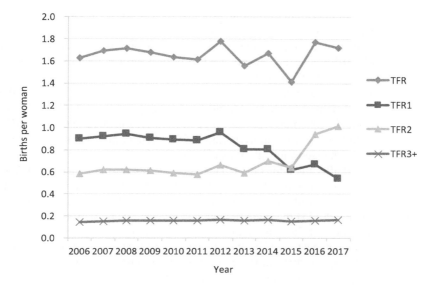

Figure 10.1 Trends in overall TFR and parity-specific TFR in China, 2006–2017

Note: The survey was taken in the middle of 2017, and we inflate the births in the first half year of 2017 by multiplying by 2 to estimate the fertility rate in 2017. This applies to the calculations in fertility rates in all parities and in all socio-demographic groups.

2017 witnessed the second-child fertility surpassing 1 in the context of low fertility, exactly the result of implementing the two-child policy. It was the fertility accumulation where women of different ages chose to have the second child at the same time upon the promulgation of the two-child policy. This phenomenon can be described as a "spurt" of fertility desires that were suppressed by the former fertility policy. In this sense, the two-child policy is highly effective. But the increase in the second-child fertility brought about by such fertility accumulation is only temporary and will not last. The long-term effects of this policy will have to depend on the new generation who has come to the age of marriage and childbearing. However, if the decline in women's the first marriage rate and the first childbirth rate continues in the coming years, or if they do not go down further but maintain at such a low level, the effects of the two-child policy will be severely weakened or offset.

Figure 10.1 also shows that the fertility rate of the third or subsequent child has remained at around 0.15 for almost the entire period without either excessive fluctuations or significant increase along with the implementation of the two-child policy. This shows that although the fertility policy still forbids the birth of the third or subsequent child, it is more important to see that fertility intentions are extremely low already, and the proportion of women who wish to have more children is rather low. Meanwhile, it also reminds us that couples who wish to have more children will spare no effort to have more children no matter how the fertility policy is written.

One question of interest in evaluating low fertility levels is addressing the impact of "tempo effect". When taking account of the "tempo effect" behind the dramatic fluctuations and changes employing the parity progression fertility model to adjust the first-child fertility and the second-child fertility, followed also by the adjustment of the "tempo effect" in the first marriage rate, it was found that although the overall trend after adjustment was similar to the trend before such adjustment, the rates changed substantially. The first-child fertility dropped from 0.97 in 2012 to 0.90 in 2017, and the first marriage rate dropped from 0.97 in 2012 to 0.82 in 2017; the second-child fertility went up from 0.55 in 2015 to 0.74 in 2017. It can be seen that the dramatic change in fertility under the unadjusted "tempo effect" has been greatly weakened after the adjustment. That is to say, the postponement in the age of first marriage has substantially depressed the first marriage rate and first childbirth rate, while the fertility accumulation where women of different ages choose to have the second child at the same time exaggerates the increase of the two-child fertility. As a matter of fact, the adjustment of the "tempo effect" is a measure adopted from the perspective of lifetime marriage and lifetime fertility, indicating that although the age of first marriage is significantly postponed, 90% of women will eventually get married, and 74% of women will give birth to the second child under the two-child policy. This is very similar to the situations in the times of the "one-child policy" – although China's fertility rate has been much lower than the replacement level since the 1990s, most couples actually gave birth to two children from the perspective of lifetime fertility. According to Coale (1989), in the period from 1950 to 1981, even if the lifetime fertility in married couples had remained at the actual number of their children, another 104 million people would have been born if the age of first marriage had not been postponed in these 31 years. This is a surprising result brought about by the postponement in the age of first marriage – even if such postponement is slow but chronic. Therefore, the postponement in the age of first marriage in Chinese women over the past ten years and the implementation of the two-child policy from 2016 onward might not seem to have significant effects from the perspective of lifetime marriage and lifetime fertility, but they do have huge implications for the period effect of the policy.

Second-Child Fertility: Patterns and Determinants

As mentioned above, the second-child fertility rate in China has been soaring in recent years, which is the result of implementing the two-child policy. However, the effects of this policy must be substantially different between different population groups. The question is: Who are giving birth to the second child upon implementation of the two-child policy and what factors affect women's fertility behavior to have the second child?

The influencing factors of fertility behaviors are rather complicated, and the fertility behavior of having the second child under the two-child policy is naturally the result of a combination of multiple factors at multiple levels. According to the theories of demographic transition and microeconomics, and based on Bongaarts low fertility model, this study establishes a theoretical framework to identify the influencing factors of fertility behaviors from macro, meso and micro perspectives. The theory of demographic transition explains the causes of the changes in fertility behaviors from a macro perspective. The microeconomic theory explains the factors affecting family's fertility choice from a micro perspective – the cost and utility of raising a child, while the low fertility model proposed by Bongaarts (2001) explains the direct influencing factors of fertility behaviors. The macroscopic social environment (including the level of modernization, the fertility policy and the cultural norm) acts on the family factors at the meso level and individuals at the micro level, affecting not only the characteristics of the family and the individual, but also people's attitude toward fertility. In the meantime, the combined effects of social environment, family factors and individual characteristics have led to the different understanding of the cost and utility of raising a child among different families and different population groups, thus shaping their distinct fertility intentions and fertility behaviors. Based on this theoretical framework and in conjunction with the data from 2017 Fertility Survey, we define the variables separately at the macro, meso and micro levels. At the macro level, because the survey only collected micro-level case data, there are no corresponding macro-level variables. We use the region of residence instead and define six major regions with the variable of province. In addition, we also use the type of sample point (neighborhood committee or village committee) to define urban and rural variables. The meso-level family variables include total family income and housing area. The micro-level individual variables include age, education level, occupation, type of employer, desired number of children and the age and gender of the first child.

Socio-Demographic Profile of Women Having the Second Child

The two-child policy acts directly on those women who have given birth to their first child but cannot have the second child under the former fertility policy, also including of course those who have just given birth to a child and who have just come to the age of marriage and childbearing. The former group exhibits substantial age differences and is dominated by women with relatively higher ages. According to the sample data, among these women, 65% were aged 35 or above, and 45% were 40 years old or above. Upon implementation of the two-child policy, women who have had a child in different times and who intend to have the second child will probably give birth to their second child at the same time, thus leading to the simultaneous increase in second-child fertility among women of different ages. Figure 10.2 shows that after the implementation of the two-child policy, except for the two lowest age groups, the other five age groups (25 years or older) all saw an increase in the second-child fertility. The greatest absolute increase incurred in the 30–34 and 35–39 age groups, and the greatest relative increase incurred in the 40–45 age group. Women above the age of 40, even if they want to have the second child, are often unable to do so due to their declined fecundity. In the 25–39 age groups, the increase in fertility as a result of the two-child policy has basically reached the level of age-specific second-child fertility rates when the overall TFR was as high as 2.5–3.0 in China.

146 *The Two-Child Policy and Fertility*

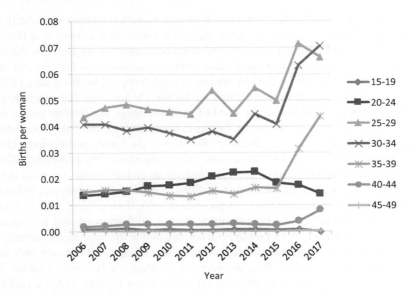

Figure 10.2 Second-child fertility rates by age in China, 2006–2017

   Women with characteristics associated with low fertility tend to be the groups in which the two-child policy has the best effects. Urban residence, higher levels of education, a job in state-owned institution, and higher incomes are generally associated with low fertility. During the times of the one-child policy, these women were subject to stricter fertility control, thus leading to lower fertility. The implementation of the two-child policy imposes the greatest impact on these groups. For the groups already with higher fertility before the two-child policy was introduced, their fertility behaviors are less constrained by the fertility policy adjustment, and thus, the policy adjustment won't have much effect in these groups. Figures 10.3–10.6 compare the second-child fertility between women with urban/rural residence, different levels of education, different occupations and different income levels.

   The two-child policy brought about a marked increase in second-child fertility in both urban and rural areas (Figure 10.3). The second-child fertility in rural areas rose from 0.82 in 2015 to 1.17 in 2017, and that in urban areas went up from 0.47 in 2015 to 0.88 in 2017. The growth rates of second-child fertility are very close between urban and rural areas, though the growth rate in urban areas is slightly higher implying higher policy effects. Before the implementation of the two-child policy, the educational level was negatively correlated with the second-child fertility. That is, the higher the educational level, the lower the fertility rate. The group holding a master plus degree had a second-child fertility rate close to 0. After the launch of the two-child policy, the educational level became positively correlated with the increase in second-child fertility. It can be observed from Figure 10.4 that women with the highest educational level (master's degree and over) not only witnessed the fastest and the greatest increase in second-child fertility but also topped

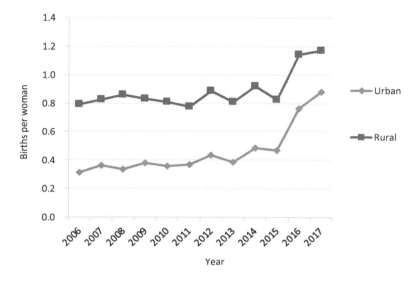

Figure 10.3 Second-child fertility rates in urban and rural areas in China, 2006–2017

in 2017 the list of women with different educational levels. It is further observed that the second-child fertility in women with the lowest educational level (primary school or below) remained at around 1, indicating that they have always been giving birth to the second child. In women with other educational levels, the second-child fertility has basically been rising since 2006 – slow in the early years but accelerating in the later years, especially upon the implementation of the two-child policy (rising continuously during the period from the Selective to the Universal Two-Child Policy). In general, women with higher educational levels tend to have lower fertility intentions, and they are subject to stricter control under the previous fertility policy. Moreover, their age of marriage and childbearing also tends to be older. Therefore, after the implementation of the two-child policy, they tend to have the second child faster and contribute more to fertility accumulation.

The second-child fertility rates and its growth rates are also quite different by occupation (Figure 10.5). By dividing the six occupations into two categories – non-manual occupations (senior executives, professionals and technicians and clerks and related personnel) and manual occupations (commercial service workers, industrial workers and peasants), we can see that before the implementation of the two-child policy, the second-child fertility in women with a non-manual occupation was much lower than those with a manual occupation. The two-child policy has greatly boosted the second-child fertility in women with a non-manual occupation. As for those with a manual occupation, the second-child fertility increased slightly in commercial service workers but dropped in industrial workers. In fact, by comparing between Figures 10.4 and 10.5, we can see that the two are closely connected. Women with a non-manual occupation tend to have a higher level of education, while those with a manual occupation tend to have a lower level

148 *The Two-Child Policy and Fertility*

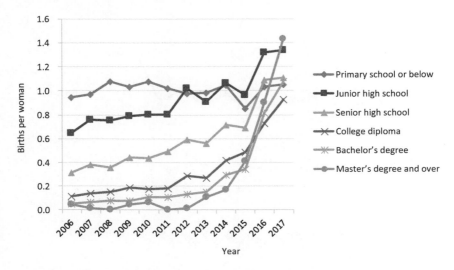

Figure 10.4 Second-child fertility rates by educational level in China, 2006–2017

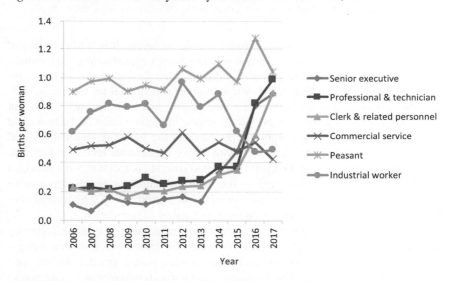

Figure 10.5 Second-child fertility rates by occupation in China, 2006–2017

of education. According to the sample data, 75% of non-manual female workers hold a college diploma or above, while 90% of manual female workers hold a high school diploma or below. Therefore, women with higher educational levels and women with lower educational levels as shown in Figure 10.4 basically correspond to the women with a non-manual occupation and women with a manual occupation as shown in Figure 10.5, and the changes in their second-child fertility rates are basically consistent. In addition, the differences in the second-child fertility rates by occupation also largely reflect the influencing role played by their employers. The sample data shows that the senior executives, professionals and technicians and clerks and related personnel mainly work in state-owned organizations, including party and government organs, people's associations, state-owned public institutions and state-owned enterprises, with proportion reaching as high as 60%. The state-owned organizations are more fertility-friendly and do better in implementing national policies, such as maternity leave, maternity insurance, childcare services and even gender equality in recruitment, which are more conducive to promoting work-life balance for couples, who can then have the second child more easily.

Increasing income was once an important factor contributing to the decline in fertility. However, given the increasing cost of raising a child and the growing financial pressure, the increase in income has become a factor conducive to the second-child fertility. Figure 10.6 shows the relations between total family income and second-child fertility. It can be seen that upon implementation of the two-child policy, the high-income group saw the fastest and the greatest increase in second-child fertility. In contrast, the low-income group witnessed the decline in second-child fertility. Before this, the second-child fertility was negatively correlated with income. In the 2017 Fertility Survey, when the respondents were asked why they chose not to have another (more) child, they referred to "heavy financial burden" as the primary reason, which was also an overwhelming reason. It seems that income has become the most important determinant of the decision to have the second child.

The relationship between housing and fertility has been extensively studied in Western countries. According to the theory of fertility economics, there is a close relationship between housing and fertility (Becker, 1960, 1965; Willis, 1973). The maximization of household utility depends on income and time constraints. As a

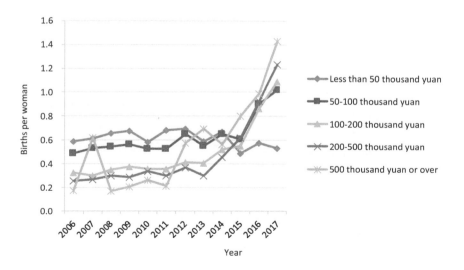

Figure 10.6 Second-child fertility rates by income in China, 2006–2017

150 *The Two-Child Policy and Fertility*

main cost of raising a child, housing is incorporated into the household production function and becomes an important influencing factor of fertility. Therefore, the rise in housing prices can either bring down the fertility rate by reducing the demand for children due to the increase in the cost of raising a child or boost the fertility rate by increasing the demand for children due to the growth in household wealth. Both positive and negative effects have been verified in different countries. For those who buy their house for the first time or who want to upgrade their existing house to a larger one, the surge in housing prices has a negative impact on their fertility. For those who already have a house and do not need to upgrade their house, the surge in housing prices will have a positive impact on their fertility, because the increase in housing wealth leads to higher probability for them to have another child (Lovenheim and Mumford 2013; Dettling and Kearney, 2014). Since housing is an important prerequisite for childbearing, people are more willing to have a child when they are capable for providing better living conditions and living environment for their child(ren). Figure 10.7 confirms the relationship between housing area and second-child fertility in China. It's not about how the fertility will be affected when people have or do not have a house. It only shows that the larger housing area brings about higher fertility. Generally speaking, the larger the housing area, the more likely for the family to have a higher income. In the meantime, when housing prices remain high and continue to rise, the household wealth will increase as well. This is an important factor contributing to the increase in second-child fertility when "heavy financial burdens" have become the dominant reason that people choose not to have another child. In fact, Figure 10.7 shows that families with larger housing areas are always associated with higher second-child fertility. They are also the group exhibiting the fastest and the greatest increase in second-child fertility after the implementation of the two-child policy. Although

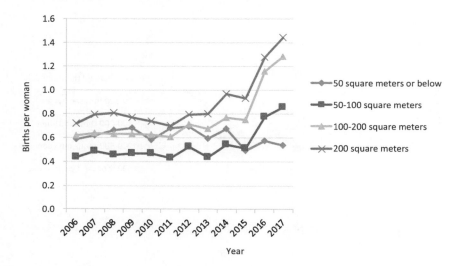

Figure 10.7 Second-child fertility rates by housing area in China, 2006–2017

women with the smallest housing area (less than 50 square meters) are not associated with the lowest second-child fertility, their second-child fertility fell instead of rising after the launch of the two-child policy. This also shows that in today's Chinese society, financial capabilities have become the main determinant of the decision to have the second child.

Factors Affecting the Second-Child Fertility

The previous section describes the socio-demographic characteristics of women choosing to have the second child; yet, certain characteristics are highly correlated. In order to examine the independent effects of the above-mentioned influencing factors, regression analysis will be conducted in this section. The discrete-time logit model is adopted to avoid proportional risk assumptions. Data on individual women will need to be converted to data in women's person-years. The dependent variable is whether the second children are born in each person-year, while the independent variables include the macro-level variables of region (six administrative regions, with Northeast China as the reference group) and urban/rural residence (with rural residence as the reference group), meso-level (family) variables of household income (with household income less than RMB 100,000 as the reference group) and housing area (with housing area less than 50 square meters as the reference group) and micro-level (individual) variables of age (continuous variable), educational level (with educational level of primary school or below as the reference group), occupation (with industrial workers as the reference group), type of employer (with private employers as the reference group), age of the first childbirth (continuous variable), gender of the first child (with girl as the reference group) and the desired number of children (continuous variable).

Table 10.1 shows the results of the regression analysis of factors affecting second-child fertility. It includes two models. The first model covers all women, exhibiting factors affecting second-child fertility in all women in the period from 2006 to 2015. The second model only covers women who were not allowed to have the second child under the former policy but now can do so under the new two-child policy, exhibiting factors affecting second-child fertility in these women in the period from 2016 to 2017. The comparison between the results of these two models reveals not only the laws of factors affecting second-child fertility but also the obvious differences between the two. In these two models, factors exerting the same direction impact on second-child fertility are two macro-level variables: urban/rural residence and the residence divided by the six administrative regions. The impact of urban/rural residence shows that urban women have lower second-child fertility than rural women. This impact is significant in all women model but insignificant in the model of women who can only now have a second child under the new policy. That is, the implementation of the two-child policy has made the significant urban-rural difference in second-child fertility no longer significant, mainly because of the larger surge in second-child fertility in urban women. This also shows that the two-child policy has seen more obvious outcomes in urban areas. In regard to the six regions, the second-child fertility in other regions was all

152 *The Two-Child Policy and Fertility*

Table 10.1 Factors Affecting the Second-Child Fertility in China, 2006–2017

		All Women				Women Who Were Not Allowed to Have the Second Child Under the Former Policy			
		Coefficient	Standard Error	Odds Ratio		Coefficient	Standard Error	Odds Ratio	
Age		0.255	0.026	1.291	***	0.716	0.057	2.045	***
Age squared		−0.003	0.000	0.997	**	−0.013	0.001	0.987	***
Ethic group	Han	−0.049	0.027	0.952	+	0.031	0.133	1.032	
Educational level	Junior high	−0.052	0.026	0.949	***	0.421	0.127	1.524	***
	Senior high	−0.284	0.037	0.753	***	0.501	0.136	1.650	***
	College diploma	−0.636	0.054	0.529	***	0.421	0.146	1.524	**
	Bachelor's degree	−0.890	0.070	0.411	***	0.685	0.152	1.983	***
	Master's degree and over	−0.690	0.152	0.502	***	1.061	0.188	2.888	***
Occupation	Senior executive	−0.034	0.112	0.967		0.342	0.142	1.408	**
	Professional and technician	−0.054	0.051	0.947		0.333	0.107	1.395	**
	Clerk and related personnel	−0.144	0.056	0.866	***	0.192	0.107	1.212	+
	Commercial service	−0.061	0.033	0.941	+	0.081	0.094	1.085	
	Industrial worker								
	Peasant	0.132	0.033	1.141	***	0.940	0.104	2.559	***
Type of employer	State-owned organization	−0.169	0.045	0.845	***	0.183	0.062	1.201	**
Age of first childbirth		−0.186	0.005	0.830	***	−0.024	0.009	0.976	**
Gender of first child	Girl	0.354	0.019	1.424	***	0.181	0.047	1.198	***
Desired number of children		0.014	0.003	1.014	***	0.015	0.006	1.015	**
Total household income	RMB 100,000–200,000	−0.146	0.032	0.864	***	0.029	0.055	1.030	
	RMB 200,000–500,000	−0.033	0.059	0.968		0.098	0.078	1.102	
	RMB 500,000+	0.235	0.144	1.265		0.395	0.171	1.485	*
Housing area	50–100 square meters	−0.169	0.036	0.845	***	−0.033	0.099	0.967	

Table 10.1 Continued

		All Women			Women Who Were Not Allowed to Have the Second Child Under the Former Policy		
		Coefficient	Standard Error	Odds Ratio	Coefficient	Standard Error	Odds Ratio
	100–200 square meters	−0.029	0.035	0.972	0.273	0.097	1.314 **
	200+ square meters	0.017	0.039	1.017	0.337	0.112	1.401 **
Urban/rural residence	Urban residence	−0.272	0.027	0.762 ***	−0.003	0.063	0.997
Region	North China	0.867	0.061	2.381 ***	1.111	0.135	3.037 ***
	East China	0.977	0.059	2.657 ***	1.306	0.128	3.690 ***
	Central and Southern China	1.260	0.058	3.525 ***	1.643	0.129	5.171 ***
	Southwest China	1.007	0.061	2.737 ***	1.360	0.138	3.894 ***
	Northwest China	1.113	0.061	3.045 ***	1.133	0.150	3.104 ***
Constant		−5.418	0.446	0.004 ***	−16.115	0.957	0.000 ***

Note: ***indicates statistically significant at the level of 0.001; **indicates statistically significant at the level of 0.01; *indicates statistically significant at the level of 0.05; and †indicates statistically significant at the level of 0.10.

higher than that in Northeast China, and after the launch of the two-child policy, the increase in the second-child fertility in other regions became much stronger than that in Northeast China.

At the individual level, there are also factors exerting the same direction impact on the second-child fertility, i.e. age, age of first childbirth, gender of the first child and the desired number of children. The effect of age on second-child fertility is not linear. In fact, the age-specific fertility of each parity is characterized by high in the middle and low at both ends. By adding age and age squared to the models, we obtained both significant results, indicating that the effect of age is non-linear. It is obvious that older women are more likely to have the second child. However, for women who can only have the second child under the new policy, their age coefficient is nearly three times that in all women, a result that can be expected. Women who can only have the second child under the new policy are generally older because of the long-term restriction under the former policy. The sample data show that in these women, those aged 40 or above account for 45%. Upon implementation of the two-child policy, their long-accumulated desires for the second child are suddenly released, leading to the "eruption" of second-child fertility and the rising possibility of older women giving birth to their second child.

The age of first childbirth is negatively correlated with second-child fertility. That is, the older the age of first childbirth, the less likely for the woman to have the second child. Women with older age of first childbirth are generally older in age, and they tend to have a lower fertility intention and declined fecundity. However, for women who can only have the second child under the two-child policy, the odds ratio is almost 1, indicating that in spite of the statistical significance, it basically exerts no physical impact. The gender of first child has a significant impact on women's decision to have the second child. For all women, compared to those with first child being a boy, women with first child being a girl are 42% more likely to have the second child and 20% higher for women who can only have the second child under the two-child policy. This result echoes with some previous studies, revealing that the preference for son is still an important factor affecting second-child fertility (Chen Wei and Jin Yongai, 2014). The strong preference for son still exists nowadays in China. The data from the NBS censuses and population sample surveys also suggest that China's sex ratio at birth is still among the highest in the world despite its continuous decline over the past decade. The desired number of children is another individual factor exerting the same direction impact on second-child fertility. It is obvious that women with a higher desired number of children are more likely to have the second child. Although the impact is significant, the actual influence is not that big. Basically, for every increase in the desired number of children, the odds of women giving birth to the second child will only rise by 1%.

In terms of the factors at the meso level (family) and others at the micro level (individual), there have been large differences and even opposite results between the all women model and the model of women who can only have the second child under the new policy. Ethnic group used to have a significant impact on the fertility rate of Chinese women. Due to the differences in the level of socio-economic development, the region of residence and the family planning policy, ethnic minorities tend to have higher fertility rates. However, the results of regression analysis see no significant impact from ethnic group. For all women, the second-child fertility in Han women is only about 5% lower than that in minority women, and it is only significant at the level of 0.10. For women who can only give birth to the second child under the new policy, the impact of ethnic group is insignificant, and Han women are more likely to have the second child.

The educational level has been confirmed by extensive studies to have a significant impact on fertility rate and is often the most important influencing factor among individual characteristics. The results in Table 10.1 also show that the educational level has a strong impact on the second-child fertility. An interesting fact is that the educational level exerts just opposite impacts on these two groups of women. For all women, the higher the level of education, the less likely for them to have the second child (despite turning to slightly higher odds in women holding a master plus degree). Women holding a college diploma, bachelor's degree and master plus degree are 47%, 59% and 50% less likely to have the second child than those who only received primary or lower education. For women who can only have the second child under the new policy, the educational level is positively correlated with the second-child fertility – the higher the level of education, the more likely for them to have the second child. Women holding a college diploma, bachelor's degree and master plus degree are 1.5 times, 2 times and 3 times more likely to have the second child than those who only received primary or lower education. This further confirms the results shown in Figure 10.4.

The occupation and the type of employer also exert opposite impacts on these two groups of women. This might also be closely related to the level of education. Non-manual workers tend to have a higher educational level and a lower fertility rate. This is basically the fact in the all women model. Still, among the three types of non-manual occupations, only clerks and related personnel have significantly lower second-child fertility than the industrial workers. Senior executives and professionals and technicians are not significantly different from industrial workers. This might be associated with the fact that the group of all women includes women who can only have the second child under the new policy. The second-child fertility in industrial workers dropped significantly after 2014, thus narrowing the difference. For all women, women working in a state-owned organization are 15% less likely to have the second child than women working in a private organization. For women who can only have the second child under the new policy, the impact of these factors is more obvious and significant. Women engaged in the three types of non-manual occupations have significantly higher second-child fertility than women as industrial workers. In particular, senior executives and professionals and technicians are 40% more likely to have the second child than industrial workers. Women working in a state-owned organization are 20% more likely to have the second child than women working in a private organization. Moreover, peasants are always characterized by the highest rate of second-child fertility. It must be pointed out that although the educational level, occupation and the type of employer are highly correlated to a large extent, which allows them to exert comparatively stable and consistent impact, the results in Table 10.1 show their different impacts after they are subject to mutual control, well revealing their respective and independent effects.

The meso-level (family) factors also exert quite different impacts on the two groups of women. For all women, the total household income and housing area exert a negative impact; yet, their relationship with the second-child fertility is not monotonously decreasing but exhibiting a U-shaped curve. That is, along with the increase in household income and housing area, the two-child fertility drops first and then rises again. Such a relationship between family economy and fertility has also been confirmed in other studies (Chen Wei and Jin Yongai, 2014). However, for women who can only have the second child under the new policy, the total household income and the housing area basically exert a monotonously positive impact; yet, significant impact only exists under the conditions of high household income and large housing area. The coefficient of income increases gradually and becomes significant when reaching the level of RMB 500,000+. These families are 40% more likely to have the second child than families having a household income of less than RMB 100,000. The housing area will only have a significant impact after exceeding 100 square meters. Families with a housing area of 100–200 square meters and 200+ square meters, respectively, are 31% and 40% more likely to have the second child than families with a housing area less than 50 square meters. This once again confirms that in today's Chinese society, financial capabilities have become the main determinant of the decision to have the second child.

Concluding Remarks

Without question, the launch of the Universal Two-Child Policy has dramatically increased the rate of second-child fertility in China. In the meantime, the effects of this policy vary greatly among different population groups. Factors that used to be negatively correlated with fertility, such as age, educational level, occupation, type of employer, income and housing area, are now positively correlated with fertility under the new policy. In women with the highest level of education, the highest income and the highest housing area, the increase in second-child fertility is amazingly significant, revealing the long-term accumulation of fertility desires. Formerly associated with a higher rate of second-child fertility, women with the lowest education level, the lowest income and the smallest housing area are insusceptible to the two-child policy, and we even observe the decline in their second-child fertility. This shows that in today's Chinese society, financial capability has become the main determinant of the decision to have the second child, which echoes with the fact that "heavy financial burdens" has become the dominant reason that people choose not to have another child in the 2017 fertility survey. At the same time, it should be noted that senior executives, professionals and technicians and clerks and related personnel, as well as those working in a state-owned organization, are generally associated with a higher rate of second-child fertility. This also reveals that the occupations and employers that are conducive to work-life balance are also key factors contributing to the increase in second-child fertility. Therefore, designing and improving the social support policies that focuses on both financial and institutional arrangements will help increase the fertility rate. This has also been confirmed by the experience of developed countries.

It must be noted that the hike in second-child fertility under the two-child policy is like a volcanic eruption – it is simply the sudden release of long-accumulated desires. It might be dazzling, but it won't last. In spite of the obvious short-term effects of the two-child policy, its long-term prospects look dim. An important reason for this is the continuous postponement in women's age of first marriage since the beginning of this century. During the past decade, the first marriage rate among women has dropped sharply. This quiet revolution might ruin the fruits of fertility policy adjustments in an invisible way. We must also notice that from now till 2030, the birth cohorts 1990–2005 will gradually come to the age of marriage and childbearing, and yet, during the period from 1990 to 2005, China's fertility rate dropped dramatically and remained far below the replacement level. The sudden shrinkage in the number of women of marriageable and reproductive age and their tendency to continuously postpone the age of first marriage will inevitably lead to further decline in the first marriage rate and the first childbirth rate, making the second-child fertility even lower. Therefore, it is necessary to incorporate marriage promotion into the further adjustment and improvement of the fertility policy and the design of the social support policies. So far, China is still a universal marriage society, and Western scholars used to believe that China is the biggest challenger of the marriage transition theory. However, from the major changes observed in recent years, we can see that although China's marriage revolution began late, it is likely to advance at a faster pace. The Chinese Government must further adjust and improve its fertility policy and build a strong policy and institutional system capable of promoting marriage and fertility as soon as possible, or else it will be difficult for China to avoid the huge risk of running into ultra-low fertility.

References

Allison, P. D. 2010. *Survival Analysis Using SAS: A Practical Guide* (2nd Ed.). Cary, NC: SAS Institute Inc.

Becker, G. S. 1960. An Economic Analysis of Fertility. Pp. 209–240 in *Demographic and Economic Change in Developed Countries*. New York, NY: Columbia University Press.

Becker, G. S. 1965. A Theory of the Allocation of Time. *The Economic Journal*, 75493–517.

Bongaarts, J. 2001. Fertility and Reproductive Preferences in Post-Transitional Societies. *Population and Development Review* 27(Suppl.): 260–281.

Chen Wei and Jin Yongai. 2014. The Implementation of China's Family Planning Policy and Its Influencing Factors: From a Micro Perspective. *Population and Economics* 4: 118–128.

Chen Wei and Yang Shenghui. 2014. China's Fertility in 2010: An Indirect Estimation Using Brass P/F Ratio Method. *Population Research* 6: 16–24.

Coale, A. J. 1989. Marriage and Childbearing in China Since 1940. *Social Forces* 67(4): 833–850.

Dettling, L. J. and Kearney, M. S. 2014. House Prices and Birth Rates: The Impact of the Real Estate Market on the Decision to Have a Baby. *Journal of Public Economics* 110(1): 82–100.

Lovenheim, M. F. and Mumford, K. J. 2013. Do Family Wealth Shocks Affect Fertility Choices? Evidence from the Housing Market Boom and Bust. *Social Science Electronic Publishing* 95(2): 464–475.

Willis, R. J. 1973. A New Approach to the Economic Theory of Fertility Behavior. *Journal of Political Economy* 81(2, Part 2): S14–S64.

Yang Fan and Zhao Menghan. 2013. Estimation of the Fertility Level in China Since 2000. *Population Research* 2: 54–65.

Zhai Zhenwu, Chen Jiaju, and Li Long. 2015. China's Recent Total Fertility Rate: New Evidence from the Household Registration Statistics. *Population Research* 6: 22–34.

Zhao Z. W. 2015. Closing a sociodemographic chapter of Chinese history. *Population and Development Review* 4:681–686.

11 Demographic Trends under the Two-Child Policy

Population situation is a key consideration in formulating economic and social strategies and making resource and environmental policies. Many scholars have estimated the demographic trends since the adjustment of the fertility policy. Generally speaking, they have reached almost the same conclusion, that is, the implementation of the two-child policy will increase the population peak, but it will not bring about an upsurge in the birth rate or a violent rebound of the population; it will keep negative population growth down to some extent, but it will not change the fact that China's total population will be shrinking; it will help slow down the population aging, but it cannot reverse the trend of population aging, and even it will increase the total dependency burden on the society.

Population projection is of great significance both academically and practically. It is based on assumptions, hence full of uncertainties. With the update of data and changes in population-related factors, it is necessary to constantly adjust the parameters to maximize the accuracy of projection. Therefore, this study combines the fertility changes after the two-child policy and the other factors of economic and social development to predict the demographic trend in China from 2015 to 2100 and analyze the trends in population size, population structure and dependency ratio of China in the 21st century, to provide basic data for evaluating the economic and social impact of the two-child policy in the following chapters.

Data and Methods

This research uses the data of 2015 national 1% population sample survey, with the cohort-component method, to predict the trend of China's population size and structure from 2015 to 2100 under three sets of scenarios – low-, medium- and high-fertility variants. All the tables and figures presented in this chapter are produced from these population projections and, thus, their data sources are no longer further noted.

The parameters for the population projections are set as follows:

1 The starting population

Since 2015 is the starting point for the implementation of the two-child policy, the projection in this study takes the data of 2015 national 1% population

DOI: 10.4324/9781003429661-11

sample survey as the base year data, and the age-specific and sex-specific population data as the starting population for the projection.

2 Mortality parameters

The mortality parameters include mortality level and mortality pattern. Mortality level is mainly measured by the average life expectancy. The starting data comes from the life expectancy published by the National Bureau of Statistics in 2015, that is, 73.64 years for men and 79.43 years for women, and the life expectancy for each year thereafter is set according to the United Nations' rapid pace increment model. Mortality pattern adopts the Coale-Demeny West Model Life Tables (Coale et al. 1983).

3 Fertility parameters

Fertility parameters are the most important in population projection. Like mortality, fertility parameters also include fertility level and fertility pattern. In the process of setting the total fertility rate, it is necessary to determine the total fertility rate of the base year and also to make assumptions about the total fertility rate of the future calendar years.

China's total fertility rate has always been the focus of attention from all walks of life. The data of the Sixth National Census in 2010 showed that China's total fertility rate was only 1.18, which was at an extremely low level. Many scholars questioned the rate and used various methods to estimate it. The estimates of the total fertility rate since 2010 by the scholars are mainly between 1.5 and 1.7.

For the estimation of the total fertility rate after 2015, many scholars have set different values in related population projection studies. Sun Mingzhe (2014) set the total fertility rate at 1.3, 1.44, 1.8 and 2.3, respectively, to compare the impacts of different fertility levels on China's population size in the next 50 years; Yang Ge (2016) set the rate after 2020 at 1.7 and 1.9; Chen Ning (2017) set it at 1.6, 1.9 and 2.1; Gu Hejun and Li Qing (2017) set the low, medium and high scenarios of the total fertility rate at 1.64, 1.85 and 1.75, with the total fertility rate increasing by 0.02 every five years until 2050; and Jinying Wang and Yanxia Ge (2016) set China's total fertility rate from 2010 to 2100 by urban and rural areas and by stage.

Taking the existing research results into consideration, this study set the total fertility rate in 2015 at 1.6 and make assumptions of the total fertility rate from 2016 to 2100 in three scenarios. The low scenario assumes that the two-child policy is not implemented, and the fertility rate will drop from 1.6 in 2015 to 1.35 in 2035, remaining unchanged until 2100; the medium and high scenarios are based on the actual situation from 2015 to 2018, which is that the fertility rate rises, then falls and then rises again. Specifically, the medium scenario assumes that the fertility rate rises from 1.6 in 2015 to 1.7 in 2016–2017, then falls to 1.6 in 2035 and remains at 1.6 after 2035; the high scenario is similar to the medium one, but the fertility rate rises to 1.85 in 2035 and remains unchanged at 1.85 thereafter. Data of other years are obtained by interpolation. This study adjusts the age-specific fertility rate from 2015 national 1% population sample survey as the fertility pattern for projection.

4 Sex ratio at birth
    Normally, the sex ratio at birth stands between 103 and 107, which is internationally recognized. China's sex ratio at birth has been high for a long time, especially after the implementation of the one-child policy when people cannot give births as they want. Therefore, the sex ratio at birth increase and becomes abnormally high. However, in the past ten years, China's sex ratio at birth has continued to decline. Considering the relaxation of the birth control, economic and social development and changes in cultural values and other factors, this study assumes that sex ratio at birth declines to a normal level of 107 in 2025 and remains unchanged thereafter.
5 Migration
    China is not a nation of immigrants, and the annual amount of international migration is relatively small, and almost insignificant compared to its huge population base. Besides, the international migration data are difficult to obtain. So, neglecting the international net migration makes little difference to the projection results.

Trends of China's Total Population

Table 11.1 shows the projection results of the low, medium and high scenarios of China's total population size from 2015 to 2100. The low scenario shows the population size of China in the future without the implementation of the two-child policy. The results show that if the birth control policy is not liberalized, China's population will peak at about 1.404 billion in 2023 and then begin to experience negative growth and continue to decline, falling below 1.2 billion in the mid-century, below 1 billion in 2073, and to 684 million in 2100. The medium scenario assumes the total fertility rate after 2035 is 1.6. The results show that in 2024, the total population will peak at 1.409 billion and then decline steadily, falling below 1.4 billion in 2036, below 1.3 billion in 2058 and below 1 billion in 2083 and finally will drop to 863 million in 2100. The high scenario assumes that the total fertility rate after 2035 is 1.85. The results show that if the total fertility rate of 1.85 is maintained, the population will reach the peak of 1.416 billion in 2034. Like the two scenarios above, it will gradually decline after the peak, falling below 1.4 billion in 2045, below 1.3 billion in 2059 and below 1.2 billion in 2074 and will drop to 1.060 billion in 2100. The total population in this century will anyway be above 1 billion.

Figure 11.1 shows the change of China's population size from 2015 to 2100 more clearly. Regardless of the low, medium and high scenarios, the trends are similar that they all experience a small increase and then gradually decrease and only the times of change and the rates of descent are different. Compared with the low scenario without the two-child policy, by 2100, the medium one will have 179 million more people, and the high one will have 376 million more people. Although the policy adjustment will delay the peak of population, the trend of negative population growth in the future will not change.

162 Demographic Trends under the Two-Child Policy

Table 11.1 Projection of China's Total Population Size from 2015 to 2100 (Million)

Year	Low	Medium	High	Year	Low	Medium	High
2015	1,374.6	1,374.6	1,374.6	2058	1,170.8	1,241.2	1,303.5
2016	1,383.0	1,383.0	1,383.0	2059	1,158.4	1,231.4	1,296.5
2017	1,390.6	1,390.6	1,390.6	2060	1,146.1	1,221.7	1,289.8
2018	1,396.0	1,396.0	1,396.0	2061	1,134.0	1,212.2	1,283.2
2019	1,399.4	1,399.9	1,399.9	2062	1,121.9	1,202.8	1,276.8
2020	1,401.5	1,403.0	1,403.2	2063	1,110.0	1,193.5	1,270.5
2021	1,402.9	1,405.4	1,405.9	2064	1,098.1	1,184.2	1,264.2
2022	1,403.6	1,407.1	1,408.0	2065	1,086.2	1,175.0	1,258.0
2023	1,403.7	1,408.2	1,409.6	2066	1,074.2	1,165.7	1,251.7
2024	1,403.2	1,408.8	1,410.8	2067	1,062.2	1,156.3	1,245.3
2025	1,402.2	1,409.0	1,411.7	2068	1,050.1	1,146.8	1,238.7
2026	1,400.8	1,408.8	1,412.2	2069	1,037.9	1,137.1	1,231.9
2027	1,399.2	1,408.4	1,412.6	2070	1,025.5	1,127.2	1,224.9
2028	1,397.3	1,407.8	1,413.0	2071	1,012.9	1,117.2	1,217.7
2029	1,395.2	1,407.1	1,413.3	2072	1,000.2	1,107.0	1,210.4
2030	1,393.0	1,406.3	1,413.7	2073	987.5	1,096.7	1,202.9
2031	1,390.6	1,405.5	1,414.2	2074	974.6	1,086.4	1,195.4
2032	1,388.0	1,404.6	1,414.7	2075	961.7	1,076.0	1,187.9
2033	1,385.2	1,403.5	1,415.2	2076	948.8	1,065.5	1,180.4
2034	1,382.1	1,402.3	1,415.6	2077	936.0	1,055.2	1,173.0
2035	1,378.8	1,400.9	1,416.0	2078	923.2	1,044.9	1,165.8
2036	1,375.1	1,399.3	1,416.3	2079	910.6	1,034.9	1,158.8
2037	1,371.1	1,397.2	1,416.2	2080	898.3	1,025.1	1,152.3
2038	1,366.8	1,394.8	1,415.8	2081	886.2	1,015.7	1,146.1
2039	1,361.9	1,391.9	1,414.9	2082	874.5	1,006.6	1,140.4
2040	1,356.5	1,388.4	1,413.4	2083	863.0	997.8	1,135.0
2041	1,350.5	1,384.4	1,411.2	2084	851.9	989.3	1,130.0
2042	1,343.9	1,379.8	1,408.4	2085	841.0	981.1	1,125.3
2043	1,336.6	1,374.4	1,404.8	2086	830.3	973.1	1,120.9
2044	1,328.6	1,368.4	1,400.6	2087	819.8	965.3	1,116.7
2045	1,319.9	1,361.7	1,395.7	2088	809.4	957.7	1,112.7
2046	1,310.6	1,354.4	1,390.3	2089	799.1	950.1	1,108.7
2047	1,300.7	1,346.6	1,384.3	2090	788.9	942.5	1,104.8
2048	1,290.4	1,338.3	1,377.9	2091	778.7	935.0	1,100.9
2049	1,279.6	1,329.6	1,371.0	2092	768.4	927.4	1,096.8
2050	1,268.4	1,320.5	1,363.9	2093	758.1	919.7	1,092.7
2051	1,256.9	1,311.0	1,356.4	2094	747.8	911.9	1,088.4
2052	1,245.0	1,301.3	1,348.8	2095	737.3	903.9	1,083.9
2053	1,232.8	1,291.3	1,341.0	2096	726.7	895.9	1,079.3
2054	1,220.5	1,281.2	1,333.2	2097	716.1	887.6	1,074.6
2055	1,208.1	1,271.1	1,325.5	2098	705.4	879.4	1,069.7
2056	1,195.6	1,261.1	1,318.0	2099	694.7	871.0	1,064.8
2057	1,183.2	1,251.1	1,310.6	2100	684.0	862.7	1,059.8

Changes in the Size and Proportion of Child Population

In demography, the total population is often divided into three broad age groups: the child population (ages 0–14), the working-age population (ages 15–59 or 15–64) and the elderly population (age 60 and above or 65 and above). Among them,

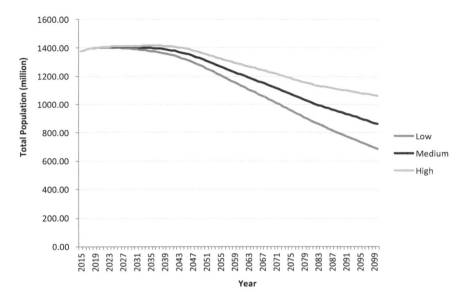

Figure 11.1 Trends of China's total population from 2015 to 2100

the child population has always been the focus in demography. The child group is the beginning of population development, and its size directly affects the future population size and the sustainable development of the nation. The fertility policy works on the birth numbers directly, so first of all, the implementation of the two-child policy affects the child group aged 0–14.

Figures 11.2 and 11.3, respectively, show the trends of the population size and proportion of children aged 0–14 years in China from 2015 to 2100. Different from the change of the total population, the population size of children shows fluctuating changes in the future and eventually declines. In 2018, the third year of the implementation of the two-child policy, the size of child population peaks at about 256 million, accounting for 18.35% of the total population. The implementation of the two-child policy cause the fertility potential which has been restrained for many years to explode. The fertility accumulative effect brings about a peak of the population size. After that, this fertility potential gradually subsides, and the population enters a period of negative growth. What is special is that the child population size is affected not only by the fertility policy but also by the size of women of childbearing age. The birth cohort in the 1960s was baby boomers. Over time, the birth cohort in the 1960s and 1970s gradually retired from the childbearing age and were replaced by the birth cohort after 1980 who grew up under the strict fertility policy, which directly reduces the size of the childbearing age group. Therefore, even if the two-child policy is implemented, the reduction in the size of childbearing age group will directly lead to a decline in the size of future birth numbers. The population of the baby boom and the baby bust will alternately enter the childbearing age, which will also lead to fluctuations in the future birth

164 *Demographic Trends under the Two-Child Policy*

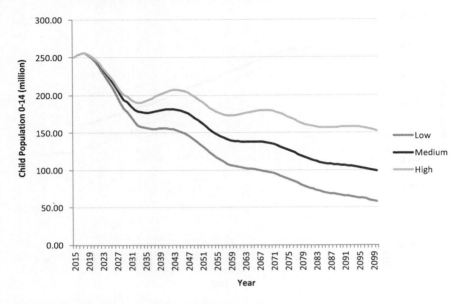

Figure 11.2 Trends of the child population aged 0–14 in China from 2015 to 2100

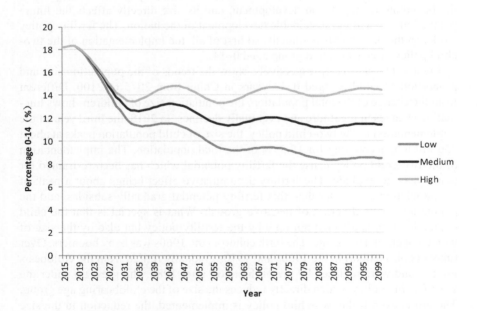

Figure 11.3 Trends of the proportion of child population aged 0–14 in China from 2015 to 2100

numbers. Therefore, the trend of the child population in the future will be a decline with fluctuations.

After peaking in 2018, the total child population begins to decline rapidly. If the two-child policy is not implemented (low scenario), the first trough of the child population appears in 2037, which is 155 million people, accounting for 11.34% of the total population; if the total fertility rate remains 1.6 from 2035 to 2100 (medium scenario), the first trough of the child population appears two years earlier, but the decline is smaller than the former, dropping to 177 million in 2035, accounting for 12.65%; if the total fertility rate stabilizes at 1.85 from 2035 to 2100, the first trough of the child population occurs in 2033, about 190 million people, accounting for 13.44%. Although the troughs of the medium and high scenarios appear earlier than that of the low scenario, the population sizes are larger than that of the low scenario, 22 million and 35 million more than that, respectively. After the first trough appears, due to the influence of the population size of women of childbearing age, the size of China's child population begins to show a rebounding trend. The rebounding period in the low scenario is quite short, and it will decline again after maintaining at about 156 million people from 2039 to 2041. It will fall below 100 million in 2068, accounting for less than 10% of the total population. Until the end of this century, the child population drops to 58 million, accounting for 8.48%. In the medium scenario, the child population increases to 182 million and begins to decrease after keeping this size for two years and drops below 100 million in 2100, which is 98 million, accounting for 11.41%. In the high scenario, it continues to decline after rising to 207 million between 2043 and 2045, reaching a second trough of 173 million in 2060, then slowly rising, and falling again after reaching 180 million in 2067. After a small increase in 2090, the child population finally drops to 153 million in 2100, accounting for 14.39% of the total population. Compared with the low and medium scenarios, the fluctuations in the high scenario last longer. The implementation of the two-child policy may at least increase the number of children by 40 million by 2100. If the total fertility rate of 1.85 remains until the end of this century, the child population in China may increase by 95 million, and the difference of nearly 100 million people will inevitably bring different impacts on China's economic and social development.

Trends of the Size and Proportion of the Working-Age Population

When defining the elderly population, internationally the age of 65 is often set as the threshold for the elderly, while it is set at 60 in China. The difference in the classification criteria directly affects the size of the working-age population and the elderly population. This study predicts the size and proportion of the working-age population in China from 2015 to 2100 according to the domestic standard (15–59 years old) and the international standard (15–64 years old), respectively.

The size and structure of the working-age population is an important indicator for analyzing economic activities and is used to measure the potential and actual labor resources of a nation or region. Figures 11.4 and 11.5, respectively, show that the size and proportion of the working-age population aged 15–59 in China from

2015 to 2100 show a gradual downward trend. 2015 is the starting year of this study, and also the year with the largest working-age population in this 85-year period of projection, reaching 906 million, accounting for 65.92% of the total population. After that, it begins to decline, with a small increase in 2021. After reaching 902 million people, China's working-age population goes downward completely. In 2036, the working-age population falls below 800 million. The low scenario shows that it falls below 500 million in 2069, to 400 million in 2079 and to 283 million in 2100 which accounts for 41.43% of the total population and is 623 million less than the peak population. In the medium scenario, it drops below 500 million in 2076, and to 392 million in 2100 which accounts for 45.43%. The data in the high scenario are relatively moderate that the working-age population keeps above 500 million until the end of this century, and it is 511 million in 2100 which accounts for 48.24% and is 395 million less than the peak.

Before 2040, the adjustment of the fertility policy did not have a significant impact on the working-age population. But over time, the birth cohort under the policy adjustment moves to the working age, and the cumulative effect brought by the policy begins to work. Especially by the end of this century, the implementation of the two-child policy can increase the size of China's working-age population by about 109 million to 228 million.

If the working-age population is set to be 15–64 years old according to international standards, its trend is the same as that of the 15- to 59-year-old working-age population (see Figures 11.6 and 11.7). In the 21st century, whether it is based on domestic or international standard, China's working-age population shrinks gradually anyway.

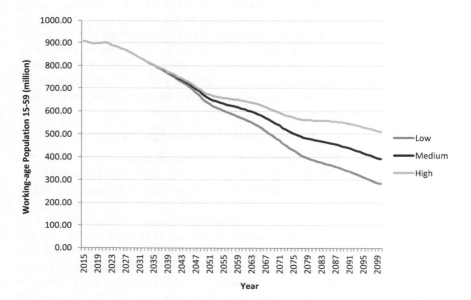

Figure 11.4 Trends of the working-age population aged 15–59 in China from 2015 to 2100

Demographic Trends under the Two-Child Policy 167

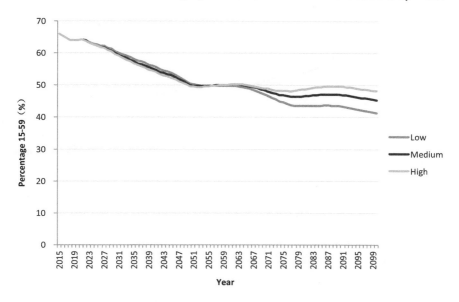

Figure 11.5 Trends of the proportion of working-age population aged 15–59 in China from 2015 to 2100

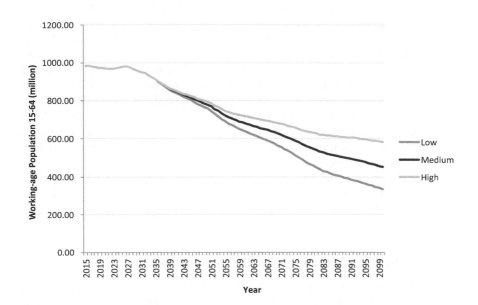

Figure 11.6 Trends of the working-age population aged 15–64 in China from 2015 to 2100

168 *Demographic Trends under the Two-Child Policy*

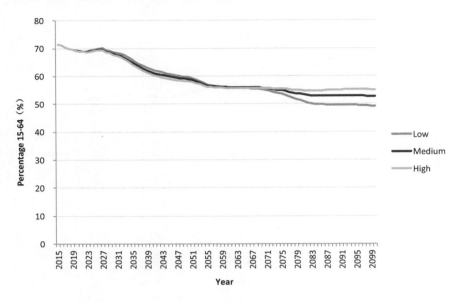

Figure 11.7 Trends of the proportion of working-age population aged 15–64 in China from 2015 to 2100

Based on international standards, China's working-age population peaks in 2015 at 983 million people, accounting for 75.51% of the total population, and then begins to decline. It rebounds when it reaches 968 million in 2023 and rises to 980 million in 2026 and keeps declining since then. The low scenario shows that the working-age population drops below 500 million in 2077, below 400 million in 2089, and reaches the lowest point of this century at 335 million in 2100 which accounts for 48.95% and declines by 26.56% compared with the peak. In the medium scenario, it falls below 500 million in 2090, and to 453 million in 2100 which accounts for about 52.50%. The working-age population in the high scenario is always above 500 million, and the lowest point is in 2100, about 582 million people, accounting for about 54.90%. By the end of this century, compared with the working age of domestic standard (15–59 years old), the international standard will make China's working-age population increase by 51–71 million. However, the sharp reduction of the labor force in this century is an indisputable fact. The labor-intensive industries relying on the huge labor force in the past are no longer suitable for the future development trend. The new situation of population will also force the transformation and upgrading of the industry.

Trends in the Size and Proportion of the Elderly Population

Similar to the analysis of the working-age population, the elderly population is set differently according to two different age classification standards, namely the domestic standard (over 60 years old) and the international standard (over 65 years old). This study analyzes the trends of China's elderly population from 2015 to 2100 under both standards, respectively.

Figures 11.8 and 11.9 show the trends of the size and the proportion, respectively, of the population aged over 60 in China from 2015 to 2100. Since 2015, the size of the elderly population has gradually increased, reaching a peak around the middle of the 21st century and then steadily declining. The projection shows that the population of the elderly over 60 years old is the smallest in 2015, with 218 million people, accounting for about 15.89% of the total population. After that, the increase accelerates, reaching 300 million in 2025, 400 million in 2033 and a peak of 495 million in 2051 which accounts for about 48% of the total population. After maintaining a size of more than 400 million for 40 years, it begins to decline slowly. The low scenario shows that it drops below 400 million in 2086, and in the medium and high scenarios, it falls below 400 million in 2088 and 2090, respectively. By 2100, the population size of the elderly over 60 years old predicted in the low, medium and high scenarios is 343, 372 and 396 million, respectively.

Unlike the child and working-age groups, the results of projection in the low, medium and high scenarios for the elderly population have been the same, and only a small difference appears between the three scenarios until 2080. By the end of this century, the difference in the size of the elderly population between the three scenarios is far less than that of the child population and that of the working-age population, which means the two-child policy has little impact on the size of the elderly population in this century. However, it cannot be ignored that the cumulative effect of the policy on the elderly population will also work over time, but it

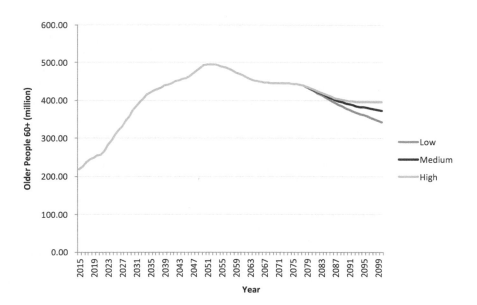

Figure 11.8 Trends of the elderly population aged 60 and over in China from 2015 to 2100

170 *Demographic Trends under the Two-Child Policy*

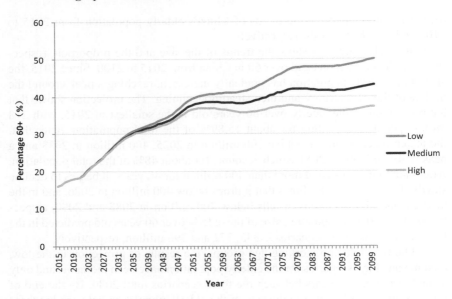

Figure 11.9 Trends of the proportion of the elderly population aged 60 and over in China from 2015 to 2100

takes a long time. Therefore, the formulation of population policies should be more proactive and forward-looking.

The trend of the size of the elderly population in China from 2015 to 2100 of the international classification standard (over 65 years old) is the same as that of the domestic standard (over 60), both rising rapidly at first, peaking in the middle of this century and then declining slowly (see Figures 11.10 and 11.11). Compared with the domestic standard, the elderly populations in three scenarios under the international standard will not be different until 2084. That is to say, the two-child policy under the international standard has a later impact on the size of the elderly population than the domestic standard. From the perspective of the total elderly population, in 2100, the elderly populations of the low, medium and high scenarios under the international standard are, respectively, 291, 311 and 325 million, 51–71 million less than those of the domestic standard.

A country will enter an aging society if the population over the age of 65 exceeds 7% of the total population or the population over the age of 60 exceeds 10% of the total population. At the end of this century, the proportions of the elderly over 60 years old in low, medium and high scenarios in China are 50.09%, 43.17% and 37.37%, respectively, and the proportions of the elderly over 65 years old are 42.56% and 36.10% and 30.71%, far exceeding the standard of an aging society. In the future, the main demographic challenge in China will be the severe aging situation.

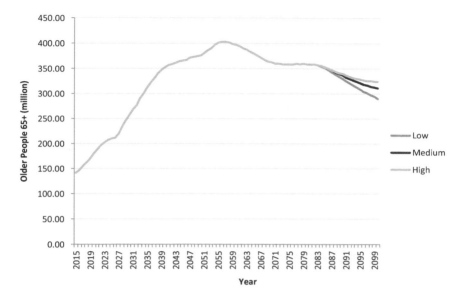

Figure 11.10 Trends of the elderly population aged 65 and over in China from 2015 to 2100

Trends of the Dependency Ratio

The socioeconomic impact of the age structure of the population is usually measured by the population dependency ratio, which is divided into total dependency ratio (TDR), child dependency ratio (CDR), and old-age dependency ratio (ODR). Considering that China's average life expectancy has continued to increase in recent years, and policies calling for delayed retirement have become stronger, the age group of 15–64 years is used as the working-age population, and the age of the elderly population is set to be over 65 years old in the analysis of the dependency ratio in this study.

CDR is measured by the proportion of the child population aged 0–14 to the working-age population aged 15–64. Figure 11.12 shows that the CDR in China fluctuates from 2015 to 2100. Between 2015 and 2020, China's CDR is the highest, reaching a peak of 26.23% in 2018, which is mainly due to the impact of policy adjustments and the growth of the birth rapidly increases the CDR in the short term. After that, it begins to decline and there is a trough around 2033. The CDRs of the low, medium and high scenarios are 17.09%, 19.10% and 20.21%, respectively. It continues to increase after that and enters a second rising period. The CDRs of the three scenarios begin to vary. In 2044, the CDRs of the low, medium and high scenarios are 18.91%, 22.06% and 25.13%. After a second peak appears around 2045, it falls again and reaches a third peak around the 2070s. This kind of fluctuation has always existed in the CDR, mainly due to the changes in the size of births brought about by the adjustment of the fertility policy, and the birth cohorts of different periods entering the childbearing age lead to fluctuations in the size of

172 *Demographic Trends under the Two-Child Policy*

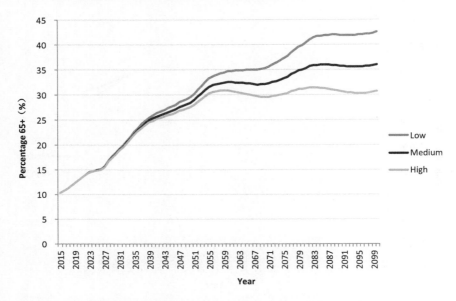

Figure 11.11 Trends of the proportion of the elderly population aged 65 and over in China from 2015 to 2100

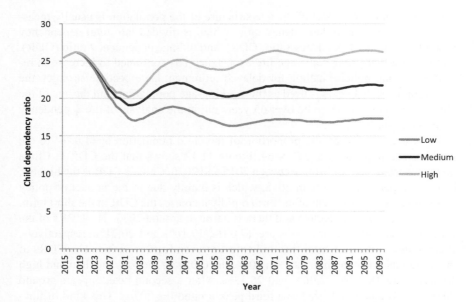

Figure 11.12 Trends of child dependency ratio in China from 2015 to 2100

Demographic Trends under the Two-Child Policy 173

the childbearing age population, which feeds back to the next generation population. According to the line chart, the projection for CDR of the high scenario is the highest, with an average of 24.67%, followed by the medium one, with an average of 21.62%, and the low scenario is always the lowest, about 18.45%, indicating that the implementation of the two-child policy has increased the CDR to a certain extent.

Figure 11.13 shows the trend of China's ODR from 2015 to 2100. In the future, the ODR will continue to rise in a quite rapid way. The ODR is the lowest in 2015 at 14.4%. After that, it continues to rise, exceeding 20% in 2022, 30% in 2033, 40% in 2039 and 50% in 2051. On average, the ODR in China increases by about 10% every ten years. After the mid-21st century, the ODRs of the low, medium and high scenarios gradually vary from each other. The low scenario shows that the ODR will basically continue to increase at a rate of 10% every ten years, exceeding 60% in 2057 and 70% in 2076, 80% in 2082 and reaching 86.94% in 2100. Although in the medium and high scenarios, it also maintains growth, the growth is smaller and the rate is slower than that of the low scenario. In the medium scenario, it has been stable at around 67% after exceeding 60% in 2074. In the high scenario, it exceeds 50% in the mid-21st century and remains between 50% and 60% until the end of this century and has been stable at around 55% in the decade from 2090 to 2100. By the end of this century, China's ODR will be 12.82–31% less than that if the two-child policy is not implemented. Although the aging of China's population

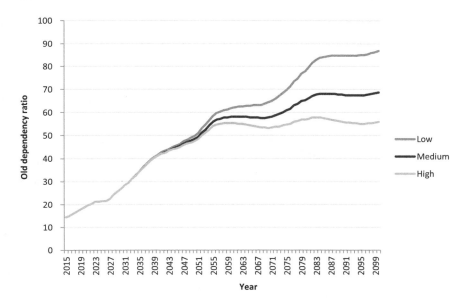

Figure 11.13 Trends of the old dependency ratio in China from 2015 to 2100

cannot be reversed, the implementation of the two-child policy can reduce the burden of support for the old age to a certain extent.

The CDR and the ODR together determine the future trend of China's TDR. From 2015 to 2100, China's TDR will continue to rise (see Figure 11.14), mainly because China has already entered an aging society, the adjustment of the fertility policy has increased the size of the birth population, and the expansion of the two ends of the population pyramid has increased the size of the dependent population. In 2015, the TDR is the lowest at 39.84%, and it continues to rise after that, exceeding 50% around 2034 and 70% in 2050. In 2084, the TDR predicted by the low scenario exceeds 100%, which seriously exceeds the normal dependency burden. By 2100, the TDR of the low scenario will reach 104.27%. Although the results of projection in the medium and high scenarios are relatively moderate, the total dependency burden is still very large. In 2100, the TDRs of the medium and high scenarios are 90.49% and 82.15%, respectively. China's TDR at the end of this century is more than twice the initial value in 2015. If the two-child policy is not implemented, the dependency ratio will be even more than 2.5 times that of 2015.

In the first half of the 21st century, the projected TDR of the high scenario has been higher than that of the low and medium scenarios, and in 2065, the TDR of the low scenario exceeds that of the medium scenario and is equal to that of the high scenario, and in 2069, the TDR of the low scenario exceeds that of the high scenario. That is to say, in the early period, the increase in the size of the birth population brought about by the adjustment of the fertility policy will increase the TDR, but the population born under the influence of the two-child policy will

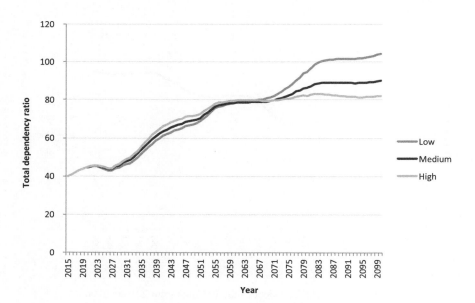

Figure 11.14 Trends of the total dependency ratio in China from 2015 to 2100

gradually move to the working-age population in the future, changing from a dependent population into a supporting population. Therefore, in the later period, the TDR without policy adjustment will be higher than that under policy adjustment. It will decrease by 13.78–22.12% in 2100 compared with the situation that the policy is not implemented. Therefore, in the long run, the implementation of the two-child policy will help ease the social burden of support in the future. The policy effect will be late, but it will come eventually.

In addition, according to the predicted trend of the TDR in Figure 11.14, it can be found that the trend of China's TDR from 2015 to 2100 is basically the same as that of the ODR, but it is not the same as that of the CDR, indicating that the increasing size of the elderly population will cause a more serious social burden in the future than the child population. Meanwhile, due to the different trends of the CDR and the ODR, the composition of the TDR borne by the working-age population in different periods is different. In the early period, the burden of caring for children brought about by the adjustment of the fertility policy is the main part, but it is generally not too large, fluctuating slightly between 20% and 26%, and the burden of caring for the old age will exceed that for children around 2027. Since then, the burden of caring for the old age has maintained strong growth and, therefore, it will become the main burden after about 2030.

Concluding Remarks

Based on the current new situation of population in China, this chapter predicts the trends of the population size, structure, and dependency ratio from 2015 to 2100 with consideration of the adjustment of fertility policy and the influencing factors of economic development.

The adjustment of the fertility policy will delay the arrival of the population peak, but it will not change the trend of gradual shrinking of the population in the future. After the policy adjustment, China's population peak will appear at the earliest in 2024 and at the latest in 2034. It is about 0.5–12 million people more than the peak without the policy adjustment, which is not a big increase. But the change in policy will increase the population by 179–376 million by 2100.

From 2015 to 2100, the population of children aged 0–14 and the population of working age in China show a downward trend, while the size of the elderly population gradually increases. In the early days of the implementation of the two-child policy, the child population reached a maximum of 256 million and then gradually declined with fluctuations. In 2015, the working-age population reaches a peak of 906 million, accounting for 65.92% of the total population, and it begins to enter a downward period after 2021. By the end of this century, the implementation of the two-child policy will increase the working-age population by about 109 million to 228 million. From 2015, the elderly population will gradually increase, reaching a peak of about 495 million people in 2051, and then decline steadily. However, it should be noted that from 2015 to 2100, when the total population decreases by an average of 569 million people, the number of elderly people over 60 years old increases by an average of 152 million people, and the number of elderly people over 65 years old increases by an average of 169 million people, and the proportion of the elderly population has been increasing.

From 2015 to 2100, the CDR shows fluctuating changes. In the future, the ODR and GDR will always be on the rise, and the increase will be large. The early support burden is mainly from the burden of caring for children brought about by the adjustment of the fertility policy, but the ODR will exceed the CDR around 2027 and will maintain strong growth, and therefore, it will become the main burden in the future.

When the proportion of the population aged 0–14 in a country is less than 30%, and the proportion of the population aged 65 and above is more than 7%, it has entered an aging society. According to this standard, China has entered an aging society in 2015. No matter how the fertility policy changes in the future, the trend of aging is irreversible. This is an inevitable result of economic and social development and population transformation. Adjusting the fertility policy can alleviate the aging process to a certain extent, but its effect is minimal. With the development of economy and society, the effect of fertility policies on fertility itself will become smaller and smaller, and it will no longer be the main determinant of fertility. Policies and systems in the future should focus on addressing the growing challenges of aging actively.

References

Chen Ning. 2017. Research on the Impact of Comprehensive Two-Child Policy on the Aging of Chinese Population. *Journal of Huazhong University of Science and Technology (Social Science Edition)* 2: 96–103.

Coale, A. J., Demeny, P., and Vaughan, B. 1983. *Regional Model Life Tables and Stable Populations (Studies in Population)* (2nd Ed.). Cambridge, MA: Academic Press.

Gu Hejun and Li Qing. 2017. The Impact of Universal Two-Child Policy on the Size and Structure of Working-Age Population in China: 2017–2050. *Population and Economics* 4: 1–9.

Jinying Wang and Yanxia Ge. 2016. China's Population Development under the Universal Two-Child Policy. *Population Research* 6: 3–21.

Sun Mingzhe. 2014. Prediction of the Future Trend of China's Population Using Six Census Data. *Beijing Social Sciences* 5: 85–92.

Yang Ge. 2016. Population Expectation and Policy Outlook after Universal Two-Child Policy. *Journal of Beijing University of Technology (Social Sciences Edition)* 4: 25–33.

12 Labor Supply

Sufficient supply and effective utilization of labor force are important for sustainable economic development. Currently, with fertility rate below the replacement level, China is having a larger number of aging population and lesser labor force. The implementation of the universal two-child policy will have a profound impact on China's population development and labor market. Based on the universal two-child policy, this chapter will discuss the policy's impact on the future labor supply. The supply of labor force is affected by the size of the total population, the size of the labor force, the labor force structure and the labor force participation rate. In addition, effective labor force is related to not only the quantity of labor force but also its quality. This chapter accurately estimates and analyzes the future labor supply in a comprehensive way by creating an effective labor supply model incorporating human capital, which considers the quantity, structure and quality of labor force and makes use of population forecast, labor participation rate forecast and human capital index forecast. This chapter will also show the contribution rate of each factor to the change of labor supply through factor decomposition and analyze the impact of demographic factors and non-demographic factors on labor supply.

Research Methods and Data

Concept Definition

Working-age population refers to the legal adult population minus the total number of persons above the legal retirement age. In this chapter, the international standard for working-age population is adopted, that is, the population aged 15–64.

The working population includes the economically active and the economically inactive population. The National Bureau of Statistics defines the economically active population as those aged 16 and above who have the ability to participate in or require to participate in social and economic activities, including the employed and unemployed. The economically inactive population refers to the population aged 16 years and older who has the ability to work and does not participate in or is not required to participate in social and economic activities. It reflects the number of people who quit the labor market in a certain region in a certain period, such as pursuing higher education or not working after graduation, and are potential labor

DOI: 10.4324/9781003429661-12

178 Labor Supply

resources. The labor force studied in this chapter is the economically active population of working age (15–64 years old), that is, the effective labor supply.

The labor force participation rate is the ratio of the economically active population to the working-age population and is used to measure people's participation in economic activities. There are differences in the labor force participation rate among people of different ages, so age should be fully considered in calculating the labor force participation rate.

Research Methods

Based on the above concepts, this chapter use the mathematical notations as follows: P_t represents the total population; t represents time; $P_{i,t}$ means the working-age population of people aged i in t year (the population aged 15–64 is divided into ten groups at intervals of five years old, $i = 1,2,\ldots\ldots 10$); WP_t means the total number of working-age population in year t, i.e. $WP_t = \sum_i^j P_{i,t}$; $S_{i,t}$ represents the proportion of working-age population in age group i in the total population in year t, namely $S_{i,t} = P_{i,t}/P_t$; $w_{i,t}$ shows the proportion of the working-age population in age group i in the total working-age population in year t, i.e. $w_{i,t} = P_{i,t}/WP_t$; $PR_{i,t}$ means the labor force participation rate of age group i in year t. PR_t is the total labor force participation rate, i.e. $PR_t = \sum_i^j w_{i,t} PR_{i,t}$, and L_t is the number of effective labor supply, and the formula is $L_t = \sum_i^j P_{i,t} PR_{i,t} = P_t \sum_i^j s_{i,t} PR_{i,t} = WP_t PR_t$.

An effective labor supply model incorporating human capital can be constructed by considering human capital factors on the basis of effective labor force. h_t is for human capital index in year t, so the effective labor force model including human capital can be written as follows:

$$HL_t = h_t L_t = h_t \sum_i^j P_{i,t} PR_{i,t} = h_t P_t \sum_i^j s_{i,t} PR_{i,t} \tag{1}$$

This formula shows that the effective labor supply incorporating human capital depends on four factors: population number, population structure, labor participation rate and human capital. With factor decomposition, the influence of these factors on the effective labor supply incorporating human capital can be further studied.

Let the effective labor supply incorporating human capital in the initial year be HL_0, and $HL_{t/0}$ is the change of HL from period 0 to period t, so the formula can be written as follows:

$$HL_{t/0} = \frac{HL_t}{HL_0} = \frac{h_t P_t \sum_i^j s_{i,t} \times PR_{i,t}}{h_0 P_0 \sum_i^j s_{i,0} \times PR_{i,0}} \tag{2}$$

Multiply the numerator and denominator at the right end of the above equation, and the factorization formula can be written as follows:

$$HL_{t/0} = \frac{P_t}{P_0} \frac{\sum_i^j s_{i,t} \times PR_{i,0}}{\sum_i^j s_{i,0} \times PR_{i,0}} \times \frac{\sum_i^j s_{i,t} \times PR_{i,t}}{\sum_i^j s_{i,t} \times PR_{i,0}} \frac{h_t}{h_0} \qquad (3)$$

$$HL_{t/0} = PNI \times PSI \times PRI \times HI = PI \times NPI_o$$

Formula (3) decomposes the change of effective labor force including human capital into four factors: population number, population structure, labor participation rate and human capital, denoted by PNI, PSI, PRI and HI, respectively. Among them, population number and structure are demographic factors represented by PI, while labor participation and human capital are non-demographic factors represented by NPI. Thus, the formula can be written as follows $HL_{t/0} = PNI \times PSI \times PRI \times HI = PI \times NPI$.

Assuming that the effective labor supply incorporating human capital increases exponentially over time and all factors are independent from each other, so $HL_t = HL_0 \times \exp\left(t \sum_i^j r_i\right)$ and $HL_{t/0} = e^{tr} = e^{t(r_{PN} + r_{PS} + r_{PR} + r_H)}$. Therefore, the growth rate of effective labor supply with human capital will be as follows:

$$r = r_{PN} + r_{PS} + r_{PR} + r_H \qquad (4)$$

In this formula, mathematical denotations are as follows: r denotes the growth rate of effective labor supply incorporating human capital, $r = \sum r_i$; r_{PN} is the contribution rate of population number; r_{PS} is the contribution rate of population structure; r_{PR} represents the contribution rate of labor participation and r_H means the contribution rate of human capital. Each factor can also be expressed in the form of exponential growth, so as to calculate the contribution of each factor to the growth rate of effective labor supply incorporating human capital. The related formulas are as follows: the contribution rate of population structure can be calculated by $r_{PS} = \frac{1}{t}\ln(\text{PSI})$; the contribution rate of population number can be calculated by $r_{PN} = \frac{1}{t}\ln(\text{PNI})$; the contribution rate of labor participation rate can be calculated by $r_{PR} = \frac{1}{t}\ln(\text{PRI})$, and the contribution rate of human capital can be calculated by $r_H = \frac{1}{t}\ln(\text{HI})$.

Data

This chapter aims to investigate the effect of the universal two-child policy on the future labor supply in China and the development of future labor force. It is also

180 *Labor Supply*

of interest to examine the impact of labor force participation and human capital on the changes of labor supply. The research is mainly based on forecast, including population forecast, labor force participation forecast and human capital forecast, thus data sources of the tables and figures are not further noted.

Forecasts of Labor Force, Labor Force Participation Rate and Human Capital

Labor Force Forecast

There are three population forecast scenarios by different levels of fertility rates. The one with low level of fertility rate forecast assumes that the universal two-child policy is not implemented, and the fertility rate will drop from 1.6 in 2015 to 1.35 in 2035, and then remain unchanged to 2100. The one with medium level of fertility rate shows that the TFR in China will rise from 1.6 in 2015 to 1.7 in 2016–2017, then fall to 1.6 in 2035 and remain unchanged thereafter. The one with high level of fertility rate indicates that the TFR rose from 1.6 in 2015 to 1.7 in 2016–2017, and then to 1.85 in 2035, which will remain unchanged thereafter. In addition, there is only one scenario for mortality, that is, the net international migration assumption is 0, according to the United Nations empirical data. The specific results of population forecast are presented in Chapter 11.

According to the forecast, China's total population will first increase slowly for nearly a decade, and then decrease constantly (Table 11.1). The scenario with low fertility rate is made under the assumption that the universal two-child policy is not implemented. Under this scenario, the total population will increase to 1.402 billion by 2025 and then continue to decline. According to that scenario, the population will be 1.27 billion in the middle of the century and will fall to 680 million by the end of the century. The other two scenarios are based on the universal two-child policy. According to the scenario with medium level fertility rate, the population will increase slowly until 2027 (1.408 billion) and then start to decline rapidly. The total population will be 1.32 billion by the middle of the century and 860 million by the end of the century. The scenario with high fertility rate assumes a relatively high rate. Under this scenario, the size of our population will slowly increase to 2036 (1.416 billion) and then decline slowly. In the middle of the century, the population is projected to be 1.36 billion, and by the end of the century, the total will be 1.06 billion.

According to the forecast, the working-age population will continue to decrease from 2020. Under the scenario with low fertility rate (assuming no universal two-child policy), the working-age population is projected to fall to 760 million by mid-century and further to 330 million by the end of the century. In the scenario with medium fertility rate, the working-age population will continue to decline rapidly, from 780 million by mid-century to 450 million by the end of the century. Under the high scenario, the working-age population declines at a slightly slower rate, from 790 million by mid-century to 580 million by the end of the century. There is little difference in the results of the three scenarios before 2040, and then the difference becomes prominent, and the scenario with low rate becomes increasingly different from the one with medium and high rate. According to the forecast, by the end of the century, the scenario with low rate will have 120 million fewer people than the medium one, and the latter one will have 130 million fewer people than the high scenario (Figure 11.6).

According to the forecast, the proportion of the working-age population will be generally decreased in the future. It is expected to fall to 55% by mid-century. In the scenario with high fertility rate, the proportion will remain at 55% after the 1950s. In the medium one, the working-age share will fall to 52% by the end of the century. As for the scenario with low rate, the working-age share will fall to 49% by the end of the century (Figure 11.7).

Labor Force Participation Rate Forecast

Based on the 2010 Sixth National Census, the changes of labor participation rate in developed countries such as Japan and the social and economic development in China, the future labor participation rate by age is effectively predicted (China's labor participation rate in 2010 is equivalent to Japan's labor participation rate in 1970) (OECD, 2016). The forecast fully considered the impact of education development and the increase of enrollment rate on the reduction of labor force participation rate of the younger age group and took into account the impact of delaying retirement age on improving labor force participation rate of the older age group. The labor force participation rate of the 25–49 age group remained unchanged at the 2010 Sixth National Census (85% for 25–29 and 90% for 30–49). As for the forecast for the younger age group, due to the similarities and different developmental speed of in social economy, education and between China and Japan, China's labor participation rate in 2050 can refer to the level of Japan in 2010. Therefore, the assumptions are as follows: (1) in 2050, the labor force participation rate of the younger age group in China will fall to the level of Japan in 2010. The labor force participation rate of the 15–19 age group will be 16%, and the labor force participation rate of the 20–24 age group will be 69%; (2) The labor force participation rate shows geometric changes with decreasing speed. So between 2010 and 2050, the labor force participation rate of 15- to 19-year olds will fall by

Table 12.1 Labor Force Participation Rate Forecast for Younger Age Group, 2010–2050

	15–19	20–24
2010	33.5	72.8
2015	30.6	72.3
2020	27.9	71.9
2025	25.5	71.4
2030	23.3	70.9
2035	21.3	70.5
2040	19.4	70.0
2045	17.7	69.6
2050	16.2	69.1

1.8% per year, from 33.5% to 16.2%, a decline of 17.3 percentage points. The labor force participation rate for those aged 20 to 24 will decline by 0.13% annually, or 3.7 percentage points, from 72.8% to 69.1% (Table 12.1). After 2050, the level of labor force participation is assumed to remain unchanged.

Due to the similarities between China and Japan in terms of aging and delayed retirement, the labor participation rate of China's advanced age group can be predicted by referring to the situation of Japan (Zhang Shibin, 2014). In addition, considering the gradual approach to delaying retirement, the specific assumptions are as follows: In 2050, the labor participation rate of the aged group will rise to the current level of Japan, and it is assumed that the labor participation rate will increase geometrically, with the growth rate increasing year by year. Thus, from 2010 to 2050, the labor force participation rate of the 50–54 age group will increase from 76.3% to 84.8%, with an annual growth rate of 0.27%. The labor force participation rate of the 55–59 age group will rise from 67.1% to 80.2%, with an annual growth rate of 0.46%. The labor force participation rate of the 60–64 age group will be 62.5%, with an annual growth rate of 0.6%. In addition, the labor force participation rate of the older age group is assumed to remain the same after 2050. The forecast results are as follows (Table 12.2):

In addition, with the formula of the total labor force participation rate of the working-age population, $PR_t = \sum_i^j w_{i,t} PR_{i,t}$, the changes of the total labor force participation rate over time under each forecast scenario can be further calculated. The forecast results showed that from 2015 to 2040, the developmental trend in total labor force participation rate will be like the shape of "V", declining first and then rising, and then fluctuated in stages. The peaks are in 2045, 2065 and 2095, respectively (Figure 12.1). Therefore, the impact of the universal two-child policy on the total labor participation rate should be investigated in different stages, and the impact of age-specific labor participation rate and changes in the age structure of the labor population on the total labor participation rate should be investigated at the same time. By comparing three different fertility scenarios, the one with low fertility rate (based on the assumption that the universal two-child policy had

Table 12.2 Labor Force Participation Rate Forecast for the Older Population Group, 2010–2050

	50–54	55–59	60–64
2010	76.3	67.1	49.5
2015	77.3	68.6	51.0
2020	78.3	70.2	52.5
2025	79.4	71.7	54.0
2030	80.4	73.4	55.6
2035	81.5	75.0	57.3
2040	82.6	76.7	59.0
2045	83.7	78.4	60.7
2050	84.8	80.2	62.5

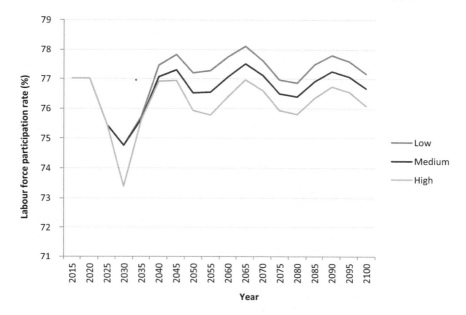

Figure 12.1 Changes in labor force participation rate of working-age population under the low-medium-high scenarios, 2015–2100

not been implemented) has higher total labor force participation than that in the other two scenarios, as the newly born population under the accumulation effect gradually becoming the working-age population after the universal two-child policy fully implemented make the proportion of labor force in younger aged group. Therefore, the total labor force participation rate of the working-age population will decrease significantly.

Human Capital Forecast

The historical data of human capital come from the China Population and Employment Statistics Yearbook. The future human capital data are based on the development of Chinese education and the experience of developed countries. With the data, the human capital index is constructed to reflect the relative changes of human capital level. In this chapter, the average years of education of the employed people are taken as a proxy variable for the level of human capital. With the increase of education expenditure, China's education will continue to rise. However, with the popularization of compulsory education, the popularization of higher education will become difficult and relatively slower, so the growth rate of the average years of schooling will gradually decrease. This chapter makes segmented assumptions about future growth rates. The annual growth rate of the average number of years of education in the workforce is assumed to be 2% from 2015 to 2020, 1% from 2021 to 2030, 0.5% from 2031 to 2040 and 0.25% from 2041 to 2050, and the growth after 2050 remains at 0.1%. Based on the above assumptions, the average years of schooling for employees from 2015 to 2100 is estimated to be 13.57 years by 2050, which is equivalent to the first-year college or university, catching up with developed countries. By the end of this century, the average years of schooling for Chinese employees will reach 14.27. Therefore, from 2015 to 2100, the highest education of the Chinese employed will change from junior high school to senior high school education, and then gradually to college or university, and thus the level of human capital will be significantly improved. The details are as follows (Table 12.3):

In order to have a longitudinal comparison, the human capital index h_t is constructed. The average years of schooling for the employed in 2015 was 10.32 as cardinal number 1, and the human capital index of the following years is equal to the ratio of the average years of schooling of the employed in that year to 10.32. Human capital index can clearly reflect its relative development and thus affect the effective labor supply incorporating human capital. According to the forecast, China's human capital index will increase slowly from 2020 to 2100, but with the

Table 12.3 Average Years of Schooling for the Employed, 2015–2050

Year	Annual Growth Rate (%)	Average Number of Years of Schooling
2015	2.00	10.32
2020	2.00	11.40
2025	1.00	11.98
2030	1.00	12.59
2035	0.50	12.91
2040	0.50	13.23
2045	0.25	13.40
2050	0.25	13.57
2060	0.1	13.71
2070	0.1	13.85
2080	0.1	13.99
2090	0.1	14.13
2100	0.1	14.27

Table 12.4 Human Capital Index for the Employed, 2015–2100

Year	Human Capital Index	Year	Human Capital Index
2015	1.00	2060	1.33
2020	1.10	2065	1.33
2025	1.16	2070	1.34
2030	1.22	2075	1.35
2035	1.25	2080	1.36
2040	1.28	2085	1.36
2045	1.30	2090	1.37
2050	1.31	2095	1.38
2055	1.32	2100	1.38

development of social economy, the growth of education level will slow down after reaching a certain level. The country's human capital index will reach 1.31 in 2050 and 1.38 in 2100. The results are as follows (Table 12.4):

Effective Labor Supply with Human Capital

As purely effective labor supply cannot fully reflect the real level of labor supply, it is necessary to use human capital to evaluate the quality of labor force. This chapter will show the model of effective labor supply incorporating human capital to comprehensively investigate the quantity, structure and quality of labor force. According to the model, effective labor supply incorporating human capital depends on four factors: population number, population structure, labor participation rate and human capital index.

The results of population forecast can be used to calculate the effective labor supply incorporating human capital from 2020 to 2100 (Figure 12.2). It is predicted that the trend of effective labor supply incorporating human capital is similar to that of total population and working-age population. Before 2030, the effective labor supply increases slowly, and there is almost no difference between the three scenarios with different fertility rate. After 2030, the difference gradually becomes prominent, and the overall size continues to shrink. Under the scenario with low fertility rate (assuming no universal two-child policy), the effective labor supply incorporating human capital is projected to be 759 million in 2050 and 357 million

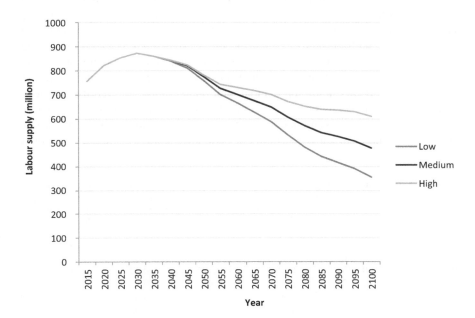

Figure 12.2 Effective labor supply incorporating human capital under the low-medium-high scenarios, 2015–2100

in 2100. Under the scenario with medium fertility rate, the effective labor supply incorporating human capital will be 775 million in 2050 and further decrease to 479 million in 2100. In contrast, under the high fertility scenario, the supply declines more slowly. The supply in 2050 will be 783 million and 611 million in 2100, 132 million more than in the medium fertility rate scenario and 254 million more than the low fertility rate scenario. It can be seen that the implementation of the universal two-child policy can effectively improve the labor supply incorporating human capital.

Decomposition of Influences on Labor Supply

According to the effective labor supply model incorporating human capital, labor supply is influenced by the population number, population structure, labor participation rate and human capital, and each influence is different. This chapter classifies the influence of population number and population structure as demographic influence, and the labor force participation rate and human capital as the non-demographic influence. The influence decomposition under the three scenarios is as follows:

Under the low fertility scenario (assuming that the universal two-child policy is not implemented), various factors have different effects at different stages (Table 12.5). The effective labor supply incorporating human capital in 2030 is 1.15 times that of 2015, an increase of 15%. Demographic factors have a slight convergent effect, in which population number has the amplification effect and population structure has the convergent effect. The amplification effect of non-demographic factors is more significant, among which the labor participation decomposition index is 1.008, and the human capital decomposition index is 1.220, indicating that the amplification effect of human capital is better and more significant. From 2030 to 2050, the effective labor supply incorporating human capital decreases on the whole. At this time, non-demographic factors have an amplifying effect, while demographic factors have a significant convergence effect, which is mainly affected by the population number and demographic structure. From 2015 to 2050, since the population first increase until 2030 and then begin to decrease, the amount

Table 12.5 Influence Decomposition at Each Stage under the Low Fertility Scenario (Based on the Assumption That the Universal Two-Child Policy Is Not Implemented)

Influence Decomposition	2015–2030	2030–2050	2015–2050	2050–2100	2015–2100
HL changes	1.150	0.870	1.002	0.470	0.470
PI	**0.937**	**0.798**	**0.745**	**0.431**	**0.321**
PNI	1.013	0.911	0.923	0.539	0.498
PSI	0.925	0.877	0.807	0.800	0.645
NPI	**1.230**	**1.098**	**1.347**	**1.053**	**1.430**
PRI	1.008	1.022	1.036	1.000	1.036
HI	1.220	1.074	1.300	1.053	1.380

of effective labor supply incorporating human capital is almost the same during this period, while non-demographic factors, especially human capital, have a significant amplifying effect and demographic factors show a convergent effect. Effective labor supply, including human capital, almost decrease by a half between 2050 and 2100 due to a large convergence of demographic factors, while non-demographic factors still play an amplifying role. From 2015 to 2100, the overall effective labor including human capital decreases by nearly half, which is mainly caused by demographic factors and greatly amplified by the influence of human capital.

In the medium fertility scenario with the universal two-child policy implemented, the amount of overall effective labor supply incorporating human capital increases to a certain extent compared with the scenario in which the universal two-child policy is not implemented, and the developmental trend also increases until 2030, and then start to decrease (Table 12.6). From 2015 to 2030, the population growth rate is 15.3%, among which the decomposition index of demographic influence is 0.924, and the decomposition index of non-demographic influence is 1.227, among which the amplification effect of human capital is obvious. From 2030 to 2050, effective labor including human capital decreases in an overall way, with demographic influence having convergence effect and non-demographic influence having slight amplification effect. The growth rate of effective labor force including human capital is 2.3% from 2015 to 2050, mainly due to the amplifying effect of non-demographic influence, while demographic influence is still convergent, with a decomposition index of 0.754. After 2050, efficient labor including human capital declines rapidly, and the total amount in 2100 is 61.9% of the total amount in 2050. At this time, the convergence effect of demographic influence is very significant, and the decomposition index of non-demographic influence is 1.053. Overall, at the end of this century, the effective labor supply incorporating human capital is 63.3% of that in 2015. Demographic influence has a great convergence effect, while non-demographic influence, especially human capital, has a great amplification impact. Its 1.38 decomposition index indicates that human capital is of great significance to effective labor supply.

In the high fertility scenario with the universal two-child policy implemented, the effective labor supply incorporating human capital still increases first and then decreases, and the speed of change in each stage is slow (Table 12.7). At the end of

Table 12.6 Influence Decomposition at Each Stage under the Medium Fertility Scenario

Influence Decomposition	2015–2030	2030–2050	2015–2050	2050–2100	2015–2100
HL changes	1.153	0.887	1.023	0.619	0.633
PI	**0.924**	**0.826**	**0.754**	**0.583**	**0.443**
PNI	1.023	0.939	0.955	0.653	0.628
PSI	0.903	0.880	0.790	0.892	0.705
NPI	**1.227**	**1.096**	**1.342**	**1.053**	**1.424**
PRI	1.006	1.021	1.033	1.000	1.032
HI	1.220	1.074	1.300	1.053	1.380

188　Labor Supply

Table 12.7 Influence Decomposition at Each Stage under the High Fertility Scenario

Influence Decomposition	2015–2030	2030–2050	2015–2050	2050–2100	2015–2100
HL changes	1.153	0.897	1.035	0.780	0.807
PI	**0.937**	**0.826**	**0.773**	**0.735**	**0.571**
PNI	1.028	0.965	0.992	0.777	0.771
PSI	0.911	0.856	0.779	0.945	0.740
NPI	**1.230**	**1.095**	**1.339**	**1.053**	**1.414**
PRI	1.008	1.019	1.030	1.000	1.024
HI	1.220	1.074	1.300	1.053	1.380

the century, the effective workforce including human capital is 80.7% of its 2015 level. In 2050, effective labor supply including human capital is 1.035 times that of 2015, an increase of 3.5%. The analysis at different stages shows the developmental trend and rule same as that of the medium fertility scenario.

In short, the implementation of universal two-child policy has a significant role in improving the effective labor supply incorporating human capital. On the whole, the decomposition results show the decomposition index of population influence less than 0 and the decomposition index of non-population influence greater than 0 in the three scenarios with different fertility rates. It can be seen that population influence has a convergent effect on the effective labor supply with human capital, while the non-population influence has an amplifying effect. Among them, the impact of population number increases after the implementation of the universal two-child policy, a sign that indicate the important role of the universal two-child policy in boosting the population number. In addition, the amplification effect of human capital is very significant, which shows the importance of human capital to effective labor supply.

In addition, the contribution of each influence to the growth rate of efficient labor force including human capital is further investigated. When the contribution rate of each influence is greater than 0, it means that its contribution is positive. When the factor contribution rate is less than 0, it means that its contribution is negative. The decomposition results of growth rate are as follows (Table 12.8):

At different stages, the contribution of each influence to the growth rate of effective labor supply incorporating human capital is different. In the three scenarios, the growth rate of effective labor supply incorporating human capital from 2015 to 2050 is positive, while the rate from 2050 to 2100 is negative. This result is related to the changes of the total population number and the trend of the effective labor force including human capital. On the whole, the contribution of demographic influence to the growth rate of effective labor supply with human capital is negative, while the contribution of non-demographic influence is positive. In addition, with the implementation of the universal two-child policy, the growth rate of effective labor supply incorporating human capital significantly increases.

Table 12.8 Influence Decomposition of the Growth Rate of Effective Labor Supply Incorporating Human Capital under the Low-Medium-High Scenarios

	Scenario with Low Fertility Rate		Scenario with Medium Fertility Rate		Scenario with High Fertility Rate	
Influence decomposition	2015–2050	2050–2100	2015–2050	2050–2100	2050–2100	2050–2100
HL growth rate r	0.0100	−1.5800	0.0337	−0.9758	0.0984	−0.5125
PI	**−0.8411**	**−1.6833**	**−0.8068**	**−1.0791**	**−0.7356**	**−0.6158**
Population number r_{PN}	−0.2289	−1.2361	−0.1316	−0.8524	−0.0229	−0.5046
Population structure r_{PS}	−0.6127	−0.4463	−0.6735	−0.2286	−0.7136	−0.1131
NPI	**0.8511**	**0.1033**	**0.8405**	**0.1033**	**0.8341**	**0.1033**
Labor participation rate r_{PR}	0.1010	0.0000	0.0928	0.0000	0.0845	0.0000
Human capital r_H	0.7496	0.1033	0.7496	0.1033	0.7496	0.1033

Concluding Remarks

China is experiencing a great population transition, and the changes in population number and population structure directly affect the labor supply. The number of working-age population has a downward trend. Demographic dividend turns into population debt, and labor shortage and structural aging will become obstacles to economic development, and the implementation of the universal two-child policy will alleviate this situation to a certain extent. In addition, labor supply is not only related to the number and structure of population but also related to the population quality, and human capital is very critical. Therefore, this chapter constructs an effective labor supply model incorporating human capital from four aspects of population number, structure, labor participation rate and human capital, so as to compare the total population size, working-age population size and labor supply with human capital under the three scenarios with low, medium and high fertility rates. Furthermore, the four influences on changing effective labor supply incorporating human capital are investigated through influence decomposition.

According to the forecast, the working-age population will continue to decline after 2020. Under the low fertility rate scenario (based on the assumption that universal two-child policy is not implemented), the working-age population is projected to fall to 760 million by mid-century and further to 330 million by the end of the century. Under the medium fertility rate scenario, the working-age population will continue to decline rapidly, from 780 million by mid-century to 450 million by the end of the century. Under the high fertility rate scenario, the working-age population declines at a slightly slower rate, from 790 million by mid-century to 580 million by the end of the century. There is little difference among the results of the three scenarios before 2040, but after 2040 the difference becomes prominent, and the result of low fertility rate scenario will be far more different from the medium and high fertility rate scenarios. By the end of the century, the low rate scenario will have 120 million fewer people than the medium one, and the latter will have 130 million fewer people than the high fertility rate scenario. Therefore, the implementation of the universal two-child policy can significantly improve the scale of China's labor force population. In the scenario with medium fertility rate, the working-age population will be 12 million more in 2050 and 118 million more in 2100 than if the universal two-child policy were not implemented. Under the scenario with high fertility rate, the working-age population will be 37 million more in 2050 and 246 million more in 2100 than without the universal two-child policy.

Changes in labor force participation affect the effective labor supply. The trend of labor force participation rate in the future is that the development of education and the improvement of enrollment rate make the labor force participation rate of the younger group (15–24 years old) decrease, while the delayed retirement policy makes the labor force participation rate of the older group (50–64 years old) increase. From 2015 to 2040, the development of total labor participation rate shows a "V" shape, whose trend first shows decreasing and then increasing, and then has periodical fluctuation, with peaks in 2045, 2065 and 2095, respectively. Therefore, the impact of the universal two-child policy on the total labor participation rate should be investigated in stages. At the same time, the influence of the age-specific labor force participation rate and the change of the age structure of the labor force on the total labor force participation rate is investigated. By comparing three different scenarios, the one with low rate (based on the assumption that the universal two-child policy is not implemented) has higher total labor participation rate than the scenario with medium fertility rate, and the latter has higher participation rate than the scenario with higher fertility rate, as the newly born population under the accumulation effect gradually becoming the working-age population after the universal two-child policy fully implemented make the proportion of labor force in younger aged group. Therefore, the total labor force participation rate of the working-age population decreases significantly.

With the development of education, science and technology, the development of human capital has become an important factor affecting labor productivity. As a proxy variable of human capital, the average years of schooling for the employed can effectively reflect labor quality. The forecast shows that the average years of schooling for future workers will increase year by year, reaching 13.57 years in 2050, and the human capital index will be 1.31 (1.31 times of 2015), and 14.27 years in 2100, and the human capital index will be 1.38 (1.38 times of 2015). As can be seen, human capital increases significantly.

Effective labor supply with human capital can better reflect the development of labor force. With human capital, the effective labor supply improves obviously. In 2050, the effective labor supply with human capital in the medium scenario increases by 160 million compared with the low scenario, and the supply in the high plan increases by 240 million compared with the low plan. In 2100, the supply in the medium scenario increases by 120 million compared with that in the low scenario, and the supply in the high plan increases by 250 million compared with that in the low plan. It can be seen that the universal two-child policy improves the effective labor supply incorporating human capital. In addition, after considering the influence of human capital, the total effective labor supply increases significantly, indicating that the improvement of human capital can greatly makes up for the negative impact of the decline in the number of working-age population.

The implementation of universal two-child policy can significantly improve the effective labor supply incorporating human capital. On the whole, the population influence decomposition results are all less than 0, while the non-population influence decomposition are all greater than 0 under the three scenarios. It can be seen that the population influence has a convergent effect on the effective labor supply with human capital, while the non-population factor has an amplifying effect. Among them, the impact of population number has increased after the implementation of the universal two-child policy, a sign that indicate the important role of the universal two-child policy in boosting the population number. In addition, the amplification effect of human capital is very significant, which shows the importance of human capital to effective labor supply.

Stable labor supply is necessary for economic growth, which involves many aspects of the size, structure and quality of labor force. At present, fully implementing the two-child policy is conducive to slowing down the decline in labor force size and aging structure in the future, which is of great significance for stabilizing labor supply. However, the impact of the universal two-child policy on the labor force cannot be shown in the short term. The negative impact of declining labor force can be well compensated by improving labor participation rate and human capital. Education is a double-edged sword. On the one hand, it can reduce the participation rate of young workers, and on the other hand, it can improve the knowledge and skills of the workforce. In the long run, the promotion of human capital is crucial for promoting labor productivity and economic growth. Therefore, with current universal two-child policy, it is necessary to increase investment in education, promote the development of human capital to promote qualitative change by giving full play to the advantage of China's labor supply and to fuel the shift from extensive economic development to intensive development.

References

OECD. 2016. OECD Labour Force Statistics 2016. https://doi.org/10.1787/oecd_lfs-2016-en.

Zhang Shibin. 2014. Retirement Age Policy Adjustment: Japan's Experience and Implications for China. *Modern Japanese Economy* 1: 66–75.

13 Aging Population

China is entering a period of rapid population aging featuring with huge size and rapid growth of the elderly population, and rapid pace of aging. With the largest elderly population in the world, China's aging trend will be the fastest of any comparable population, a trend that is determined by the process of its demographic transition. It has been shown in the previous chapters that the universal two-child policy has a weak impact on population aging and has no impact on the size of the elderly population before 2075–2080. The change in the size of the elderly population is more important than aging in terms of the design and improvement of medical and social security system, and the impact on economic and social development. Therefore, this chapter will discuss the future evolution process and characteristics of China's aging population and the size of the elderly population based on the trend of population aging and the size of the elderly population against the backdrop of the universal two-child policy.

Research Methods and Data

In order to reveal the relationship between the rate of fertility transition and the rate of population aging, we used macropopulation simulation method, based on the stable population model, to investigate the trend of population aging under different processes of fertility decline. While promoting population aging, fertility decline also changes the family and kinship structure of the elderly population. Within the elderly population at different life stages and under different fertility levels, we also used population microsimulation method to examine the family structure, the number and structure of relatives. In examining the heterogeneity of the elderly population, we used forecasting cohort analysis to reveal different trends in health and education among the elderly population.

In addition to our research group's long-term trend projections of China's population development, this chapter also used the global population projections of the United Nations Population Division. The United Nations Population Division updates global, regional and country population estimates and projections every two years, with the latest revisions released in June 2019 (United Nations, 2019). In this chapter, we used the results of population projections. At the same time, the difference between the two sets of population projections is mainly reflected in the

DOI: 10.4324/9781003429661-13

assumption of the fertility rate. The fertility rate given by the UN medium scenario is 1.70–1.77 in this century, while the fertility rate of our research group is about 1.6. Nevertheless, the two sets of population forecast data are consistent in reflecting the evolution pattern and long-term trend of population aging in China.

Irreversible Aging Population

Demographic Transition Will Inevitably Lead to Aging Population

Population aging is the inevitable result of population transition. The demographic transition, consisting of an initial decline in mortality from a high level to a low level, followed by a same sustained decline in fertility, brings about not only major changes in population size and growth but also profound changes in the age structure. Demographic transition is a universal law of human society. In the 21st century, all countries in the world have been or are being affected by demographic transition. Some scholars believe that population transition is an exogenous process, which occurs in different social and economic environments with various cultural and political systems. Population transition is one of the most significant changes in human society in the past 300 years. It has been playing an important role in urbanization, urban development, the formation of the modern world and social and economic development, etc. These effects come from two inevitable trends of the transition. One is population growth, and the other is population aging.

Fertility rate remains high even as the mortality rate has fallen, and the speed of the decline in mortality rate and the time gap between the declines in mortality rate and fertility rate exert impact on population growth. Therefore, a decline in mortality rates can trigger a demographic transition and population growth. The surge in world population since the 1950s is largely the result of a rapid decline in mortality rates and the high fertility rates for a long time in developing regions. Population growth brought about by declining mortality rate puts pressure on the survival and development of families and societies, gradually creating incentives for fertility decline. Fertility decline has an important impact on population growth and structure. The impact also depends on the rate of fertility decline. Declining fertility has changed the trend of population growth, and it has also led to an aging population.

Population aging is the inevitable trend and result of population transition. The causal relationship between demographic transition or fertility transition and population aging is deterministic. The decline in fertility leads directly to fewer births. As fertility rates continue to fall and remain low, the number of births each year continues to decline, and cohort shifts result in a smaller population of children and adolescents. The population pyramid shows population aging at the bottom, that is, shrinking at the bottom, which will lead to a higher proportion of the elderly population. Besides, as the birth cohort in the high fertility period before the fertility decline gradually grows old, the size of the elderly population expands, leading to the aging at the top of the population pyramid and further significantly increasing the proportion of the elderly population. In the post-demographic transition phase, when birth and death rates are at a low level, the growth of population is very slow or even stops, and the elderly population of all age groups is the fastest. This is also related to the fact that most of the decline in mortality occurred in older age groups. Many developed countries have gone through this process, and China is going through this.

The process and pace of population aging varies widely across the world. History and related experience show that the later a country modernizes, the faster it modernizes. Countries that have a later demographic transition tend to have a faster transition, and thus, they experience faster-aging population. Post-modernization countries directly use the modernization achievements created by developed countries, so that their population transition is much faster. At the same time, the government's intervention can also greatly accelerate the process of population transition.

China's demographic transition began with a decline in mortality, even before the founding of the People's Republic of China. After the founding, China enjoyed peace and security without war and greatly improved its medical and health conditions, and its mortality rate declined rapidly, ushering in a substantial demographic transition. The fertility rate remained high in the 1950s and 1960s as the mortality rate continued to decline. Although the rapid transition from high to low fertility rates began with the introduction of the national family planning policy in the 1970s, studies have shown that fertility declines began in the 1950s among certain segments of the population, such as the more educated. As the Chinese government vigorously implemented the family planning policy across the country in the early 1970s, China's fertility rate has fallen rapidly. Studies have shown that since the 1990s, when there was a continuous decline in fertility, the role of family planning policy has been weakened, while the role of social and economic development has been strengthened. Since 2000, social and economic development has played a decisive role in the trend of low fertility. Despite the fact that the Chinese government has continuously adjusted the family planning policy since 2013 and implemented the selective and universal two-child policy, especially the latter one, China's second-child fertility rate has risen significantly, leading the increase in overall fertility rate. However, the effect would last for a short time, and the low fertility level and its developmental trend would remain. Therefore, China's population aging trend will not change. And the transition has been greatly accelerated by the government's one-child policy. So an accelerated fertility transition is bound to lead to an accelerated population aging.

In order to further understand the relationship between the rate of fertility decline and the rate of population aging, Figure 13.1 shows the simulation results of the relationship. The initial simulated population shows stability with a total fertility rate (TFR) of 6.1 and an average life expectancy of 40 years for women and 37.3 years for men (The mortality level 9 in Coale-Demeny west regional model life table). Less than 5% of the population is aged 60 or above. In the simulation from this initial population, the mortality rate is only calculated in one scenario, that is, from the initial year (year 0), and the rate continues to decline in accordance with the United Nations medium-high speed decline, therefore, the average female life expectancy will rise from 40 years in year 0 to 87.1 years in the 150th year, whereas that of men will rise from 37.3 years in year 0 to 81.9 years in the 150th year. The fertility rate is set up in four scenarios, namely, the TFR will decline from the 20th year to the replacement level (2.1 TFR) in 20 years (fast), 40 years (medium fast), 60 years (medium slow) and 80 years (slow) and then remain at the replacement level until the end of the simulation.

Figure 13.1 clearly shows that although the four fertility scenarios have simultaneous fertility decline, the faster the fertility decline, the earlier and faster the aging occurred. For example, under the scenario of rapid decline, the proportion of the population aged 60 and above reaches 10% in the 60th year when the rate has been declining for 40 years. The proportion of the population aged 60 and above reaches 10% in the 68th, 76th and 83rd years, respectively, under the conditions of rapid, moderate and slow decline in fertility rate. The difference between the four scenarios is about eight years, and the fertility transition has been completed under the fast and medium fast scenario, while the fertility transition is close to completion under the medium and slow scenarios. It takes 23 years, 24 years, 26 years and 29 years, respectively, for the proportion of the population aged 60 and above to increase from 10% to 20%. The faster the fertility rate falls, the less time it takes for the proportion of the elderly population to double. Across the world, the rate of fertility decline in China is similar to the fast scenario. The rate of fertility decline in many developing countries is similar to the scenarios between fast and medium fast ones, while that rate in a few developed countries is between medium and slow, and the rate in most developed countries is above slow. Figure 13.1

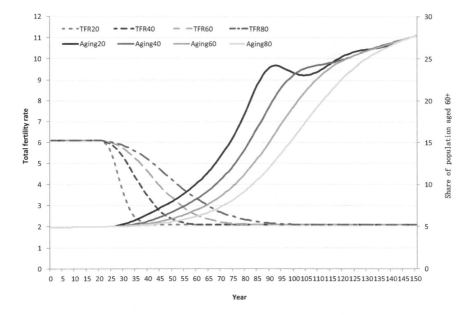

Figure 13.1 Simulation of the relationship between fertility decline and population aging

Source: Author's simulation results.

could reflect the relationship between fertility decline and aging in most countries around the world.

Universal Population Aging in the 21st Century

The 21st century is a century of aging populations. With the globalization of fertility transition and the continuous decline in middle-aged and elderly mortality, population aging will continue to occur globally, and the aging process is accelerating. According to the data from the United Nations, in 1950, the elderly above 65 only took up 5.1% of the world's population, whereas this proportion had increased to 8.3% by 2015 (Figure 13.2). The number of elderly people in the world increased from 130 million in 1950 to 610 million in 2015. Before the 1980s, the growth rate of the world's elderly population was basically same as the world's total population, and since the 1980s, the former one has been increasingly faster than the latter one. In 2015, the world's population grew by 1.1%, while the elderly population grew by 3.2%. By the end of the century, more than one-fifth (22.7%) and possibly 30% of the world's population will be aged 65 or above.

Developed regions are leading the process of global population aging. In 1950, the proportion of elderly people in the developed regions was 7.7%. In 2015, it rose by 10 percentage points to 17.65%. The size of the elderly population has correspondingly increased from 63 million to 220 million. In 1950, the elderly population in the rich world was just a quarter of the size of the young; now they

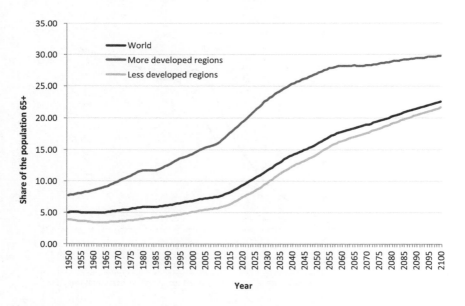

Figure 13.2 Aging trends in the world, more developed and less developed regions, 1950–2100

Source: United Nations. World Population Prospects: The 2019 Revision.

are about the same. Europe is the oldest of the developed regions, with 17.6% of the population elderly. Indeed, of all ages in Europe, only the elderly are growing. Japan has the oldest population in the world, with 26.3% of its population in 2015 to be older people and a median age of 46.5 years (that is, half of its population is over 46 years old).

Developed regions are also moving from aging to advanced aging. In developed regions, the proportion of people aged 80 or above rose from less than 1% in 1950 to 4.7% in 2015. The proportion of the advanced older population (age 80+) in the elderly population increased from 12.9% in 1950 to 26.8% in 2015. The size of the advanced older population increased more than sixfold during that period. The elderly aged 80+ are the fastest-growing population of all age groups.

Compared with developed regions, the aging rate in developing regions is still slow. From 1950 to 2015, the proportion in developing regions only rose from 3.8% to 6.4%. However, the growth rate of the elderly population is significantly faster than that in developed regions. From 1950 to 2015, the size of the elderly population increased from 66 million to 390 million. In 1950, the size of the elderly population in developing and developed regions was almost equal. By 2015, the size of the elderly population in developing regions was 1.8 times that in developed regions. The rate of aging in many developing countries is increasing and will continue to increase. In some countries with high fertility rate and high population growth rate, the potential of aging in the future will be huge.

Figure 13.2 shows that the world aging accelerates. The next 40 years will be the fastest-aging period in developed regions, while developing regions are experiencing fast population aging until the end of the century, especially in the last half century. In the next 40 years, the proportion of elderly people in the world's population will double. Their proportion in developed regions will exceed 20% by 2022 and close to 30% by the end of the century. The proportion of the elderly population in developing regions will double in the next 30 years to more than 20% by the 2080s. Even countries with the youngest population today will become an aging society by the end of the century.

China's Irreversible Aging Population

Since the early 1990s, China's fertility has been below replacement level and continued to decline to very low level. In this context the age structure of China's population has changed greatly. The proportion of working-age population has increased significantly, and the proportion of children population continued to decline. The proportion of working-age population reached 70% during the fifth census in 2000. The median age has been rising since the 1980s, and the population is aging.

Since the 1970s, the proportion of Chinese older population has been rising slowly, but it started to accelerate in the 1990s. According to the results of the fifth National Census in 2000, the proportion of the population aged 65 and above reached 7%, an increase of 1.4 percentage points over 1990. At the same time, the proportion of children in the population fell by nearly 5 percentage points, and that of working-age population rose by nearly 4 percentage points. In 2000 the bottom of the population pyramid shrank further, while the top expanded. According to international practice, in 2000, China started to become an aging society.

Since 2000, China's fertility rate has been at a very low level, with the TFR remaining at about 1.6, much lower than the replacement level of 2.1, and the trend of population growth has been sluggish. The results of the sixth census in 2010 show that the age structure of the Chinese population continues to become old, and the proportion of children aged 0–14 years continues to decrease, reaching 16.6% in 2010, while the proportion of working-age population increases to 74.5%, and the median age continues to rise to about 35 years old.

At the same time, the fifth census in 2000 marked that since China entered the aging society, the aging population has been deepening, and the speed has been accelerating. According to the sixth National Census in 2010, the number of people aged 60 and above in China reached 178 million, accounting for 13.26% of the total population, an increase of 3 percentage points over 2000. Among them, the population aged 65 or above was 119 million, accounting for 8.87%, an increase of 1.7 percentage points over 2000. Both the elderly population and its proportion grew faster than those in the previous decade.

With the fertility rate decreasing, the people born in the baby boom during the early years of the People's Republic gradually become old, and thus, aging population is accelerating. According to the population forecast of the United Nations medium variant (Table 13.1), by 2041, the elderly population aged 60 years and above will account for more than 30% of the total, and China will become a severely aging country at that time with that proportion increasing to 34.6% by 2050. The proportion of the population aged 65 and above will reach 26.1% in 2050. The number of elderly people aged 60 and above will exceed 200 million in 2014, 300 million in 2026, 400 million in 2034, and nearly 500 million in 2050. The number of elderly people aged 65 and above will exceed 200 million in 2025, 300 million in 2036 and 370 million in 2050.

The long-term development of China's population from author's population projections is slightly different from that of the United Nations (Table 13.1). The United Nations' median variant assumes the TFR between 1.7 and 1.77, while in our prediction the fertility rate is assumed to be around 1.6. Our prediction shows that by 2024, China will have 300 million people aged 60 and above, accounting for nearly 20% of the total population. Among them, the number of people aged 65 or above will reach 200 million by 2022, accounting for 14.36%. By 2041, the population aged 60 and above will account for more than 30% of the total population, at which time China will be heavily aging, and the proportion will further increase to 34.6% by 2050. The proportion of the population aged 65 and above will reach 26.7% in 2050. The number of people aged 60 and above will exceed 400 million in 2032 and nearly 500 million in 2050. The number of people aged 65 and above will exceed 300 million by 2034 and 380 million by 2050.

Although the speed of aging in China fluctuates, the aging in the next 40 years will be at a high speed. It accelerated significantly from 2010 to 2020 and will be increasingly faster from 2020 to 2035. From 2035 to 2050, it will develop in depth

Table 13.1 Trends of Elderly Population in China (Million), 2017–2100

	United Nations			Author		
	60+	*65+*	*80+*	*60+*	*65+*	*80+*
2017	227	147	24	241	158	29
2018	234	156	25	249	167	31
2019	241	164	26	253	177	32
2020	250	172	27	257	186	33
2025	300	205	31	315	215	41
2030	364	247	41	380	265	54
2035	414	302	60	426	321	75
2040	434	344	72	444	358	85
2045	449	356	90	460	367	109
2050	485	366	115	492	376	134
2055	488	397	132	486	402	145
2060	479	398	131	464	394	140
2065	465	388	133	441	372	139
2070	454	376	155	431	351	156
2075	448	367	155	428	345	151
2080	442	363	149	419	345	138
2085	431	360	142	402	339	128
2090	420	353	141	383	327	131
2095	410	346	146	369	313	139
2100	403	339	151	359	301	141

Source: Author's prediction and the United Nations. World Population Prospects: The 2019 Revision.

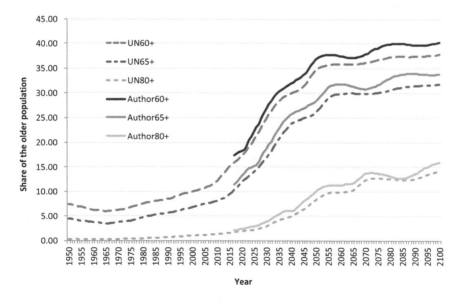

Figure 13.3 Trend of population aging in China, 1950–2100

Source: Author's prediction of population and the United Nations. World Population Prospects: The 2019 Revision.

(Figure 13.3). According to the prediction of the United Nations, before 2020, the proportion of the elderly population aged 60 years old and above will increase by 0.4–0.5 percentage points every year. It will continue to climb after 2020 from 0.5 percentage points every year to the peak in 2029 with an increase of 0.90 percentage points. After that, it will still develop rapidly but will slow down. As the birth cohort of the third birth boom after the founding of the People's Republic is becoming old, the aging speed will accelerate again. In 2048, the proportion of the elderly population aged 60 years and above will increase by 0.74 percentage points compared with the previous year, which will become another peak.

In the next 40 years, as the baby boomers after the founding of the People's Republic are becoming old, the proportion of the elderly population aged 60–79 years old will gradually rise, among which the number of the young aged 60–64 years old will fluctuate and remain at about 100 million after 2040. The elderly population aged 65–79 years will continue to grow in the next 30 years, but there will be a decline in growth rate. After 2040, The growth rate will be negative and their numbers began to dwindle. In the next 40 years, the number and proportion of the elderly aged 80 and above will continue to increase, and the population growth rate will be very high. When the baby boomers turn 80 in 2025, the proportion of elderly of advanced older age will rise rapidly. China will face an increasingly aging population.

The life expectancy in China reached 76.3 years in 2015. With the rapid medical development, the life expectancy will increase as before, and the growth of longevity and health will further accelerate the aging trend. By 2050, the number of Chinese aged 80 and above will rise to 120 million, nearly seven times that of 2010. From 2030, there will be a large number of people of advanced older age. The proportion of people aged 80 years and over in the elderly population aged 60 years and over will increase from 11.6% in 2030 to 24.5% in 2050, which will more than double in 20 years.

In the next four decades, the aging rate will be accelerated twice. The proportion of the population aged 60 and above will increase by 12 percentage points between 2020 and 2035, with an average annual increase of 0.5 to 0.9 percentage points. From 2035 to 2045, the added value of percentage will decrease and the aging rate will slow down. After 2045, the rate of aging will accelerate again. From 2045 to 2052, the proportion of the population aged 60 and above will increase by 5 percentage points, with an average annual increase of 0.5–0.8 percentage points. The two changes in the rate of aging correspond to the time when the baby boom cohorts reach old age.

After the rapid aging from 2020 to 2045, the proportion of the population aged 60 and above will reach more than 30% and the proportion of the population aged 65 and above will reach more than 25%. The proportion of the elderly aged 80 and above will exceed 5% and will close to 9% by the middle of this century. By 2050, one in three people in China will be over 60 years old, one in four will be over 65 years old and one in ten will be over 80 years old. The acceleration will make population aging severe.

In the second half of this century, China's aging population will be at a high level. The proportion of the population aged 60 and over will continue to increase by 3 percentage points, reaching 38% by the end of the century. The share of the population aged 65 and over and 80 and over will both continue to increase by about 6 percentage points, reaching 32% and 14%, respectively, by the end of the century. The aging trend will be driven mainly by declining mortality rates, as fertility will remain stable at low levels, and meanwhile, UN assumes a slow, slight increase in fertility and, therefore, there will be a small increase in aging upon its high level.

The aging population will have a significant impact on the potential support ratio. The potential support ratio is the ratio between the population aged 25–64 and the population aged 65 and above, that is, each elderly people aged 65 and above can receive the support from how many people aged 25–64, reflecting the burden of the elderly population on the population that can provide support. Figure 13.4 shows that the potential support ratio increased until 1965 and then turned to decline sharply until 2050. It is now down to around 5, half of what it was before 1965. Compared with Japan and Europe, China's potential support ratio is still high. Japan has the lowest potential support ratio in the world at 1.8. European countries are mostly below 3. By 2050, 48 countries in Europe, North America, East and Southeast Asia including China will have potential support ratios below 2. Actually by the 1990s, China's potential support ratio had fallen further to 1.4.

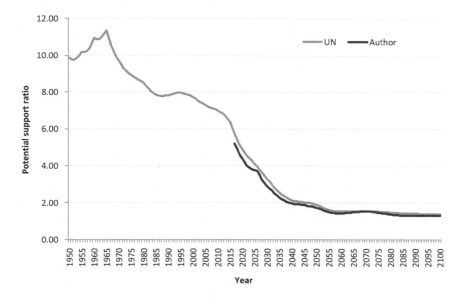

Figure 13.4 China's potential support ratio, 1950–2100

Source: Author's prediction of population and the United Nations. World Population Prospects: The 2019 Revision.

Wavy Development of Aging

Wavy Process of Fertility Transition Determines the Wavy Development of Aging

The process of population aging is closely related to population transition. On the one hand, the rate of population aging depends mainly on the rate of fertility decline during the demographic transition. On the other hand, the growth and change of the elderly population reflects the movement of the birth cohorts under different fertility rate. During the 200 years of population transition in Western countries, the decline of fertility rate was relatively slow, and thus, the size of birth cohorts did not undergo drastic changes, resulting in a relatively gradual population aging. The situation in China is very different from that in the West. Before the fertility transition in the 1950s and 1960s, due to political, economic and social changes, the fertility rate experienced huge fluctuations and the size of birth cohorts have huge differences. In the process of fertility transition from 1970s to 1990s, due to the change of fertility policy, the influence of population inertia and the rapid development of economy and society, fertility and size of the birth cohorts fluctuated considerably. Since the 21th century, China has been experiencing stable changes of fertility rate. Although the low fertility rate fluctuated due to the zodiac preference and the implementation of the two-child policy, but the fluctuation was much less than the previous ones. The magnitude of fluctuations in fertility during the demographic transition will essentially determine the magnitude of fluctuations in the size of older people cohort decades later. Therefore, the changes and fluctuations of the scale of the birth cohorts reflected in Figure 13.5 in the past few decades, to a great extent, also reflect the changes and fluctuations of China's elderly population cohort after 2010.

It is noted that some studies using census and mini-census data asserted that the China's low fertility trends were characterized by constantly falling fertility rate as they found that the TFR in 2000, 2010 and 2015 was falling to increasingly lower levels (Guo Zhigang 2013, 2017; Gu Baochang et al., 2019). In fact, it is not scientific to look at just three years of data to judge the trend of fertility. According to the annual population survey conducted by the National Bureau of Statistics over the years, the fertility rate also experienced great fluctuations during the 15 years, instead of continuous decreasing. The 2017 National Fertility Survey provided more data to show that China's low fertility process showed fluctuations under the influence of various factors (Chen Wei and Duan Yuanyuan, 2019). The trend of China's low fertility presents a wavy process, which more or less reflects a cyclical fluctuation. However, fluctuations in fertility at low levels have little impact on the future wavy development of population aging. This wavy development will mainly be reflected in the wavy development of the elderly population cohort after several decades due to the alternating evolution of the birth peak and trough in the last century, thus leading to the wavy trend of the elderly growth and proportion.

Wavy Development of the Elderly Population and Aging

Figure 13.5 shows the trend in the size of older population at ages 60, 65 and 80 and the contrast with the number of births a few decades ago. Naturally, these changing patterns are similar, with baby boomers born 60 years ago becoming old after 60 years and living at an advanced older age after 65 and 80 years later, respectively, and vice versa. However, as time went on and mortality rates declined, especially the decline of mortality rate among the middle- and old-age people, cohort attrition reduced substantially. Of those born in the early 1950s, only half lived to old age (60) and only a quarter to advanced older age (80). At present, the elderly cohort has reached nearly 70% of the birth population. The share living to advanced older age takes up 40% of births. By the 2060s, the older population cohort will account for 90% of births, and the population cohort at advanced older age will account for 70% of births. The older population cohort at the end of the century will account for nearly 95% of births, and three-quarters of births will live to the advanced older age. The improvement of survival rates from birth to old age and to advanced older age not only plays an important role in the aging process and the size of growth but also contributes to the wavy development process.

Unlike the cohorts entering old age have obvious fluctuations, the overall size of the elderly population fluctuates only slightly due to the mixing of different cohorts. However, as can be seen from Figure 13.6, the spikes in births in the 1950s, 1960s and the late 1980s all lead to the corresponding peak of the elderly population later. The decline in fertility after the 1990s and the long period of low

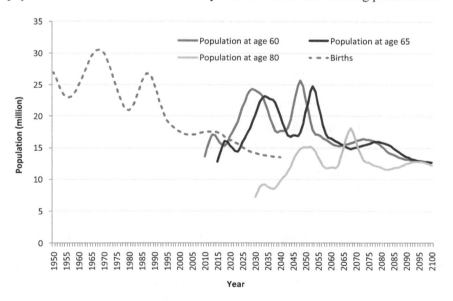

Figure 13.5 Trend of births, population aged 60, 65 and 80 in China, 1950–2100
Source: United Nations. World Population Prospects: The 2019 Revision.

204 Aging Population

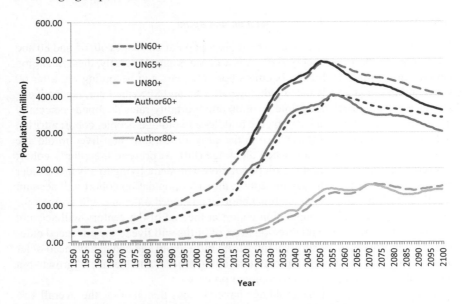

Figure 13.6 Developmental trend of China's elderly population, 2010–2100

Source: Author's prediction of population and the United Nations. World Population Prospects: The 2019 Revision.

fertility will lead to the declining size of the elderly population in the second half of the century.

Increasingly Prominent Advanced Aging Population

The Trend of Advanced Aging Population

As the saying goes hundreds years ago, "there are few people who can live to be 70 years old." However, there are many people of 80 or 90 years old now. Demography often refers to the age of 80 and older as advanced age. With the continuous increasing of life expectancy, the trend of aging and advanced aging are accelerating. Based on the projections of the United Nations, Figure 13.7 calculates and compares the growth rates of the elderly aged 80 years and above, the elderly aged 60 years and above and the elderly aged 60–79 years. In developed countries and developing countries including China, the growth rate of the elderly population is the fastest compared with that of the younger elderly population. Especially from 2030 to 2050, the growth rate of the older elderly population is several times that of the younger elderly population. Accordingly, the proportion of the advanced age in the whole population is rising rapidly. In China, in the first 30 years of this century, the proportion of the elderly aged 80 and above in the elderly population aged 60 and above will be between 10 and 12% and will reach a quarter by the middle of this century, then a third by 2070, and nearly 38% by the end of this century. From

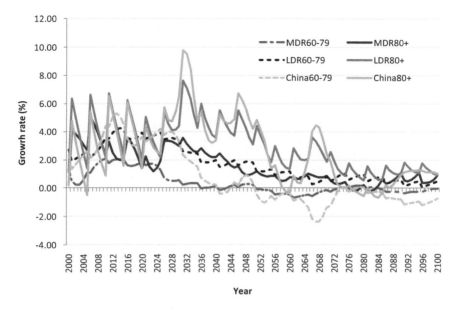

Figure 13.7 Trends in the growth rate of China's elderly population, 2000–2100
Source: United Nations. World Population Prospects: The 2019 Revision.

2030 to 2050, the elderly population will quadruple from 40 million to nearly 120 million. After 2070, it will basically stabilize at 140–150 million (Figure 13.6).

Growing Trend of Centenarians

A further breakdown of the advanced age reveals an even more dramatic increase in centenarians and older. Figure 13.8 shows that in the 21st century, except for some years, the growth rate of centenarians is several times that of the elderly, leading to a trend of substantial growth in the number and proportion of centenarians. According to UN estimates and projections, there were 10,000 centenarians in China at the beginning of the century, rising to 100,000 in 2024, while the number will rise to 1 million by the middle of the century and close to 5 million by the 2090s. At the beginning of the century, centenarians accounted for 0.1% of the advanced age and will rise to 1% in 2060, 2% in 2080 and 3% in 2088. The highest level, 3.4%, will be seen in 2091. The number of centenarians per 10,000 people in the total population is currently 0.05, rising to 0.1 in 2030 and 1.0 in 2060, and above 4.0 in the 1990s. China has the largest population of centenarians in the world in this century, but the number of centenarians per 10,000 people is much lower than that of developed countries such as Japan, the United States and Italy.

As for the number of centenarians after the 2070s, there is a large difference between our research group's population projections and those of the United Nations (Figure 13.9). In fact, until the 2070s, our projections were slightly higher

206 Aging Population

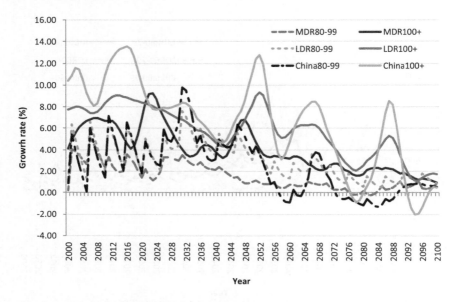

Figure 13.8 Trends in growth rate of centenarian population in China, 2000–2100

Source: United Nations. World Population Prospects: The 2019 Revision.

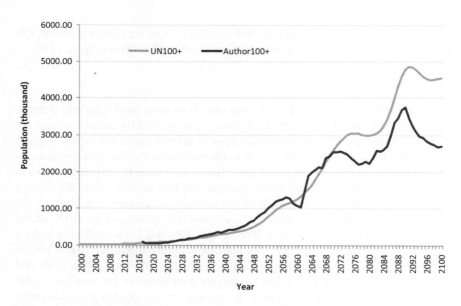

Figure 13.9 Trend of the proportion of centenarians in the elderly population in China, 2000–2100

Source: Author's prediction of population and United Nations. World Population Prospects: The 2019 Revision.

than those of the United Nations. By 2069, the United Nations give higher projections, and the difference is growing. However, even if the difference is large, it will have little effect on the difference in aging and even aging trends, as the population size of centenarians is small. Even based on the low number of centenarians in our study group, the growth rate is still very high. The advanced aging and extremely aging of China's population are very prominent.

Increasing Heterogeneity

Heterogeneity of the Elderly Population

The elderly is a subpopulation of the total one. The so-called "the elderly" just generally summarize the people of that age. In fact, there is no consistent or common problem, as increasingly prominent heterogeneity in this group has brought various problems and needs with different cohorts, situation, condition. Heterogeneity has been shown before when the elderly population is distinguished by their age, i.e. the old, the advanced age and the centenarians. In China, there are significant differences between urban and rural areas, between regions, between rural areas with different levels of development and between different socioeconomic classes. Institutional policy design and services need to address the heterogeneity.

Population aging is about not only the changes in the size and proportion of the elderly population but also the changes of the economic and social structure of the elderly population. Some scholars have proposed the concept of "gerontological transition" to explain the changes in the number and characteristics of the elderly population over time (Rowland, 2012). Gerontological transition interprets the process of population aging as a process of cohort movement: in the cohorts of older population, their number and proportion increase, and in the cohorts of older population with different characteristics such as marriage, occupation, education, income and health condition, cohort movement will further change the composition of the elderly population. The growing elderly population is increasingly heterogeneous.

It is a common phenomenon that the heterogeneity of the elderly population increases in the process of aging, but the situation in China will make this heterogeneity more prominent. China's population transition is very rapid. The rapid decline in fertility rate leads to rapidly decreasing births of different cohorts, and the structure of family relatives under high fertility rate and low fertility rate is very different. Over the past 40 years of reform and opening-up, China has witnessed rapid economic development and become the world's second largest economy. Its per capita GDP has increased by more than 60 times. People's wage income and property income have also increased dramatically, and the gap between the rich and the poor has widened. The income and wealth of China's population are highly heterogeneous. The policy of university enrollment expansion and returns to higher education implemented by China in the late 1990s has effectively make Chinese more educated, ranging from the cohort of younger people to the cohort of older population. Among all levels of education, college-educated population shows the strongest growth. With 120 million people with a college education or above, China has the world's largest college-educated population, according to the Sixth National Population Census of the People's Republic of China. As the cohort moves, the elderly population will also be vastly more educated. The great changes of China's society and population are rare in human history, and its aging process will also be rare in the world. In this process, the heterogeneity will also be very prominent.

Aging Population and Increasing Heterogeneity in the Elderly Population

With the aging process, the heterogeneity in China's elderly population will continue to increase. The heterogeneity involves many aspects such as economy, society and population. However, due to limited data, it is impossible to analyze all aspects, even the very important ones. According to the data and the feasibility of prediction, we selected the health condition, education background and family structure of the elderly population for analysis and prediction and investigated the differences and changing trends in these aspects of the elderly population in the aging process.

Data from the 2005 mini-census, the 2010 mini-census and the 2015 mini-census show that the health condition of China's elderly population has remained basically unchanged over the past ten years and even slightly decreased from the self-rated health condition. Data from the Chinese Longitudinal Healthy Longevity Study also showed that their health condition did not improve from 2002 to 2014 in terms of self-rated health, activities of daily living and instrumental activities of daily living. In addition, two international studies have shown that the health condition of the elderly has improved very little in both developed and developing countries, while in some low- and middle-income countries, including China, between the early 2000s and early 2010s, disease expansion happened among the elderly (Sudharsanan and Bloom, 2018). But life expectancy has risen in various degrees. Even if the spread of disease leads to an increase in unhealthy life expectancy, with the development of medical technology, older people will have more means of subsistence rather than less.

Data from the 2015 Mini-census show that 2.6% of people aged 60 and above are unable to take care of themselves. Of course, there are big differences among the elderly. The proportion of people aged 60 to 64 who fail to take care of themselves is only 0.8%, while the proportion of people aged 80 and over who cannot take care of themselves is nearly 10%. In 2015, the number of elderly people aged 60 and above who could not take care of themselves is 5.15 million. According to the trend calculation, the proportion of elderly people who cannot take care of themselves remained unchanged and the proportion of elderly people who cannot take care of themselves continued to decline. How to explain the proportion of the elderly who cannot take care of themselves? According to data from the 2010 census, the rate is highly correlated with mortality. Figure 13.10 shows that although there is not a linear relationship between the rate and the mortality rate, there is a strong quadratic relationship. Therefore, we predicted the decline in the

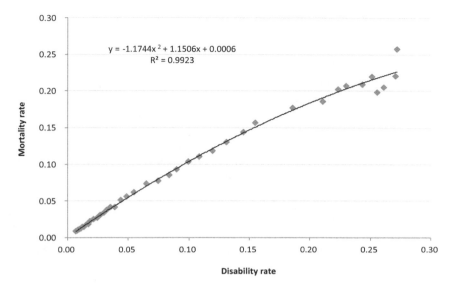

Figure 13.10 Relationship by age between disability rate and mortality rate of the elderly in China, the 2010 Chinese Census

rate of self-reliance based on the decline in the future mortality rate of the elderly population.

The United Nations World Population Prospects 2019 provides the life tables of each country within the forecast period. Figure 13.11 shows the death probability of the elderly population by age in China's life table in each period of this century. The absolute decline in the death probability of the advanced older age is significantly larger than that of the relatively younger people, while the relative decline is smaller. According to the decreasing proportion of the death probability of China's elderly population in each period, the rate and the number of the elderly population who cannot take care of themselves are calculated. Table 13.2 shows the prediction of the proportion of elderly people who cannot take care of themselves. By the middle of this century, the proportion of elderly people under 75 years old who cannot take care of themselves will drop by 50%, and by the end of this century it will drop by more than 70%. In these two years, the rate of dependency among the population aged 75 and over will fall by about 40% and 60%. Accordingly, the size of the elderly population who cannot take care of themselves in the future was calculated according to the United Nations Population Projections (Table 13.3). The results show that with the movement of the cohort, the number of dependent elderly people at all ages increases first and then decreases. In 2015, the number of elderly people who cannot take care of themselves was 5.15 million, which will continue to rise to 10.22 million in 2040, nearly doubling. As China's aging population reaches its peak in the middle of this century, the size of the elderly population declines (Figure 13.6), and the size of the elderly population who cannot take care of themselves also declines slowly.

210 Aging Population

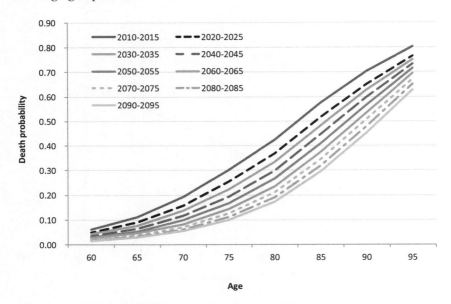

Figure 13.11 Age-specific death probability of China's elderly population in the future

Table 13.2 Prediction of Proportion of Elder Dependents Chinese, 2015–2090

	2015	2030–2035	2050–2055	2070–2075	2090–2095
60–64	0.80	0.56	0.39	0.28	0.21
65–69	1.33	0.92	0.66	0.47	0.36
70–74	2.26	1.60	1.15	0.84	0.64
75–79	3.87	2.86	2.14	1.62	1.27
80+	9.82	7.70	6.14	4.89	4.01

Table 13.3 Scale of Elder Dependents in China (Ten Thousand), 2015–2090 (Decline in the Rate of Elder Dependents)

Year	60–64	65–69	70–74	75–79	80+	Total
2015	64	69	77	93	212	515
2020	58	92	95	96	249	589
2025	65	82	127	121	280	676
2030	74	93	116	167	347	798
2035	65	106	133	156	479	939
2040	48	94	153	183	543	1022
2045	46	69	137	215	639	1107
2050	54	66	102	198	774	1194
2060	31	55	118	148	779	1131
2070	25	40	70	132	829	1096
2080	22	37	60	101	723	942
2090	16	28	53	97	620	814

Table 13.4 Scale of Elder Dependents in China (Ten Thousand), 2015–2090 (Unchanged Rate of Elder Dependents)

Year	60–64	65–69	70–74	75–79	80+	Total
2015	64	69	77	93	212	515
2020	62	99	102	103	261	627
2025	76	96	147	138	309	767
2030	94	118	145	204	405	966
2035	90	146	180	204	588	1209
2040	72	141	225	258	706	1401
2045	75	113	219	325	881	1613
2050	96	118	177	321	1132	1845
2060	65	116	242	280	1283	1986
2070	63	98	166	285	1523	2135
2080	63	105	163	246	1464	2040
2090	53	93	165	267	1387	1965

If the rate of dependent elderly is assumed to remain unchanged, which means the scale of dependent elderly population is calculated based on the rate by age in 2015, the results are shown in Table 13.4. Although with the movement of the cohort, the number of elderly people of all ages who could not take care of themselves also increased first and then decreased, but the decline obviously happened later than before. And the number has increased dramatically. By 2050, the number of dependent elderly is 6.5 million higher than in the previous scenario, and after 2070, it will almost double to more than 20 million.

Education exerts an important impact on the health, career and income. Since the implementation of the higher education expansion policy in the late 1990s, Chinese people have experienced an unprecedentedly rapid rise in education. This implies that the future elderly people will have had far better education compared with that of the elderly today. The heterogeneity of education of the elderly in China will be greatly enhanced. Table 13.5 shows at least half a century spanning from the oldest cohort to the youngest cohort, and the illiteracy rate dropped from nearly half to less than 1%. The share of those with higher education is already more than a fifth in the youngest cohort, almost ten times that of the oldest. By the age of 30, most people have graduated from school, and many even older people will have received higher education, especially postgraduate education. Thus the younger cohorts in Table 13.5 will continue to pursue higher education. We assume that if the cohorts of elder population will have had unchanged education same as they had when they were young, what will be the number of lower and higher-educated older people in the future?

We also estimate the number and changes of Chinese elderly population with different education in the future by using the future elderly population data from the United Nations and the proportion of different education in each cohort in Table 13.5. Table 13.6 shows the prediction results. By the middle of the century, the number of elder illiteracy will drop from 45.64 million to 18.12 million, a drop of

212　Aging Population

Table 13.5 Proportion of Chinese Population with Different Education by Age, 2015

Age	Illiteracy	Primary School	Junior High School	Senior High School	College and Above
25–29	0.62	4.78	43.59	23.51	27.51
30–34	0.97	7.52	48.60	20.22	22.70
35–39	1.44	12.10	50.73	19.17	16.56
40–44	2.00	17.96	52.90	15.85	11.30
45–49	2.82	24.96	51.36	12.98	7.87
50–54	3.89	27.55	45.67	16.05	6.84
55–59	7.28	35.85	36.02	16.30	4.56
60–64	11.79	46.06	29.99	8.80	3.36
65–69	17.26	50.76	22.20	6.80	2.97
70–74	25.16	47.37	17.46	6.76	3.25
75–79	34.24	44.01	12.17	5.77	3.82
80+	48.66	37.00	8.18	3.67	2.49

Table 13.6 Distribution of Elderly Population with Different Education, 2015–2050

	Illiteracy	Primary School	Junior High School	Senior High School	College and Above	Total
Number Distribution (Ten Thousand)						
2015	4,564	9,779	4,611	1,504	678	21,137
2020	3,984	10,812	6,748	2,527	906	24,978
2025	3,375	11,384	10,100	3,693	1,405	29,956
2030	2,922	11,989	14,622	4,698	2,124	36,355
2035	2,567	11,603	18,384	5,760	3,108	41,422
2040	2,209	10,428	20,106	6,434	4,176	43,352
2045	1,964	9,101	21,019	7,140	5,676	44,899
2050	1,812	7,828	21,990	8,767	8,152	48,549
Percentage Distribution(%)						
2015	21.59	46.26	21.82	7.12	3.21	100.00
2020	15.95	43.29	27.02	10.12	3.63	100.00
2025	11.27	38.00	33.71	12.33	4.69	100.00
2030	8.04	32.98	40.22	12.92	5.84	100.00
2035	6.20	28.01	44.38	13.90	7.50	100.00
2040	5.09	24.05	46.38	14.84	9.63	100.00
2045	4.37	20.27	46.81	15.90	12.64	100.00
2050	3.73	16.12	45.29	18.06	16.79	100.00

60%. The number of elderly with college degrees or above will rise 11-fold from 6.78 million to 81.52 million. Accordingly, the illiteracy rate of the elderly population will fall from 21.6% in 2015 to less than 4% in 2050, and the proportion of the population with higher education will rise from 3.2% to nearly 17%. In addition, the number and proportion of people with high school education will continue to rise, while the number and proportion of people with middle school education will continue to rise and become stable after 2040. Primary education will rise and then fall, but its share falls from 46% to 16%.

Home care will be the major pattern for the elderly support in China in a long period of time. Many surveys and studies have shown that support and children are the main caregivers for the elderly. Due to the rapid decline and long-term low fertility rate in China, the family structure and living style of the elderly have undergone great changes. With the continuous adjustment and improvement of the fertility policy, the heterogeneity of China's population will continue to increase. In the future, people will be able to have as many children as they need and can afford. Although there will be a majority of couples with fewer children, it is likely to have more couples with more children. The increase of fertility heterogeneity will inevitably

Table 13.7 Number of Relatives at Different Fertility Rates

	50	60	70	80	90
High TFR(TFR=5.9)					
Wife	0.96	0.94	0.82	0.57	0.28
Parent	0.59	0.16	0.02	.	.
Sibling	5.51	5.01	4	2.49	1.08
Child	5.5	5.64	5.65	5.46	5.38
Grandparent					
Grandchild	0.17	3.98	14.46	24.84	29.83
Great-grandparent					
Great-grandchild			0.01	1.37	13.97
Aunt/uncle	8.8	4.09	1.36	0.38	0.08
Cousin	60.23	54.3	43.72	30.37	16.06
Nephew/niece	29.41	32.07	32.27	31.03	29.78
Replacement fertility(TFR=2.2)					
Wife	0.96	0.94	0.83	0.59	0.28
Parent	0.9	0.32	0.04		
Sibling	1.44	1.33	1.04	0.58	0.19
Child	2.05	2.08	2.08	1.96	1.81
Grandparent	0.01				
Grandchild	0.48	2.95	4.02	4.09	3.93
Great-grandparent					
Great-grandchild			0.06	2.31	6.13
Aunt/uncle	2.92	1.29	0.36	0.07	0.02
Cousin	5.76	5.19	4.12	2.44	1.08
Nephew/niece	3.12	3.11	3.05	2.81	2.41
Low TFR(TFR=1.6)					
Wife	0.96	0.94	0.83	0.59	0.24
Parent	0.97	0.36	0.05	.	.
Sibling	1.02	0.93	0.73	0.39	0.11
Child	1.53	1.54	1.52	1.47	1.39
Grandparent	0.01	.	.	.	.
Grandchild	0.39	1.83	2.3	2.38	2.6
Great-grandparent					
Great-grandchild			0.06	1.33	3.09
Aunt/uncle	2.2	0.98	0.27	0.06	0.01
Cousin	3.21	2.92	2.3	1.36	0.55
Nephew/niece	1.67	1.68	1.62	1.49	1.31

promote the heterogeneity of family structure and living arrangement. In order to investigate the influence of different fertility levels on family kinship structure, we used population microsimulation (Zhao Zhongwei and Chen Wei, 2008). In the simulation, a death and marriage scenario and three fertility scenarios were designed to explore the number of relatives that people have at different life stages under different fertility rates. The age-specific probabilities of death and marriage are based on the Chinese census 2000, and the three fertility scenarios were set based on TFR at 5.9, 2.2 and 1.6, respectively. The simulations were carried out from the perspective of male, which looked at the number of average relatives that a man has at different life stages under different fertility rates.

Table 13.7 shows the simulation results. There is a big difference in the number of different relatives under high fertility and low fertility scenarios. Compared with the high fertility rate (TFR=5.9) similar to that in the 1950s and 1960s, a man aged 60 and above had on average five siblings, 5.6 children, four grandchildren, as well as 54 cousins and more than 30 nephews. Under current low fertility rate (TFR=1.6), the number of relatives other than children fell much more than the fertility rate, sometimes over 10-fold reduction. The average number of children and grandchildren dropped to 1.5 and 1.8, while the number of cousins and nephews dropped 17 times. If fertility returns to the replacement level (TFR=2.2) in the future, and the number of relatives of all kinds will certainly increase. Compared with the low birth rate, the average number of children will increase by 0.5, and

Table 13.8 Family Structure at Different Fertility Rates

	50	60	70	80
High TFR(TFR=5.9)				
Two or more married sons	0.85	34.03	65.09	69.7
One married son	7.82	30.89	19.16	16.12
One or more unmarried son	79.56	23.74	3.7	0.94
Having daughters but no sons	5.94	5.69	5.91	6.42
No children but having spouse	2.94	2.77	2.53	2.07
No spouse and children	2.89	2.89	3.61	4.75
Replacement fertility (TFR=2.2)				
Two or more married sons	1.34	18.75	25	22.47
One married son	13.46	40.59	42.39	43.34
One or more unmarried son	55.34	10.73	2.84	2
Having daughters but no sons	22.96	22.83	22.55	24.4
No children but having spouse	4.15	4.26	3.81	2.9
No spouse and children	2.74	2.85	3.42	4.89
Low fertility rate (TFR=1.6)				
Two or more married sons	0.87	10.41	13.44	13.28
One married son	12.33	40.20	41.82	41.03
One or more unmarried son	46.22	8.48	2.91	2.04
Having daughters but no sons	30.75	30.73	30.43	29.45
No children but having spouse	6.65	6.74	6.88	7.1
No spouse and children	3.18	3.44	4.51	7.1

the number of grandchildren will increase by more than one, and the number of cousins and nephews will increase more.

Differences in fertility rate also have a significant impact on family structure (Table 13.8). Under high fertility rate, it is easy to form large families. By age 60, more than a third of the elderly have at least two married sons, 90% have at least one son, fewer than 6% had daughters but no sons, and fewer than 6% had no children or spouse. At current low fertility rate, the proportion having at least one son falls to less than 60%, the proportion having daughters but no sons exceeds 30%, and the proportion having no children or spouse exceeds 10%. If the fertility rate can be raised to replacement level in the future, the family structure will also be significantly different from that at the low fertility rate. The proportion with at least one son will rise by 10 percentage points, the proportion with only daughters and no sons will fall by 8 percentage points, and the proportion with no children or spouse will fall by 3 percentage points. Different fertility rates between 1.6 and 2.2 also make a significant difference in access to family care from children. The increase of fertility heterogeneity in the future will undoubtedly promote the heterogeneity of relatives and family structure of the elderly.

Concluding Remarks

The wave of aging has swept across every corner of the world. The speed and extent of population aging in the future will be unprecedented in human history, and the aging process will have a marked impact on economic and social development. Although the current aging problem is more prominent in developed countries, it will be more severe in developing countries and will bring huge pressure and contradiction. As the norm in human society, the aging process will not be reversed as long as the birth rate remains at a low level and life expectancy will be further extended. The common, long-lasting aging process will exert a profound impact on human society and bring about challenges to human life.

China plays a pivotal role in the global landscape of aging population, as it has the largest population and the elderly population and will also have the fastest-aging population. Although the current level of aging in China is still relatively low, it is in the middle of rapid aging that will last for 40 years. By the second half of this century, less than one in three people in China will be over 60 years old, one in three will be over 65 years old, and one in six will be over 80 years old. The accelerated aging process will make it a country with severe aging population and advanced aging population. In this process, the working-age population will be also aging and the size of labor force will decline. Population aging in China is an inevitable result of modernization, and the family planning policy has promoted and accelerated the aging process to some extent. However, the implementation of the universal two-child policy has little effect on alleviating the rapid population aging.

Population aging in China is characterized by not only the elderly people's large size, rapid growth and fast aging process but also the wavy development of population aging and the elderly. These are determined by the speed of China's fertility transition and the wavy process of low fertility. In the process of aging transition, the advanced aged among the elderly are increasing, and the heterogeneity of the elderly will continue to increase. China's rapid fertility transition leads to rapid aging at the macro level, and it also profoundly changes the family and kinship structure of the elderly at the micro level. The increase of fertility heterogeneity in the future will also promote the heterogeneity of relatives and family structure among the elderly.

Declining fertility, longer life expectancy and an aging population are inevitable and irreversible trends. Throughout history, the social and economic systems and human structures have been established, developed and perfected based on the society of young population. The modernization, population transformation and aging of developed countries are endogenous and gradual, and thus, their social and economic systems can gradually accumulate strong economic, organizational and institutional resources to adapt to the population change. However, as the population transition and aging occur rapidly in the post-modern countries like China, the socioeconomic system and population structure have intense conflicts. In the process of coping with the conflicts, we should focus on changing the social and economic system to adapt to the population change and aging, instead of adjusting and changing the developmental trend of population. World experience shows that it is ineffective to increasing fertility by changing population and aging trends through fertility policy. It is to be expected that China's universal two-child policy, or even the full abolition of the birth control in the future, and then, the implementation of the birth encouragement policy will have only a limited effect. A comprehensive framework system of economic, social and population policies based on social integration fulled by long-term development strategy is needed to adapt, cope with and even lead China's aging society.

References

Chen Wei and Duan Yuanyuan. 2019. Recent Levels and Trends of Fertility in China. *Population Research* 1: 3–17.

Gu Baochang, Hou Jiawei, and Wu Nan. 2019. Why is China's Total Fertility Rate So Low? Interplay between Postponement and Recuperation. *Population and Economics* 1: 49–62.

Guo Zhigang. 2013. How Low is China's Fertility Level: Based on the Analysis of the Sixth Census Data. *Chinese Journal of Population Science* 2: 2–10.

Guo Zhigang. 2017. Main Characteristics of the Low Fertility Process in China: Implications from the Results of the 1% Population Sample Survey in 2015. *Chinese Journal of Population Science* 4: 2–14.

Rowland, D. T. 2012. *Aging in Asia*. Netherland: Springer.

Sudharsanan, N. and Bloom, D. E. 2018. The Demography of Aging in Low- and Middle-Income Countries: Chronological versus Functional Perspectives. Pp. 309–338. *Future Directions for the Demography of Aging: Proceedings of a Workshop*. Washington, DC: National Academies Press.

United Nations. 2019. World Population Prospects: The 2019 Revision. https://population.un.org/wpp/Download/Standard/Population/

Zhao Zhongwei and Chen Wei. 2008. Changes in Household Formation and Composition in China since the Mid-twentieth Century. *Journal of Population Research* 25(3): 1–20.

14 The Impact of the Two-Child Policy on Demand for Maternal and Child Health Services

The adjustment of the fertility policy has wide and far-reaching impacts on the society, with the immediate and direct effects on the demand for basic public services. The implementation of the two-child policy may bring about an increase in the number of births, infants and pregnant women in the short term. Within five years after the implementation of the policy, about 2.3–4.2 million extra new births are likely to be born each year (Wang Guangzhou, 2016), which will extra increase the demand for maternal and child health services and medical care. And in the long run, this growth will continue with demographic inertia.

The initial consequence of the two-child policy is an increase in the number of pregnant women and births. The increase in pregnant women has led to an increase in the demand for prenatal care, eugenic guidance and other services. For example, generally, you should go to the hospital to confirm whether you are pregnant and the specific gestational week within 6–8 weeks of pregnancy and then check every four gestational weeks until 28 weeks of pregnancy; at 28–38 weeks of pregnancy, check every two weeks; after 38 weeks of pregnancy, weekly examinations are required.

Obviously, the demand for examination and health care during pregnancy will increase significantly. At the same time, the age of pregnant women also needs to be distinguished, because the conception rate of older women decreases and the spontaneous abortion rate increases, so the prenatal examination and pregnancy care of older women have certain particularity.

An increase in the number of births would also naturally lead to an increase in the demand for obstetric and pediatric medical services. The rate of hospital births in China has reached more than 99%. The accumulation of births and the increase in the number of births after the implementation of the two-child policy will lead to a significant increase in the demand for obstetric medical services. Over time, the increase in demand for obstetric health services will gradually transfer to the increase in demand for child health services. In terms of hardware indicators, it is mainly reflected in the demand for the number of beds, doctors and nurses at all levels of medical and health institutions.

After the adjustment of the one-child policy, the National Health Commission successively issued the Notice on Implementing the Opinions of the CPC Central Committee and The State Council on Adjusting and Improving the Fertility

DOI: 10.4324/9781003429661-14

Policy and the Guidance on Providing Maternal and Child Health Services under the New Situation, stressing that under the background of the adjustment of the fertility policy, it is necessary to promptly carry out a survey of maternal and child resources, and the construction of corresponding maternal and child resources and the strengthening of maternal and child health services according to the change of service demand. After the implementation of the two-child policy, maternal and child health services will also face a new round of challenges and should be paid enough attention. In order to improve and adjust the health service resources in time, it needs to be based on clear demand measurement. Therefore, this chapter builds on the changing number of births under the two-child policy produced from population projections. According to the current medical and health resources, the number and age structure of pregnant women, the proportion, type and standard of prenatal examination and pregnancy care and the standard of the matching degree of beds, doctors and nurses will be combined to measure the impact of the two-child policy on the demand for pediatrics, obstetrics and gynecology and other medical and health services.

Data and Methods

The data of population projections in this chapter are from the results of Chapter 11. The relevant data of national obstetric and gynecological and pediatric medical institutions, number of beds, number of doctors and nurses and hospitalization are derived from China Health Statistical Yearbook 2018 and China Maternal and Child Health Development Report 2019 released by the Department of Maternal and Child Health of the National Health Commission.

In this chapter, the population-resource density method is used to measure the impact of changing births on the demand for maternal and child health services. Population-resource density is defined as the amount of a certain resource per 1,000 or 10,000 population. When measuring the impact of the new-born population growth on the demand for maternal and child health services, population-resource density refers to the number of medical institutions, specialized hospitals, beds, doctors and nurses per 1,000 births or per 1,000 children. The standard of population-resource density is determined according to domestic and foreign experiences, and the total demand for various health services is estimated, namely the impact on the demand for maternal and child health services. Data sources of all the tables and figures are not further noted as they are produced from forecasting results.

The Size and Structure of the Births, Maternal and Child Populations

The predicted results of the trends in births under the two-child policy are shown in Figure 14.1. The peak of the births was in 2016, reaching 17.59 million, and then fell to 16.98 million and 15.01 million in 2017 and 2018, respectively. On the whole, the two-child policy does not seem to result in a strong short-term accumulation of births, which may be affected by the decrease of the number of women of childbearing age, delayed marriage and childbearing and other factors. For maternal and child health care services, it also means that there is no short-term substantial increase in demand, giving more sufficient time to adjust the allocation of resources.

According to the low scenario, that is, if the family planning policy remains unchanged, the total number of births from 2016 to 2020 would be 74.94 million. Under the two-child policy, the total number of births from 2016 to 2020 under the medium and high scenarios are predicted to be 76.39 million and 76.62 million, respectively, which is 1.45 million and 1.68 million more than that under the low scenario. It is necessary to increase the corresponding allocation of medical and health resources. In the long run, by 2050, 52.45 million and 96.17 million more babies will be born in the medium and high scenarios than in the low scenario, with an average of 1.5 million to 2.7 million each year, which is a great challenge for medical and health services.

It is also worth noting that although the number of births will start to decline after only one year's increase, there will still be a small peak of births around 2035 under the effect of population inertia, especially in the results of the high scenario. The small peak of births under the low, medium and high scenarios will be 10.81 million, 12.8 million and 14.75 million, respectively. The sudden increase in the number of births in 2016, resulting in a shortage of medical and health resources for mothers and children. This provides important policy implications for preparing in advance for the coming of the next baby boom.

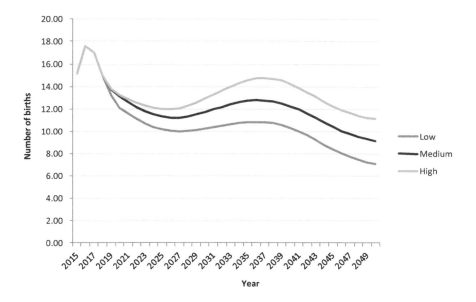

Figure 14.1 Trends in number of births in China, 2015–2050

220 Maternal and Child Health Services

The number of births can largely represent the number of pregnant women. In cases where the proportion of twins or multiple births is very low, the number of births is a rough proxy for the number of mothers. Then, the number of pregnant women also peaked in 2016 and will have another small peak around 2035.

Let's take a look at the change in the number of children aged 0–14. See Figure 14.2 for the predicted results. Corresponding to the peak in births, the peak in the number of children aged 0–14 occurred in 2018, reaching 256 million, an increase by 6.07 million over 2015. This would increase the pressure on the pediatrics resources which are understaffed and seriously drained. From 2016 to 2020, the number of children aged 0–14 under the medium and high scenarios will be 1.938 million and 2.227 million higher than that under the low scenario, respectively. The adjustment of the fertility policy will significantly increase the demand for pediatric medical and health resources in the short term.

It is also noted that the number of children aged 0–14 will also have a small peak after 2017. Under the low, medium and high scenarios, the small peak will be reached in 2040, 2042 and 2044, respectively, and the small peak size will reach 156 million, 182 million and 207 million, respectively. There will be 26.29 million more in the medium and 51.56 million more in the high scenario than in the low scenario. It can be seen that although the increase of births only occurred in 2016 and then began to decline, under the effect of population inertia, the adjustment of fertility policy has a more significant impact on the growth of the number of children aged 0–14 in the medium and long term.

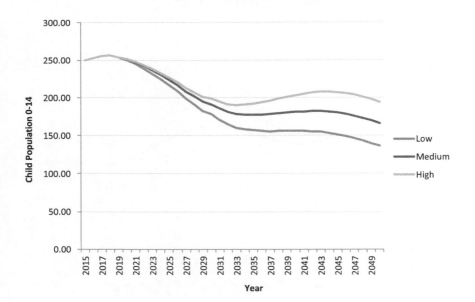

Figure 14.2 Trends in child population aged 0–14 in China, 2015–2050

The Impact of Births on the Demand for Maternal and Child Health Services

1 The impact on the demand for obstetric and gynecological medical services

The implementation of the two-child policy and the increase in the number of pregnant women and newborns will first lead to an increase in the demand for prenatal examinations, health care during pregnancy, eugenic guidance, delivery, postpartum care and other services, and correspondingly, the demand for service facilities and personnel allocation will also increase.

1 Evaluation of existing obstetric and gynecological medical resources in China

In 2017, there were 773 maternity hospitals nationwide, including 576 in cities and 197 in rural areas. There were 3,077 maternal and child health institutions, of which 1,160 were in urban areas and 1,917 in rural areas. There were 3,850 maternity hospitals and maternal and child health care institutions in total, and 20,812 general hospitals of the first grade or higher with at least obstetrics and gynecology departments. In 2018, the number of maternity hospitals increased to 807 and the number of maternity and child health institutions increased to 3,080. The number of maternity hospitals and maternity and child health institutions totaled 3,887, and there were 26,000 midwifery institutions nationwide. In 2017, there were 729,900 beds in obstetrics and gynecology nationwide. According to the calculation that obstetrics beds accounted for 35% of the total number of obstetrics and gynecology beds in 2014, there were about 255,500 beds nationwide in 2017. On average, there are about 9.82 maternity beds per midwifery facility.

In 2017, there were 312,000 practicing (assistant) physicians of obstetrics and gynecology in China, including 255,000 practicing physicians, 185,000 practicing (assistant) physicians of obstetrics and gynecology in medical institutions and 127,000 practicing (assistant) physicians of maternal and child health institutions. In 2018, there were nearly 210,000 obstetricians in China.

In 2017, there were 380,000 registered nurses in China. If the number of registered nurses in obstetrics and gynecology is calculated according to the proportion of practicing (assistant) physicians in obstetrics and gynecology, there were 350,000 registered nurses in obstetrics and gynecology in 2017, including 155,000 in maternal and child health institutions. In 2018, there were 180,000 midwives nationwide.

According to the above statistical data of various obstetric medical resources and the calculated results, the density of obstetric medical resources (medical resources/per 1,000 births) was calculated based on the national births of 16.89 million in 2017 and 15.01 million in 2018.

a Institutional density: in 2017, there were 0.23 maternity institutions per 1,000 live births and 1.46 midwifery institutions per 1,000 live births; In

2018, there were 0.26 maternity facilities per 1,000 live births and 1.73 midwifery facilities per 1,000 live births.
b Bed density: 15.1 maternity beds per 1,000 live births in 2017.
c Doctor density: 14.0 obstetricians per 1,000 live births in 2018.
d Nurse density: 12.0 midwives per 1,000 live births in 2018.

2 Supply and demand of obstetric and gynecological medical services

According to the general standard of China's third-class A hospitals, each pregnant woman should perform at least ten times of prenatal examinations during pregnancy. In 2018, 15.01 million pregnant women needed 150 million times of prenatal examinations. On average, each medical institution conducted 5,773 prenatal examinations, 15.8 examinations per day, and each doctor conducted 2.7 pregnancy examinations for each working day. Based on the hospital delivery rate being 99.7%, 14.96 million newborns were delivered in medical institutions in 2018, with an average of 575.6 live births delivered in each institution, 1.6 live births delivered in each institution per day, 71.3 live births delivered by an obstetrician, or one birth delivered every five days. The average nurse cares for 83.1 infants and 83.1 parturients, or 0.23 infants and parturients per day. The rate of cesarean section in 2018 was 36.7%, and a total of 5.492 million cesarean sections were performed in 2018, with an average of 262,000 cesarean sections performed by each obstetrician. According to the average length of stay in obstetrics and gynecology hospitals of 5.7 days in 2017, 14.97 million women who gave birth in hospital were hospitalized 85.3 million individual days in 2018, an average of 234,000 people were hospitalized every day and 468,000 mothers and children were hospitalized every day in total.

3 Forecast of obstetric medical service demand

In 2018, the rate of hospital deliveries and prenatal visits reached 99.7% and 96.6%, respectively. It can be seen that the supply and demand of obstetric medical resources in China are basically balanced in total quantity. Therefore, the density of all kinds of obstetric medical resources mentioned above is taken as the parameter to predict the change of obstetric medical resource demand after the implementation of the two-child policy. According to the population projection results, the demand for obstetric and gynecological medical resources under the two-child policy is as follows:

First, the need for obstetric institutions. According to the density of obstetric and gynecological medical institutions in 2018 (see Table 14.1), the peak of births between 2015 and 2050 and the peak of demand for obstetric and gynecological institutions in 2016 has passed. However, we should also pay attention to the fact that around 2037, the demand for obstetric and gynecological institutions will reach a small peak. According to the forecast results of medium and high scenarios, the peak demand for obstetric and gynecological institutions will be 22,145 and 25,526, respectively, among which the peak demand for obstetric and gynecological specialized hospitals will be 3,328 and 3,836. The difference between the predicted results of medium and high scenario demand and the results of low scenario demand will continue to increase, and the difference will be largest in 2050. The demand gap of obstetric and gynecological institutions will be 3,627 and 7,005, respectively, and the demand gap of obstetric and gynecological specialized hospitals will be 545 and 1,053, respectively.

Table 14.1 Forecast of Demand of Obstetric and Gynecological Institutions, 2015–2050 (Million)

| | Obstetric and Gynecological Institutions ||||||
| | Low || Medium || High ||
	Specialized Hospitals	All Institutions	Specialized Hospitals	All Institutions	Specialized Hospitals	All Institutions
2015	39.33	261.70	39.33	261.70	39.33	261.70
2016	45.75	304.38	45.75	304.38	45.75	304.38
2017	44.15	293.74	44.15	293.74	44.15	293.74
2018	39.03	259.69	39.03	259.69	39.03	259.69
2019	34.34	228.52	35.61	236.95	35.77	237.98
2020	31.57	210.09	34.09	226.83	34.53	229.75
2021	30.22	201.09	32.83	218.42	33.54	223.15
2022	28.97	192.73	31.69	210.83	32.68	217.43
2023	27.88	185.50	30.70	204.29	32.01	212.98
2024	27.03	179.83	29.93	199.17	31.49	209.56
2025	26.44	175.93	29.43	195.82	31.20	207.60
2026	26.10	173.69	29.20	194.29	31.17	207.39
2027	25.99	172.95	29.23	194.50	31.37	208.71
2028	26.10	173.64	29.50	196.31	31.92	212.39
2029	26.34	175.29	29.96	199.37	32.75	217.88
2030	26.68	177.51	30.52	203.05	33.64	223.80
2031	27.04	179.92	31.11	206.99	34.53	229.76
2032	27.38	182.16	31.72	211.08	35.43	235.73
2033	27.69	184.25	32.31	214.99	36.31	241.63
2034	27.96	186.01	32.82	218.38	37.15	247.20
2035	28.11	187.03	33.19	220.85	37.86	251.95
2036	28.11	187.03	33.28	221.45	38.30	254.84
2037	28.09	186.89	33.22	221.02	38.36	255.26
2038	27.92	185.75	33.03	219.80	38.20	254.17
2039	27.41	182.41	32.54	216.50	37.79	251.42
2040	26.74	177.95	31.84	211.88	36.99	246.11
2041	25.99	172.96	31.11	207.02	36.01	239.61
2042	25.11	167.09	30.20	200.97	35.02	233.01
2043	24.00	159.66	29.18	194.13	33.92	225.72
2044	22.87	152.17	28.15	187.32	32.86	218.64
2045	21.88	145.57	27.16	180.70	31.87	212.08
2046	20.92	139.21	26.22	174.44	30.99	206.18
2047	20.08	133.58	25.40	169.01	30.24	201.23
2048	19.42	129.20	24.74	164.64	29.66	197.32
2049	18.87	125.54	24.23	161.22	29.22	194.40
2050	18.40	122.43	23.85	158.70	28.93	192.48

Second, demand for maternity beds. Based on the maternity bed density of 15.1 beds per 1,000 live births in 2017, similarly the peak in demand will occur in 2016, followed by a small peak around 2037 (Table 14.2). According to the prediction results of medium and high scenarios, the minimum peak demand of obstetric beds is 193,200 and 228,800, respectively. The difference between the predicted results of medium and high scenario demand and the results of the low scenario demand also continues to increase, and the number of obstetric beds in 2050 will be 317 and 61,100 in medium and high scenarios demand and 61,100 in the low scenario demand.

Third, the demand for obstetricians and nurses. In 2018, the density of obstetricians was 14.0 per 1,000 live births and the density of nurses was 12.0 per 1,000 live births. According to the prediction results of medium and high scenarios, the small peak demand for obstetricians was 179,200 and 206,600, respectively (Table 14.2). The demand for obstetric nurses peaked at 153,600 and 177,100, respectively. By 2050, the demand difference between the number of obstetricians under the medium and high scenarios and under the low scenario is 29,700 and 56,700, and the demand difference of obstetric nurses is 25,200 and 48,600, respectively. It should be noted that the ratio of obstetric care in 2018 was inverted, with the number of nurses less than that of physicians. Although the prediction was made according to the resource density in 2018, the investment in the number of obstetric nurses should be further increased compared with that of physicians to achieve a balanced ratio of medical care.

2 The impact on pediatric medical service demand

1 Evaluation of existing pediatric medical resources in China

Statistics from the National Health Commission show that by the end of 2018, there were 228 specialized children's hospitals, more than 20,000 hospitals offering pediatric medical services, and 154,000 pediatricians nationwide. According to China Health Statistics Yearbook, in 2017, there were 517,000 pediatric beds in China, and the number of registered pediatric nurses was 223,000 in 2017 and 257,000 in 2018, based on the ratio of doctors to nurses of 0.6 in national children's hospitals.

The number of children aged 0–14 in 2017 was 254.95 million, and the number of children aged 0–14 in 2018 was 256.11 million. According to this calculation, the density of pediatric medical resources is as follows:

a Institutional density: In 2018, 0.08 pediatric medical institutions per 1,000 children.
b Bed density: In 2017, 2.03 pediatric beds per 1,000 children.
c Doctor density: 0.60 pediatricians per 1,000 children in 2018.
d Nurse density: In 2018, there were 1.00 pediatric nurses per 1,000 children.

2 Supply and demand of pediatric medical services

In 2017, there were 542 million outpatient and emergency visits to pediatrics nationwide, including 319 million in hospitals, 15.788 million in

Table 14.2 Forecast of Demand of Maternity Beds, Obstetricians and Nurses in China, 2015–2050 (Million)

	Beds			Obstetricians			Nurses		
	Low	Medium	High	Low	Medium	High	Low	Medium	High
2015	2,284.2	2,284.2	2,284.2	2,117.8	2,117.8	2,117.8	1,815.3	1,815.3	1,815.3
2016	2,656.7	2,656.7	2,656.7	2,463.2	2,463.2	2,463.2	2,111.3	2,111.3	2,111.3
2017	2,563.8	2,563.8	2,563.8	2,377.1	2,377.1	2,377.1	2,037.5	2,037.5	2,037.5
2018	2,266.6	2,266.6	2,266.6	2,101.5	2,101.5	2,101.5	1,801.3	1,801.3	1,801.3
2019	1,994.6	2,068.1	2,077.2	1,849.3	1,917.5	1,925.9	1,585.1	1,643.6	1,650.8
2020	1,833.7	1,979.9	2,005.3	1,700.2	1,835.6	1,859.3	1,457.3	1,573.4	1,593.6
2021	1,755.2	1,906.5	1,947.7	1,627.3	1,767.6	1,805.8	1,394.8	1,515.1	1,547.8
2022	1,682.2	1,840.2	1,897.8	1,559.7	1,706.2	1,759.6	1,336.9	1,462.4	1,508.2
2023	1,619.1	1,783.1	1,859.0	1,501.2	1,653.2	1,723.6	1,286.7	1,417.0	1,477.3
2024	1,569.6	1,738.5	1,829.1	1,455.3	1,611.8	1,695.9	1,247.4	1,381.6	1,453.6
2025	1,535.5	1,709.2	1,812.0	1,423.7	1,584.7	1,680.0	1,220.3	1,358.3	1,440.0
2026	1,516.0	1,695.9	1,810.2	1,405.6	1,572.3	1,678.3	1,204.8	1,347.7	1,438.6
2027	1,509.6	1,697.6	1,821.7	1,399.6	1,573.9	1,689.0	1,199.7	1,349.1	1,447.7
2028	1,515.6	1,713.5	1,853.8	1,405.2	1,588.7	1,718.8	1,204.4	1,361.7	1,473.2
2029	1,530.0	1,740.2	1,901.8	1,418.6	1,613.4	1,763.2	1,215.9	1,382.9	1,511.3
2030	1,549.4	1,772.3	1,953.4	1,436.5	1,643.2	1,811.1	1,231.3	1,408.4	1,552.4
2031	1,570.4	1,806.7	2,005.4	1,456.0	1,675.1	1,859.3	1,248.0	1,435.8	1,593.7
2032	1,590.0	1,842.4	2,057.6	1,474.1	1,708.2	1,907.7	1,263.5	1,464.1	1,635.2
2033	1,608.2	1,876.5	2,109.0	1,491.1	1,739.8	1,955.4	1,278.1	1,491.2	1,676.1
2034	1,623.6	1,906.1	2,157.6	1,505.3	1,767.2	2,000.4	1,290.3	1,514.8	1,714.7
2035	1,632.5	1,927.6	2,199.1	1,513.6	1,787.2	2,038.9	1,297.3	1,531.9	1,747.6
2036	1,632.4	1,932.9	2,224.4	1,513.5	1,792.1	2,062.3	1,297.3	1,536.1	1,767.7
2037	1,631.2	1,929.1	2,228.0	1,512.4	1,788.6	2,065.7	1,296.3	1,533.1	1,770.6
2038	1,621.2	1,918.5	2,218.5	1,503.1	1,778.7	2,056.9	1,288.4	1,524.6	1,763.0
2039	1,592.1	1,889.7	2,194.5	1,476.1	1,752.1	2,034.6	1,265.2	1,501.8	1,744.0
2040	1,553.2	1,849.4	2,148.1	1,440.0	1,714.6	1,991.6	1,234.3	1,469.7	1,707.1
2041	1,509.7	1,807.0	2,091.4	1,399.7	1,675.3	1,939.1	1,199.8	1,436.0	1,662.1
2042	1,458.4	1,754.1	2,033.8	1,352.2	1,626.3	1,885.6	1,159.0	1,394.0	1,616.2
2043	1,393.6	1,694.4	1,970.2	1,292.0	1,571.0	1,826.7	1,107.5	1,346.6	1,565.7
2044	1,328.2	1,635.0	1,908.4	1,231.4	1,515.9	1,769.3	1,055.5	1,299.3	1,516.6
2045	1,270.6	1,577.2	1,851.1	1,178.0	1,462.3	1,716.2	1,009.7	1,253.4	1,471.1
2046	1,215.1	1,522.6	1,799.6	1,126.6	1,411.7	1,668.5	965.6	1,210.0	1,430.1
2047	1,165.9	1,475.2	1,756.4	1,081.0	1,367.7	1,628.5	926.6	1,172.3	1,395.8
2048	1,127.7	1,437.0	1,722.3	1,045.6	1,332.3	1,596.8	896.2	1,142.0	1,368.7
2049	1,095.7	1,407.2	1,696.7	1,015.9	1,304.6	1,573.1	870.8	1,118.3	1,348.4
2050	1,068.6	1,385.2	1,680.1	990.8	1,284.3	1,557.7	849.2	1,100.8	1,335.1

community health service centers and 82.126 million in township health centers. In 2017, the average number of outpatient and emergency consultations for each child was 2.13, with an average of 4,044.78 sick children treated by each pediatrician and 15.51 children treated every working day. In 2017, a total of 23.6,058 million discharged pediatric patients were hospitalized, including 16.6,716 million in hospitals, 110,000 in community health service centers and 3.1,050 million in township health centers. The average length of stay in children's hospitals was 7.0 days, and the bed occupancy rate was 95.9%.

3 Forecast of pediatric medical service demand

In 2018, the neonatal visit rate reached 93.7%, 91.2% of children under the age of three were under systematic management and 92.7% of children under the age of seven were under health management. Thus, the utilization rate of pediatric medical resources is high in China. Therefore, in scheme I, the density of pediatric medical resources mentioned above is taken as the parameter to predict the change of pediatric medical resource demand after the implementation of the two-child policy. According to the Opinions on Strengthening the Reform and Development of Children's Medical and Health Services, scheme II sets that by 2020, "the number of practicing (assistant) physicians for every 1,000 children's pediatrics shall reach 0.69". The number of beds and the number of pediatric nurses are estimated according to the current ratios. Scheme III employs the median value of 1.07 according to the standard of the ratio of doctors to the number of children per 1,000 in major developed countries. According to the population projection results, the demand for obstetric and gynecological medical resources after the implementation of the two-child policy is estimated.

a Results of Scheme I

First, pediatric facilities and bed demand (Table 14.3). The density of pediatric medical institutions in 2018 and the density of pediatric beds in 2017 were calculated. The demand for pediatric medical institutions and pediatric beds peaked in 2018 at 20,489 and 519,900, respectively. The demand in the low scenario will continue to decline by 2050, while the secondary peaks in the medium and the high scenarios will be 14,565 and 369,600 in 2042 and 16,586 and 420,900 in 2044, respectively. The demand difference between the predicted results of medium and high scenarios and the results of low scenario will continue to increase. In 2050, the demand gap of pediatric medical institutions will be 2,398 and 4,668, and the demand gap of pediatric beds will be 60,800 and 118,500, respectively.

Second, the demand for pediatricians and nurses (Table 14.4). Based on the 2018 pediatricians density of 0.60 per 1,000 children and nurses density of 1.0 per 1,000 children, the demand for pediatricians and nurses peaked in 2018 at 154,000 and 256,000, respectively. The demand under the low scenario will continue to decline by 2050, and the secondary peak of the medium and high scenarios will be in 2042 and 2044, respectively, with the peaks of 109,200 physicians, 182,100 nurses and 124,400 physicians and 207,300 nurses, respectively. The difference between the projected demand under the medium and high scenarios and the low scenario continues to increase, with the demand gap for pediatricians reaching 18,000 and 35,000, respectively, and the demand gap for pediatric nurses reaching 30,000 and 58,400, respectively, in 2050.

b Results of Scheme II

Based on the estimates according to 0.69 pediatricians per 1,000 children and 2.2 beds per 1,000 children (Table 14.5), the peak demand for

Table 14.3 Forecast of Demand of Pediatric Medical Institutions and Beds in China, 2015–2050 (Million)

	Institutions			Beds		
	Low	Medium	High	Low	Medium	High
2015	200.03	200.03	200.03	0.508	0.508	0.508
2016	202.28	202.28	202.28	0.513	0.513	0.513
2017	203.96	203.96	203.96	0.518	0.518	0.518
2018	204.89	204.89	204.89	0.520	0.520	0.520
2019	202.64	203.03	203.08	0.514	0.515	0.515
2020	199.71	200.87	201.05	0.507	0.510	0.510
2021	195.70	197.66	198.06	0.497	0.502	0.503
2022	190.65	193.44	194.14	0.484	0.491	0.493
2023	185.17	188.82	189.93	0.470	0.479	0.482
2024	179.13	183.67	185.25	0.455	0.466	0.470
2025	173.09	178.55	180.67	0.439	0.453	0.458
2026	166.74	173.14	175.86	0.423	0.439	0.446
2027	159.01	166.39	169.77	0.403	0.422	0.431
2028	152.94	161.37	165.48	0.388	0.409	0.420
2029	146.18	155.71	160.67	0.371	0.395	0.408
2030	142.35	153.05	158.97	0.361	0.388	0.403
2031	136.68	148.62	155.59	0.347	0.377	0.395
2032	131.60	144.87	152.97	0.334	0.368	0.388
2033	128.17	142.85	152.17	0.325	0.362	0.386
2034	126.24	142.03	152.63	0.320	0.360	0.387
2035	125.21	141.78	153.67	0.318	0.360	0.390
2036	124.59	141.94	155.15	0.316	0.360	0.394
2037	124.34	142.43	156.92	0.316	0.361	0.398
2038	124.37	143.17	158.83	0.316	0.363	0.403
2039	124.50	143.98	160.77	0.316	0.365	0.408
2040	124.61	144.73	162.56	0.316	0.367	0.412
2041	124.59	145.33	164.05	0.316	0.369	0.416
2042	124.33	145.65	165.18	0.315	0.370	0.419
2043	123.70	145.56	165.81	0.314	0.369	0.421
2044	122.65	145.02	165.86	0.311	0.368	0.421
2045	121.19	144.00	165.33	0.308	0.365	0.420
2046	119.33	142.52	164.26	0.303	0.362	0.417
2047	117.11	140.60	162.69	0.297	0.357	0.413
2048	114.59	138.30	160.67	0.291	0.351	0.408
2049	111.82	135.68	158.26	0.284	0.344	0.402
2050	108.86	132.84	155.54	0.276	0.337	0.395

pediatric beds, pediatricians and pediatric nurses was 563,400, 176,700 and 294,500, respectively. According to this standard, the number of the demand gap of pediatric beds, physicians and nurses is 49,000, 24,000 and 37,000, respectively. The demand under the low scenario will continue to decline by 2050, while the secondary peak of the medium and high scenarios will be 405,000 beds, 125,600 physicians, 209,400 nurses and 456,100 beds, 143,100 physicians and 238,400 nurses, respectively. In 2050, the difference between the predicted demand under the medium

Table 14.4 Forecast of Demand of Pediatricians and Nurses in China, 2015–2050 (Million)

	Pediatricians			Nurses		
	Low	Medium	High	Low	Medium	High
2015	0.150	0.150	0.150	0.250	0.250	0.250
2016	0.152	0.152	0.152	0.253	0.253	0.253
2017	0.153	0.153	0.153	0.255	0.255	0.255
2018	0.154	0.154	0.154	0.256	0.256	0.256
2019	0.152	0.152	0.152	0.253	0.254	0.254
2020	0.150	0.151	0.151	0.250	0.251	0.251
2021	0.147	0.148	0.149	0.245	0.247	0.248
2022	0.143	0.145	0.146	0.238	0.242	0.243
2023	0.139	0.142	0.142	0.231	0.236	0.237
2024	0.134	0.138	0.139	0.224	0.230	0.232
2025	0.130	0.134	0.136	0.216	0.223	0.226
2026	0.125	0.130	0.132	0.208	0.216	0.220
2027	0.119	0.125	0.127	0.199	0.208	0.212
2028	0.115	0.121	0.124	0.191	0.202	0.207
2029	0.110	0.117	0.121	0.183	0.195	0.201
2030	0.107	0.115	0.119	0.178	0.191	0.199
2031	0.103	0.111	0.117	0.171	0.186	0.194
2032	0.099	0.109	0.115	0.164	0.181	0.191
2033	0.096	0.107	0.114	0.160	0.179	0.190
2034	0.095	0.107	0.114	0.158	0.178	0.191
2035	0.094	0.106	0.115	0.157	0.177	0.192
2036	0.093	0.106	0.116	0.156	0.177	0.194
2037	0.093	0.107	0.118	0.155	0.178	0.196
2038	0.093	0.107	0.119	0.155	0.179	0.199
2039	0.093	0.108	0.121	0.156	0.180	0.201
2040	0.093	0.109	0.122	0.156	0.181	0.203
2041	0.093	0.109	0.123	0.156	0.182	0.205
2042	0.093	0.109	0.124	0.155	0.182	0.206
2043	0.093	0.109	0.124	0.155	0.182	0.207
2044	0.092	0.109	0.124	0.153	0.181	0.207
2045	0.091	0.108	0.124	0.151	0.180	0.207
2046	0.089	0.107	0.123	0.149	0.178	0.205
2047	0.088	0.105	0.122	0.146	0.176	0.203
2048	0.086	0.104	0.121	0.143	0.173	0.201
2049	0.084	0.102	0.119	0.140	0.170	0.198
2050	0.082	0.100	0.117	0.136	0.166	0.194

and high scenarios and the low scenario is 65,900 and 128,400 pediatric beds, 20,700 and 40,300 pediatricians and 34,500 and 67,100 pediatric nurses, respectively.

c Results of Scheme III

Based on the standard of 1.07 pediatricians per 1,000 children in the world's major developed countries, the peak demand for pediatric beds, pediatricians and pediatric nurses was 927,200, 274,000 and 456,700, respectively (Table 14.6). According to this standard, the number of demand

Table 14.5 Forecast of Pediatric Beds, Obstetricians and Nurses in China under Scheme II, 2015–2050 (Million)

	Beds			Obstetricians			Nurses		
	Low	Medium	High	Low	Medium	High	Low	Medium	High
2015	0.550	0.550	0.550	0.173	0.173	0.173	0.288	0.288	0.288
2016	0.556	0.556	0.556	0.174	0.174	0.174	0.291	0.291	0.291
2017	0.561	0.561	0.561	0.176	0.176	0.176	0.293	0.293	0.293
2018	0.563	0.563	0.563	0.177	0.177	0.177	0.295	0.295	0.295
2019	0.557	0.558	0.558	0.175	0.175	0.175	0.291	0.292	0.292
2020	0.549	0.552	0.553	0.172	0.173	0.173	0.287	0.289	0.289
2021	0.538	0.544	0.545	0.169	0.170	0.171	0.281	0.284	0.285
2022	0.524	0.532	0.534	0.164	0.167	0.167	0.274	0.278	0.279
2023	0.509	0.519	0.522	0.160	0.163	0.164	0.266	0.271	0.273
2024	0.493	0.505	0.509	0.155	0.158	0.160	0.258	0.264	0.266
2025	0.476	0.491	0.497	0.149	0.154	0.156	0.249	0.257	0.260
2026	0.459	0.476	0.484	0.144	0.149	0.152	0.240	0.249	0.253
2027	0.437	0.458	0.467	0.137	0.144	0.146	0.229	0.239	0.244
2028	0.421	0.444	0.455	0.132	0.139	0.143	0.220	0.232	0.238
2029	0.402	0.428	0.442	0.126	0.134	0.139	0.210	0.224	0.231
2030	0.391	0.421	0.437	0.123	0.132	0.137	0.205	0.220	0.229
2031	0.376	0.409	0.428	0.118	0.128	0.134	0.196	0.214	0.224
2032	0.362	0.398	0.421	0.114	0.125	0.132	0.189	0.208	0.220
2033	0.352	0.393	0.418	0.111	0.123	0.131	0.184	0.205	0.219
2034	0.347	0.391	0.420	0.109	0.122	0.132	0.181	0.204	0.219
2035	0.344	0.390	0.423	0.108	0.122	0.133	0.180	0.204	0.221
2036	0.343	0.390	0.427	0.107	0.122	0.134	0.179	0.204	0.223
2037	0.342	0.392	0.432	0.107	0.123	0.135	0.179	0.205	0.226
2038	0.342	0.394	0.437	0.107	0.123	0.137	0.179	0.206	0.228
2039	0.342	0.396	0.442	0.107	0.124	0.139	0.179	0.207	0.231
2040	0.343	0.398	0.447	0.107	0.125	0.140	0.179	0.208	0.234
2041	0.343	0.400	0.451	0.107	0.125	0.141	0.179	0.209	0.236
2042	0.342	0.401	0.454	0.107	0.126	0.142	0.179	0.209	0.237
2043	0.340	0.400	0.456	0.107	0.126	0.143	0.178	0.209	0.238
2044	0.337	0.399	0.456	0.106	0.125	0.143	0.176	0.208	0.238
2045	0.333	0.396	0.455	0.105	0.124	0.143	0.174	0.207	0.238
2046	0.328	0.392	0.452	0.103	0.123	0.142	0.172	0.205	0.236
2047	0.322	0.387	0.447	0.101	0.121	0.140	0.168	0.202	0.234
2048	0.315	0.380	0.442	0.099	0.119	0.139	0.165	0.199	0.231
2049	0.308	0.373	0.435	0.096	0.117	0.137	0.161	0.195	0.228
2050	0.299	0.365	0.428	0.094	0.115	0.134	0.156	0.191	0.224

gap of pediatric beds, physicians and nurses were 413,200, 120,000 and 199,700, respectively. The demand under the low scenario will continue to decline by 2050, while the secondary peaks for the medium and high scenarios are 659,100 beds, 194,800 physicians, 324,700 nurses and 750,500 beds, 228,800 physicians and 369,700 nurses, respectively. In 2050, the difference between the predicted demand under the medium and high scenarios and that under the low scenario is 108,500 and 212,200 pediatric beds, 32,100 and 62,400 pediatricians and 53,500 and 104,100 pediatric nurses, respectively.

Table 14.6 Forecast of Pediatric Beds, Obstetricians and Nurses in China under Scheme III, 2015–2050 (Million)

	Beds			Obstetricians			Nurses		
	Low	Medium	High	Low	Medium	High	Low	Medium	High
2015	0.905	0.905	0.905	0.268	0.268	0.268	0.446	0.446	0.446
2016	0.915	0.915	0.915	0.271	0.271	0.271	0.451	0.451	0.451
2017	0.923	0.923	0.923	0.273	0.273	0.273	0.455	0.455	0.455
2018	0.927	0.927	0.927	0.274	0.274	0.274	0.457	0.457	0.457
2019	0.917	0.919	0.919	0.271	0.272	0.272	0.452	0.453	0.453
2020	0.904	0.909	0.910	0.267	0.269	0.269	0.445	0.448	0.448
2021	0.886	0.894	0.896	0.262	0.264	0.265	0.436	0.441	0.442
2022	0.863	0.875	0.879	0.255	0.259	0.260	0.425	0.431	0.433
2023	0.838	0.854	0.859	0.248	0.253	0.254	0.413	0.421	0.423
2024	0.811	0.831	0.838	0.240	0.246	0.248	0.399	0.409	0.413
2025	0.783	0.808	0.818	0.232	0.239	0.242	0.386	0.398	0.403
2026	0.755	0.783	0.796	0.223	0.232	0.235	0.372	0.386	0.392
2027	0.720	0.753	0.768	0.213	0.223	0.227	0.354	0.371	0.378
2028	0.692	0.730	0.749	0.205	0.216	0.221	0.341	0.360	0.369
2029	0.661	0.705	0.727	0.196	0.208	0.215	0.326	0.347	0.358
2030	0.644	0.693	0.719	0.190	0.205	0.213	0.317	0.341	0.354
2031	0.618	0.673	0.704	0.183	0.199	0.208	0.305	0.331	0.347
2032	0.595	0.656	0.692	0.176	0.194	0.205	0.293	0.323	0.341
2033	0.580	0.646	0.689	0.171	0.191	0.204	0.286	0.318	0.339
2034	0.571	0.643	0.691	0.169	0.190	0.204	0.281	0.317	0.340
2035	0.567	0.642	0.695	0.167	0.190	0.206	0.279	0.316	0.343
2036	0.564	0.642	0.702	0.167	0.190	0.208	0.278	0.316	0.346
2037	0.563	0.645	0.710	0.166	0.191	0.210	0.277	0.318	0.350
2038	0.563	0.648	0.719	0.166	0.191	0.212	0.277	0.319	0.354
2039	0.563	0.652	0.728	0.167	0.193	0.215	0.278	0.321	0.358
2040	0.564	0.655	0.736	0.167	0.194	0.217	0.278	0.323	0.362
2041	0.564	0.658	0.742	0.167	0.194	0.219	0.278	0.324	0.366
2042	0.563	0.659	0.747	0.166	0.195	0.221	0.277	0.325	0.368
2043	0.560	0.659	0.750	0.165	0.195	0.222	0.276	0.324	0.370
2044	0.555	0.656	0.751	0.164	0.194	0.222	0.273	0.323	0.370
2045	0.548	0.652	0.748	0.162	0.193	0.221	0.270	0.321	0.369
2046	0.540	0.645	0.743	0.160	0.191	0.220	0.266	0.318	0.366
2047	0.530	0.636	0.736	0.157	0.188	0.218	0.261	0.313	0.363
2048	0.519	0.626	0.727	0.153	0.185	0.215	0.255	0.308	0.358
2049	0.506	0.614	0.716	0.150	0.181	0.212	0.249	0.302	0.353
2050	0.493	0.601	0.704	0.146	0.178	0.208	0.243	0.296	0.347

Concluding Remarks

In this chapter, we investigated the demand for maternal and child health services by the population-resources density method according to the changing number of births produced in the population projections in Chapter 11.

The results show that birth accumulation under the two-child policy is not large in the short term. Births peaked in 2016, at 17.59 million, before falling back. On the whole, the two-child policy does not seem to have a strong short-term accumulation of births, which also means that obstetric health services do not face a tense situation of continuous increase in demand in the short term. However, by 2050, a cumulative 52.45 million and 96.17 million more babies will be born under the medium and high scenarios than under the low scenario, with an annual average of 1.5 million to 2.7 million, which should also be paid attention to and corresponding supporting health services need to be increased. Although the number of births began to decline after only one year's increase, due to the effect of demographic inertia, there will still be a small peak of births around 2035, which needs to be prepared in advance.

The number of children aged 0–14 peaked in 2018 at 256 million, an increase by 6.07 million over 2015, putting increased pressure on pediatric resources. Between 2016 and 2020, the number of children aged 0–14 under the medium and high scenarios was 1.938 million and 2.227 million higher than that under the low scenario. The number of children aged 0–14 also has a small peak. Under the low, medium and high scenarios, the small peak will be reached in 2040, 2042 and 2044, and the small peak size will reach 156 million, 182 million and 207 million, respectively. The number of children in the medium and high scenarios is 26.29 million and 51.56 million more than that in the low scenario, respectively.

The implementation of the two-child policy has increased the demand for medical and health services for pregnant women in the long run. According to the resource density in 2018, the small peak of births around 2037 will produce demand of 22,145 and 25,526 maternity hospitals, including 3,328 and 3,836 specialized maternity hospitals, and 179,200 and 206,600 obstetricians, respectively. The demand for the number of obstetric nurses is 153,600 and 177,100, respectively. By 2050, the difference between the predicted demand under medium and high scenarios and that under low scenario will reach the maximum. The difference between the demand for obstetric and gynecological institutions will be 3,627 and 7,005, respectively, among which the demand difference of specialized hospitals in obstetrics and gynecology will be 545 and 1,053, respectively, and the demand difference of obstetricians will be 29,400 and 56,700, respectively. The demand difference of obstetric nurses will be 25,200 and 48,600, respectively.

With the implementation of the two-child policy, children's medical services need to be met urgently. According to Scheme I, the peak demand for pediatric medical institutions and pediatric beds in 2018 was 20,489 and 519,900, respectively, and the secondary peaks will be 14,565 and 369,600 and 16,586 and 420,900, respectively, in the medium and high scenarios. In 2050, the difference in demand for pediatric medical institutions between the medium and high scenarios and the low scenario is 2,398 and 4,668, respectively, and the difference in demand for beds is 60,800 and 118,500, respectively. According to the estimation of Scheme II, the peak demand for pediatric beds, pediatricians and nurses was 563,400, 176,700 and 294,500, respectively, and the gap in pediatric beds, physicians and nurses will be 49,000, 24,000 and 37,000, respectively. In 2050, the difference between the results of the medium and high scenarios and the low scenario will be 65,900 and 128,400 pediatric beds, 20,700 and 40,300 pediatricians and 34,500 and 67,100 pediatric nurses, respectively. According to the estimation of Scheme III, the peak demand for pediatric beds, pediatricians and nurses was 927,200, 274,400 and 456,700, respectively, and the gap will be 413,200, 120,000 and 199,700, respectively. In 2050, the difference between the results of the medium and high scenarios and the low scenario will be 108,500 and 212,200 pediatric beds, 32,100 and 62,400 pediatricians and 53,500 and 104,100 pediatric nurses, respectively.

In view of the population trends under the two-child policy and the further liberalization of the family planning policy, it is important to meet the demand for maternal and child health services. Great challenges exist in especially constructing maternity departments and children's specialized hospitals, increasing the number of obstetric and pediatric beds, training obstetricians and pediatricians, midwives and nurses and increasing the number of pediatric nurses, improving the ratio of doctor to nurse in pediatric care.

Reference

Wang Guangzhou. 2016. Analysis of Several Key Factors Affecting the Size of Newborns under the Universal Two-Child Policy. *Academia Bimestris* 1: 82–89.

15 The Impact of the Two-Child Policy on Preschool- and School-Age Populations and the Demand for Teachers

With the implementation of the universal two-child policy, the number of births will increase. The accumulation of births will in recent years lead to an increase in the demand for child care, preschool and primary education, more specifically, in the demand for facilities or seats and teachers. While China's existing public services related to education cannot satisfy the need for the time being. The changes in population structure give the education structure a severe challenge. Current contradiction between the supply and demand of education and long-term social coordinative and sustainable development both decide that education is a basic and important part, and it is of profound practical significance to study the impact of population structure changes on education. This chapter measures the impact on education-related demands by the demographic changes after the universal two-child policy and by indicators such as enrollment rates in kindergartens and in compulsory education, teacher–student ratio and education spending index.

Data and Methods

First, according to the population projection results, the preschool population and the school-age populations at each stage are calculated, respectively, from 2015 to 2050. "Regulations on Kindergarten Work" implemented in 2016 stipulates that "kindergarten-age children are generally 3 to 6 years old",[1] and Article 11 of "Compulsory Education Law of the People's Republic of China" stipulates that

> when children have reached the age of six, their parents or guardians shall send them to school to receive compulsory education for the prescribed number of years; in areas where that is not possible, the beginning of schooling may be postponed to the age of seven.[2]

China's primary schools implement autumn enrollment. Children who are six years old before August 31 are eligible for admission and those born between September and December need to be enrolled in the following year. As a result, some children who have reached the age of six are receiving preschool education and meanwhile others are receiving primary education. When making population projections, it

DOI: 10.4324/9781003429661-15

is impossible to accurately classify the populations around September each year. Therefore, in the study of the school-age population, it has been controversial whether six-year-old children are classified as preschool-age population or primary school-age population. Based on relevant laws, regulations and systems in China, this chapter defines those under three years old as nursery-age children and those from 3 to 6 years old as preschool children. As for children of compulsory education age, primary school education age is defined as 6–11 years old, and junior high school education age as 12–14 years old.

Second, in the prediction of the care services for infants and young children under the age of 3, due to the incomplete childcare services in China, there are no relevant regulations to make clear requirements for the enrollment rate of nurseries. So here taking the experience of the EU countries as reference, the enrollment rate of nurseries is set at 30%, and the teacher-to-child ratio is set to be 1:5.

Third, when studying the impact of the universal two-child policy on the preschool population, two enrollment rates are set to infer the demand for preschool seats. The first one is a conservative estimate based on national regulations, that is, the enrollment rate will remain unchanged at 85% from 2020 to 2050; the second one is an ideal setting based on the enrollment rate of developed countries, that is, it will increase from 85% in 2020 to 95% in 2050 at a constant rate. In the research on the number of preschool teachers, two teacher-to-child ratios are set to predict the demand for teachers under the influence of the "comprehensive second-child policy". The first ratio is based on China's target requirement, that is, the ratio of full-time teachers to children is 1:8; the second one is the lowest level in estimation, which is 1:15. Two standards are also used to estimate the number of kindergartens needed in the future. One is based on the current average number of children in kindergartens, that is, 175 children per kindergarten, and the other is based on the minimum requirement of the "Regulations on Kindergarten Work", that is, 360 children per kindergarten. As for the financial investment in preschool education, the index of 2016 preschool education expenditure per student, which is 16%, is used for projection. The impact of the policy on preschool education will be measured all together by the demand for enrollment seats, teachers, kindergartens and financial investment.

Fourth, when studying the impact of the universal two-child policy on the school-age population of compulsory education, the enrollment rate is set at 100% due to China's popularization of compulsory education, and then, the number of seats needed by the school-age population of compulsory education is estimated. Further, the school-age population of compulsory education is divided into primary school-age population and junior high school-age population. According to different teacher–student ratios (1:19 for primary school, 1:13.5 for junior high school) and the indexes of education expenditure per student (21% for primary school and 29% for junior high school), the number of teachers and financial investment needed for primary and junior high schools in the future are estimated. All the tables and figures based on forecasting results are not further noted with data sources.

Forecast of Demand for Child-Care Services for Children under Age Three

The age of being admitted by public kindergartens in China is three years old and above. The infants and young children under three years old are mainly excluded from the public education system and mainly rely on the informal family care. In some developed countries, childcare services is important in the public service, but in our country, the nursery service should be improved. Family care often refers to mother's care or grandparents' care. To a certain extent, this affects mother's labor participation rate. Although grandparents' care has played a supporting role, it fails to give more professional education. The Outline of the National Program for Medium- and Long-term Education Reform and Development (2010–2020) published in 2010 attached importance to the education of children aged 0 to 3. In 2013, the Ministry of Education issued the Notice on Pilot Early Education for Infants and Children aged 0 to 3, which launched pilot early education for infants and children aged 0 to 3 in 14 regions including Beijing and Shanghai. It proposed that with the help of kindergartens and maternal and child health care institutions, an education system for community and parents educating infants and children will be built by fully integrating public education, health and community resources. The two-child policy first affects the born population, so the related demand for infant care services is urgent and has important practical significance. According to the forecast, after the implementation of the two-child policy, the total size of infants and toddlers under the age of three years in China from 2015 to 2050 is as follows (see Table 15.1).

Overall, from 2015 to 2050, the number of children under three years old shows a decreasing trend. Although it begins to rise around 2029, the overall trend was downward. At the end of 2015, China implemented the two-child policy. Limited by the 10-month pregnancy, the two-child policy took effect in 2017. The stock and increment of infants under the age of three years old overlapped and reached a peak in 2017, that is, 49,471,800 people. By 2050, the number of children under the age of three will be 21,748,500 in the Low scenario, which reduces by more than half from the peak, with 27.940,700 in the Medium scenario and 33.686,600 in the High scenario.

According to China's Special Provisions on Female Worker Labor Protection, female workers enjoy 98 days of maternity leave.[3] However, female workers do not enjoy parental leave. Mothers have to choose between child care and work, which brings difficulties to child care. Imperfect public services for infant and child care are a key factor limiting fertility. In some developed countries, there will be special childcare facilities to provide scientific and professional care of babies. This supporting policy can help mother effectively alleviate the conflict between work and family responsibilities. With the improvement of women's labor participation rate, household demand for nursery as a kind of public service is increasing. In 2015, 33% of children in Organization for Economic Cooperation and Development (OECD) countries enjoy formal government care. Nordic countries, in particular, are exemplary in child care, with the majority of children under the age of

236 Preschool- and School-Age Populations

Table 15.1 Projections of Demand for Care of Children under 3, 2015–2050 (Million)

	Number of Infants under Three			Demand for Child-Care Seats			Demand for Child-Care Teachers		
Year	Low	Medium	High	Low	Medium	High	Low	Medium	High
2015	51.31	51.31	51.31	15.39	15.39	15.39	3.08	3.08	3.08
2016	51.19	51.19	51.19	15.36	15.36	15.36	3.07	3.07	3.07
2017	49.47	49.47	49.47	14.84	14.84	14.84	2.97	2.97	2.97
2018	49.34	49.34	49.34	14.80	14.80	14.80	2.96	2.96	2.96
2019	44.98	45.47	45.53	13.49	13.64	13.66	2.70	2.73	2.73
2020	40.18	41.63	41.86	12.05	12.49	12.56	2.41	2.50	2.51
2021	36.81	39.26	39.76	11.04	11.78	11.93	2.21	2.36	2.39
2022	34.76	37.76	38.58	10.43	11.33	11.57	2.09	2.27	2.31
2023	33.34	36.47	37.62	10.00	10.94	11.29	2.00	2.19	2.26
2024	32.12	35.36	36.84	9.64	10.61	11.05	1.93	2.12	2.21
2025	31.16	34.50	36.28	9.35	10.35	10.88	1.87	2.07	2.18
2026	30.48	33.93	35.96	9.14	10.18	10.79	1.83	2.04	2.16
2027	30.09	33.66	35.91	9.03	10.10	10.77	1.81	2.02	2.15
2028	29.96	33.69	36.19	8.99	10.11	10.86	1.80	2.02	2.17
2029	30.06	33.99	36.80	9.02	10.20	11.04	1.80	2.04	2.21
2030	30.32	34.49	37.67	9.10	10.35	11.30	1.82	2.07	2.26
2031	30.69	35.10	38.68	9.21	10.53	11.60	1.84	2.11	2.32
2032	31.08	35.78	39.71	9.33	10.73	11.91	1.87	2.15	2.38
2033	31.47	36.47	40.74	9.44	10.94	12.22	1.89	2.19	2.44
2034	31.83	37.13	41.74	9.55	11.14	12.52	1.91	2.23	2.50
2035	32.11	37.69	42.68	9.63	11.31	12.80	1.93	2.26	2.56
2036	32.27	38.07	43.44	9.68	11.42	13.03	1.94	2.28	2.61
2037	32.32	38.22	43.91	9.70	11.47	13.17	1.94	2.29	2.63
2038	32.25	38.16	44.04	9.68	11.45	13.21	1.94	2.29	2.64
2039	31.99	37.88	43.85	9.60	11.36	13.15	1.92	2.27	2.63
2040	31.47	37.36	43.32	9.44	11.21	13.00	1.89	2.24	2.60
2041	30.74	36.62	42.48	9.22	10.99	12.75	1.84	2.20	2.55
2042	29.86	35.73	41.43	8.96	10.72	12.43	1.79	2.14	2.49
2043	28.80	34.71	40.25	8.64	10.41	12.08	1.73	2.08	2.42
2044	27.61	33.57	39.05	8.28	10.07	11.71	1.66	2.01	2.34
2045	26.37	32.41	37.84	7.91	9.72	11.35	1.58	1.94	2.27
2046	25.19	31.27	36.72	7.56	9.38	11.02	1.51	1.88	2.20
2047	24.12	30.22	35.72	7.24	9.07	10.71	1.45	1.81	2.14
2048	23.18	29.29	34.87	6.95	8.79	10.46	1.39	1.76	2.09
2049	22.39	28.53	34.19	6.72	8.56	10.26	1.34	1.71	2.05
2050	21.75	27.94	33.69	6.52	8.38	10.11	1.30	1.68	2.02

three being cared for in formal institutions. Due to the imperfect development of childcare institutions in China, there is no formal mechanism for childcare services at present. According to the standards of developed countries, the enrollment rate is set as 30%, and the teacher–child ratio is set as 1:5. The forecast of the demand for childcare seats and the demand for childcare teachers in China from 2015 to 2050 are shown in Table 15.1.

The forecast shows that every year, China basically needs more than 10 million childcare seats, and especially in the early period of the two-child policy, the demand reached its highest, more than 15 million, which brought great challenges to the immature infant care services. As time goes by, the effect of two-child policy will become more and more obvious. By 2050, the demand will decrease year by year, with the demand dropping to 6,524,500 people in the Low scenario and dropping by around 10 million people in the medium and High scenarios, which are 8.382,200 people and 10.106 million people, respectively. Compared with no two-child policy, the policy increases demand for childcare seats by 1.85 million to 3.58 million. Due to the particularity of infants and young children, preschool services require more professional full-time teachers and more concentrated care, which are different from other education. According to the standard of teacher–child ratio of 1:5, the demand for preschool teachers is predicted (see Table 15.1). In the early days, more than 3 million teachers were needed, and then the demand for teachers decreased with the decline of required seats. If there were no two-child policy, the teachers demand in 2024 will drop below 2 million. According to the Medium scenario, the implementation of two-child policy makes the demand for teachers just drop below 2 million until 2044. In High scenario, the demand for teachers will remain above 2 million until 2050.

With the further understanding toward the importance of child care and the growing demand for early education in our country, infant childcare services will become a kind of basic, rigid, the universal livelihood needs but also have positive externalities. Child-care services can effectively encourage couples to have two children and promote female employment so as to improve the economic efficiency of the whole society. In May 2019, the Guiding Opinions on Promoting the Development of Care Services for Infants under 3 Years Old issued by the General Office of the State Council points out that by 2020, policies, regulations and standards for infant care services will be preliminarily established, and a number of infant care service institutions with exemplary effects will be established. The Guiding Opinions also points that a diversified infant care service system covering both urban and rural areas will be basically built by 2025, which will meet the needs of infant care.[4] The Guiding Opinions provides a direction for the development of future childcare services and clarify the roles of the government, the market, society and families in caring children under the age of three. Child care is the responsibility of not only families but also the state and society.

Forecast of Demand for Preschool Education

As the start of lifelong learning, Preschool education is an important part of the national educational system, and also an important public welfare cause. A good preschool education environment is of great significance for the physical and mental health of children. However, "low kindergarten enrollment" and "high tuition" are the existing problems in preschool education in China. After the implementation of the two-child policy, the size of the born population has been increasing rapidly in the short term, which will undoubtedly make the previous problems worse. Therefore, solving the structural contradiction between supply and demand of preschool education is an urgent task to improve the quality of preschool education. According to the population prediction after the implementation of the two-child policy, the total population of 3–6 years old is selected as the preschool-age population. After calculation, the prediction of preschool-age population under low, medium and high scenarios from 2015 to 2050 are as follows (see Table 15.2).

Since the low scenario is about the estimation without the implementation of the two-child policy, the comparison between the medium and the high scenarios shows that after the implementation of the two-child policy, the size of the preschool-age population is always larger than the size of the population without

Table 15.2 Forecast of Preschool-Age Population, 2015–2050 (Million)

Year	Low	Medium	High
2015	73.03	73.03	73.03
2016	72.72	72.72	72.72
2017	73.62	73.62	73.62
2018	70.68	70.68	70.68
2019	68.52	68.52	68.52
2020	67.78	67.78	67.78
2021	64.13	64.13	64.13
2022	62.23	62.72	62.78
2023	56.84	58.28	58.51
2024	51.54	53.98	54.48
2025	47.72	51.19	52.07
2026	45.26	49.33	50.64
2027	43.53	47.75	49.49
2028	42.09	46.46	48.61
2029	41.01	45.52	48.04
2030	40.30	44.97	47.80
2031	39.95	44.81	47.97
2032	39.92	45.02	48.57
2033	40.14	45.53	49.52
2034	40.55	46.25	50.74
2035	41.04	47.11	52.08
2036	41.56	48.01	53.45
2037	42.06	48.90	54.80
2038	42.47	49.70	56.08
2039	42.76	50.30	57.19
2040	42.91	50.65	57.98
2041	42.90	50.74	58.39
2042	42.64	50.50	58.36
2043	42.12	49.95	57.87
2044	41.33	49.15	56.98
2045	40.26	48.08	55.77
2046	38.96	46.80	54.29
2047	37.48	45.39	52.72
2048	35.91	43.88	51.14
2049	34.31	42.36	49.61
2050	32.81	40.92	48.20

the implementation of the two-child policy, and the number of the population is fluctuating. As a whole, preschool-age population experiences a downward trend and then increases and then decreases. After the implementation of the two-child policy, the number of preschool-age children peaked in 2017, reaching 73.62 million. Part of the reason is that the willing of childbearing can be achieved after the implementation of the policy. Since then, the effect of the policy is gradually weakened, the size of preschool-age children each year is shrinking. However, in 2032, which is a turning point, the population starts to grow. At the same time, the population of preschool education is estimated to be 39.92 million in the low scenario, 45.2 million in the medium scenario, and 48.57 million in the high scenario. The population of fertile women in different periods lead to fluctuations in the size of the birth population. The population of preschool-age children reaches the second peak in 2041, with 42.9 million, 50.74 million and 58.39 million in the low, medium and high scenarios, respectively. Since then, the size of the preschool population declines year by year, and by 2050, the population under low, medium and high scenarios are predicted to be 32.81 million, 40.92 million and 48.2 million, respectively.

Forecast of the Demand for Preschool Education Seats

According to the above prediction of the preschool-age population, the demand for preschool education seats can be estimated and compared with the current scale of seats, so as to analyze how much seats are needed because of the two-child policy. In 2010, the Outline of the National Plan for Medium- and Long-term Education Reform and Development (2010–2020) stated that preschool education should become universal education, and the main goal for the development of preschool education is to reach 95% of the gross enrollment rate for the first preschool grade, 80% for second grade and 70%[5] for third grade by 2020. However, according to the 2017 National Statistical Bulletin on the Development of Education, the gross enrollment rate of preschool education was 79.6%[6] in 2017, which proves that the goal has been realized ahead of schedule. In 2017, the 13th Five-Year Plan for the Development of National Education (No. 4, 2017) issued by the National Development and Reform Commission of the People's Republic of China set the main goals for the development of education and human resources in the 13th Five-Year Plan. It points that the goal of first three-year preschool enrollment rate in 2020 is 85%.[7] When forecasting the demand for preschool education seats, this chapter will set the enrollment rate of 2020 as 85% according to the development goals of the 13th Five-Year Plan for the Development of National Education. The enrollment rate of 2015–2020 will be predicted based on the data interpolation with published data and 85% target data from 2018 Education Statistics Report. However, from 2020 to 2050, the 30-year time span will definitely change. According to the current development trend and the experience of developed countries, there is still room for the growth of the enrollment. Thus, the enrollment rate of 2020–2050 needs to be predicted.

At present, there are a number of researchers predicting the kindergarten enrollment over the next few decades. Shi Wenxiu (2018), referring to the experience and development process of preschool education in developed countries, estimates that in 2025, the gross enrollment rate of preschool for the first, second and third year will reach 99%, 96% and 90%, respectively. Yang Shunguang and Li Ling (2016) assume that by the end of the 16th Five-Year Plan, the universal three-year preschool education will be achieved, that is, the gross enrollment rate of preschool students will reach 100% by 2035. Pang Lijuan, Wang Honglei, and Lv Wu (2016) make regional forecasts, assuming that by 2020, the average gross enrollment rate in eastern regions can be 95% or above, in central regions, it can reach about 85% and, in western regions, it will strive to achieve 75–85%.

According to UNESCO's Sustainable Development Goals database, preschool enrollment rates vary widely in more than 200 countries around the world. At present, the global rate is close to 50%, over 92% in European countries, and over 100% in some developed countries, especially OECD countries such as France, the Netherlands and Ireland in the 1980s (see Table 15.3). In China, according to the 2017 National Statistical Bulletin on the Development of Education, the rate in China in 2015, 2016 and 2017 was 75%, 77.4% and 79.6%, respectively.[8] From the perspective of inter-provincial differences, the rate of each province is different,

Table 15.3 Kindergarten Enrollment Rates in Major Areas and Countries in the World in Recent Years

	2010	2011	2012	2013	2014	2015	2016
World	38.68	40.84	43.56	45.68	45.98	46.88	49.33
Europe	87.86	88.63	89.45	89.14	90.82	90.75	92.21
East Asia	58.01	63.46	71.19	75.56	78.78	80.78	84.12
United Kingdom	81.82	84.98	83.95	79.23	90.26	96.18	110.89
Australia	78.79	95.53	108.09	109.45	114.37	125.26	168.61
China	54.88	61.01	69.57	74.31	77.96	80.15	83.70
United States	70.10	70.15	70.93	71.52	72.54	72.03	71.94
Japan	–	–	–	87.32	86.42	86.06	86.76
Korea	–	–	–	92.88	93.33	94.77	97.86
France	105.92	105.66	104.96	104.81	105.07	105.06	105.11
Germany	–	–	–	107.39	107.79	107.47	108.46
Iceland	96.32	95.81	96.40	96.32	97.86	97.49	95.17
Ireland	–	–	103.56	110.48	110.93	102.11	116.00
Italy	99.67	100.10	100.31	99.88	99.09	98.88	98.20
Netherlands	–	89.80	90.47	92.83	93.57	94.37	95.11
New Zealand	–	–	–	–	90.67	91.94	91.50
Norway	98.80	98.99	99.06	98.67	97.89	97.38	95.90
Portugal	87.06	90.28	90.36	89.83	91.08	92.93	93.38
Sweden	95.19	94.93	94.84	95.01	95.57	93.89	94.08
Switzerland	98.78	99.65	99.20	102.61	105.22	104.71	104.79

Source: UNESCO's Sustainable Development Goals [EB/OL]. http://data.uis.unesco.org/

and the rate of eastern regions is higher than that of central and western regions. In 2011, Beijing's Three-year Action Plan for Preschool Education (2011–2013) set a target of achieving 90% kindergarten enrollment of school-age children as permanent residents.[9] And the Outline of Tianjin's Medium- and long-term Education Reform and Development Plan (2010–2020) set 98% by 2020 as its goal in three-year gross enrollment rate.[10]

In the estimation of the kindergarten enrollment rate from 2020 to 2050, this chapter refers to two assumptions about the rate from 2015 to 2050 by referring to the rate in developed countries and the currently well-developed cities in China. The first assumption (Scheme I) is to make the enrollment rate reach 85% after 2020 and remain unchanged until 2050 in accordance with the development goal of the 13th Five-Year Plan for the Development of National Education. As for the second assumption (Scheme II), according to the average development level of European countries, assuming that the rate in China will grow by 0.37% a year, which is based on the premise that the rate in China reaches 95% of the current average level of OECD countries in 2050 according to the average developmental level of European countries. The enrollment rates from 2015 to 2020 are based on the data published in the 2017 National Educational Development Statistical Report. The enrollment rates in 2015, 2016 and 2017 were 75%, 77.4% and 79.6%, respectively.[11] With a target of 85% by 2020, the growth rate for 2017–2020 is calculated to be 2.2%. According to the above two methods of calculating enrollment rate, we have made two sets forecast of preschool education seats demand in low, medium and high scenarios. According to 2018 Education Statistics, there were 46,564,204 preschool students.[12] The number has been taken to calculate the demand for preschool education seats in 2018, and as a reference, it helps calculate two predictions of each year's gap between the supply and demand of preschool education seats from 2015 to 2050 (see Tables 15.4 and 15.5).

As can be seen from Table 15.4, according to Scheme I, the enrollment rate will remain unchanged at 85% from 2020 to 2050. In 2017, the demand for preschool education seats in China had the largest number, and the gap between supply and demand also reached the largest, and then the demand started to decline. From the perspective of the low scenario, in 2032, the demand for preschool seats reaches the lowest, which has 33,929,600 people, and then it slowly rises, reaching the second peak in 2040 at 36,475,200 people, and then it gradually drops to 27,891,300 people in 2050. The trend of medium and high scenarios is consistent with that of low scenario. The medium scenario decreases to 2031 after 2017, and the demand for seats plummets to the all-time low, which is at 38,087,100, and then rises to the second peak of 43,128,800 in 2041. In the high scenario, the demand drops to its lowest point in 2030, at 40,633,300, before rising again in 2041, to 49,629,100. From the perspective of the gap between supply and demand, from the implementation of the two-child policy to 2023, demand for kindergarten in China exceeds its supply, and especially in 2020, the gap between supply and demand reaches 1,052,600 people, which is the largest number. From then on, there is a stage of oversupply. But from 2037 to 2045, the prediction under the high scenario shows

Table 15.4 Forecast of Demand and Gap Between Supply and Demand for Preschool Education Seats from 2015 to 2050 (Scheme I) (Million)

Year	Enrollment rate	Demand Low	Demand Medium	Demand High	Gap Low	Gap Medium	Gap High
2015	0.75	54.77	54.77	54.77	8.21	8.21	8.21
2016	0.77	56.29	56.29	56.29	9.72	9.72	9.72
2017	0.80	58.60	58.60	58.60	12.03	12.03	12.03
2018	0.81	57.50	57.50	57.50	10.94	10.94	10.94
2019	0.83	56.97	56.97	56.97	10.40	10.40	10.40
2020	0.85	57.62	57.62	57.62	11.05	11.05	11.05
2021	0.85	54.51	54.51	54.51	7.94	7.94	7.94
2022	0.85	52.90	53.31	53.36	6.33	6.75	6.80
2023	0.85	48.32	49.54	49.73	1.75	2.98	3.17
2024	0.85	43.81	45.88	46.31	−2.75	−0.68	−0.26
2025	0.85	40.56	43.51	44.26	−6.01	−3.05	−2.31
2026	0.85	38.47	41.93	43.05	−8.09	−4.64	−3.52
2027	0.85	37.00	40.59	42.07	−9.56	−5.98	−4.50
2028	0.85	35.78	39.49	41.32	−10.78	−7.07	−5.25
2029	0.85	34.86	38.69	40.84	−11.71	−7.87	−5.73
2030	0.85	34.25	38.22	40.63	−12.31	−8.34	−5.93
2031	0.85	33.96	38.09	40.78	−12.61	−8.48	−5.79
2032	0.85	33.93	38.27	41.29	−12.63	−8.30	−5.28
2033	0.85	34.12	38.70	42.09	−12.44	−7.87	−4.47
2034	0.85	34.47	39.31	43.13	−12.10	−7.25	−3.44
2035	0.85	34.89	40.04	44.27	−11.68	−6.52	−2.29
2036	0.85	35.33	40.81	45.44	−11.24	−5.76	−1.13
2037	0.85	35.75	41.56	46.58	−10.82	−5.00	0.02
2038	0.85	36.10	42.24	47.67	−10.46	−4.32	1.11
2039	0.85	36.34	42.75	48.61	−10.22	−3.81	2.05
2040	0.85	36.48	43.05	49.28	−10.09	−3.51	2.72
2041	0.85	36.47	43.13	49.63	−10.10	−3.44	3.06
2042	0.85	36.24	42.92	49.61	−10.32	−3.64	3.05
2043	0.85	35.81	42.46	49.19	−10.76	−4.10	2.62
2044	0.85	35.13	41.78	48.43	−11.43	−4.78	1.87
2045	0.85	34.22	40.87	47.40	−12.34	−5.70	0.84
2046	0.85	33.11	39.78	46.15	−13.45	−6.79	−0.41
2047	0.85	31.86	38.58	44.81	−14.71	−7.98	−1.75
2048	0.85	30.52	37.30	43.47	−16.04	−9.27	−3.09
2049	0.85	29.16	36.01	42.17	−17.40	−10.56	−4.40
2050	0.85	27.89	34.78	40.97	−18.67	−11.78	−5.59

that the demand for seats is in short supply again, while the low and medium scenarios show that the current supply meets the demand in the future.

According to Table 15.5, the data in Scheme II is based on the experience of developed countries from 2020 to 2050, and thus, the result is same with Scheme I. In 2017, the demand for preschool education seats and the gap between supply and demand reaches the largest, after which the demand decreases and then increases, and then decreases again. In terms of the low scenario, the low demand and the

Table 15.5 Forecast of Demand and Gap Between Supply and Demand of Preschool Education Seats from 2015 to 2050 (Scheme II) (Million)

Year	Enrollment Rate	Demand Low	Medium	High	Gap Low	Medium	High
2015	0.75	54.77	54.77	54.77	8.21	8.21	8.21
2016	0.77	56.29	56.29	56.29	9.72	9.72	9.72
2017	0.80	58.60	58.60	58.60	12.03	12.03	12.03
2018	0.81	57.50	57.50	57.50	10.94	10.94	10.94
2019	0.83	56.97	56.97	56.97	10.40	10.40	10.40
2020	0.85	57.62	57.62	57.62	11.05	11.05	11.05
2021	0.85	54.71	54.71	54.71	8.15	8.15	8.15
2022	0.86	53.29	53.70	53.76	6.73	7.14	7.19
2023	0.86	48.85	50.09	50.29	2.29	3.53	3.72
2024	0.86	44.46	46.57	47.00	−2.10	0.00	0.43
2025	0.87	41.31	44.32	45.08	−5.25	−2.24	−1.48
2026	0.87	39.33	42.87	44.01	−7.23	−3.70	−2.55
2027	0.87	37.97	41.65	43.17	−8.59	−4.91	−3.39
2028	0.88	36.85	40.68	42.56	−9.71	−5.89	−4.01
2029	0.88	36.04	40.00	42.22	−10.53	−6.56	−4.35
2030	0.88	35.54	39.66	42.16	−11.02	−6.91	−4.40
2031	0.89	35.36	39.67	42.47	−11.20	−6.90	−4.10
2032	0.89	35.47	40.00	43.16	−11.10	−6.56	−3.41
2033	0.89	35.80	40.60	44.16	−10.76	−5.96	−2.40
2034	0.90	36.30	41.40	45.41	−10.27	−5.16	−1.15
2035	0.90	36.87	42.32	46.79	−9.69	−4.24	0.23
2036	0.90	37.48	43.29	48.20	−9.08	−3.27	1.64
2037	0.91	38.06	44.25	49.60	−8.50	−2.31	3.04
2038	0.91	38.58	45.15	50.95	−7.98	−1.42	4.38
2039	0.91	38.98	45.86	52.14	−7.58	−0.70	5.58
2040	0.92	39.27	46.35	53.06	−7.29	−0.21	6.50
2041	0.92	39.41	46.61	53.63	−7.16	0.04	7.07
2042	0.92	39.31	46.55	53.81	−7.25	−0.01	7.24
2043	0.93	38.98	46.22	53.55	−7.58	−0.34	6.98
2044	0.93	38.39	45.65	52.92	−8.18	−0.91	6.35
2045	0.93	37.53	44.82	51.99	−9.03	−1.75	5.42
2046	0.94	36.45	43.79	50.80	−10.11	−2.78	4.24
2047	0.94	35.20	42.63	49.51	−11.37	−3.94	2.95
2048	0.94	33.85	41.36	48.21	−12.72	−5.20	1.64
2049	0.95	32.46	40.08	46.93	−14.10	−6.49	0.37
2050	0.95	31.16	38.86	45.77	−15.40	−7.71	−0.79

high demand for seats appear in 2031 and 2041, respectively, which are 35,363,300 and 39.407,400, respectively. The low demand falls to 39.6,586 million in 2030, and the high one rises to 46.6,068 million in 2041, according to the medium scenario. While the high scenario shows that the demand has its lowest point in 2030, at 42,162,100, and the highest in 2042, at 538,082. From the perspective of the gap between supply and demand, from the implementation of the two-child policy to 2024, the demand for preschool education seats in China is much higher than the supply, and after 2025, the supply of preschool seats is basically greater than the demand. The gap turns from negative to positive between 2035 and 2049, which means that according to the prediction under the high scenario, the demand for preschool education seats is in short supply again.

Forecast of the Demand for Preschool Education Institutions

According to the 2018 Education Statistics Yearbook, China has 266,677 kindergartens in 2018 and 46,564,204 students.[13] Thus, every kindergarten has around 175 children on average. Article 11 on Kindergarten Work Procedures proposes that the size of a kindergarten, whose size generally is no more than 360 people, should bring benefits to children's physical and mental health and management.[14] On the basis of different enrollment rates, the kindergarten number demand in each year is predicted according to the standards of kindergarten capacity, which are 175 students/school and 360 students/school, respectively. With cross-analysis, a total of four schemes are made, and the gap of supply and demand for the number of kindergarten in each scheme is calculated.

In Scheme I, the enrollment rate is set at 85% with 175 children per school. The forecast results are presented in Table 15.6.

In Scheme II, the enrollment rate is set at 85% with 360 children per school. The forecast results are presented in Table 15.7.

In Scheme III, the enrollment rate is set at 95% with 175 children per school. The forecast results are presented in Table 15.8.

In Scheme V, the enrollment rate is set at 95% with 360 children per school. The forecast results are presented in Table 15.9.

Judging from the above forecast, the enrollment rate does not make a big difference in much demand for kindergartens, whether it's 85% or 95%. The gap is mainly caused by the size of kindergarten. The average capacity of a kindergarten in China is 175 children, and the minimum national standard is 360 children per kindergarten. The latter is more than twice the former.

According to the 175 students per school, the largest demand for kindergartens in China is more than 330,000. After 2030, the demand basically remains within 200,000, and by 2050, it is close to 150,000. According to the current supply of kindergartens, before 2023, there will be insufficient kindergartens with the most serious shortage of nearly 70,000, but there will also be a surplus of kindergarten when the demand is small. In 2030, there are 30,000 surplus kindergartens at most.

With 360 students per school, the demand for kindergartens in the future will be reduced by more than half compared with the standard of 175 students per school. Even if the maximum enrollment rate is 95%, the predicted results show that the current kindergartens are sufficient to meet the needs brought by the two-child policy. From 2015 to 2050, the highest demand for kindergartens is 162,800. Apart from that, the demand is basically below 150,000. Especially in the mid and late 2040s, the demand for kindergartens is below 100,000. By 2050, the demand under the low scenario is 86,600, and even under the high scenario, it is 127,100, less

Table 15.6 Forecast Results of Demand and Gap Between Supply and Demand for Kindergartens from 2015 to 2050 (Million)

Year	Demand for Kindergartens Low	Medium	High	Gap Low	Medium	High
2015	0.313	0.313	0.313	0.046	0.046	0.046
2016	0.322	0.322	0.322	0.055	0.055	0.055
2017	0.335	0.335	0.335	0.068	0.068	0.068
2018	0.329	0.329	0.329	0.062	0.062	0.062
2019	0.326	0.326	0.326	0.059	0.059	0.059
2020	0.329	0.329	0.329	0.063	0.063	0.063
2021	0.312	0.312	0.312	0.045	0.045	0.045
2022	0.302	0.305	0.305	0.036	0.038	0.038
2023	0.276	0.283	0.284	0.009	0.016	0.018
2024	0.250	0.262	0.265	−0.016	−0.005	−0.002
2025	0.232	0.249	0.253	−0.035	−0.018	−0.014
2026	0.220	0.240	0.246	−0.047	−0.027	−0.021
2027	0.211	0.232	0.240	−0.055	−0.035	−0.026
2028	0.205	0.226	0.236	−0.062	−0.041	−0.031
2029	0.199	0.221	0.233	−0.068	−0.046	−0.033
2030	0.196	0.218	0.232	−0.071	−0.048	−0.035
2031	0.194	0.218	0.233	−0.073	−0.049	−0.034
2032	0.194	0.219	0.236	−0.073	−0.048	−0.031
2033	0.195	0.221	0.241	−0.072	−0.046	−0.026
2034	0.197	0.225	0.246	−0.070	−0.042	−0.020
2035	0.199	0.229	0.253	−0.067	−0.038	−0.014
2036	0.202	0.233	0.260	−0.065	−0.034	−0.007
2037	0.204	0.238	0.266	−0.062	−0.029	−0.001
2038	0.206	0.241	0.272	−0.060	−0.025	0.006
2039	0.208	0.244	0.278	−0.059	−0.022	0.011
2040	0.208	0.246	0.282	−0.058	−0.021	0.015
2041	0.208	0.247	0.284	−0.058	−0.020	0.017
2042	0.207	0.245	0.284	−0.060	−0.021	0.017
2043	0.205	0.243	0.281	−0.062	−0.024	0.014
2044	0.201	0.239	0.277	−0.066	−0.028	0.010
2045	0.196	0.234	0.271	−0.071	−0.033	0.004
2046	0.189	0.227	0.264	−0.078	−0.039	−0.003
2047	0.182	0.221	0.256	−0.085	−0.046	−0.011
2048	0.174	0.213	0.248	−0.092	−0.054	−0.018
2049	0.167	0.206	0.241	−0.100	−0.061	−0.026
2050	0.159	0.199	0.234	−0.107	−0.068	−0.033

than 130,000. From the perspective of supply, according to the capacity of 360 students per school, oversupply always happens, and even in the period of the largest demand, there are still more than 100,000 kindergartens. That is to say, the current supply has met the national minimum level. However, it is worth noting that this figure only represents the average level of China. As there are big differences between urban and rural areas in China, the current supply fails to meet some regions' needs even though it can conform to the national standard.

Table 15.7 Forecast of Demand and Gap Between Supply and Demand for Kindergartens from 2015 to 2050 (Million)

Year	Demand for Kindergartens			Gap		
	Low	Medium	High	Low	Medium	High
2015	0.152	0.152	0.152	−0.115	−0.115	−0.115
2016	0.156	0.156	0.156	−0.110	−0.110	−0.110
2017	0.163	0.163	0.163	−0.104	−0.104	−0.104
2018	0.160	0.160	0.160	−0.107	−0.107	−0.107
2019	0.158	0.158	0.158	−0.109	−0.109	−0.109
2020	0.160	0.160	0.160	−0.107	−0.107	−0.107
2021	0.151	0.151	0.151	−0.115	−0.115	−0.115
2022	0.147	0.148	0.148	−0.120	−0.119	−0.119
2023	0.134	0.138	0.138	−0.133	−0.129	−0.129
2024	0.122	0.128	0.129	−0.145	−0.139	−0.138
2025	0.113	0.121	0.123	−0.154	−0.146	−0.144
2026	0.107	0.117	0.120	−0.160	−0.150	−0.147
2027	0.103	0.113	0.117	−0.164	−0.154	−0.150
2028	0.099	0.110	0.115	−0.167	−0.157	−0.152
2029	0.097	0.108	0.113	−0.170	−0.159	−0.153
2030	0.095	0.106	0.113	−0.172	−0.161	−0.154
2031	0.094	0.106	0.113	−0.172	−0.161	−0.153
2032	0.094	0.106	0.115	−0.173	−0.160	−0.152
2033	0.095	0.108	0.117	−0.172	−0.159	−0.150
2034	0.096	0.109	0.120	−0.171	−0.158	−0.147
2035	0.097	0.111	0.123	−0.170	−0.156	−0.144
2036	0.098	0.113	0.126	−0.169	−0.153	−0.141
2037	0.099	0.115	0.129	−0.167	−0.151	−0.137
2038	0.100	0.117	0.132	−0.166	−0.149	−0.134
2039	0.101	0.119	0.135	−0.166	−0.148	−0.132
2040	0.101	0.120	0.137	−0.165	−0.147	−0.130
2041	0.101	0.120	0.138	−0.165	−0.147	−0.129
2042	0.101	0.119	0.138	−0.166	−0.148	−0.129
2043	0.100	0.118	0.137	−0.167	−0.149	−0.130
2044	0.098	0.116	0.135	−0.169	−0.151	−0.132
2045	0.095	0.114	0.132	−0.172	−0.153	−0.135
2046	0.092	0.111	0.128	−0.175	−0.156	−0.139
2047	0.089	0.107	0.125	−0.178	−0.160	−0.142
2048	0.085	0.104	0.121	−0.182	−0.163	−0.146
2049	0.081	0.100	0.117	−0.186	−0.167	−0.150
2050	0.078	0.097	0.114	−0.189	−0.170	−0.153

Forecast of the Demand for Preschool Education Teachers

Teacher–child ratio is one of the important structural indicators to measure the quality of preschool education. The OECD's PISA tests for 15-year-olds suggest that a longer preschool, a low pupil–teacher ratio and higher public spending of each child all exert a positive impact on preschool education. A reasonable teacher–child ratio is helpful to improve the quality of preschool education, so as to promote the development of children.

Table 15.8 Forecast of Demand and Gap Between Supply and Demand for Kindergartens from 2015 to 2050 (Million)

Year	Demand for Kindergartens			Gap		
	Low	Medium	High	Low	Medium	High
2015	0.313	0.313	0.313	0.046	0.046	0.046
2016	0.322	0.322	0.322	0.055	0.055	0.055
2017	0.335	0.335	0.335	0.068	0.068	0.068
2018	0.329	0.329	0.329	0.062	0.062	0.062
2019	0.326	0.326	0.326	0.059	0.059	0.059
2020	0.329	0.329	0.329	0.063	0.063	0.063
2021	0.313	0.313	0.313	0.046	0.046	0.046
2022	0.305	0.307	0.307	0.038	0.040	0.041
2023	0.279	0.286	0.287	0.013	0.020	0.021
2024	0.254	0.266	0.269	−0.013	−0.001	0.002
2025	0.236	0.253	0.258	−0.031	−0.013	−0.009
2026	0.225	0.245	0.252	−0.042	−0.022	−0.015
2027	0.217	0.238	0.247	−0.050	−0.029	−0.020
2028	0.211	0.232	0.243	−0.056	−0.034	−0.024
2029	0.206	0.229	0.241	−0.061	−0.038	−0.026
2030	0.203	0.227	0.241	−0.064	−0.040	−0.026
2031	0.202	0.227	0.243	−0.065	−0.040	−0.024
2032	0.203	0.229	0.247	−0.064	−0.038	−0.020
2033	0.205	0.232	0.252	−0.062	−0.035	−0.014
2034	0.207	0.237	0.260	−0.059	−0.030	−0.007
2035	0.211	0.242	0.267	−0.056	−0.025	0.001
2036	0.214	0.247	0.275	−0.053	−0.019	0.009
2037	0.218	0.253	0.283	−0.049	−0.014	0.017
2038	0.221	0.258	0.291	−0.046	−0.009	0.024
2039	0.223	0.262	0.298	−0.044	−0.005	0.031
2040	0.224	0.265	0.303	−0.042	−0.002	0.037
2041	0.225	0.266	0.307	−0.042	0.000	0.040
2042	0.225	0.266	0.308	−0.042	−0.001	0.041
2043	0.223	0.264	0.306	−0.044	−0.003	0.039
2044	0.219	0.261	0.302	−0.047	−0.006	0.036
2045	0.215	0.256	0.297	−0.052	−0.011	0.030
2046	0.208	0.250	0.290	−0.058	−0.017	0.024
2047	0.201	0.244	0.283	−0.066	−0.023	0.016
2048	0.193	0.236	0.276	−0.073	−0.030	0.009
2049	0.186	0.229	0.268	−0.081	−0.038	0.002
2050	0.178	0.222	0.262	−0.089	−0.045	−0.005

There are huge differences in the teacher–child ratio between countries in the world. According to the data from Sustainable Development Goals Database released by UNESCO, the average teacher–child ratio in the world in recent years is 1:18, and the average ratio in European countries is 1:11 (see Table 15.10). Nordic countries ranks high in the world in preschool teacher–child ratio, and some countries have maintained the ratio at about 1:5 years ago, such as Iceland and Sweden. According to the educational statistics of the Department of Development and Planning of the Ministry of Education, the number of teachers and full-time

248   Preschool- and School-Age Populations

Table 15.9 Forecast of Demand and Gap Between Supply and Demand for Kindergartens from 2015 to 2050 (Million)

	Demand for Kindergartens			Gap		
Year	Low	Medium	High	Low	Medium	High
2015	0.152	0.152	0.152	−0.115	−0.115	−0.115
2016	0.156	0.156	0.156	−0.110	−0.110	−0.110
2017	0.163	0.163	0.163	−0.104	−0.104	−0.104
2018	0.160	0.160	0.160	−0.107	−0.107	−0.107
2019	0.158	0.158	0.158	−0.109	−0.109	−0.109
2020	0.160	0.160	0.160	−0.107	−0.107	−0.107
2021	0.152	0.152	0.152	−0.115	−0.115	−0.115
2022	0.148	0.149	0.149	−0.119	−0.118	−0.117
2023	0.136	0.139	0.140	−0.131	−0.128	−0.127
2024	0.124	0.129	0.131	−0.143	−0.137	−0.136
2025	0.115	0.123	0.125	−0.152	−0.144	−0.142
2026	0.109	0.119	0.122	−0.157	−0.148	−0.144
2027	0.106	0.116	0.120	−0.161	−0.151	−0.147
2028	0.102	0.113	0.118	−0.164	−0.154	−0.149
2029	0.100	0.111	0.117	−0.167	−0.156	−0.149
2030	0.099	0.110	0.117	−0.168	−0.157	−0.150
2031	0.098	0.110	0.118	−0.169	−0.157	−0.149
2032	0.099	0.111	0.120	−0.168	−0.156	−0.147
2033	0.099	0.113	0.123	−0.167	−0.154	−0.144
2034	0.101	0.115	0.126	−0.166	−0.152	−0.141
2035	0.102	0.118	0.130	−0.164	−0.149	−0.137
2036	0.104	0.120	0.134	−0.163	−0.146	−0.133
2037	0.106	0.123	0.138	−0.161	−0.144	−0.129
2038	0.107	0.125	0.142	−0.160	−0.141	−0.125
2039	0.108	0.127	0.145	−0.158	−0.139	−0.122
2040	0.109	0.129	0.147	−0.158	−0.138	−0.119
2041	0.110	0.130	0.149	−0.157	−0.137	−0.118
2042	0.109	0.129	0.150	−0.158	−0.137	−0.117
2043	0.108	0.128	0.149	−0.158	−0.138	−0.118
2044	0.107	0.127	0.147	−0.160	−0.140	−0.120
2045	0.104	0.125	0.144	−0.162	−0.142	−0.122
2046	0.101	0.122	0.141	−0.165	−0.145	−0.126
2047	0.098	0.118	0.138	−0.169	−0.148	−0.129
2048	0.094	0.115	0.134	−0.173	−0.152	−0.133
2049	0.090	0.111	0.130	−0.177	−0.155	−0.136
2050	0.087	0.108	0.127	−0.180	−0.159	−0.140

teachers in preschools in recent years has been increasing, and the ratio has been gradually decreasing (see Table 15.11). The ratio falls from 1:24 in 2001 to 1:11 in 2017. The reason why there is a decline is that kindergarten staff includes full-time teachers, childcare workers, administrative personnel, health care personnel, support staff, etc., but it is only full-time teachers and childcare workers that are truly engaged in preschool teaching. Therefore, the ratio that only involves full-time teachers can better reflect the real quality of preschool education. From the

Table 15.10 Ratio of Preschool Educators to Children in Major Areas and Countries of the World

	2012	2013	2014	2015	2016
World	18	18	18	18	18
Europe	11	11	11	11	11
East Asia	23	22	21	20	19
China	23	22	21	20	19
The United States	13	14	14	14	–
Japan	☐	26	25	25	27
Korea	–	15	14	13	13
Germany	–	8	8	8	8
Italy	–	13	13	12	12

Table 15.11 Number of Teachers and Teacher–Student Ratio in Preschools in China from 2000 to 2017

Year	Teaching and Administrative Staff	Full-Time Teachers	Students	Teaching and Administrative Staff–Student Ratio	Full-Time Teacher–Student Ratio
2000	114	86	2,244.2	1:20	1:26
2001	86	55	2,021.8	1:24	1:37
2002	90	57	2,036.0	1:23	1:36
2003	97	61	2,003.9	1:21	1:33
2004	105	66	2,089.4	1:20	1:32
2005	115	72	2,179.0	1:19	1:30
2006	124	78	2,263.9	1:18	1:29
2007	132	83	2,348.8	1:18	1:28
2008	143	90	2,475.0.	1:17	1:28
2009	157	99	2,657.8	1:17	1:27
2010	185	114	2,976.7	1:16	1:26
2011	220	132	3,424.5	1:16	1:26
2012	249	148	3,685.8	1:15	1:25
2013	283	166	3,894.7	1:14	1:23
2014	314	184	4,050.7	1:13	1:22
2015	350	205	4,264.8	1:12	1:21
2016	382	223	4,413.9	1:12	1:20
2017	419	243	4,600.1	1:11	1:19

perspective of that ratio, China has reduced from 1:37 in 2001 to 1 in 2017: 19. This is a significant progress, but compared with other countries, the ration is still too high in China, which is much lower than the average level of OECD countries.

Education at a Glance released by OECD sets 1:15 as the minimum standard for the appropriate teacher–child ratio. In 2013, the Interim Standards for the Staffing of Kindergarten Staff and Children issued by the Ministry of Education gives standards and ratio of teaching and administrative staff to students. Specific standards and ratio are as follows: each class in kindergarten has 30 students, with two

250 *Preschool- and School-Age Populations*

full-time teachers and one childcare worker, or three full-time teachers, and each class in half-day kindergartens should have two full-time teachers and, if conditions allow, one childcare worker for each class. That is, the ratio of teacher to child should be at least 1:15. At the same time, it is clearly proposed that in full-time preschools, the ratio of teacher and administrative staff to child should be 1:5–1:7, and the ratio of nursery staff to child should be 1:7–1:9.[15]

In the process of predicting the number of teachers under the influence of the two-child policy, the 1:8 teacher–child ratio and 1:15 teacher–child are, respectively, used to estimate the demand for preschool education staff, and the two ratios are cross-calculated with the previous two enrollment rates. According to China's Education Statistics 2018, there were 4,531,454 preschool teaching and administrative staff in 2018, including a total of 2,581,363 full-time teachers.[16] On the basis of 2018 data, the gap between supply and demand for faculty and full-time teachers has been calculated.

1 According to the ideal standard, the teacher–child ratio is set to 1:8.

From the perspective of the world, the teacher–child ratio of 1:8 is a high standard, surpassing that of most countries. Only a few countries can reach this level, such as France, New Zealand. According to the ratio of nursery staff to child set in the Interim Standards for the Staffing of Kindergarten Staff and Children, in order to calculate the average value, the ratio of teaching and administrative staff to child is 1:6, and the ratio of nursery staff and child is 1:8, which is at an ideal level. According to the previous prediction results of the demand for two kinds of preschool seats obtained by different enrollment rates, two schemes of preschool teacher demand with low, medium and high scenarios have been made. Tables 15.12 and 15.13 show the demand for teaching and administrative staff and full-time teachers and their respective supply gap in the ideal situation, based on the predicted demand for preschool seats with an enrollment rate of 85%, and teaching and administrative staff–student ratio of 1:6 and nursery staff–student ratio of 1:8. Tables 15.14 and 15.15 show demand for teaching and administrative staff and full-time teachers and their respective supply gap in the ideal situation, based on the predicted demand for preschool seats with different enrollment rates, and teaching and administrative staff–student ratio of 1:6 (Scheme I) and nursery staff–student ratio of 1:8 (Scheme I).

From 2015 to 2050, according to the ideal teacher–child ratio, China's teaching force is far from enough to meet the demand for seats brought about by the two-child policy. When the enrollment rate remains 85% (Scheme I), from the perspective of teaching and administrative staff (see Table 15.12), the average demand for teachers under the low, middle and high scenarios is 6.685 million, 7.3,603 million and 7.911 million, respectively. However, the average demand for full-time teachers under the low, medium and high scenarios is 5,013,800, 5,520,300 and 5,933,200, respectively, and the corresponding average supply difference is 2,432,400, 2,938,900 and 3,351,800, respectively (see Table 15.13). If the number of teachers in 2018 is taken as the standard, there is a

Table 15.12 Ideal Demand and the Gap Between Supply and Demand for Teaching and Administrative Staff under Scheme I (Million)

Year	Demand for Teaching Administrative Staff Low	Medium	High	Supply and Demand for Teaching Administrative Staff Low	Medium	High
2015	9.13	9.13	9.13	4.60	4.60	4.60
2016	9.38	9.38	9.38	4.85	4.85	4.85
2017	9.77	9.77	9.77	5.23	5.23	5.23
2018	9.58	9.58	9.58	5.05	5.05	5.05
2019	9.49	9.49	9.49	4.96	4.96	4.96
2020	9.60	9.60	9.60	5.07	5.07	5.07
2021	9.08	9.08	9.08	4.55	4.55	4.55
2022	8.82	8.88	8.89	4.28	4.35	4.36
2023	8.05	8.26	8.29	3.52	3.73	3.76
2024	7.30	7.65	7.72	2.77	3.12	3.19
2025	6.76	7.25	7.38	2.23	2.72	2.84
2026	6.41	6.99	7.17	1.88	2.46	2.64
2027	6.17	6.76	7.01	1.64	2.23	2.48
2028	5.96	6.58	6.89	1.43	2.05	2.35
2029	5.81	6.45	6.81	1.28	1.92	2.27
2030	5.71	6.37	6.77	1.18	1.84	2.24
2031	5.66	6.35	6.80	1.13	1.82	2.26
2032	5.65	6.38	6.88	1.12	1.85	2.35
2033	5.69	6.45	7.02	1.16	1.92	2.48
2034	5.74	6.55	7.19	1.21	2.02	2.66
2035	5.81	6.67	7.38	1.28	2.14	2.85
2036	5.89	6.80	7.57	1.36	2.27	3.04
2037	5.96	6.93	7.76	1.43	2.40	3.23
2038	6.02	7.04	7.95	1.49	2.51	3.41
2039	6.06	7.13	8.10	1.53	2.59	3.57
2040	6.08	7.18	8.21	1.55	2.64	3.68
2041	6.08	7.19	8.27	1.55	2.66	3.74
2042	6.04	7.15	8.27	1.51	2.62	3.74
2043	5.97	7.08	8.20	1.44	2.55	3.67
2044	5.85	6.96	8.07	1.32	2.43	3.54
2045	5.70	6.81	7.90	1.17	2.28	3.37
2046	5.52	6.63	7.69	0.99	2.10	3.16
2047	5.31	6.43	7.47	0.78	1.90	2.94
2048	5.09	6.22	7.25	0.56	1.68	2.71
2049	4.86	6.00	7.03	0.33	1.47	2.50
2050	4.65	5.80	6.83	0.12	1.27	2.30

shortage of preschool teaching staff in the next 35 years, and there is a most serious shortage of full-time teachers from 2015 to 2022, more than 4 million teachers needed. After 2025, the gap is roughly more than 1 million under the low scenario, over 2 million under the medium scenario and over 2 million under the high scenario between 2025 and 2035. After 2035, the number will rise again to over 3 million. If the enrollment rate is predicted to reach 95% in 2050

Table 15.13 Ideal Demand and the Gap Between Supply and Demand for Full-Time Teachers under Scheme I (Million)

Year	Demand for Full-Time Teachers Low	Medium	High	Supply of and Demand for Full-Time Teachers Low	Medium	High
2015	6.85	6.85	6.85	4.26	4.26	4.26
2016	7.04	7.04	7.04	4.45	4.45	4.45
2017	7.32	7.32	7.32	4.74	4.74	4.74
2018	7.19	7.19	7.19	4.61	4.61	4.61
2019	7.12	7.12	7.12	4.54	4.54	4.54
2020	7.20	7.20	7.20	4.62	4.62	4.62
2021	6.81	6.81	6.81	4.23	4.23	4.23
2022	6.61	6.66	6.67	4.03	4.08	4.09
2023	6.04	6.19	6.22	3.46	3.61	3.64
2024	5.48	5.74	5.79	2.90	3.15	3.21
2025	5.07	5.44	5.53	2.49	2.86	2.95
2026	4.81	5.24	5.38	2.23	2.66	2.80
2027	4.63	5.07	5.26	2.04	2.49	2.68
2028	4.47	4.94	5.16	1.89	2.36	2.58
2029	4.36	4.84	5.10	1.78	2.26	2.52
2030	4.28	4.78	5.08	1.70	2.20	2.50
2031	4.24	4.76	5.10	1.66	2.18	2.52
2032	4.24	4.78	5.16	1.66	2.20	2.58
2033	4.27	4.84	5.26	1.68	2.26	2.68
2034	4.31	4.91	5.39	1.73	2.33	2.81
2035	4.36	5.01	5.53	1.78	2.42	2.95
2036	4.42	5.10	5.68	1.83	2.52	3.10
2037	4.47	5.20	5.82	1.89	2.61	3.24
2038	4.51	5.28	5.96	1.93	2.70	3.38
2039	4.54	5.34	6.08	1.96	2.76	3.50
2040	4.56	5.38	6.16	1.98	2.80	3.58
2041	4.56	5.39	6.20	1.98	2.81	3.62
2042	4.53	5.37	6.20	1.95	2.78	3.62
2043	4.48	5.31	6.15	1.89	2.73	3.57
2044	4.39	5.22	6.05	1.81	2.64	3.47
2045	4.28	5.11	5.93	1.70	2.53	3.34
2046	4.14	4.97	5.77	1.56	2.39	3.19
2047	3.98	4.82	5.60	1.40	2.24	3.02
2048	3.82	4.66	5.43	1.23	2.08	2.85
2049	3.65	4.50	5.27	1.06	1.92	2.69
2050	3.49	4.35	5.12	0.91	1.77	2.54

(Scheme II), preschool education is urgently needed in factors such as teaching and administrative staff and full-time teachers. The average demand for full-time teachers under low, medium and high scenarios is 5.225,800, 5.768,900 and 6.214,400, respectively. The corresponding average gap is 2.6,444 million, 3.1,875 million and 3.633 million (see Table 15.15). Compared with the prediction in Scheme I, teaching staff supply gap in Scheme II increases by more than 200,000 on average.

Table 15.14 Ideal Demand and the Gap Between Supply and Demand for Teaching Administrative Staff under Scheme II (Million)

Year	Demand for Teaching Administrative Staff			Supply of and Demand for Teaching Administrative Staff		
	Low	Medium	High	Low	Medium	High
2015	9.13	9.13	9.13	4.60	4.60	4.60
2016	9.38	9.38	9.38	4.85	4.85	4.85
2017	9.77	9.77	9.77	5.23	5.23	5.23
2018	9.58	9.58	9.58	5.05	5.05	5.05
2019	9.49	9.49	9.49	4.96	4.96	4.96
2020	9.60	9.60	9.60	5.07	5.07	5.07
2021	9.12	9.12	9.12	4.59	4.59	4.59
2022	8.88	8.95	8.96	4.35	4.42	4.43
2023	8.14	8.35	8.38	3.61	3.82	3.85
2024	7.41	7.76	7.83	2.88	3.23	3.30
2025	6.89	7.39	7.51	2.35	2.86	2.98
2026	6.56	7.14	7.34	2.02	2.61	2.80
2027	6.33	6.94	7.20	1.80	2.41	2.66
2028	6.14	6.78	7.09	1.61	2.25	2.56
2029	6.01	6.67	7.04	1.47	2.14	2.50
2030	5.92	6.61	7.03	1.39	2.08	2.50
2031	5.89	6.61	7.08	1.36	2.08	2.55
2032	5.91	6.67	7.19	1.38	2.14	2.66
2033	5.97	6.77	7.36	1.44	2.24	2.83
2034	6.05	6.90	7.57	1.52	2.37	3.04
2035	6.15	7.05	7.80	1.61	2.52	3.27
2036	6.25	7.22	8.03	1.72	2.68	3.50
2037	6.34	7.38	8.27	1.81	2.84	3.74
2038	6.43	7.52	8.49	1.90	2.99	3.96
2039	6.50	7.64	8.69	1.97	3.11	4.16
2040	6.55	7.73	8.84	2.01	3.19	4.31
2041	6.57	7.77	8.94	2.04	3.24	4.41
2042	6.55	7.76	8.97	2.02	3.23	4.44
2043	6.50	7.70	8.92	1.97	3.17	4.39
2044	6.40	7.61	8.82	1.87	3.08	4.29
2045	6.26	7.47	8.66	1.72	2.94	4.13
2046	6.08	7.30	8.47	1.54	2.77	3.94
2047	5.87	7.10	8.25	1.33	2.57	3.72
2048	5.64	6.89	8.03	1.11	2.36	3.50
2049	5.41	6.68	7.82	0.88	2.15	3.29
2050	5.19	6.48	7.63	0.66	1.94	3.10

2 According to the minimum standard, the teacher–child ratio is set to 1:15.

Although China's related policy requires that the ratio of teacher to child should be between 1:7 and 1:9, it is difficult to achieve this ideal standard due to many limitations in real life. The ratio of 1:15 is taken as the minimum standard in the *Starting Well: Benchmarking Early Education Across the World* and The Interim Standards for the Staffing of Kindergarten Staff and Children issued by

Table 15.15 Ideal Demand and the Gap Between Supply and Demand for Full-Time Teachers under Scheme II (Million)

Year	Demand for Full-Time Teachers			Supply of and Demand for Full-Time Teachers		
	Low	Medium	High	Low	Medium	High
2015	6.85	6.85	6.85	4.26	4.26	4.26
2016	7.04	7.04	7.04	4.45	4.45	4.45
2017	7.32	7.32	7.32	4.74	4.74	4.74
2018	7.19	7.19	7.19	4.61	4.61	4.61
2019	7.12	7.12	7.12	4.54	4.54	4.54
2020	7.20	7.20	7.20	4.62	4.62	4.62
2021	6.84	6.84	6.84	4.26	4.26	4.26
2022	6.66	6.71	6.72	4.08	4.13	4.14
2023	6.11	6.26	6.29	3.53	3.68	3.70
2024	5.56	5.82	5.87	2.98	3.24	3.29
2025	5.16	5.54	5.64	2.58	2.96	3.05
2026	4.92	5.36	5.50	2.34	2.78	2.92
2027	4.75	5.21	5.40	2.16	2.62	2.81
2028	4.61	5.08	5.32	2.03	2.50	2.74
2029	4.50	5.00	5.28	1.92	2.42	2.70
2030	4.44	4.96	5.27	1.86	2.38	2.69
2031	4.42	4.96	5.31	1.84	2.38	2.73
2032	4.43	5.00	5.39	1.85	2.42	2.81
2033	4.47	5.08	5.52	1.89	2.49	2.94
2034	4.54	5.18	5.68	1.96	2.59	3.10
2035	4.61	5.29	5.85	2.03	2.71	3.27
2036	4.68	5.41	6.03	2.10	2.83	3.44
2037	4.76	5.53	6.20	2.18	2.95	3.62
2038	4.82	5.64	6.37	2.24	3.06	3.79
2039	4.87	5.73	6.52	2.29	3.15	3.94
2040	4.91	5.79	6.63	2.33	3.21	4.05
2041	4.93	5.83	6.70	2.34	3.24	4.12
2042	4.91	5.82	6.73	2.33	3.24	4.14
2043	4.87	5.78	6.69	2.29	3.20	4.11
2044	4.80	5.71	6.61	2.22	3.13	4.03
2045	4.69	5.60	6.50	2.11	3.02	3.92
2046	4.56	5.47	6.35	1.98	2.89	3.77
2047	4.40	5.33	6.19	1.82	2.75	3.61
2048	4.23	5.17	6.03	1.65	2.59	3.44
2049	4.06	5.01	5.87	1.48	2.43	3.29
2050	3.89	4.86	5.72	1.31	2.28	3.14

the Ministry of Education. The predicted number of teachers based on the ratio represents the minimum demand for teachers in China, which is a conservative estimate. It should be emphasized that the ratio of 1:15 only involves full-time teachers, not teaching and administrative staff. Therefore, the number of needed full-time teachers and the supply and demand gap can be predicted only based on the ratio 1:15. Similarly, according to the cross-allocation in different scenarios, two schemes of preschool teacher demand under low, medium and high scenarios can be made. Table 15.16 shows the gap between the demand and supply of full-time teachers in a conservative scenario based on the predicted demand for preschool seats with an enrollment rate of 85% (Scheme I) and the 1:15 ratio of full-time teachers to children. Table 15.17 shows the projections of the number of teachers based on achieving an enrollment rate of 95% by 2050 (Scheme II).

Table 15.16 Minimum Demand for and the Gap in Demand-Supply of Full-Time Preschool Teachers under Scheme I (Million)

Year	Demand for Full-Time Preschool Teachers			Gap		
	Low	Medium	High	Low	Medium	High
2015	3.65	3.65	3.65	1.07	1.07	1.07
2016	3.75	3.75	3.75	1.17	1.17	1.17
2017	3.91	3.91	3.91	1.33	1.33	1.33
2018	3.83	3.83	3.83	1.25	1.25	1.25
2019	3.80	3.80	3.80	1.22	1.22	1.22
2020	3.84	3.84	3.84	1.26	1.26	1.26
2021	3.63	3.63	3.63	1.05	1.05	1.05
2022	3.53	3.55	3.56	0.95	0.97	0.98
2023	3.22	3.30	3.32	0.64	0.72	0.73
2024	2.92	3.06	3.09	0.34	0.48	0.51
2025	2.70	2.90	2.95	0.12	0.32	0.37
2026	2.56	2.80	2.87	−0.02	0.21	0.29
2027	2.47	2.71	2.80	−0.11	0.12	0.22
2028	2.39	2.63	2.75	−0.20	0.05	0.17
2029	2.32	2.58	2.72	−0.26	0.00	0.14
2030	2.28	2.55	2.71	−0.30	−0.03	0.13
2031	2.26	2.54	2.72	−0.32	−0.04	0.14
2032	2.26	2.55	2.75	−0.32	−0.03	0.17
2033	2.27	2.58	2.81	−0.31	0.00	0.22
2034	2.30	2.62	2.88	−0.28	0.04	0.29
2035	2.33	2.67	2.95	−0.26	0.09	0.37
2036	2.36	2.72	3.03	−0.23	0.14	0.45
2037	2.38	2.77	3.11	−0.20	0.19	0.52
2038	2.41	2.82	3.18	−0.17	0.23	0.60
2039	2.42	2.85	3.24	−0.16	0.27	0.66
2040	2.43	2.87	3.29	−0.15	0.29	0.70
2041	2.43	2.88	3.31	−0.15	0.29	0.73
2042	2.42	2.86	3.31	−0.17	0.28	0.73
2043	2.39	2.83	3.28	−0.19	0.25	0.70
2044	2.34	2.79	3.23	−0.24	0.20	0.65
2045	2.28	2.72	3.16	−0.30	0.14	0.58
2046	2.21	2.65	3.08	−0.37	0.07	0.50
2047	2.12	2.57	2.99	−0.46	−0.01	0.41
2048	2.03	2.49	2.90	−0.55	−0.09	0.32
2049	1.94	2.40	2.81	−0.64	−0.18	0.23
2050	1.86	2.32	2.73	−0.72	−0.26	0.15

Table 15.17 Minimum Demand for and the Gap in Demand-Supply of Full-Time Preschool Teachers under Scheme II (Million)

Year	Demand for Full-Time Teachers Low	Medium	High	Gap Low	Medium	High
2015	3.65	3.65	3.65	1.07	1.07	1.07
2016	3.75	3.75	3.75	1.17	1.17	1.17
2017	3.91	3.91	3.91	1.33	1.33	1.33
2018	3.83	3.83	3.83	1.25	1.25	1.25
2019	3.80	3.80	3.80	1.22	1.22	1.22
2020	3.84	3.84	3.84	1.26	1.26	1.26
2021	3.65	3.65	3.65	1.07	1.07	1.07
2022	3.55	3.58	3.58	0.97	1.00	1.00
2023	3.26	3.34	3.35	0.68	0.76	0.77
2024	2.96	3.10	3.13	0.38	0.52	0.55
2025	2.75	2.95	3.01	0.17	0.37	0.42
2026	2.62	2.86	2.93	0.04	0.28	0.35
2027	2.53	2.78	2.88	−0.05	0.20	0.30
2028	2.46	2.71	2.84	−0.12	0.13	0.26
2029	2.40	2.67	2.81	−0.18	0.09	0.23
2030	2.37	2.64	2.81	−0.21	0.06	0.23
2031	2.36	2.64	2.83	−0.22	0.06	0.25
2032	2.36	2.67	2.88	−0.22	0.09	0.30
2033	2.39	2.71	2.94	−0.19	0.13	0.36
2034	2.42	2.76	3.03	−0.16	0.18	0.45
2035	2.46	2.82	3.12	−0.12	0.24	0.54
2036	2.50	2.89	3.21	−0.08	0.30	0.63
2037	2.54	2.95	3.31	−0.04	0.37	0.73
2038	2.57	3.01	3.40	−0.01	0.43	0.82
2039	2.60	3.06	3.48	0.02	0.48	0.89
2040	2.62	3.09	3.54	0.04	0.51	0.96
2041	2.63	3.11	3.58	0.05	0.53	0.99
2042	2.62	3.10	3.59	0.04	0.52	1.01
2043	2.60	3.08	3.57	0.02	0.50	0.99
2044	2.56	3.04	3.53	−0.02	0.46	0.95
2045	2.50	2.99	3.47	−0.08	0.41	0.88
2046	2.43	2.92	3.39	−0.15	0.34	0.81
2047	2.35	2.84	3.30	−0.23	0.26	0.72
2048	2.26	2.76	3.21	−0.32	0.18	0.63
2049	2.16	2.67	3.13	−0.42	0.09	0.55
2050	2.08	2.59	3.05	−0.50	0.01	0.47

If the scale of preschool teachers is predicted based on the lowest teacher–child ratio 1:15, the number of preschool teachers in China still fails to meet the demand for seats under the influence of the two-child policy, though there are a lot of improvements compared with the standard 1:8. If the scale of preschool teachers is predicted based on the enrollment rate of 85% (Scheme I) and there is no two-child policy under low scenario, preschool teachers will be insufficient from 2015 to 2025, and then, there will be a surplus of the teachers. Under the medium scenario, the gap in supply-demand of teachers is changing, with insufficient teachers from 2015 to 2028, surplus teachers from 2029 to 2033, insufficient teachers again from 2034 to 2046, and then the supply rises again. The most serious shortage of teachers is about 1,325,200, and the most serious surplus occurs in 2050, with 262,700 extra teachers. Under the high scenario, the supply of preschool teachers has been insufficient, with a maximum of 1,325,200 and a minimum of 150,100 (see Table 15.16).

According to the enrollment rate of 95% (Scheme II) (see Table 15.17) under the low scenario, the gap in demand-supply of preschool teachers will change in a curve shape without the effect of two-child policy, and the shortage remains from 2015 to 2026. There is a surplus between 2027 and 2038 and insufficiency between 2039 and 2043, with a modest gap. The results under the medium and high scenarios show that after the implementation of the two-child policy, there has been a lack of teachers, whose number is fluctuating, and the gap is varying. However, China is always in short of preschool teachers.

For a long time, there has been a shortage of full-time kindergarten teachers in our country, and the implementation of the universal two-child policy has posed a challenge to the existing size of preschool teachers, which is too small to ensure the sound development of preschool education. Although the number of full-time teachers in kindergarten in China has been increasing in recent years, it fails to meet the needs of China's large number of preschool children. In fact, there are many factors affecting the teacher–child ratio. The size of the teacher–child ratio does not mean the economic development or the investment in education. Instead, it depends on cultural concepts. For example, Japan advocates large-size class teaching. We should sensibly view preschool education and rationally formulate education development plans according to objective needs and changing trends so as to avoid the shortage or blind expansion of the size of teachers.

Forecast of Financial Investment in Preschool Education

The Outline of the National Program for Medium - and Long-term Education Reform and Development (2010–2020) states that the investment in education is basic and strategic to support the long-term development of the country, and it is the material foundation of education and also an important area of public finance.[17] To a certain extent, the government's financial investment in education reflects the country's emphasis on education and is also the most basic material guarantee for education. Sufficient, effective, fair investment is related to the sustainable, stable and sound development of education. National financial education funds refer to all financial funds obtained by schools, and public financial education funds are the main source of national educational financial investment. International organizations such as the OECD also look at the index of "public financial education funds" when measuring fiscal revenue of a country. In the international community, the ratio of national fiscal expenditure on education to GDP is usually used to measure the national support for education. According to the 2017 China Education Expenditure Statistical Yearbook, from 2012 to 2016, China's fiscal expenditure on education accounted for 4.28%, 4.11%, 4.10%, 4.24% and 4.22% of GDP, respectively.[18] According to the data of OECD, China's current fiscal expenditure on education is above the medium scenario. In recent years, the expenditures in Australia, Canada, France and the United Kingdom account for more than 5% of the total fiscal investment, and the proportion in Finland, Iceland, Norway and Sweden is more than 7%.

UNESCO recommends the index of education expenditure per preschool student, which refers to the ratio of education expenditure per student to GDP per capita, to make a horizontal comparison between regions at different levels of economic development. According to the 2017 China Education Expenditure Statistical Yearbook, the education expenditure per preschool student in China in 2016 is 8,588.80 yuan,[19] and the GDP per capita of that year is 53,680 yuan,[20] and thus, the index of education expenditure per student is 16%. When estimating the future fiscal investment in education, it is necessary to first forecast the GDP per capita in the next 35 years. According to the existing GDP per capita from 2000 to 2016, it is calculated that the annual growth rate of China's GDP is about 9%. Assuming that its annual growth rate is 5% in the future, the GDP per capita from 2015 to 2050 can be calculated. At the same time, it is assumed that the annual index of education expenditure per preschool student in the future is same as that of 2016, that is, 16%. therefore, the average education expenditure per preschool student in the future can be obtained by the multiplication of the two percentages. And the future education expenditure per preschool student can be calculated by multiplying the result by the predicted demand for preschool education seats in the two schemes. Finally, two schemes of demands of financial expenditure for preschool education under low, medium and high levels from 2015 to 2050 can be made (see Tables 15.18 and 15.19).

According to the 85% enrollment rate in Scheme I or the 95% enrollment rate in Scheme II, China's future financial investment in preschool education is increasing. According to the 2017 China Education Statistics Yearbook, national financial education expenditure of kindergarten in 2016 in China is 132.607 billion yuan, and the forecast shows that in 2016, the need for education investment is 483.428 billion yuan, a shortfall of more than 350 billion yuan. As time goes by, the gap will continue to increase. By 2034, compared with the non-implementation of the two-child policy, the financial investment in preschool education will exceed 1 trillion yuan after the implementation of the policy. By 2045, the investment in the high scenario will exceed 2 trillion yuan. If measured by the share of preschool education in GDP, the result also reflects that the investment is extremely sufficient. For example, the GDP in 2016 is 740,061 billion yuan, and the proportion of fiscal expenditure on preschool education in GDP is 0.18%. According to official data from UNESCO's Sustainable Development Database, China has a low proportion in the international community, a proportion that is far lower than that of some developed countries, especially Nordic countries. The proportion is 0.23% in Australia, 0.32% in the United States, 0.42% in South Korea, 0.46% in Germany, and 0.23% in the United States. It is 0.69% in France, 0.74% in Norway, 0.76% in Finland, 0.85% in Iceland, and 1.29% in Sweden.[21] If measured by the percentage

Table 15.18 Forecast of Financial Investment in Preschool Education in China from 2015 to 2050 (Scheme I)

Year	GDP per Capita (Yuan)	Index of Education Expenditure per Preschool Student	Education Expenditure per Preschool Student (Yuan)	Low (100 Million Yuan)	Medium (100 Million Yuan)	High (100 Million Yuan)
2015	50,028.00	0.16	8,004.48	4,384.10	4,384.09	4,384.10
2016	53,680.00	0.16	8,588.80	4,834.28	4,834.28	4,834.28
2017	59,201.00	0.16	9,472.16	5,550.53	5,550.53	5,550.53
2018	64,644.00	0.16	10,343.04	5,947.46	5,947.46	5,947.46
2019	67,876.20	0.16	10,860.19	6,186.53	6,186.53	6,186.53
2020	71,270.01	0.16	11,403.20	6,570.16	6,570.16	6,570.16
2021	74,833.51	0.16	11,973.36	6,526.44	6,526.44	6,526.44
2022	78,575.19	0.16	12,572.03	6,650.43	6,702.04	6,708.41
2023	82,503.95	0.16	13,200.63	6,377.96	6,539.87	6,565.32
2024	86,629.14	0.16	13,860.66	6,072.68	6,359.75	6,418.37
2025	90,960.60	0.16	14,553.70	5,902.80	6,332.56	6,440.91
2026	95,508.63	0.16	15,281.38	5,878.68	6,407.16	6,577.95
2027	100,284.06	0.16	16,045.45	5,937.01	6,512.35	6,750.13
2028	105,298.26	0.16	16,847.72	6,028.24	6,653.49	6,961.13
2029	110,563.18	0.16	17,690.11	6,166.47	6,844.67	7,223.79
2030	116,091.34	0.16	18,574.61	6,362.16	7,099.34	7,547.49
2031	121,895.90	0.16	19,503.34	6,622.44	7,428.25	7,953.00
2032	127,990.70	0.16	20,478.51	6,948.29	7,836.29	8,454.66
2033	134,390.23	0.16	21,502.44	7,336.89	8,321.17	9,050.86
2034	141,109.74	0.16	22,577.56	7,781.67	8,876.13	9,736.63
2035	148,165.23	0.16	23,706.44	8,270.45	9,492.07	10,494.92
2036	155,573.49	0.16	24,891.76	8,794.00	10,157.72	11,309.65
2037	163,352.17	0.16	26,136.35	9,343.35	10,862.60	12,175.12
2038	171,519.78	0.16	27,443.16	9,907.01	11,592.80	13,082.76
2039	180,095.77	0.16	28,815.32	10,472.12	12,319.85	14,007.48
2040	189,100.55	0.16	30,256.09	11,035.98	13,026.55	14,910.98
2041	198,555.58	0.16	31,768.89	11,585.03	13,701.53	157,66.62
2042	208,483.36	0.16	33,357.34	12,090.33	14,317.58	165,48.31
2043	218,907.53	0.16	35,025.20	12,540.96	14,871.48	17,228.25
2044	229,852.91	0.16	36,776.46	12,919.37	15,365.36	17,810.57
2045	241,345.55	0.16	38,615.29	13,214.94	15,780.18	18,303.89
2046	253,412.83	0.16	40,546.05	13,426.55	16,127.73	18,712.07
2047	266,083.47	0.16	42,573.36	13,563.01	16,424.88	19,078.35
2048	279,387.64	0.16	44,702.02	13,644.24	16,672.86	19,432.85
2049	293,357.03	0.16	46,937.12	13,688.31	16,899.72	19,791.08
2050	308,024.88	0.16	49,283.98	13,745.96	17,141.38	20,192.87

of preschool education expenditure on the total education expenditure, the investment in preschool education is also obviously insufficient. In 2016, the government spends 3,139.625 billion yuan on education, accounting for 4.22% of the total education expenditure. In the same year, the proportion in many countries is more than

Table 15.19 Forecast of Financial Investment in Preschool Education in China from 2015 to 2050 (Scheme II)

Year	GDP per Capita (Yuan)	Index of Education Expenditure per Preschool Student	Education Expenditure per Preschool Student (Yuan)	Low (100 Million Yuan)	Medium (100 Million Yuan)	High (100 Million Yuan)
2015	50,028.00	0.16	8,004.48	4,384.10	4,384.09	4,384.10
2016	53,680.00	0.16	8,588.80	4,834.28	4,834.28	4,834.28
2017	59,201.00	0.16	9,472.16	5,550.53	5,550.53	5,550.53
2018	64,644.00	0.16	10,343.04	5,947.46	5,947.46	5,947.46
2019	67,876.20	0.16	10,860.19	6,186.53	6,186.53	6,186.53
2020	71,270.01	0.16	11,403.20	6,570.16	6,570.16	6,570.16
2021	74,833.51	0.16	11,973.36	6,550.59	6,550.59	6,550.59
2022	78,575.19	0.16	12,572.03	6,699.74	6,751.73	6,758.14
2023	82,503.95	0.16	13,200.63	6,449.02	6,612.73	6,638.47
2024	86,629.14	0.16	13,860.66	6,163.06	6,454.40	6,513.89
2025	90,960.60	0.16	14,553.70	6,012.81	6,450.58	6,560.95
2026	95,508.63	0.16	15,281.38	6,010.40	6,550.72	6,725.34
2027	100,284.06	0.16	16,045.45	6,092.49	6,682.90	6,926.91
2028	105,298.26	0.16	16,847.72	6,209.00	6,853.00	7,169.86
2029	110,563.18	0.16	17,690.11	6,374.88	7,076.00	7,467.93
2030	116,091.34	0.16	18,574.61	6,601.52	7,366.43	7,831.44
2031	121,895.90	0.16	19,503.34	6,897.02	7,736.24	8,282.74
2032	127,990.70	0.16	20,478.51	7,263.15	8,191.39	8,837.78
2033	134,390.23	0.16	21,502.44	7,697.74	8,730.42	9,496.01
2034	141,109.74	0.16	22,577.56	8,194.60	9,347.14	10,253.30
2035	148,165.23	0.16	23,706.44	8,741.54	10,032.74	11,092.72
2036	155,573.49	0.16	24,891.76	9,329.31	10,776.03	11,998.08
2037	163,352.17	0.16	26,136.35	9,948.77	11,566.46	12,964.02
2038	171,519.78	0.16	27,443.16	10,587.98	12,389.65	13,982.03
2039	180,095.77	0.16	28,815.32	11,233.35	13,215.39	15,025.69
2040	189,100.55	0.16	30,256.09	11,882.00	14,025.16	16,054.05
2041	198,555.58	0.16	31,768.89	12,519.28	14,806.47	17,038.09
2042	208,483.36	0.16	33,357.34	13,113.67	15,529.44	17,948.98
2043	218,907.53	0.16	35,025.20	13,652.78	16,189.91	18,755.62
2044	229,852.91	0.16	36,776.46	14,116.78	16,789.46	19,461.30
2045	241,345.55	0.16	38,615.29	14,493.17	17,306.53	20,074.35
2046	253,412.83	0.16	40,546.05	14,779.73	17,753.15	20,597.94
2047	266,083.47	0.16	42,573.36	14,985.19	18,147.14	21,078.85
2048	279,387.64	0.16	44,702.02	15,130.71	18,489.28	21,549.95
2049	293,357.03	0.16	46,937.12	15,235.74	18,810.19	22,028.42
2050	308,024.88	0.16	49,283.98	15,356.52	19,149.77	22,558.79

5% or even more than 10%. For example, the UK accounts for 10.77%, Iceland 11.35%, Italy 11.65%, France 12.79% and Sweden 16.81%.[22] As for the present fiscal expenditure on preschool education in China, there is a big gap compared with the international level. Therefore, China should increase the investment in preschool education so as to provide guarantee for the sustainable development of preschool education.

Forecast of Demand for the Primary School Education

The nine-year compulsory education system implemented in China requires children to accept compulsory education, as well as to fulfill the obligation. Compulsory education is the most important part of China's education system. It consists of primary school and junior high school, which last for nine years. The research on predicting and analyzing the students who have reach the age of receiving compulsory education is carried out separately. One is about the primary school population, and the other is about junior middle school population.

Forecast of Seats Demand for Primary School Education

According to the forecast of the population size from 2015 to 2050 under the influence of the two-child policy, the forecast of the primary school-age population under low, medium and high scenarios is made with population aged 6–11 years as the primary school-age population. According to the Compulsory Education Law of the People's Republic of China, as public welfare, compulsory education is enforced by China to require that all school-age children and adolescents must receive the education.[23] Based on the law, the primary school enrollment rate is set at 100%. In fact, according to UNESCO data, the primary school enrollment rate is 105.23% in 2012, 103.88% in 2013, 99.20% in 2014, 99.33% in 2015, 100.85% in 2016 and 102.05% in 2017, which is already over 100%. However, China's Education Statistics 2018 shows that the primary school enrollment rate in recent years is above 99.9%. For better calculation, the enrollment rate in this research is set at 100%. Thus, the demand for primary school seats from 2015 to 2050 is shown in Table 15.20.

According to the forecast, the peak of China's primary school-age population appears in 2020, about 109 million, and then, the population falls year by year. Around 2036, it reduces to the lowest point. Compared with the peak, the population roughly reduces by 30–40 million, and then it will rise slightly. According to China's Education Statistics 2018, there are 103.39 million primary school students in China.[24] With this number, the gap between supply and demand of primary school seats between 2015 and 2050 can be calculated. The biggest shortfall is in 2020, requiring another 5.58 million primary school seats. After that, the supply of primary seats continues to outnumber the demand by as much as 43.25 million.

Forecast of the Demand for Primary School Teachers

According to the data of UNESCO, the world average teacher–child ratio in recent years is stable at about 1:23, and the average ratio in European countries is at 1:14, while China, South Korea and Japan close to 1:16. There are some countries

Table 15.20 Primary School-Age Population and Seats Demand from 2015 to 2050 (Million)

Year	Demand for Seats Low	Medium	High	Supply-Demand Gap Low	Medium	High
2015	100.7	100.7	100.7	−2.7	−2.7	−2.7
2016	102.4	102.4	102.4	−1.0	−1.0	−1.0
2017	104.6	104.6	104.6	1.3	1.3	1.3
2018	107.7	107.7	107.7	4.3	4.3	4.3
2019	107.9	107.9	107.9	4.5	4.5	4.5
2020	109.0	109.0	109.0	5.6	5.6	5.6
2021	106.1	106.1	106.1	2.7	2.7	2.7
2022	105.9	105.9	105.9	2.5	2.5	2.5
2023	104.8	104.8	104.8	1.4	1.4	1.4
2024	100.1	100.1	100.1	−3.3	−3.3	−3.3
2025	95.6	96.1	96.2	−7.8	−7.3	−7.2
2026	89.2	90.6	90.8	−14.2	−12.8	−12.6
2027	85.7	88.1	88.6	−17.7	−15.3	−14.8
2028	79.3	82.8	83.7	−24.1	−20.6	−19.7
2029	73.2	77.7	79.1	−30.2	−25.7	−24.3
2030	68.6	74.3	76.2	−34.8	−29.2	−27.2
2031	65.6	71.9	74.5	−37.8	−31.5	−28.9
2032	63.5	70.1	73.2	−39.9	−33.3	−30.2
2033	61.9	68.7	72.4	−41.5	−34.7	−31.0
2034	60.8	67.9	72.1	−42.6	−35.5	−31.3
2035	60.3	67.6	72.4	−43.1	−35.8	−31.0
2036	60.1	67.8	73.3	−43.3	−35.6	−30.1
2037	60.4	68.5	74.5	−43.0	−34.9	−28.9
2038	60.9	69.5	76.2	−42.5	−33.9	−27.2
2039	61.5	70.7	78.1	−41.9	−32.7	−25.3
2040	62.3	71.9	80.1	−41.1	−31.5	−23.3
2041	62.9	73.2	82.1	−40.5	−30.2	−21.3
2042	63.5	74.2	83.8	−39.9	−29.2	−19.6
2043	63.9	75.1	85.3	−39.5	−28.3	−18.1
2044	64.1	75.6	86.4	−39.3	−27.8	−17.0
2045	64.0	75.7	87.0	−39.4	−27.7	−16.4
2046	63.6	75.3	86.9	−39.8	−28.1	−16.5
2047	62.8	74.5	86.2	−40.6	−28.9	−17.2
2048	61.6	73.4	85.0	−41.8	−30.0	−18.4
2049	60.1	71.8	83.3	−43.3	−31.6	−20.1
2050	58.2	70.0	81.3	−45.2	−33.4	−22.1

with high teacher–child ratio, such as Greece, Norway and Iceland, whose ratio are around 1:9 (see Table 15.21).

The Notice on Unifying the Pay Packages of teaching and administrative staff in Urban and Rural Primary and Junior High Schools issued by the Central Compilation Office makes the pay packages of teaching and administrative staff in counties, towns and rural primary and secondary schools same as that in urban areas, and the ratio of primary school teaching and administrative staff to student is 1:19.[25] China's current ratio of full-time teachers to children has realized the goal set by the

Table 15.21 Primary School Teacher–Child Ratio in World's Major Regions and Countries in Recent Years

	2010	2011	2012	2013	2014	2015	2016	2017
World	24.31	24.07	24.19	23.54	23.29	23.10	23.47	23.64
Europe	13.75	13.79	14.03	14.31	14.27	14.13	14.01	14.04
East Asia	17.06	16.95	16.94	16.89	16.30	16.34	16.55	16.60
China	16.84	16.79	16.85	16.85	16.23	16.29	16.55	16.59
Korea	20.92	19.05	17.88	16.85	16.50	16.55	16.31	–
Japan	–	–	–	16.73	16.45	16.18	15.87	–
The United Kingdom	17.53	17.27	18.31	18.44	17.39	–	15.05	–
The United States	13.59	14.29	14.42	14.45	14.54	14.46	–	–
Greece	–	–	9.20	9.49	9.45	9.64	9.27	–
Iceland	–	9.70	9.93	9.86	9.99	10.14	–	–
Norway	–	–	–	8.96	8.85	8.87	9.01	–

Source: UNESCO's Sustainable Development Goals [EB/OL]. http://data.uis.unesco.org/

country. According to the 2018 Education Statistics Yearbook, there are 5,309,694 primary school staff in China in 2018.[26] Table 15.22 shows the demand and the demand-supply gap of primary school teaching and administrative staff in China in the next 35 years according to the teacher–child ratio set by China and the data on primary school teaching and administrative staff in 2018.

The forecast in Table 15.22 shows that the existing size of teachers in primary and secondary schools in China can basically deal with the pressure brought by the policy. Compared with the kindergarten teachers, there is a relative surplus of primary school teachers. The only shortage of primary school teachers happens from 2016 to 2023, and the most urgent shortage is in 2019, with a shortage of 370,100 teachers. Later, the shrinking size of the school-age population leads to a surplus of primary school teaching and administrative staff.

Forecast of the Fiscal Expenditure on Primary School Education

The method of calculating the index of preschool education expenditure per student, which is used in predicting the fiscal expenditure on preschool education, is used again to see the investment in primary education from 2015 to 2050. The estimated GDP per capita is same as the previous one. According to the 2017 China Education Expenditure Statistical Yearbook, the average primary school education expenditure per student in 2016 is 11,397.25 yuan,[27] and the GDP per capita in 2016 is 53,680 yuan, and thus, the index is 21%. According to the Education at a Glance of UNESCO, China has a relative high index in the world, which is same as the index in the United States, Canada and Australia, close to the index in Finland, Iceland, Japan and New Zealand (22%). However, China still ranks low on the index, such as the United Kingdom (27%), Norway (25%) and South Korea (30%). The fiscal investments in primary schools from 2015 to 2050 under low, medium

Table 15.22 Forecast of Demand and the Supply-Demand Gap of Primary Teaching and Administrative Staff, 2015–2050

Year	Demand for Teaching and Administrative Staff			Supply-Demand Gap		
	Low	Medium	High	Low	Medium	High
2015	5.30	5.30	5.30	−0.01	−0.01	−0.01
2016	5.39	5.39	5.39	0.08	0.08	0.08
2017	5.51	5.51	5.51	0.20	0.20	0.20
2018	5.67	5.67	5.67	0.36	0.36	0.36
2019	5.68	5.68	5.68	0.37	0.37	0.37
2020	5.74	5.74	5.74	0.43	0.43	0.43
2021	5.58	5.58	5.58	0.27	0.27	0.27
2022	5.57	5.57	5.57	0.26	0.26	0.26
2023	5.52	5.52	5.52	0.21	0.21	0.21
2024	5.27	5.27	5.27	−0.04	−0.04	−0.04
2025	5.03	5.06	5.06	−0.28	−0.25	−0.25
2026	4.69	4.77	4.78	−0.62	−0.54	−0.53
2027	4.51	4.64	4.66	−0.80	−0.67	−0.65
2028	4.18	4.36	4.40	−1.13	−0.95	−0.91
2029	3.85	4.09	4.16	−1.46	−1.22	−1.15
2030	3.61	3.91	4.01	−1.70	−1.40	−1.30
2031	3.45	3.78	3.92	−1.86	−1.53	−1.39
2032	3.34	3.69	3.85	−1.97	−1.62	−1.46
2033	3.26	3.62	3.81	−2.05	−1.69	−1.50
2034	3.20	3.57	3.80	−2.11	−1.74	−1.51
2035	3.17	3.56	3.81	−2.14	−1.75	−1.50
2036	3.17	3.57	3.86	−2.14	−1.74	−1.45
2037	3.18	3.61	3.92	−2.13	−1.70	−1.39
2038	3.20	3.66	4.01	−2.11	−1.65	−1.30
2039	3.24	3.72	4.11	−2.07	−1.59	−1.20
2040	3.28	3.79	4.22	−2.03	−1.52	−1.09
2041	3.31	3.85	4.32	−2.00	−1.46	−0.99
2042	3.34	3.91	4.41	−1.97	−1.40	−0.90
2043	3.36	3.95	4.49	−1.95	−1.36	−0.82
2044	3.37	3.98	4.55	−1.94	−1.33	−0.76
2045	3.37	3.98	4.58	−1.94	−1.33	−0.73
2046	3.35	3.96	4.57	−1.96	−1.35	−0.74
2047	3.30	3.92	4.54	−2.01	−1.39	−0.77
2048	3.24	3.86	4.47	−2.07	−1.45	−0.84
2049	3.16	3.78	4.38	−2.15	−1.53	−0.93
2050	3.06	3.68	4.28	−2.25	−1.63	−1.03

and high scenarios are calculated based on the index of education expenditure per student in 2016 (see Table 15.23).

The forecast shows that compared with the fiscal investment in preschool education, the investment in primary education increases greatly, and the change is also increasing. In 2015, the fiscal investment in primary education exceeds 1 trillion yuan. In 2034, the investment under the medium and high scenarios exceeds 2 trillion yuan, in 2041, it exceeds 3 trillion yuan and, in 2046, it is over 4 trillion

Table 15.23 Forecast of China's Fiscal Investment in Primary School from 2015 to 2050

Year	GDP per Capita (Yuan)	Index of Preschool Education Expenditure per Student	Preschool Education Expenditure per Student (Yuan)	Low (100 Million Yuan)	Medium (100 Million Yuan)	High (100 Million Yuan)
2015	50,028.00	0.21	10,505.88	10,574.30	10,574.30	10,574.30
2016	53,680.00	0.21	11,397.25	11,671.57	11,671.57	11,671.57
2017	59,201.00	0.21	12,432.21	13,008.86	13,008.86	13,008.86
2018	64,644.00	0.21	13,575.24	14,622.75	14,622.75	14,622.75
2019	67,876.20	0.21	14,254.00	15,382.26	15,382.26	15,382.26
2020	71,270.01	0.21	14,966.70	16,309.09	16,309.09	16,309.09
2021	74,833.51	0.21	15,715.04	16,672.92	16,672.92	16,672.92
2022	78,575.19	0.21	16,500.79	17,472.85	17,472.85	17,472.85
2023	82,503.95	0.21	17,325.83	18,158.61	18,158.61	18,158.61
2024	86,629.14	0.21	18,192.12	18,208.87	18,208.87	18,208.87
2025	90,960.60	0.21	19,101.73	18,268.09	18,360.22	18,371.57
2026	95,508.63	0.21	20,056.81	17,880.97	18,170.04	18,215.47
2027	100,284.06	0.21	21,059.65	18,047.66	18,560.24	18,664.89
2028	105,298.26	0.21	22,112.64	17,541.02	18,308.44	18,501.92
2029	110,563.18	0.21	23,218.27	16,983.61	18,039.24	18,358.01
2030	116,091.34	0.21	24,379.18	16,721.93	18,100.41	18,580.20
2031	121,895.90	0.21	25,598.14	16,790.51	18,406.29	19,067.57
2032	127,990.70	0.21	26,878.05	17,073.00	18,829.33	19,680.54
2033	134,390.23	0.21	28,221.95	17,475.07	19,387.64	20,435.05
2034	141,109.74	0.21	29,633.05	18,028.09	20,114.27	21,375.18
2035	148,165.23	0.21	31,114.70	18,750.91	21,036.11	22,535.44
2036	155,573.49	0.21	32,670.43	19,648.55	22,164.40	23,933.12
2037	163,352.17	0.21	34,303.96	20,713.13	23,496.24	25,569.92
2038	171,519.78	0.21	36,019.15	21,927.34	25,021.85	27,438.24
2039	180,095.77	0.21	37,820.11	23,272.56	26,721.62	29,528.82
2040	189,100.55	0.21	39,711.12	24,721.80	28,564.74	31,802.88
2041	198,555.58	0.21	41,696.67	26,242.65	30,511.18	34,212.87
2042	208,483.36	0.21	43,781.51	27,797.79	32,503.66	36,708.55
2043	218,907.53	0.21	45,970.58	29,375.51	34,503.76	39,222.18
2044	229,852.91	0.21	48,269.11	30,947.90	36,475.53	41,699.74
2045	241,345.55	0.21	50,682.57	32,445.99	38,348.65	44,075.38
2046	253,412.83	0.21	53,216.69	33,826.40	40,072.86	46,252.00
2047	266,083.47	0.21	55,877.53	35,070.96	41,638.51	48,175.14
2048	279,387.64	0.21	58,671.41	36,157.56	43,036.03	49,854.63
2049	293,357.03	0.21	61,604.98	37,006.88	44,242.17	51,308.85
2050	308,024.88	0.21	64,685.22	37,614.42	45,253.17	52,560.87

yuan. In 2050, the investment reaches 4.525,317 trillion yuan under medium scenario, reaches 5.256,087 trillion yuan under high scenario. According to the 2017 China Education Statistical Yearbook, the national fiscal expenditure on primary education in 2016 is 1,031.742 billion yuan, which is close to the prediction in 2015, and since then, there has been a gap. Of course, this is closely related to the annual growth of GDP per capita. In 2016, China's government expenditure on education amounted to 3,139.625 billion yuan, with a GDP of 740,061 billion yuan. The government's expenditure on primary schools accounts for 1.39% of the GDP and 32.86% of the total education expenditure of that year. According to the database of UNESCO, China has exceeded that of many countries. In France, the proportion is 1.13%, while in Japan it is 1.12%.

Forecast of Demand for Junior High School Education

Forecast of the Demand for Junior High School Seats

Junior high school education is the last stage of the nine-year compulsory education. In this chapter, the age of receiving junior high school education is set at 12–14 years old, and thus, the population aged 12–14 is the total junior high school students. China's education statistics in recent years show that the enrollment rate of junior high schools in China is above 98% (see Table 15.24). According to the Compulsory Education Law of the People's Republic of China, the junior high school-age population has the right and obligation to receive a three-year education. Therefore, the method of estimating the demand for junior high school seats is same as the method used in calculating primary school enrollment rate, that is, the enrollment rate is expected to be 100% (see Table 15.25).

The forecast in Table 15.25 shows that the demand for junior high school education seats in China gradually increases from 2015 to 2026, reaching the maximum in 2026, which is 55.5,669 million, and then declining and reaching the minimum around 2040. The forecast under the low scenario is 29.8,049 million on the basis of no two-child policy. The minimum demand under the medium scenario is 33.4,831 million, and the minimum demand under the high scenario is 35.7,214 million. The demand picks up again with modest change. As for the gap, the seats are in short supply from 2018 to 2030. After 2030, there is a surplus of seats, and the biggest gap in supply-demand happens during the time from 2037 to 2040, which exceeds tens of millions.

Forecast of the Demand for Junior High School Teachers

At present, the average ratio of junior high school teachers to students in the world is about 1:17. The ratio in European countries is 1:10, East Asia 1:13, China and Japan basically 1:12, which is even higher than that in the United Kingdom and the United States and other developed countries. Greece, Switzerland, Norway and other countries rank high in the preschool, primary school or junior high school ratio, which is basically around 1:8 (Table 15.26).

Table 15.24 China's Junior High School Enrollment Rate in Recent Years

Year	2010	2011	2012	2013	2014	2015	2016	2017	2018
Enrollment rate	98.7	98.3	98.3	98.3	98	98.2	98.7	98.8	99.1

Table 15.25 Forecast of the Demand for Junior High School Seats and the Supply-Demand Gap (Million)

Year	Demand for Seats Low	Medium	High	Supply-Demand Gap Low	Medium	High
2015	42.91	42.91	42.91	−3.62	−3.62	−3.62
S2016	44.17	44.17	44.17	−2.36	−2.36	−2.36
2017	45.12	45.12	45.12	−1.40	−1.40	−1.40
2018	47.96	47.96	47.96	1.43	1.43	1.43
2019	49.43	49.43	49.43	2.91	2.91	2.91
2020	51.23	51.23	51.23	4.71	4.71	4.71
2021	52.57	52.57	52.57	6.05	6.05	6.05
2022	52.85	52.85	52.85	6.33	6.33	6.33
2023	53.29	53.29	53.29	6.76	6.76	6.76
2024	55.02	55.02	55.02	8.50	8.50	8.50
2025	54.94	54.94	54.94	8.42	8.42	8.42
2026	55.57	55.57	55.57	9.04	9.04	9.04
2027	50.96	50.96	50.96	4.44	4.44	4.44
2028	50.84	50.84	50.84	4.32	4.32	4.32
2029	49.14	49.14	49.14	2.61	2.61	2.61
2030	49.03	49.03	49.03	2.51	2.51	2.51
2031	44.71	45.19	45.25	−1.82	−1.34	−1.28
2032	39.93	41.37	41.60	−6.59	−5.15	−4.93
2033	36.59	39.02	39.52	−9.93	−7.50	−7.01
2034	34.55	37.54	38.35	−11.97	−8.99	−8.17
2035	33.15	36.26	37.40	−13.37	−10.27	−9.12
2036	31.94	35.16	36.63	−14.58	−11.36	−9.89
2037	30.99	34.31	36.08	−15.54	−12.22	−10.45
2038	30.32	33.74	35.76	−16.21	−12.78	−10.76
2039	29.93	33.48	35.72	−16.60	−13.04	−10.80
2040	29.80	33.52	36.00	−16.72	−13.01	−10.52
2041	29.90	33.81	36.61	−16.62	−12.71	−9.92
2042	30.17	34.31	37.48	−16.36	−12.22	−9.04
2043	30.53	34.93	38.48	−15.99	−11.60	−8.04
2044	30.93	35.61	39.51	−15.59	−10.92	−7.01
2045	31.32	36.30	40.54	−15.20	−10.23	−5.98
2046	31.68	36.95	41.55	−14.85	−9.57	−4.98
2047	31.96	37.52	42.48	−14.56	−9.01	−4.04
2048	32.13	37.90	43.25	−14.40	−8.63	−3.28
2049	32.18	38.05	43.72	−14.34	−8.47	−2.81
2050	32.11	38.00	43.85	−14.41	−8.53	−2.67

According to the Notice on Unifying the Pay Packages of teaching and administrative staff in Urban and Rural Primary and Junior High Schools jointly issued by State Commission Office of Public Sectors Reform, Ministry of Education and Ministry of Finance, the ratio of junior high teaching and administrative staff to students is required to be 1:13.5.[28] With the ratio, the predicted number of junior high school seats, the demand for junior high school teachers under low, medium and high scenarios can be calculated. The 2018 Education Statistical Yearbook shows that there are 2.779,555 million junior high school teaching and administrative

Table 15.26 Ratio of Junior High School Teacher–Student in the World's Major Regions and Countries in Recent Years

	2010	2011	2012	2013	2014	2015	2016	2017
World	17.59	17.74	17.80	17.41	17.33	17.19	16.89	16.84
Europe	10.43	10.30	10.33	10.37	10.21	10.16	10.31	10.33
East Asia	14.99	14.56	13.97	13.56	12.81	12.63	12.45	12.42
China	14.91	14.47	13.85	13.42	12.61	12.46	12.30	12.27
Japan	–	–	–	12.96	12.79	12.64	12.40	–
Korea	19.28	18.06	17.33	16.78	15.81	15.08	14.17	–
The United Kingdom	–	–	–	16.29	15.27		21.34	–
The United States	13.38	14.52	14.67	14.71	14.80	14.71	–	–
Greece	–	–	–	7.35	7.84	8.14	7.69	–
France	14.15	14.23	14.79	14.68	–	–	–	–
Sweden	9.58	9.48	9.50	10.93	11.08	11.22	11.40	–
Switzerland	–	–	8.18	7.55	7.97	–	8.29	–
New Zealand	14.85	14.85	14.85		14.70	14.74	14.83	15.02
Norway	–	–	–	8.53	8.36	8.51	8.42	–
Iceland	–	–	–	9.89	10.02	9.88	–	–

staff at the beginning of 2018,[29] and the gap of teacher supply in different years is finally calculated (see Table 15.27). In 2026, the demand for junior high school teachers is the largest, reaching 4.116,100 million. Based on the data in 2018, the shortfall is 1.336,500 million. The shortage lasts for a longer period of time until around 2033 compared with that of primary school teachers.

Forecast of the Fiscal Investment on Junior High Schools

The method of calculating the index of education expenditure per student is used to predict the fiscal investment in China's junior high school from 2015 to 2050. According to the 2017 Statistical Yearbook of Education Expenditure, the average expenditure per student on ordinary junior middle schools in 2016 is 16,007.22 yuan, and the GDP per capita of that year is 53,680 yuan. Thus, the index in 2016 is 29%. According to the data from Education at a Glance, China has higher index in 2016 compared with many developed countries in the world, such as the United States (23%), the United Kingdom (26%), Australia (25%), Japan (26%), France (25%) and Germany (22%). With the same method, the average education expenditure index of junior high school students in 2016 is used to predict the fiscal investment in junior high school education from 2015 to 2050. The results are shown in Table 15.28.

The forecast shows that the investment in junior high school education is much lower than that in primary school. In 2020, the investment in junior high school exceeds 1 trillion yuan for the first time, and in 2042, the investment under medium scenario exceeds 2 trillion yuan. By 2050, it is 3,394.473 billion yuan under medium scenario and 39,172.16 billion yuan under high scenario. According to

Table 15.27 Forecast of the Demand for Junior High Teachers and the Supply-Demand Gap (Million)

Year	Demand for Teachers			Gap		
	Low	Medium	High	Low	Medium	High
2015	3.18	3.18	3.18	0.40	0.40	0.40
2016	3.27	3.27	3.27	0.49	0.49	0.49
2017	3.34	3.34	3.34	0.56	0.56	0.56
2018	3.55	3.55	3.55	0.77	0.77	0.77
2019	3.66	3.66	3.66	0.88	0.88	0.88
2020	3.80	3.80	3.80	1.02	1.02	1.02
2021	3.89	3.89	3.89	1.11	1.11	1.11
2022	3.92	3.92	3.92	1.14	1.14	1.14
2023	3.95	3.95	3.95	1.17	1.17	1.17
2024	4.08	4.08	4.08	1.30	1.30	1.30
2025	4.07	4.07	4.07	1.29	1.29	1.29
2026	4.12	4.12	4.12	1.34	1.34	1.34
2027	3.78	3.78	3.78	1.00	1.00	1.00
2028	3.77	3.77	3.77	0.99	0.99	0.99
2029	3.64	3.64	3.64	0.86	0.86	0.86
2030	3.63	3.63	3.63	0.85	0.85	0.85
2031	3.31	3.35	3.35	0.53	0.57	0.57
2032	2.96	3.06	3.08	0.18	0.29	0.30
2033	2.71	2.89	2.93	−0.07	0.11	0.15
2034	2.56	2.78	2.84	−0.22	0.00	0.06
2035	2.46	2.69	2.77	−0.32	−0.09	−0.01
2036	2.37	2.60	2.71	−0.41	−0.18	−0.07
2037	2.30	2.54	2.67	−0.48	−0.24	−0.11
2038	2.25	2.50	2.65	−0.53	−0.28	−0.13
2039	2.22	2.48	2.65	−0.56	−0.30	−0.13
2040	2.21	2.48	2.67	−0.57	−0.30	−0.11
2041	2.22	2.50	2.71	−0.56	−0.27	−0.07
2042	2.23	2.54	2.78	−0.54	−0.24	0.00
2043	2.26	2.59	2.85	−0.52	−0.19	0.07
2044	2.29	2.64	2.93	−0.49	−0.14	0.15
2045	2.32	2.69	3.00	−0.46	−0.09	0.22
2046	2.35	2.74	3.08	−0.43	−0.04	0.30
2047	2.37	2.78	3.15	−0.41	0.00	0.37
2048	2.38	2.81	3.20	−0.40	0.03	0.42
2049	2.38	2.82	3.24	−0.40	0.04	0.46
2050	2.38	2.81	3.25	−0.40	0.04	0.47

the 2017 Education Statistics Yearbook, the national fiscal education expenditure on ordinary junior high schools in 2016 is 613.253 billion yuan. If this number is used to measure the gap between supply and demand of government investment in junior high schools in the future, the gap will continue to increase. In 2016, China's fiscal expenditure on ordinary junior high schools accounts for 0.83% of the GDP and 19.53% of the total education expenditure. As for the percentage of expenditure on junior high schools in GDP, China has surpassed Japan (0.66%), Norway (0.86%), South Korea (0.85%), the United States (0.83%) and the United Kingdom

Table 15.28 Forecast of Education Expenditure on Junior High Schools in China from 2015 to 2050

Year	GDP per Capita (Yuan)	Index of Preschool Education Expenditure per Student	Preschool Education Expenditure per Student (Yuan)	Low (100 Million Yuan)	Medium (100 Million Yuan)	High (100 Million Yuan)
2015	50,028.00	0.29	14,508.12	6,225.47	6,225.47	6,225.47
2016	53,680.00	0.29	16,007.22	7,069.94	7,069.94	7,069.94
2017	59,201.00	0.29	17,168.29	7,747.07	7,747.07	7,747.07
2018	64,644.00	0.29	18,746.76	8,990.75	8,990.75	8,990.75
2019	67,876.20	0.29	19,684.10	9,730.72	9,730.72	9,730.72
2020	71,270.01	0.29	20,668.30	10,589.11	10,589.11	10,589.11
2021	74,833.51	0.29	21,701.72	11,409.20	11,409.20	11,409.20
2022	78,575.19	0.29	22,786.80	12,043.71	12,043.71	12,043.71
2023	82,503.95	0.29	23,926.14	12,749.45	12,749.45	12,749.45
2024	86,629.14	0.29	25,122.45	13,823.40	13,823.40	13,823.40
2025	90,960.60	0.29	26,378.57	14,493.63	14,493.63	14,493.63
2026	95,508.63	0.29	27,697.50	15,390.64	15,390.64	15,390.64
2027	100,284.06	0.29	29,082.38	14,821.46	14,821.46	14,821.46
2028	105,298.26	0.29	30,536.50	15,525.13	15,525.13	15,525.13
2029	110,563.18	0.29	32,063.32	15,755.51	15,755.51	15,755.51
2030	116,091.34	0.29	33,666.49	16,507.71	16,507.71	16,507.71
2031	121,895.90	0.29	35,349.81	15,803.94	15,974.20	15,995.19
2032	127,990.70	0.29	37,117.30	14,822.72	15,356.94	15,440.91
2033	134,390.23	0.29	38,973.17	14,261.36	15,208.70	15,402.13
2034	141,109.74	0.29	40,921.83	14,139.83	15,361.26	15,694.58
2035	148,165.23	0.29	42,967.92	14,245.39	15,578.50	16,070.55
2036	155,573.49	0.29	45,116.31	14,411.82	15,863.77	16,526.83
2037	163,352.17	0.29	47,372.13	14,679.83	16,253.39	17,090.07
2038	171,519.78	0.29	49,740.74	15,080.56	16,784.75	17,788.92
2039	180,095.77	0.29	52,227.77	15,631.89	17,487.47	18,656.50
2040	189,100.55	0.29	54,839.16	16,344.77	18,380.66	19,743.51
2041	198,555.58	0.29	57,581.12	17,218.03	19,470.75	21,080.59
2042	208,483.36	0.29	60,460.17	18,240.28	20,744.28	22,661.44
2043	218,907.53	0.29	63,483.18	19,384.26	22,173.80	24,430.53
2044	229,852.91	0.29	66,657.34	20,619.38	23,733.81	26,338.41
2045	241,345.55	0.29	69,990.21	21,924.36	25,403.63	28,375.25
2046	253,412.83	0.29	73,489.72	23,280.91	27,158.08	30,533.59
2047	266,083.47	0.29	77,164.21	24,664.46	28,952.68	32,782.79
2048	279,387.64	0.29	81,022.42	26,030.65	30,705.43	35,041.34
2049	293,357.03	0.29	85,073.54	27,379.02	32,374.45	37,192.60
2050	308,024.88	0.29	89,327.21	28,686.34	33,944.73	39,172.16

Source: UNESCO's Sustainable Development Goals [EB/OL]. http://data.uis.unesco.org/

(0.84%). In terms of the proportion of expenditure on junior high schools in the total fiscal expenditure, China is close to Australia (19.64%), and higher than New Zealand (17.45%), Sweden (11.43%), the United Kingdom (15.36%) and Iceland (12.72%). Of course, this only reflects the relative value of each country's investment rather than the absolute value.

Concluding Remarks

Education is one of the most important social causes in China. Effective implementation of the strategy on developing a quality workforce requires quality education and related environment. The report to the 19th National Congress points out that "China continues to ensure and improve people's livelihood during its development and make new progress in providing education and enough schools seats for children". After the implementation of the two-child policy, the structural changes in population directly affects the educational structure, and the existing education has been unable to adapt to the present population structure. Thus, the population in 35 years poses varied challenges to education. both preschool education and compulsory education, the demand for education seats of preschools, primary schools and junior schools increases and then declines, repeating the pattern afterwards. However, each education stage is different in when and how demands change.

From the perspective of seats demand, after the implementation of the two-child policy, the peak of children under three years old appears in 2017, with the highest number of 49,471,800, and gradually decreases to the lowest number of 27,940,700 in 2050, according to the conservative estimate under the medium scenario. According to the experience of developed countries and the guidelines on infant care issued by China in recent years, at the same time, considering the tendency to family care, kindergarten enrollment in the future rate is 30%. There are more than 10 million people who need child care. The number is over 15 million during birth accumulation. The demand of preschool seats is 58.5,958 million in 2017, reaching its highest. And the most serious seats deficit is more than 12 million. After 2023, the deficit turns into surplus, and by 2050, there are more than 5.5,917 to 18.6,729 million seats. For primary education, the peak occurs in 2020, with 108.97 million, as the peak cohort of preschool students has moved to primary school age. Since then, primary schools see the biggest decline, reducing by nearly half from 2015 by 2050. As for junior high school, the maximum number is reached in 2026, and the demand for seats exceeds the current supply from 2018 to 2030, after which the number of seats gradually becomes surplus to more than 12 million at most.

In terms of the demand for teachers, there is a serious shortage of teachers for children under six years old in China, and there is still a big gap in teacher–child ration compared with the national standard and the ratio in developed countries. As for child care, teacher responsible for child care is urgently needed and relevant system needs to be established. For preschool education for 3–6 years old, if based on the ideal teacher–child ratio of 1:8, the demand for full-time teachers is about 7 million at most. Compared with the data in 2018, the demand for full-time preschool teachers has been in a state of shortage, with a maximum shortfall of 4 million. If based on the ratio of 1:15, the maximum shortfall is more than 1.3 million, but the supply surpasses the demand and in the end there will be a surplus. The current teacher–student ratio of primary schools ranks high in the world and also meets the national standards. Based on the ratio of 1:19, the change of teachers in primary schools is relatively stable compared with the demand in kindergartens.

Before 2023, the maximum shortage of teachers is more than 400,000, but after that, the supply outnumbers the demand by nearly 2 million, which is in sharp contrast to the shortage of kindergarten teachers. The ratio in junior high schools meets the national requirements of 1:13.5, and the days with insufficient teachers are more than the days with sufficient teachers, with the shortage of 1.33 million at most. But the surplus, with over 500,000 at most, is not as serious as that in primary schools.

As for the number of schools, based on 175 students per school, the number of kindergartens in China will be insufficient before 2023 with modest gap of 60,000 kindergartens needed at most. With 360 students per school, the number of kindergartens in China is enough to cope with the future birth peak.

From the perspective of government investment, the demands for investment of preschools, primary schools and junior schools are constantly expanding between 2015 and 2050. Among the three kinds of schools, primary schools have the largest demand for government investment, with a maximum of 5.2,560,887 trillion yuan, followed by junior high school with a maximum of 3.917,216 billion yuan, and preschools with 2.255,879 billion yuan at most. However, from the perspective of the priority of the investment, China mainly focuses on compulsory education, and thus, the share of investment in preschool education in the total education expenditure is far below the world average.

The universal two-child policy is a major change of family planning policy. The growth of birth population brought by the population policy and the existing population brings great challenge and pressure to China's educational system. In order to adapt to the new change, it is necessary to make overall, reasonable planning by balancing population prediction, urban development and public services, so as to meet the demand for higher quality and more diversified education with fairness and sustainability.

Notes

1 Regulations on Kindergarten Work [EB/OL]. https://www.sohu.com/a/273600726_768344
2 Compulsory Education Law of the People's Republic of China [EB/OL]. http://edu.people.com.cn/GB/4547065.html
3 Special Provisions on Female Worker Labor Protection [EB/OL]. http://www.gov.cn/zwgk/2012–05/07/content_2131567.htm
4 Guiding Opinions on Promoting the Development of Care Services for Infants under three Years Old [EB/OL]. http://www.gov.cn/zhengce/content/2019-05/09/content_5389983.htm
5 Outline of the National Plan for Medium- and Long-term Education Reform and Development (2010–2020) [EB/OL]. http://www.gov.cn/jrzg/2010–07/29/content_1667143.htm
6 2017 Education Statistics Report [EB/OL]. http://www.moe.gov.cn/jyb_sjzl/sjzl_fztjgb/201807/t20180719_343508.html
7 The 13th Five-Year Plan for the Development of National Education (No. 4, 2017) [EB/OL]. http://www.gov.cn/zhengce/content/2017-01/19/content_5161341.htm
8 2017 National Educational Development Statistical Report [EB/OL]. http://www.moe.gov.cn/jyb_sjzl/sjzl_fztjgb/201807/t20180719_343508.html

9 Three-year Action Plan for Preschool Education (2011–2013) [EB/OL]. https://wenku.baidu.com/view/beb70e605ef7ba0d4a733bb1.html
10 The Outline of Tianjin's Medium- and long-term Education Reform and Development Plan (2010–2020) [EB/OL]. https://max.book118.com/html/2018/0103/147000562.shtm
11 2017 National Educational Development Statistical Report [EB/OL]. http://www.moe.gov.cn/jyb_sjzl/sjzl_fztjgb/201807/t20180719_343508.html
12 China's Education Statistics 2018 [EB/OL]. http://www.moe.gov.cn/jyb_sjzl/moe_560/jytjsj_2018/
13 Ibid.
14 Kindergarten Work Procedures [EB/OL]. https://www.sohu.com/a/273600726_768344
15 The Interim Standards for the Staffing of Kindergarten Staff and Children [EB/OL]. http://www.moe.gov.cn/srcsite/A10/s7151/201301/t20130115_147148.html
16 China's Education Statistics 2018 [EB/OL]. http://www.moe.gov.cn/jyb_sjzl/moe_560/jytjsj_2018/
17 The Outline of the National Program for Medium - and Long-term Education Reform and Development (2010–2020) [EB/OL]. http://www.gov.cn/jrzg/2010-07/29/content_1667143.htm
18 2017 China Education Expenditure Statistical Yearbook.
19 Ibid.
20 National Bureau of Statistics: http://data.stats.gov.cn/easyquery.htm?cn=C01
21 Data source: UNESCO's Sustainable Development Goals [EB/OL]. http://data.uis.unesco.org/
22 Data resource: Ibid.
23 Compulsory Education Law of the People's Republic of China [EB/OL]. http://edu.people.com.cn/GB/4547065.html
24 China's Education Statistics 2018 [EB/OL]. http://www.moe.gov.cn/jyb_sjzl/moe_560/jytjsj_2018/
25 Notice on Unifying the Pay Packages of teaching and administrative staff in Urban and Rural Primary and Junior High Schools jointly issued by State Commission Office of Public Sectors Reform, Ministry of Education and Ministry of Finance [EB/OL]. http://www.moe.gov.cn/s78/A10/tongzhi/201412/t20141209_181014.html
26 Data source: 2018 Education Statistics Yearbook.
27 Data source: 2017 China Education Expenditure Statistical Yearbook.
28 Notice on Unifying the Pay Packages of teaching and administrative staff in Urban and Rural Primary and Junior High Schools jointly issued by State Commission Office of Public Sectors Reform, Ministry of Education and Ministry of Finance [EB/OL]. http://www.moe.gov.cn/s78/A10/tongzhi/201412/t20141209_181014.html
29 2018 Education Statistical Yearbook.

References

Pang Lijuan, Wang Honglei, and Lv Wu. 2016. On Development Strategies of Pre-school Education in China under the Two-Child Policy. *Journal of Beijing Normal University* (Social Sciences Edition) 6: 12–21.
Shi Wenxiu. 2017. Supply and Demand of Pre-school Education Resources under the Two-Child Policy in China: A Prediction of Pre-school Child Population 2017–2026. *Education Science* 4: 82–89.
Yang Shunguang, Li Ling, Zhang Bingjuan, and Yin Xin. 2016. The Two-Child Policy and Resource Allocation for Pre-school Education: A 20 Years Prediction of the Eligible Population. *Studies in Early Childhood Education* 8: 3–13.

16 Pro-Natalist Policies in Developed Countries and Their Effects

In the second half of the 19th century, fertility rate slid in some European countries in sympathy with the boom in industrialization and urbanization. In the second half of the 20th century, fertility decline gradually seeped into developing countries, some of which even saw their fertility rates dropping at a faster pace. In the 1970s, against the backdrop of a universal decline in fertility, European countries and regions saw their fertility tumble further to a very-low or even ultra-low level. Specifically, the fertility of Western European countries fell below the replacement level in the period 1970–1975; those of Southern European countries slipped to a very-low level below 1.5 in the period 1990–1995; and those of Eastern European countries slid to an ultra-low level below 1.3 in the period 1995–2000. To make things worse, low fertility is still spreading, and countries such as Italy, Greece, Spain and Portugal are still caught in the "low-fertility trap". While more and more countries and regions across the globe are on the cusp of a fertility transition, the year around 1970 marks a turning point for the fertility rates worldwide to make a shift "from differentiation to convergence" (Chen Youhua, 2010).

The continuation of low fertility underlines the structural problems facing different populations and even jeopardizes the reproduction of populations and brings varying crises to social development. However, is this low-fertility trend literally irreversible? A survey conducted in 15 EU countries in 2011 found that the ideal number of children exceed the replacement level among women in most countries, yet the actual fertility rate always missed the fertility expectations in respective countries (Wu Fan, 2016). The gap between the ideal number of children and the actual number of children is often used to determine the window of opportunity for overhauling the fertility policy (Anne H. Gauthier, 2007). In the 1970s, it was a common practice for European countries to institute a variety of family policies, among which pro-natalist family policies were deemed a pivotal move to address the challenges brought about by low fertility when the policy window opens.

Today, the number of countries implementing pro-natalist policies has increased from 13 countries in 1976 to 55 countries in 2015, and the percentage has surged from 9% to 28%. In particular, in the past 40 years, the number of developed countries implementing pro-natalist policies has increased from 7 to 31. By 2015, 63% of developed countries had introduced measures to encourage more births, and none had introduced measures to discourage births. In less developed countries

DOI: 10.4324/9781003429661-16

and regions, countries encouraging births and those discouraging births are both increasing in number, while countries choosing not to intervene in births are dwindling. However, in the least developed countries and regions, due to relatively low economic development, anti-natalist policies still prevail (Table 16.1).

Public policies shape family life by defining the relevant rights, responsibilities, opportunities and constraints (Anne H. Gauthier, 2007). Numerous studies have shown that pro-natalist policies have a significant effect on increasing fertility in some countries. However, there are intricate links between policy and demographic behaviors, depending largely on the policy type, economic development, government support, cultural traditions and social norms in respective countries. First, we will sort out the types of pro-natalist policies currently being implemented in developed countries. Then, we will compare various types of pro-natalist policies across countries from the perspective of fiscal support. Lastly, we will probe into the effects and functioning mechanisms of such pro-natalist policies in different countries through Leibenstein's cost-utility theory. By reviewing the pro-natalist policies and their effects in developed countries, we will summarize their implications for China's fertility policy and pro-natalist social policies.

Types of Pro-Natalist Policies in Developed Countries

Europe was the first to bear the brunt of low fertility and was also the pioneer in introducing pro-natalist policies. From the 1970s and 1980s to the present days, European countries have developed a full-fledged system of pro-natalist policies. By sorting out these policies, it's found that the existing pro-natalist policies can be roughly divided into four categories: financial incentive policies, maternity leave policies, childcare service policies and other policies. Each type of policies has a different focus and plays a different role.

Financial Incentive Policies

By directly defraying the financial costs of raising children, financial incentive policies aim to ease the financial pressure on families to raise children and narrow the gap in living standards between families with and without children (Olivier Thévenon, 2011). In general, benefits provided by the government increase with the number of children being raised (Gerda Neyer, 2003). Gauthier and Hatzius (1997) estimated that a 25% increase in family allowance could help each woman have 0.07 more children. Among all types of pro-natalist policies, financial incentive policies are the earliest and easiest way to encourage births (Wang Ying, 2017). Such incentives mainly include maternity allowance, childcare allowance and tax incentives.

Maternity Allowance

Maternity allowance aims to encourage births by providing financial incentives to ease the financial and family burdens on mothers. For example, Russia set up a

Table 16.1 Fertility Policies Worldwide (1976–2015)

	Number of Countries/Regions					Percentage				
Year	Increase	Maintain	Decrease	Not intervene	Total	Increase	Maintain	Decrease	Not intervene	Total
	World									
1976	13	19	40	78	150	9	13	27	52	100
1986	19	16	54	75	164	12	10	33	46	100
1996	27	19	82	65	193	14	10	42	34	100
2005	38	31	78	47	194	20	16	40	24	100
2015	55	30	83	29	197	28	15	42	15	100
	Developed Countries									
1976	7	7	0	20	34	21	21	0	59	100
1986	8	6	0	20	34	24	18	0	59	100
1996	16	4	1	27	48	33	8	2	56	100
2005	24	8	0	16	48	50	17	0	33	100
2015	31	5	0	13	49	63	10	0	27	100
	Less Developed Countries									
1976	6	12	40	58	116	5	10	34	50	100
1986	11	10	54	55	130	8	8	42	42	100
1996	11	15	81	38	145	8	10	56	26	100
2005	14	23	78	31	146	10	16	53	21	100
2015	24	25	83	16	148	16	17	56	11	100
	Least Developed Countries/Regions									
1976	1	2	6	33	42	2	5	14	79	100
1986	2	4	15	27	48	4	8	31	56	100
1996	0	3	32	14	49	0	6	65	29	100
2005	0	3	38	9	50	0	6	76	18	100
2015	0	1	47	0	48	0	2	98	0	100

Source: United Nations, World Population Policies 2015.

Mother Fund in 2007 to provide a tax-free allowance of RUB 250,000 to mothers who have two or more children, which was increased to RUB 450,000 in 2014 (Xu Fengcai and Liang Hongqi, 2020). The allowance can also be used to pay mortgages and to improve living conditions for families with many children. On top of this, local governments are also trying to help young families financially. Moscow set aside USD 1.3 billion for offering a lump-sum incentive of RUB 16,000 to couple who will have their first child before the age of 30. Russia's financial generosity has contributed significantly to a rebound in its fertility rate.

Childcare Allowance

Childcare allowance aims to help families pay childcare costs and increase people's fertility desire. In some countries, the amount of childcare allowance varies depending on the age or number of children. Sweden introduced its child allowance policy in 1948, according to which an allowance can be collected on a monthly basis for each child until he/she reaches the age of 16, and it will be adjusted in parallel with changes in prices. Similar policies are also being implemented in France, Russia and other countries, and basically, more children will entitle the family to more allowance, and the amount can increase progressively (Luo Chun and Song Xiaoying, 2020).

Tax Incentives

By reducing or exempting the personal income tax payable by parents, tax incentives aim to ease the burden of parents raising children, thus providing financial assistance to families indirectly. There are many types of tax incentives, including child tax credit, tax deductions, tax penalties for childless couples, etc., and these tax incentives can be used in combination. However, the complex setup and calculation of tax incentives add to the difficulties of their implementation (Wang Ying and Sun Mengzhen, 2017).

Allowance for Special Families

The allowance for special families is mainly the financial relief for families in need. Some OECD countries provide special allowances to single parents or families with disabled child(ren) to ease their financial burden, while others provide assistance to families with reproductive disabilities. For example, the Russian government appropriated USD 8 million in 2007 to provide free artificial insemination services to help couples with different infertility problems fulfill their reproductive intentions and aspirations.

Maternity Leave Policies

Leave-related childcare policies date back more than 100 years, when many Western European countries instituted conditional paid maternity leave schemes to protect the rights of female employees. Maternity leave policies have grown and diversified significantly since the 1970s (Kimberly J. Morgan, 2009), and they focus mainly on compensating parents from a time perspective, giving parents more flexibility in scheduling their time to achieve a balance between work and childcare. The types of maternity leave include maternity leave, paternity leave and parental leave, and this indicator is often measured by the total number of weeks of leave preceding and succeeding childbirth.

Maternity Leave

Maternity leave refers to the job-protected leave of absence for female employees directly around the time of childbirth. Almost all OECD countries have public income support payments tied to maternity leave, thus providing both employment protection for working mothers and care for babies at critical stages of development. The ILO convention on maternity leave stipulates that the period of leave should be at least 14 weeks.[1] In France, female employees can take 16 weeks of maternity leave after having first birth, or 26 weeks after having second or further birth.

Paternity Leave

Paternity leave is mainly for fathers. This job-protected leave is available to employed fathers around the time of childbirth. Generally, the duration of paternity leave is much shorter than that of maternity leave. Paternity leave is mainly a policy formulated from the perspective of gender equality to encourage fathers' involvement in childcare activities. In some countries, paternity leave is even mandated by law. In 1995, Sweden introduced a paternity leave of 30 days, which was increased to 60 days in 2002 and further to 90 days in 2016 (Luo Chun and Song Xiaoying, 2020).

Parental Leave

Parental leave is often supplementary to the maternity and paternity leave periods to allow parents to take care of the newborn. Generally, after childbirth, the mother can take 14 weeks of leave, and the father can take two weeks of leave, after which the parents can discuss how to take the remaining parental leave (Wang Ziyu, 2017). In some countries, fathers are required to take the parental leave and must not transfer the leave to mothers in order to promote fathers' involvement in childcare and to change the gender roles in the family. Sweden was the first country in the world to enact legislation on the parental leave for fathers. According to Sweden's Parental Leave Act, 2 months out of 16 months of the paid parental leave must be taken by the father.

Childcare Service Policies

Childcare service policies mainly aim to provide childcare facilities and services for school-aged and preschool children. Such services may be provided by the government, market, employer or non-profit organization to relieve families of the time and energy spent on childcare and to help parents achieve a balance between work and childcare. Studies have shown that a 30% increase in public childcare coverage is associated with an average increase by 0.12 more children born to each woman, not to mention the uptick in female employment (John Bongaarts and Tomas Sobotka, 2012). Furthermore, childcare also accords with the goal of promoting child development.

From a family perspective, participation in childcare services is closely linked to the accessibility and cost of childcare services, yet childcare services vary widely across countries. In Denmark, more than 60% of children under three are enrolled in registered childcare services, while this figure falls below 5% in Greece, Austria, Spain and Italy. Meanwhile, public spending on childcare varies widely across countries, with the highest spending found in the United States, and lower spending found in Southern European countries, Japan and South Korea (Anna Cristina d'Addio and Marco Mira d'Ercole, 2005).

Other Relevant Policies

Some countries have also introduced other policies to encourage births. For example, housing incentives can help families address basic housing needs, including measures to provide larger subsidized housing to families with many children or to even grant free land for housing. France has introduced a family housing allowance to help families pay for housing costs, and the amount of allowance depends on the housing area, living conditions, rent paid and family income (Ma Caichen et al., 2017). Some countries have introduced employment support policies to enable women to give birth to and raise their children without worries. In Russia, women's maternity leave can be counted into their working years, and women can choose not to work for seven years after childbirth, during which the employer must retain her original job. In France, companies are not allowed to fire a pregnant employee and must provide her with suitable working conditions.

Policy Effects in Different Types of Countries

Scholars tend to refer their categorization of welfare models to Esping-Andersen's The Three Worlds of Welfare Capitalism, according to which European and American countries are divided into three welfare models, i.e., social democratic regimes represented by Nordic countries, conservative regimes represented by Germany, and liberal regimes represented by the United Kingdom and the United States. Government, family and market are the linchpins of these three welfare regimes. Other scholars have also added the Mediterranean regime represented by Southern European countries on this basis (Anne H. Gauthier, 2002; Gerda Neyer, 2003; Suzana Bornarova et al., 2017). However, looking back at the fertility levels of different countries in the past few decades, European countries and regions diverged greatly on the pace of fertility transition. With the advent of the 21st century, the significant differences among European countries have led to the emergence of "dual fertility patterns" (Song Jian, 2017). That is, even under the same family policy model, European countries differ significantly in total fertility rate (TFR), and such difference even dwarfs the gap between countries under different policy models. For example, Denmark and Sweden both pertain to social democratic regimes. From the 1970s to the 1990s, Sweden's TFR fell from 1.9 to 1.64 and then rebounded to 1.9, while Denmark's TFR dropped from 1.96 to 1.54. Similarly, while Germany and France both pertain to the conservative regime, France has a TFR above 1.8, yet Germany has a TFR below 1.5.[2] In this chapter, we attempt to use a simpler and more direct categorization method for ease of comparison, i.e., countries with TFR rebounding significantly, countries with TFR rebounding insignificantly, countries with TFR staying above 1.5 and countries with TFR staying below 1.5.

According to the theory on the four stages of demographic transition, after entering the fourth stage of demographic transition, developed countries have seen their TFRs embarking on different trajectories – inverse J-shaped increase for Nordic countries, low-fertility trap for Southern and Western European countries, and ultra-low fertility for some East Asian countries. In certain countries, although TFR is seemingly picking up, the rebound is not strong and a fall is looming. Fertility rate is always in dynamic changes, and it's neither accurate nor rigorous to call the increase in TFR in an individual year a reversal. Some scholars have attempted to explain the difference between "rebound" and "reversal", arguing that rebound is a temporary state likely followed by a decline, while reversal is a fundamental shift in trend. They define a 10% rise in TFR over the a relative low in the preceding period as a "rebound", and a rise of more than 20% as a "reversal" (Chen Youhua and Miao Guo, 2015). According to this criterion, we will define the rise in TFR as "rebounding significantly" if it reaches the level of "reversal", or "rebounding insignificantly" if it only reaches the level of "rebound". Sweden's TFR rose from 1.558 in the period 1995–2000 to 1.902 in the period 2010–2015, an increase of 22%, which qualifies it for "reversal", and thus, it's deemed a country with TFR rebounding significantly. Germany's TFR rose from 1.345 in the period 1995–2000 to 1.586 in the period 2015–2020, an increase of less than 20%. Moreover, Germany's TFR has lingered below 1.5 since the 1980s and did not climb back above 1.5 until 2015. Due to the small magnitude of recovery, Germany is deemed a country with TFR rebounding insignificantly. France's TFR has stayed above 1.5, while South Korea and Japan have both seen their TFRs lingering below 1.5 in recent decades. In this chapter, the above-mentioned four countries are taken as the representatives of the four different types of countries, and then, we will further probe into the pro-natalist policies introduced by respective countries and their effects.

Presently, the pro-natalist policies implemented in different countries are diversified. Instead of scant measures such as direct cash allowance, countries are learning from each other to introduce mutually complementary measures. Despite the similarities between policies, the effects are widely divided. Different countries have different policy priorities and different levels of government support, so it is a daunting task to quantify the comprehensive policy support into specific indicators for cross-country comparisons. In particular, it's extremely difficult to measure the maternity leave policies. While it is possible to compare maternity leave policies across countries by the number of weeks of maternity leave, maternity leave is divided into paid and unpaid leave, not to mention the different pay rates across countries. For families, pay rate is way more important than the weeks of leave in measuring the effect of maternity leave. On average in OECD countries, maternity benefits can account for around 77% of a mother's usual average earnings, yet the pay rate tends to lower in English-speaking countries – less than 50% of average earnings in Australia, Canada, Ireland, New Zealand and the United Kingdom. In the meantime, the usage of parental leave varies from country to country. While Japan offers very generous paid paternity leave, it is used by only about 3% of fathers.[3] Social policies are usually measured by the proportions of respective social expenditures in GDP (Rebecca Ray et al., 2010). To facilitate cross-country comparison, we have specifically singled out the public spending on family benefits as percentage of GDP, the public spending on maternity and parental leave per live birth (in 2010 USD), and the public spending on childcare services as percentage of GDP to measure the level of policy support on financial incentives, maternity leave and childcare services in respective countries.

Table 16.2 summarizes the levels of fiscal support provided by each type of countries for the three kinds of pro-natalist policies in 2015. On average, OECD countries spent 2.4% of GDP on family benefits, and this indicator actually included maternity benefits and childcare allowance. Except for Japan with TFR staying below 1.5, other types of countries all outperformed this average. Although Sweden does not intervene in births, its matchless welfare policies and generous fiscal support have significantly contributed to a boost in its fertility. France provides more than 30 kinds of family benefits, which help build up a sophisticated

Table 16.2 Fiscal Support for Pro-natalist Policies in Different Types of Countries (2015)

	Financial Incentives	Maternity Leave	Childcare Services	TFR Change (1995–2000/2010–2015)
	Public Spending on Family Benefits (%GDP)	Public Spending on Maternity and Parental Leave per Live Birth (PPP$)	Public Spending on Childcare Services (%GDP)	
TFR rebounding significantly				
Sweden	3.54	26,139.97	1.60	1.56/1.90
TFR rebounding insignificantly				
Germany	3.06	11,595.45	0.60	1.35/1.43
TFR staying above 1.5				
France	3.68	7,561.45	1.32	1.76/1.98
TFR staying below 1.5				
Japan	1.61	9,655.60	0.44	1.37/1.41
OECD average	2.40	12,109.43	0.74	–

Source: OECD Family Database: Public policies for families and children. http://www.oecd.org/social/family/database.htm

TFR figures come from United Nations, World Population Prospects: The 2019 Revision.

system to defray the childbearing and childrearing costs for French families and allow employed women to source the much-needed childcare services from the market (Ma Chunhua, 2016).

In regard to the fiscal support for maternity leave, OECD countries spent on average USD 12,109.43 on maternity leave in 2015. Sweden spent more than double the OECD average. Sweden implements a very liberal leave policy that provides parents with a 480-day paid leave, and they are paid at 80% of their usual earnings for 390 days and then at a flat rate for the remaining 90 days.- Germany, though failing to reach the average level, also spent generously on maternity leave. In Germany, paternity leave and parental leave are comparatively longer and pay rates are also higher (Li Liangliang, 2013). In contrast, France, with TFR staying above 1.5, and Japan, with TFR staying below 1.5, both spent little on maternity leave.

In regard to the fiscal support for childcare services, Sweden and France spent far more than the average level, while German spent less on childcare services. In Germany, childcare services are not for free, but the fee can be reduced or exempted depending on family income, number of children, single-parent status, residence, etc. (Li Liangliang, 2013). In contrast, Japan spent the least on childcare services. Under the dual pressure from population aging and declining births, Japan has appropriated more fiscal resources for the elderly and chosen to spend less on childcare services (Ma Chunhua, 2017).

Although countries have successively introduced pro-natalist policies, these policies vary greatly from each other, not to mention their widely divided effects. While the amount of fiscal spending reflects how much weight the government gives to specific policies, the type of policies prioritized by the government mirrors a nation's development goals and priorities. Even similar policies will have different effects under different national realities.

How Do Pro-Natalist Policies Work

In 1978, Kamerman and Kahn divided family policies into "explicit" policies and "implicit" policies (Kamerman Sheila and Kahn Alfred, 1978). Explicit policies lay out direct and explicit goals, while implicit policies do not have explicit goals but do have an impact on families and cover a wider range. From the perspective of "familism" and "de-familialization", Leitner (2003) proposed a strength-based matrix model which encompasses Explicit Familialism, Optional Familialism, Implicit Familialism and De-Familialism. Drawing on the above definitions and classification standards, we divide pro-natalist policies into explicit policies and implicit policies.

Explicit policies have an explicit aim of encouraging births, such as maternity allowance and child allowance, which are directly used for subsidizing childbearing and childrearing. In contrast, the original intention of policies on parental leave and childcare services isn't to push up fertility. Parental leave policies aims to help women achieve work-life balance, while childcare service policies are meant to provide certain benefits to children. Meanwhile, these two types of

Pro-Natalist Policies and Their Effects 283

policies generally come into being and evolve over time in parallel with economic growth and social changes, and they tend to have a causal relationship with social changes. In providing other benefits, such policies indirectly accomplish the goal of encouraging births, and hence, they are deemed implicit pro-natalist policies. In his fertility cost-utility theory, Leibenstein (1974) divided fertility costs into direct and indirect costs. Direct costs includes basic necessities and everyday living expenses such as education, medical care, entertainment, etc., while indirect costs include opportunity costs such as the reduction in parents' earnings in raising the child(ren). Explicit pro-natalist policies are mainly devised to increase the family budget through financial support, thereby relieving families of the pressure from mounting living expenses and compensating the family for the direct costs of childbearing. Parental leave is more about compensating the family for time spent on childbearing and childrearing, while childcare services allow parents to remain in work and make up for the opportunity costs of childbirth. These two types of implicit pro-natalist policies compensate for the indirect costs of childbirth. Yang Juhua (2019a) once summarized the four-dimensional connotations of fertility as time, money, service and employment. Explicit and implicit pro-natalist policies jointly shape the four-dimensional connotations of fertility to encourage more births (Figure 16.1).

Building on Tables 16.2 and 16.3 outlines the childbearing costs, policy interventions on childbirth and work-life balance measures in different types of countries in 2015. If the fiscal spending associated with the three types of pro-natalist policies is higher (or lower) than the average of OECD countries, it is deemed that the country's financial compensation for the policy is large (or small), and therefore, the corresponding childbearing costs would be lower (or higher). Although Sweden has no policy intervention on childbirth, as a stellar example of welfare states, Sweden has minimized both the direct and indirect costs of childbearing through either explicit or implicit pro-natalist policies. From the early 1960s to around 1980, Sweden introduced generous fertility policies such as paid maternity

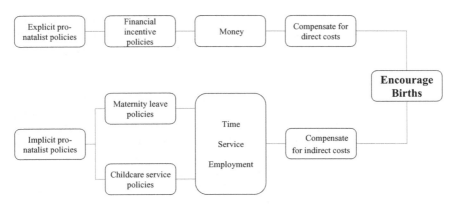

Figure 16.1 Roadmap to the functioning of pro-natalist policies

Table 16.3 Childbearing Costs and Policy Interventions on Childbirth in Respective Countries in 2015

	Direct Costs	Indirect costs		Policy Interventions	Work-Life Balance Measures
	Financial Incentives	Maternity Leave	Childcare Services		
TFR rebounding insignificantly					
Sweden	Low	Low	Low	None	123,578
Germany	Low	High	High	Encourage	135,678
TFR staying above 1.5					
France	Low	High	Low	Encourage	12,345,678
TFR staying below 1.5					
Japan	High	High	High	Encourage	135,678

Note: Work-life balance measures include: (1) job-protected maternity leave (paid or unpaid); (2) job-protected paternity leave (paid or unpaid); (3) parental leave (paid or unpaid); (4) child allowance (lump-sum payment); (5) child or family allowance; (6) tax credit for dependent children; (7) flexible working hours for parents; and (8) government-subsidized childcare services.

Source: Country-specific information on pro-natalist policies and work-life balance measures comes from United Nations, World Population Policies 2015.

leave, subsidized parenting, paid parental leave and universal child allowance to see the birth interval of its citizens narrow quickly and the effect of "speed premium" play out (Anders Bjorklund, 2006). Germany's TFR fell to around 1.5 in the 1970s and then slipped further to around 1.3 in the 1990s. Although Germany has introduced pro-natalist policies, these policies came too late. Judging from the childbearing costs in 2015 alone, indirect childbearing costs were still excessively high in Germany. As a result, Germany's TFR only picked up slightly and has been fluctuating around 1.5. France is an early adopter of pro-natalist policies. Although the indirect costs reflected in maternity leave policies remain high, France spends generously on childcare services, not to mention the flexible and diverse mix of childcare options, including public nurseries, enterprise-run nurseries, hospital-run nurseries, "temporary nurseries", "children's gardens", mother's aid and live-in nanny (Ma Chunhua, 2016), all to meet the childcare needs of different types of families and to relieve families of the pressure from childrearing. As a result, France's TFR has been remaining stable at a relatively high level. In Japan, which has been struggling for decades in the low-fertility trap, both the direct and indirect costs of childbearing are comparatively high. Although the Japanese government did introduced an array of policies to encourage births, it has seen little success.

From the above analysis, it can be concluded that lower direct and indirect costs of childbearing generally lead to higher TFR, such as the case of Sweden. In countries with low direct costs but high indirect costs (such as Germany), it is difficult to push up the fertility rate. In countries with higher direct and indirect costs (such as Japan), it's particularly difficult to reverse the fertility decline even if the government has introduced pro-natalist policies. With the passage of time and the increase in earnings, human capital enhancement is drawing increasing attention and the opportunity costs of childbearing is also getting higher and higher, not to mention the ever-mounting family spending on childrearing. According to Maslow's hierarchy of needs, both individual and family needs move from bottom to top. Financial incentives provided through explicit policies are no longer adequate to meet the childrearing needs of families at large. Instead, the "auxiliary" implicit policies appear to outperform explicit policies. The effects of a policy are linked to not only its purpose, level of support and length of implementation, but also the social and cultural environment of each country. Therefore, it is of great significance to dig into the intrinsic mechanisms behind the pro-natalist policies.

Prior to the 1950s, husband was perceived as the breadwinner of the family and wife as the housekeeper and children's caregiver. Based on such traditional gender roles, Western welfare states tended to introduce family policies encouraging men's breadwinning role and women's caregiving role in their early stage of development. In the 1970s, with the gradual uplift in women's labor force participation, more and more women came to realize their personal value beyond the family and the motherhood penalty brought about by childbearing and childrearing – that is, the more children, the greater the opportunity cost. Women began to fight for equality in the family and in the labor market, and policymakers in European countries were hence under mounting social pressures for gender equality (Zhao Fang and Chen Yan, 2014). In the wake of the reshaping of traditional values, the social environment underwent profound changes that spurred the explicit-to-implicit shift of pro-natalist policies. Some European countries began to combine welfare policies with labor policies to introduce employment-oriented fertility policies. In particular, family policies to support women's employment began to gain momentum (Emanuele Ferragina and Martin Seeleib-Kaiser, 2015). Dual-earner support policies also came into being in this context (Walter Koppi, 2000).

However, as soon as mothers leave the family and re-enter the labor market, childcare will emerge as a thorny issue facing every family. A full-fledged childcare system has become a new must for all families. Compared with the re-familiarizing characteristics of parental leave, de-familiarization policies such as childcare services attach greater importance to gender equality and help women achieve work-life balance better. Childcare service policies are also gradually shifting their focus from charitable purposes to children's education and parents' personal development. More and more public childcare institutions are replacing private institutions in supporting children's education (Gerda Neyer, 2003). The traditional family pattern of husband as breadwinner and wife as housekeeper is now giving way to the model of adult citizens participating in labor force and the government caring for their children during working hours (Huang Yuqin and Xiao Yixin, 2017). Sweden boasts the highest level of gender equality and is also the first country to experiment with implicit pro-natalist policies. In 1974, Sweden permitted parents to freely distribute income-linked paid leave according to family needs (Meng Ke, 2017), yet the pay rate for parental leave hinged largely on the pay a mother received from her full-time job prior to childbirth. The government emphasized that only families with both parents working full-time were eligible for childcare services (Anders Bjorklund, 2006), thus achieving the dual effect of encouraging births and promoting labor participation.

Implicit pro-natalist policies on promoting gender equality and work-life balance are increasingly gaining traction in more and more countries. In 2015, Sweden, Germany, France and Japan all introduced work-life balance policies, albeit in different types and combinations (Table 16.3). Basically, all these countries have rolled out leave-related policies such as maternity leave, parental leave and flexible working hours and financial incentives such as child allowance, family allowance, public subsidies for childcare, etc. Sweden and France have also adopted paternity leave policies encouraging fathers' involvement in child care activities, yet such policies are absent in Germany and Japan, a reflection of Germany and Japan's below-average performance in gender equality. Overall, France has the most comprehensive work-life balance measures, while Sweden has the most generous policies, both leading to consistently high TFRs in the two countries. In contrast, although Germany and Japan have also introduced a variety of work-life balance policies, these policies came too late and their emphasis on gender equality is not strong enough. Germany came to realize the drawbacks of gender inequality earlier than Japan and has instituted reforms since the 1980s to gradually socialize family responsibilities and move ahead with childcare services. It was not until the early 2000s that German government began to scale up employment-oriented family policies and to combine welfare policies with labor policies. Japan, however, was more conservative than Germany in policy reform, not to mention any effort to link family policies to national economic interests (Martin Seeleib-Kaiser and Tuukka Toivonen, 2011). Meanwhile, Japan's policies only target a specific group of women and therefore are not deemed universal policies (Peter Mcdonald, 2006). For example, although Japan has policies encouraging employed women to have children and raise children, Japan's tax policy and social security policy tend to support traditional families characterized by "husband as breadwinner and wife as housekeeper". The conflict between policies is deemed a major cause of the ineffectiveness of policies (Ma Chunhua, 2017).

Concluding Remarks

Low-fertility European countries have begun to experiment with pro-natalist policies since the 1970s, and soon their examples were followed by more and more countries. After more than half a century of evolution, these policies have become increasingly clear in goals and sophisticated in institutional design. Today, family policies in different countries and regions exhibit the following commonalities: (1) an ongoing shift from supporting traditional families to recognizing the diversity of family forms; (2) a universal preference for child-centric financial support; and (3) a special focus on work-life balance (Wu Fan, 2012). In particular, implicit pro-natalist policies promoting gender equality and work-life balance are gaining momentum in more and more countries. However, the following considerations must be taken into account in devising such policies.

First, policies should be aligned with the needs of the people. While families have different needs in different periods, the government should have a firm grasp of the changes in family needs and roll out the corresponding policies to meet their needs in a timely manner. For women, childbearing and employment are two important goals in their lives. Therefore, it is of paramount importance to help women improve their employment prospects and financial independence in conjunction with efforts to boost fertility. A well-designed childcare service policy should take into account the combined goals of child education, financial autonomy of mothers and gender equality (Olivier Thévenon, 2011) and relieve women of "gender-motherhood based dual taxation" (Yang Juhua, 2019b). Only then can the policy be considered best suited to the needs of the society in these days.

Second, it is crucial to grasp the right timing for introducing pro-natalist policies. As the very first country in Europe to undergo fertility decline, France was the first to weigh how to curb the fertility decline through family policies (Ma Chunhua, 2016). On the contrary, Japan and South Korea lagged far behind in adjusting their fertility policies. Even with fertility rate lingering at a low level for years, Japan only attempted to encourage births by introducing a mild fertility policy, thus missing the window of opportunity for policy adjustment. In 2005, the South Korean government enacted the Framework Act on Low Birth Rate in an Aging Society, marking a historic turn of its fertility policy from moderate and neutral intervention to proactive intervention (Zhu Hui, 2019), albeit still with little success. This is because once the low-fertility inertia is formed, it would be extremely difficult to reverse the trend.

Third, the goals of the fertility policy should span the entire life cycle. Since reproductive activities are mainly undertaken by women, pro-natalist policies should focus on women's reproductive experience and be aligned with their important events and needs over the course of life (Qi Jing and Mao Zhuo Yan, 2020). Only when such policies take into account the needs of women in different stages of their lives can they best help women solve a succession of problems brought about by childbearing.

Pro-natalist policies are not only about encouraging births but also about improving family benefits, promoting personal development, enhancing gender equality, alleviating work-life conflicts, etc. Fertility is not confined to "childbearing". It's also about "childrearing", a time-consuming process. Therefore, we cannot create a fertility-friendly and family-friendly institutional environment overnight. The fertility policy must not only be built on the present but also look into the future. Only when women's needs are truly taken into consideration can the policy be widely embraced by people.

Notes

1 Source: OECD Family Database: http://www.oecd.org/social/family/database.htm
2 Source: World Population Prospects (2019).
3 Source: OECD Family Database. PF2.4: Parental leave replacement rates.

Reference list

Anders Bjorklund. 2006. Does Family Policy Affect Fertility? Lessons from Sweden. *Journal of Population Economics* 19(1): 3–24.

Anna Cristina d'Addio and Marco Mira d'Ercole. 2005. Trends and Determinants of Fertility Rates: The Role of Policies. *OECD Social, Employment and Migration Working Papers* 6: 1–91.

Anne H. Gauthier. 2002. Family Policies in Industrialized Countries: Is There Convergence? *Population* (English Edition) 57(3): 457–484.

Anne H. Gauthier. 2007. The Impact of Family Policies on Fertility in Industrialized Countries: A Review of the Literature. *Population Research and Policy Review* 26(3): 323–346.

Anne H. Gauthier and Jan Hatzius. 1997. Family Benefits and Fertility: An Econometric Analysis. *Population Studies* 51: 295–306.

Chen Youhua. 2010. From Differentiation to Convergence: The World Fertility Transition and Its Implications for China. *Academia Bimestris* 1: 26–34.

Chen Youhua and Miao Guo. 2015. Low Fertility Trap: Concepts, OECD and BRICS Experiences and Related Issues. *Population and Development* 6: 7–18.

Emanuele Ferragina and Martin Seeleib-Kaiser. 2015. Determinants of a Silent (R)evolution: Understanding the Expansion of Family Policy in Rich OECD Countries. *Social Politics* 22(1): 1–37.

Gerda Neyer. 2003. Family Policies and Low Fertility in Western Europe. MPIDR Working Paper, WP2003–021.

Huang Yuqin and Xiao Yixin. 2017. How to Realize Fertility Reversal under the Risk of "Low Fertility Trap"? The Experience of East Asia, Europe and the United States and its Inspiration to China. *Fujian Forum (Humanities and Social Sciences Edition)* 5: 159–166.

John Bongaarts and Tomas Sobotka. 2012. A Demographic Explanation for the Recent Rise in European Fertility. *Population and Development Review* 38(1): 83–120.

Kamerman Sheila and Kahn Alfred. 1978. *Family Policy: Government and Families in Fourteen Countries.* New York, NY: Columbia University Press.

Kimberly J. Morgan. 2009. Caring Time Policies in Western Europe: Trends and Implications. *Comparative European Politics* 7(1): 37–55.

Leibenstein, H. 1974. An Interpretation of the Economic Theory of Fertility: Promising Path or Blind Alley. *Journal of Economic Literature* 12(2): 457–479.

Li Liangliang. 2013. Analysis of Family-Friendly Policies and their Effects in Four European Countries. *Journal of China Women's University* 1: 89–93.

Luo Chun and Song Xiaoying. 2020. Chinese Family Fertility Choices and Policy Changes in the Post-Family Planning Era. *Journal of Yunnan Normal University (Philosophy and Social Sciences Edition)* 2: 84–90.

Ma Caichen, Li Meng, and Na Wanqing. 2017. Policies and Laws of Family Subsidies and Tax Deductions in Developed Countries. *Social Policy Research* 6: 66–80.

Ma Chunhua. 2016. Implications of Family Policies in Sweden and France. *Journal of Women's Studies* 2: 20–23.

Ma Chunhua. 2017. Family Changes and Family Policy Reconstruction in Contemporary Japan: Intergenerational Redistribution of Public Resources. *Social Development Research* 3: 69–97.

Martin Seeleib-Kaiser and Tuukka Toivonen. 2011. Between Reforms and Birth Rates: Germany, Japan, and Family Policy Discourse. *Social Politics* 18(3): 331–360.

Meng Ke. 2017. The Change of Employment-Fertility Relationship and the Rise of Two-Salary Family Policy: Looking at China's Family Policy in the Two-Child Era from the Experience of Developed Countries. *Sociological Research* 5: 218–241.

Olivier Thévenon. 2011. Family Policies in OECD Countries: A Comparative Analysis. *Population and Development Review* 37(1): 57–87.

Peter Mcdonald. 2006. Low Fertility and the State: the Efficacy of Policy. *Population and Development Review* 32(3): 485–510.

Qi Jing and Mao Zhuo Yan. 2020. Life Course Perspective of Family Support Policy Research. *Journal of Fujian Normal University* (*Philosophy and Social Sciences Edition*) 2: 112–121.

Rebecca Ray, Janet C. Gornick, and John Schmitt. 2010. Who Cares? Assessing Generosity and Gender Equality in Parental Leave Policy Designs in 21 Countries. *Journal of European Social Policy* 20(3): 196–216.

Sigrid Leitner. 2003. Varieties of Familialism: The Caring Function of the Family in Comparative Perspective. *European Societies* 5(4): 353–375.

Song Jian. 2017. Turning Point: Where will China's Fertility Go? Based on European Experience and Implications. *Exploration and Free Views* 4: 70–75.

Suzana Bornarova, Natasha Bogoevska, and Svetlana Trbojevik. 2017. Changes in European Welfare State Regimes as a Response to Fertility Trends: Family Policy Perspective. *European Journal of Social Sciences Education and Research* 11(1): 50–57.

United Nations. 2019. *World Population Prospects: The 2019 Revision.* https://population.un.org/wpp/Publications/Files/WPP2019_Volume-I_Comprehensive-Tables.pdf

Walter Koppi. 2000. Faces of Inequality: Gender, Class, and Patterns of Inequalities in Different Types of Welfare States. *Social Politics* 7(2): 127–191.

Wang Ying and Sun Mengzhen. 2017. Fertility Policies and Their Effects: International Experience, Review and Prospect. *Journal of Zhejiang University* (*Humanities and Social Sciences Edition*) 5: 19–29.

Wang Ziyu. 2017. Family Welfare Policies and Service Systems in Nordic Countries: Experience and Development. *Social Policy Research* 6: 93–106.

Wu Fan. 2012. Family Changes and Policy Considerations in China under the Background of the Second Demographic Transition. *Guangdong Social Sciences* 2: 23–30.

Wu Fan. 2016. Family Policy and Fertility Change in Europe: Implications for the Risk of Low Fertility Trap in China. *Sociological Research* 1: 49–72.

Xu Fengcai and Liang Hongqi. 2020. Russian Population Crisis and Coping Policy. *Journal of Liaoning Normal University* (*Social Sciences Edition*) 2: 1–8.

Yang Juhua. 2019a. Fertility Support and Fertility Support Policy: Basic Implications and Future Orientation. *Shandong Social Sciences* 10: 98–107.

Yang Juhua. 2019b. "Gender – Motherhood Double Taxation" and Gender Differences in Labor Market Participation. *Population Research* 1: 36–51.

Zhao Fang and Chen Yan. 2014. Family Policy in Europe in the Past Two Decades: Changes and Continuations. *Journal of East China University of Science and Technology* (*Social Science Edition*) 1: 20–27.

Zhu Hui. 2019. A Practical Review of South Korea's Fertility Policy Based on the Incentive Compatibility Theory and Implications for China. *Population and Economics* 3: 48–61.

17 Summary and Conclusion

This study systematically investigated the trends of China's fertility transition and the patterns of low fertility in China and analyzed the impacts of the two-child policy on China's fertility. The long-term effects on population size and structure are further examined through the impact on fertility. Based on the demographic effect of the two-child policy, the possible influence on China's social and economic development is discussed. In terms of content structure, apart from the introduction of the first part and the conclusion of the fourth part, the core content is divided into two parts, namely the trend and characteristics of low fertility rate in the second part and the implementation effect of the two-child policy in the third part. This final chapter is the fourth chapter to summarize the content of this study, present the conclusions of this study and discuss policy implications.

Evolution of China's Low Fertility

Trends in Fertility Transition

China's fertility transition is one of the most momentous events in human history. This transition deviated from the predictions of the classical demographic transition theory, taking place in the world's most populous developing country with a very low level of economic development and modernization, but at a faster pace than that in any previous comparable countries.

Since the founding of the People's Republic of China, the transformation process of China's fertility can be roughly divided into four phases according to the changing fertility level: (1) The phase of high fertility level in the 1950s and 1960s. From 1949 to 1970, China's fertility level remained at a high level, with the total fertility rate basically maintaining around 6. During this period, only three years of natural disasters occurred in the late 1950s and early 1960s caused a steep decline in the total fertility rate, once dropping to a level close to 3. After the three-year period, the fertility level quickly recovered and rose to more than 7 due to the compensatory effect. After that, the total fertility rate recovered to the level that fluctuated around 6. (2) The period of plummeting fertility in the

DOI: 10.4324/9781003429661-17

1970s. From 1970 to 1980, China's total fertility rate dropped rapidly from a high level of 5.81–2.24, which was close to the replacement level. Throughout the 1970s, the average number of children born to Chinese women of childbearing age decreased by 3.6 births per woman. During this period, the total fertility rate basically showed a continuous linear decline without obvious fluctuation. (3) In the 1980s, the fertility level was hovering. In terms of the broad fertility trend, the 1980s and 1970s are completely different. In the 1970s, the total fertility rate was in a monotonous and substantial decline, while in the 1980s, the total fertility rate kept hovering at a low level, rising from 2.24 in 1980 to 2.86 in 1982. It then fell back to 2.20 in 1985, rose again to 2.59 in 1987 and, finally, fell back to 2.35 in the late 1980s. During this period, the total fertility rate rose and fell, but never crossed the "bottleneck" of replacement level. (4) Low fertility since the 1990s. Although China's total fertility rate began to approach the replacement level as early as in the early 1980s, it did not take a qualitative leap until the 1990s after nearly ten years of wandering in the 1980s. In 1992, China's total fertility rate began to fall below the replacement level and kept low steadily. Since the beginning of the 21st century, China's total fertility rate has basically stayed between 1.5 and 1.6. After 2005, due to the cyclical impact of population development, especially the further adjustment and improvement of the fertility policy after 2013, China's low fertility showed a gradual upward trend. However, according to the highest estimates of the various data, the total fertility rate still does not reach the 1.8 level.

Looking back on the changes of China's fertility level, we can find two outstanding characteristics. One is the rapidity. It only took China less than 20 years to reduce the total fertility rate from a high level of more than 6 to a replacement level of about 2. It took about 75 years on average for the total fertility rate of Britain and France to decline from the high level of 5 to the low level of 2. The second is external interference, which can be seen as the cause of the former one. The rapid fertility transition in China is obviously not only the natural result of economic and social development but also more importantly the powerful administrative intervention of the Chinese government. In addition, due to the vast area of China and the differences in the implementation of family planning policy and social and economic development in different regions, China's fertility level also shows great regional differences. On the one hand, the fertility level of urban and rural areas is obviously different, such as Beijing, Shanghai and other modern metropolises, the total fertility rate is even less than 1. It is one of the lowest levels even in the world. Meanwhile, unauthorized births are common in rural areas, and the total fertility rate is still well above the replacement level (Yuan Xin, 2014). On the other hand, there are substantial regional differences in fertility level. Some scholars estimated that in 2010, the central region had the highest fertility level and the actual fertility rate reached 1.58, followed by the western region with 1.51, while the eastern region was significantly lower, only 1.37, and the Northeast region had the lowest fertility level in China with the actual fertility rate only 0.89 (Yin Wenyao et al., 2013).

How Low Is the Fertility Rate

Both the 2000 and 2010 censuses showed that China's total fertility rate was about 1.2, while the 2015 census showed that the fertility rate was as low as 1.05, which was the lowest in the world. A small number of scholars believe that the quality of census and sample survey data is reliable and believe that China has already fallen into the "low fertility trap" and reached an extremely low fertility. But most scholars agree that these data suffer from varying degrees of under-reporting of births and population at very young ages, which means that the birth rate is not so low. Estimates and debates about China's low fertility levels over the past 20 years have never reached a consensus.

The main sources of data that can be used as basic data to estimate the low fertility level in China are census and sample surveys by the National Bureau of Statistics, household registration statistics by the Ministry of Public Security, statistics on the number of primary school students in school by the Ministry of Education, and fertility surveys by the former National Health and Family Planning Commission. Among the four major sources of data, the data from the National Bureau of Statistics reflect the lowest fertility rate, the data from education statistics imply the highest fertility rate and the data from household registration statistics and fertility surveys suggest the middle level of fertility. All four sources of data have their strengths and weaknesses. Although there is no sample bias problem in the survey data of the National Bureau of Statistics, there are serious problems of under-reporting of the newborn and the population at very young ages and over-reporting of the population at prime age groups in the census and sampling surveys after 1990. The household registration statistics of the Ministry of Public Security also have the under-reporting of the younger age groups, especially the serious incompleteness of the 0-year-old population, and the over-reporting of the older people. The Ministry of Education statistics are accurate before the introduction of compulsory education and have a high consistency with the 1982 and 1990 census data. Later data tended to overreport. The quality of the fertility survey data of the former National Health and Family Planning Commission is reliable, but there is a structural deviation in the representativeness of the samples, and it is often necessary to estimate the national fertility rate by weighting. Recognizing the characteristics and shortcomings of various types of data will help us make better use of them. On the one hand, we need to agree to disagree, on the other hand, we need to use a variety of methods and models to estimate and find the most possible results. In this case, relying on only one source of data or one method can lead to biased results.

Through the comparison and adjustment of census data, education data and public security data, using regression analysis, reversal survival and other methods, we estimated different sets of 0–10-year-old population in 2010 and then calculated the birth numbers of the corresponding years, estimated the fertility rate by different levels and trends. Comprehensively judged, in the ten years from 2000 to 2010, the fertility rate in the early period was as low as 1.5, while the fertility rate in the later period recovered to nearly 1.7. We also used the number of children born in the census and the fertility data of the year preceding the census and applied the indirect fertility estimation P/F ratio method proposed by Brass to estimate the total fertility rate of China in 2010, and the estimated value is 1.66. To further test the rationality of the above estimates, another indirect estimation method, the generalized stable population model, was used in this study to estimate the inter-censual fertility rate. This method bypasses birth data and estimates inter-censual fertility using only age distribution data from the two censuses. The two fertility estimation methods based on the generalized stable population model used in this study have different results, but the average total fertility rate from 2000 to 2010 is estimated to be about 1.6. Finally, using the data from the 2017 fertility survey by the National Health and Family Planning Commission, the estimate shows that the fertility rate from 2006 to 2017 fluctuated significantly, but with an average value of about 1.65.

The trend of low fertility in China follows a wavy course, with a sharp decline in the 1990s followed by a downturn for about a decade around 2000 and an upward trend since 2003. While the 2017 fertility survey data show a significant upward trend over the past decade, census and population sampling data show only a slight increase, not even an increase. This upward trend turned downward in the 2010s. In this process, due to the zodiac preference and the adjustment of the fertility policy, the fertility trends in the 2010s formed violent fluctuations, temporarily interrupting the continued decline of fertility. But the decline is expected to continue soon. Although the economic and social development determines the trends of fertility, the evolution of low fertility in the past 20 years also reflects a cyclical pattern of fluctuation driven by population inertia.

According to the comparison of the two sources of survey data from the National Bureau of Statistics and the former National Health and Family Planning Commission, the decline of the fertility rate at parity one caused by late marriage and late childbearing is an important feature of the process of China's low fertility rate, while the difference of the fertility rate at parity 2 and over in the two data sources is a more important feature. In the fertility gap between the two data sources since 2000, the fertility of second births or over accounts for 98% of the difference. In fact, between 1990 and 2003, the two sources of data reflect a high degree of consistency in fertility trends and relatively similar fertility levels. However, since 2003, the trends and levels of fertility derived from the two have been very different. The gap in the total fertility rate has widened from 0.2 to 0.5, and in most of the years, it is between 0.2 and 0.4.

Our estimates of fertility between the 1982–1990 censuses using the generalized stable population model show almost complete agreement with the fertility survey results of the 1980s. However, estimates of the fertility rate for the period 1990–2000 indicate that the fertility rate in the 1990s was significantly lower than what the government departments and scholars believed at that time. Fertility estimates for 2000–2010, in turn, show that they are broadly consistent with the number of births reported by the National Bureau of Statistics and are significantly higher than fertility rates directly obtained from census and population sample surveys, which is almost exactly in line with the average fertility rate from 2000 to 2010 calculated from the 2017 fertility survey.

China's Low Fertility Pattern

Structural Characteristics

The overall fertility transition and fertility change are bound to be accompanied by changes in fertility structure because the fertility transition or fertility decline process has structural differences and does not occur simultaneously in different population groups. The rapid decline of China's fertility level in the 1970s was firstly reflected in the decline of the high-parity fertility rate. In fact, in the 1970s and 1980s, the fertility rate differed in terms of the structure by high-parity fertility, while the first and second-birth fertility were basically stable. The low fertility rate since the 1990s is characterized by further drop in the fertility rate of multiple births to a very low level, while the fertility rate of second births has also declined.

The prominent feature of the fertility structure in China is that the proportion of the first-birth fertility is much higher than those in developed countries, while the proportion of childlessness and of having two or more children in the developed countries are significantly higher than those in China. From the 1990s to the middle of the 2000s, the ratio of first births stood at 0.6–0.7, and the ratio of two births at 0.23–0.32. In developed countries, the proportion of first births is mostly below 50%, and the proportion of second births is about 35%. However, in recent 10 years, the fertility structure has changed markedly. With the decline of the fertility rate of first births and the rise of the fertility rate of second births, China's fertility structure has become similar to that of the developed countries.

The transformation of the structure of fertility in China is reflected in the age pattern of fertility. In the 1970s, the fertility of the women at the older ages declined substantially, followed by the decline of the fertility at the younger ages. In the 1990s, the further change of the age pattern of fertility was manifested at the younger ages, especially the decline of fertility at the peak age. The age pattern of fertility changed from an "early, wide and high" type to a "late, narrow and low" pattern. Since 2000, the age pattern of fertility has not changed much. Compared with 2000, the age pattern of fertility became "lower" in 2010, while fertility at higher ages increased. In recent years, under the influence of the continued delay of childbearing and the two-child policy, the peak childbearing age has increased, and the fertility rate at the older ages has also increased significantly.

However, compared with developed countries, Chinese women's childbearing is not delayed as much as they did. The peak age group of Chinese fertility was 20–24 years before 2006 and has gradually changed to 25–29 years since 2006. At present, most developed countries have a peak age group of 30–34 years, and their fertility age distribution is closer to the normal distribution.

The age of marriage and childbearing and the interval of births are the important factors affecting the period fertility rate. China's family planning policy is also based on the number of children, as well as the control of the timing of births. Even if the lifetime fertility rate of each cohort remains the same, the change of birth timing will lead to different period fertility, sometimes lower and sometimes higher. China's fertility transition and low fertility trend in the past 40 years amply illustrate this point. The delay of women's age of marriage and childbearing and the lengthening of birth intervals have always been an important feature and inhibiting factor of China's low fertility trends.

On the whole, since the founding of the People's Republic, the age of women's marriage and childbearing has been gradually increasing. The increase accelerated in the 1970s due to the intervention of the family planning policy; and in the 1980s due to the amendment of the marriage law, the actual age of marriage decreased. It has been rising since the 1990s and stagnated in the early 2000s, but has been significantly delayed in the last decade. Between 1990 and 2017, the average age of first marriage for Chinese women as measured by census and population sample survey data increased by 3.5 years, while the average age of first marriage as measured by the 2017 fertility survey increased by four years. The average age of first marriage for Chinese women in 2017 was at around 26 years (25.6 years in the 2017 population sample survey and 26.1 years in the 2017 fertility survey). The trend of the average age of first births of Chinese women is very consistent with the age of first marriage, just that the average age of first births is generally 1–2 years higher than the average age of first marriage.

The interval between the first and second births for Chinese women is increasing due to the restriction on the spacing of births in China's family planning policy. From 1970 to 2010, the average age of having a second child was delayed from 25.3 years to 30.37 years, an increase of five years, which was larger than the delay in the average age of first births (the average age of first births increased by nearly three years). The average age of having a second child has been basically stable since 2010, and by 2017, the average age of Chinese women having a second child had reached 30.77. Although the average age of first births of Chinese women is lower than that of Western and Northern European countries, the average age of second births is close to those of them (30–33 years). With the continuous adjustment and improvement of the fertility policy, the average interval between the first two children for Chinese women has decreased.

The rising sex ratio at birth is a prominent feature of the changing sex structure of fertility in China and some parts of Asia. China has had the longest and most severe sex ratio at birth in the world. South Korea, Taiwan Province of China and Mainland China have experienced and are continuing to experience a change in the gender structure of childbirth. Although China's sex ratio at birth has been declining steadily in the past decade, it remains at a very high level.

The structural characteristics of China's low fertility can also be described from the driving forces of the low fertility level. The change of fertility level can be decomposed into "quantum effect" and "tempo effect", which are two driving forces. Whether fertility is falling or rising, it is either the result of one of these two driving forces or a combination of them.

Over the past 40 years, with the exception of few years, the tempo effect has been to depress the fertility rate. If the decade average is calculated, then in the 1970s, 1980s and 1990s, both the quantum effect and the tempo effect of fertility contributed to the decline in fertility. However, in the 2000s and 2010s, the quantum effect reversed to promote the increase of fertility, while the tempo effect still depressed fertility, and the tempo effect reducing fertility was larger than the quantum effect increasing fertility. Therefore, the tempo effect has been the main driving force of China's declining fertility and its sustained low fertility.

Fertility changes are influenced by economic and social factors and fertility policies, which do not directly affect reproductive behavior, but through a series of "intermediate variables" that directly control fertility: marriage, contraception, induced abortion and breastfeeding. Bongaarts developed a model of low fertility that included these four intermediate variables, which he later revised and improved. Using this model, the fertility rate in recent years is estimated again and the effects of various intermediate variables are investigated. The model estimates an average total fertility rate of 1.69 for 2012–2016, slightly higher than that calculated directly using the 2017 fertility survey data. When the four intermediate variables of the model were analyzed, the marriage index remained at a low level, suggesting that marriage had the greatest impact on fertility. The contraception index, which is close to the marriage index, is also a decisive factor in the low fertility rate. The delay in marriage and the decline in the proportion of married has been a key factor in the low fertility in China.

Institutional Characteristics

Institutional factors have always been an important and even key factor affecting the change of China's fertility rate. Although institutional factors involve many institutional arrangements and social and economic policies, the one with distinctive Chinese characteristics that has a significant impact on China's fertility transition and low fertility is the fertility policy. Numerous studies show that fertility decline and low fertility in China are jointly determined by the fertility policy and the economic and social development. In the early stage, the family planning policy plays a leading role, while in the later stage, low fertility is determined by the economic and social development.

It is recognized that the decline of China's fertility level is caused by both external factors such as the fertility policy and internal factors such as economic development and social change. Then, if the family planning policy is not implemented, what trend will China's fertility be likely to show? In this study, the long-term effects of China's family planning policy are analyzed by using the human development index data, which is a counterfactual projection of the total fertility rate in the period 1971–2100 without the influence of family planning policy based on a World Model and an East Model, respectively. The fertility rate predicted by the models can be regarded as the total fertility rate corresponding to the general development law of all or part of the countries in the world without the restriction of the family planning policy, and the difference between it and the actual total fertility rate can be regarded as the net effect of the family planning policy on the fertility level.

The World Model is fitted according to the data of all countries in the world, while the East Model is fitted according to the data of eight East and Southeast Asian countries based on the notion of "Chinese Cultural Zone". In the early 1970s,

Coale pointed out that countries with similar cultures to China are experiencing rapid fertility decline. The prediction based on the East Model can better represent the change of the fertility level under the counterfactual situation.

According to the World Model, without the one-child policy, China's total fertility rate would fall below the replacement level in 2021 and then gradually decline to 1.7 in the middle of this century and 1.5 by the end of this century. The family planning policy makes China come into low fertility and negative population growth about 30 years earlier and come into population aging nearly 20 years earlier. Looking at the East Model, the total fertility rate shows a faster pace of decline, falling below the replacement level in 2008, to 1.7 by 2025 and further to 1.4 in the middle of this century and 1.2 by the end of this century. Based on the East Model, the family planning policy has brought forward China's entry into the period of low fertility, negative population growth and aging population by about 15 years earlier.

Although China's fertility transition is based on its social and economic development, the decisive force is China's family planning policy. Although many studies have shown that the low fertility in China since the 1990s has been dominated by the exogenous factors of the fertility policy and replaced by the endogenous factors of economic development, the fertility policy still plays a role that cannot be ignored. An obvious fact is that the adjustment and improvement of the fertility policy since 2013, especially the universal two-child policy since 2015, has had a significant impact on the increase of China's fertility rate.

With the implementation of the universal two-child policy, although the overall fertility rate has not increased much, it is the result of two opposite trends. The rise in the second-child fertility was largely offset by a fall in the first-child fertility. In recent years, the rapidity of decline of the fertility rate of first child has never been seen in history. The main reason is that the age of first marriage and first births is greatly delayed and the number of newly entering the age of marriage and childbearing is significantly reduced. However, the decline of the fertility rate of first child has nothing to do with the implementation of the two-child policy, so we should only look at the change of the fertility rate of second children. The fact is that the birth rate of second children was rising rapidly. Before 2011, the fertility rate of second children basically stood at around 0.6. After 2011, it began to rise, and after 2015, it rose sharply. The second-child birth rate exceeded the first-child birth rate in 2015, reached 0.94 in 2016 and even exceeded 1 in 2017. In the history of the People's Republic, the total fertility rate of a second child exceeded 1 in the 1950s and 1960s. In the early 1950s, shortly after the People's Republic was founded, the economy gradually recovered and people's life tended to be stable. There was the first baby boom. From 1953 to 1955, the total fertility rate of second children exceeded 1. The second baby boom occurred in the 1960s largely due to the compensatory births after the natural disasters in the previous three years. In 1963–1966 and 1968, the total fertility rate of second children exceeded 1. Different from the 1950s and 1960s, the total fertility rate of second children in 2017 exceeded 1 under the background of low fertility, which is completely the result of the implementation of the two-child policy, and the fertility accumulation phenomenon caused by the two-child policy brought about women of different ages having two children at the same time. It can be described as a "blowout" release of reproductive potential restricted by the original fertility policy. In this sense, the effect of the two-child policy is very large. Without the implementation of the two-child policy, China's total fertility rate would also drop significantly along with the decline of the first-child fertility rate.

The implementation of the two-child policy has greatly improved the level of second-child birth rate in China. But the effect of the two-child policy varies greatly among different groups. Factors that were negatively correlated with fertility in the past, such as age, education level, occupation, nature of work unit, income and housing area, turned to be a positive correlation under the two-child policy. For the group with the highest education level, the highest income and the highest housing area, the increase of second-child birth rate is astonishing, showing a huge accumulation of births. However, the groups with the lowest education level, the lowest income and the lowest housing area originally had high second-child fertility rate, so the two-child policy had no effect in fact, and even their second-child fertility declined. At the same time, the implementation of the two-child policy also brought about the groups in the occupations of unit heads, professional and technical personnel and related personnel or those working in state-owned units, having a higher birth rate of the second children.

The Demographic Effects of the Two-Child Policy

Population Size and Structural Effects

The direct consequence of the two-child policy is the increase of the second-child fertility rate, which will also have a profound impact on China's population development. Using the data of the national 1% population sample survey in 2015, this study prepared three sets of population projections to analyze the future trends of China's population size, population structure and dependency ratio under the two-child policy through the cohort factor method. The three sets of population projections differ in fertility assumptions while same in mortality assumption. In the low scenario, if the two-child policy is not implemented, the total fertility rate would drop to 1.35 in 2035 and remain unchanged until 2100. The medium and high scenario is the actual situation in 2015–2018, that is, the fertility rate rises, then falls and then rises again. The medium scenario assumes that the fertility rate rises to 1.7 in 2016–2017, then falls to 1.6 in 2035 and stays at 1.6 after 2035. In the high scenario, based on the medium scenario, the fertility rate rises further to 1.85 in 2035 and remains unchanged at 1.85 thereafter.

The results show that no matter the low, medium or high scenarios, the future population trends are largely similar, which will experience a small increase and then a gradual long-term decline, but the timing and speed of negative growth are different. Under the low scenario, if the two-child policy is not implemented, China's population will peak at about 1.404 billion in 2023, then begin to experience negative growth and continue to decline, falling below 1.2 billion in the middle of this century and to 684 million in 2100. According to the medium projection, the total fertility rate after 2035 is assumed to be 1.6. The results show that the country's total population will peak at 1.409 billion in 2024 and then decline steadily to 863 million in 2100. The high scenario assumes that the total fertility rate after 2035 stands at 1.85. The results suggest that the population will peak at 1.416 billion in 2034. Same as the previous two scenarios, the total population will gradually decline after the peak and will drop to 1.06 billion in 2100. Compared with the low scenario, that is without the two-child policy, by 2100, the middle scenario will have 179 million more people, and the high scenario will have 376 million more. Although the policy adjustment will delay the population peak, the future trend of negative population growth will be irreversible.

In demographic analysis, the total population is usually divided into three broad age groups: the child population (0–14 years old), the working-age population (15–64 years old) and the elderly population (over 65 years old). Among them, the children group is the beginning of population development, and its size directly affects the future population size and the sustainable development of the country. The fertility policy mainly directly affects the number of births, so the child group is the first to be affected by the implementation of the two-child policy. What is different from the trend of total population is that the scale of child population in the future presents a waving-decreasing trend. The successive implementation of the selective two-child policy and the comprehensive two-child policy has led to the outbreak of the fertility potential that has been accumulated for many years, and the fertility accumulation effect has brought about the peak of child population size. In 2018, the child population reached the maximum, about 256 million, accounting for 18.35% of the total population. The child population is affected not only by the fertility policy but also by the size of women of childbearing age. The women of childbearing age born in the 1960s are the baby boomers, and they are also a group of people who respond positively to the two-child policy. As time goes by, the birth cohort after 1980 entered the childbearing age. However, this group of women grew up under the strict family planning policy, which directly reduced the number of women of childbearing age. The baby boomers and the baby busters alternately enter the childbearing age, which will also lead to the fluctuation of the number of births in the future. Therefore, the child population in the future will be fluctuating and declining. If the two-child policy was not introduced (low scenario), the size of the child population would drop to 58 million at the end of this century, accounting for 8.48% of the total population. According to the medium scenario, this number will drop to 98 million by 2100, accounting for 11.41%, and according to the high scenario, the fluctuation period of the child population is longer in the future, and it finally falls to 153 million people in 2100, accounting for 14.39% of the total population. Compared with not implementing the two-child policy, by 2100, this policy will at least add more than 40 million to the child population. If the total fertility rate of 1.85 continues to the end of this century, the child population will be 95 million more, this nearly 100 million extra child population is bound to bring different effects on China's economic and social development.

300 Summary and Conclusion

The size and structure of the working-age population is an important indicator for analyzing economic activity, which is used to measure the potential and actual labor resources of a country or region. Projections show that the size of China's working-age population 15–65 will start to decline after reaching 983 million in 2015. In the low scenario, the working-age population will reach its lowest point in this century in 2100, at 335 million, accounting for 48.95% of the total population. The medium scenario produces 453 million working-age population, accounting for about 52.50%. However, the working-age population of the high scenario would be always above 500 million, reaching 582 million in 2100, accounting for about 54.90%. No matter whether the fertility policy is adjusted or not, it is an indisputable fact that the scale of the labor force will be drastically reduced in the future. The labor-intensive industry that relied on the huge labor force in the past is no longer suitable for the future development, and the new situation of population will also force industrial transformation and upgrading.

The size of the elderly population increases rapidly from 2015 to 2100, reaches the peak in the middle of this century and then declines slowly. According to international standards, a country is considered to be an aging society if more than 7% of its population is over the age of 65. By the end of this century, the size of the elderly population will be 291 million, 311 million and 325 million, accounting for 42.56%, 36.10% and 30.71%, respectively. In the future, a rapidly aging population will be a great challenge in China.

The socio-economic impact of a population's age structure is usually measured using the population dependency ratio. The child dependency ratio presents a fluctuating trend from 2015 to 2100, which is mainly due to the changing number of births brought by the adjustment of the fertility policy. However, the arrival of these birth cohorts at different periods entering into the childbearing age will lead to fluctuations in the number of women of childbearing age which in turn impacts the population size of the next generation. By 2100, the old-age dependency ratio under the low, medium and high scenarios will increase to 86.94, 68.76 and 55.94, respectively. The combination of the child and old dependency ratios determines the trend of total dependency ratio in the future. Due to the expansion of the population pyramid at both ends, the total dependency ratio in China will continue to rise from 2015 to 2100. By 2100, the total dependency ratio will be 104.27, 90.49 and 82.15, respectively, under the low, medium and high scenarios. Despite a changing composition of the dependency burden borne by the working-age population in different periods, in general, the burden of child dependency is not too big, fluctuating slightly between 20 and 26. After 2030, the old-age support will become the major dependency burden.

Effective Labor Supply

The supply of labor force is affected by the size of the total population, the size of the working-age population, the structure of the labor force and labor participation rate. In addition, effective labor force is not only related to the quantity of labor force but also closely related to the quality of labor force. Further considering the labor participation rate and human capital factors, what is the effective labor supply in the future? Therefore, this study established an effective labor supply model incorporating human capital, combining the quantity, structure and quality of labor force. Data of labor participation rate forecasting and human capital index forecasting are prepared using population projections of the low, medium and high scenarios, providing a more comprehensive understanding of the future labor supply in China. In addition, through factor decomposition, this study examines the contributions of each factor (population size, population structure, labor participation rate, human capital) to the change of effective labor supply and the impact of the two-child policy on the contribution rate of each factor.

The prediction of labor participation rate is based on the sixth census data of 2010, borrowing the experiences of changing labor participation rate in Japan and considering China's future social and economic development (China's labor participation rate in 2010 is equivalent to that of Japan in 1970). In constructing the human capital index, the average number of years of schooling of employees is used as the proxy variable of human capital level. Based on the assumed growth rate, the average years of schooling of employees during 2015–2100 are predicted.

Labor participation rate first falls and then rises, then fluctuating in stages. It is predicted that the labor participation rate of the working population aged 15–24 will decrease in the future and that of the working population aged 50–64 will increase. From 2015 to 2040, the overall labor participation rate presents a V shape, first decreasing and then increasing and then fluctuating in stages, with peaks in 2045, 2065 and 2095, respectively.

The level of human capital will increase steadily in the future. The forecasting results show that the average years of schooling of future employees will increase continuously, reaching 13.57 years in 2050, which corresponds to a human capital index of 1.31 (1.31 times of 2015), and 14.27 years in 2100, which corresponds to a human capital index of 1.38 (1.38 times of 2015).

Effective labor supply adjusted for human capital is increasing significantly. It is predicted that in 2050, the medium scenario will result in an effective labor supply adjusted for human capital that is 160 million more compared with that from the low scenario, and 240 million more from the high scenario. In 2100, the effective labor supply adjusted for human capital in the medium scenario will increase by 120 million compared with that in the low scenario, and in the high scenario will increase by 250 million compared with that in the low scenario. The two-child policy further improves the effective labor supply adjusted for human capital. In addition, after incorporating the human capital factor, the total effective labor supply increases substantially, and the improvement of human capital level effectively compensates for the negative impact of the decline in the quantity of labor force.

In terms of factor decomposition, the decomposition index results of population factors are all less than 0, while those of non-population factors are all greater than 0 under the three scenarios. It can be seen that demographic factors have a convergent effect on the effective labor supply adjusted for human capital, while non-demographic factors have an amplifying effect. Among them, the effect of population size increases after the implementation of the two-child policy. In addition, the amplification effect of human capital is very significant, which shows the importance of human capital to effective labor supply.

Social and Economic Effects of the Two-Child Policy

Demand for Maternal and Child Health Services

The adjustment of the fertility policy has a wide and far-reaching impact on the society, among which the impact on the demand for basic public services is direct and important. The implementation of the two-child policy may bring about an increase in the number of births, infants and pregnant women in a short period of time, as well as an increase in the demand for maternal and child health services and medical care services. In the long run, this growth will continue with demographic inertia.

In this study, the cohort component method was used to predict the future trends in births under the two-child policy, and the population-resource density method was used to estimate the possible impact of changing number of births on the demand for maternal and child health services. The population-resource density was determined according to the current situation of maternal and child health services in China, relevant documents and policy objectives and the experiences of major developed countries.

Projections suggest that the accumulation of births will not be very large in the short term. The number of births peaked in 2016, reaching 17.59 million, and then began to fall back to 16.98 million in 2017 and 15.01 million in 2018, with a small peak still around 2035. On the whole, the two-child policy does not seem to have a strong short-term accumulation effect of births, which also means that obstetric health services do not face a tense situation of continuous increase in demand in the short term. However, by 2050, a cumulative 52.45 million and 96.17 million more babies will be born under the medium and high scenarios than under the low scenario, with an annual average of 1.5 million to 2.7 million, which should also be paid attention to and corresponding supporting health services need to be increased. Although the number of births began to decline after only one year's increase, there will still be a small peak of births around 2035 due to the effect of demographic inertia, which needs to be prepared in advance.

The number of children aged 0–14 peaked in 2018 at 256 million, an increase of 6.07 million over 2015, increasing pressure on pediatric resources. Between 2016 and 2020, the number of children aged 0–14 under the medium and high scenarios is 1.938 million and 2.227 million higher than that under the low scenario. The number of children aged 0–14 also has a small peak reached in 2040, 2042 and 2044, with 156 million, 182 million and 207 million, respectively, under the three scenarios. The number of children in the medium and high scenarios is 26.29 million and 51.56 million more than that in the low scenario, respectively.

The implementation of the two-child policy will increase the demand for maternal and child-related medical and health services in the long run. According to the resource density in 2018, the small peak of births around 2037 will produce demand for 22,145 and 25,526 medical institutions, including 3,328 and 3,836 specialized maternity hospitals, and 179,200 and 206,600 obstetricians, respectively. The number of obstetric nurses is 153,600 and 177,100, respectively. By 2050, the difference in the predicted demand between the medium and high scenarios and the low scenario will reach the maximum. The difference between the demand of obstetrics and gynecological medical institutions will be 3,627 and 7,005, respectively, among which the demand of specialized hospitals in obstetrics and gynecology will be 545 and 1,053, respectively, and the demand of obstetricians will be 29,400 and 56,700. The difference between the number of obstetric nurses and the demand is 25,200 and 48,600.

According to the current density of pediatric medical resources in China, the peak demand for pediatric medical institutions and pediatric beds in 2018 was 20,489 and 519,900, respectively, and the secondary peak demand, which is at early 2040s, was 14,565 and 369,600, respectively, in the medium scenario and 16,586 and 420,900, respectively, in the high scenario. In 2050, the difference in demand for pediatric medical institutions between the medium and high scenarios and the low scenario is 2,398 and 4,668, respectively, and the difference in demand for beds is 60,800 and 118,500, respectively. According to the standard of "the number of licensed (assistant) pediatricians per 1,000 children reaching 0.69 and the number of beds per 1,000 children increasing to 2.2" in the "Opinions on Strengthening the Reform and Development of Children's Medical and Health Services" by 2020, the peak demand for pediatric beds, pediatricians and nurses is 563,400, 176,700 and 294,500, respectively. The gap of pediatric beds, physicians and nurses was 49,000, 24,000 and 37,000, respectively. In 2050, the difference between the results of the medium and high scenarios and the low scenario is 65,900 and 128,400 pediatric beds, 20,700 and 40,300 pediatricians and 34,500 and 67,100 pediatric nurses, respectively. According to the standard of "physician ratio per 1,000 children" of 0.85–1.3 in major developed countries, the median value of 1.07 is used for estimation. The peak demand for pediatric beds, pediatricians and nurses is 927,200, 274,000 and 456,700, respectively. The shortfall is 413,200, 120,000 and 199,700, respectively. In 2050, the difference between the results of the medium and high scenarios and the low scenario is 108,500 and 212,200 pediatric beds, 32,100 and 62,400 pediatricians and 53,500 and 104,100 pediatric nurses, respectively.

School-Age Population and Demand for Teachers

With the implementation of the two-child policy, the accumulation of births will lead to an increase in the demand for child care, preschool and primary education in recent years, which is mainly reflected in the demand for infrastructure or teachers.

According to the projection results, the number of infants under the age of three will decrease from 2015 to 2050. According to the experience of European Union countries, the childcare enrollment rate is set at 30% and the teacher-child ratio is set at 1:5. By 2050, the demand for childcare will be between 6,524,500 and 10,106,000, and the demand for teachers will be between 1,300,000 and 2,021,200.

304 Summary and Conclusion

With the increasing awareness of the importance of child care and the continuous expansion of the demand for early education, infant and child care services will become a basic, rigid and universal livelihood demand, child care is no longer just a responsibility within the family, the state and society will also share the responsibility of childcare.

Preschool education is the beginning of lifelong learning and is an important part of the national education system, and a good preschool education environment for children's physical and mental health is of great significance, but "difficult to enter the kindergarten" and "expensive to enter the kindergarten" are the problems that have always existed in preschool education in China. According to the Regulations of Kindergarten Work, the total population of 3–6 years old is selected as the preschool education age group. The prediction shows that in the future, the size of 3–6 years old preschool children will first decline, then rise and then decline. When estimating the enrollment rate from 2020 to 2050, we make two assumptions. The first one is that the enrollment rate will reach 85% after 2020 and remain unchanged until 2050 according to the development goals in the 13th Five-Year Plan for the Development of National Education. Second, based on the average level of European countries, we assume that by 2050, the enrollment rate will reach 95%, which is the existing average level of OECD countries. If the 85% standard is adopted, the demand in the low, medium and high scenarios will drop to 27.8913 million, 34.7808 million and 40.9725 million, respectively, by 2050. According to the 95% standard, the numbers are 31.1593 million, 38.8556 million and 45.7731 million, respectively. The new version of the Kindergarten Work Regulations puts forward that the size of a kindergarten is generally not more than 360 children, while the current average standard of China is 175 children per school. The two standards are used to predict the demand for kindergartens in the future, respectively. It is found that if the scale of 175 children per school is adopted, the demand for kindergartens in China will reach a highest, more than 330,000, and by 2050, it will be close to 150,000. If the scale of 360 students per school is applied, the supply of kindergartens always exceeds the demand. From the perspective of preschool teachers, the Ministry of Education issued the Interim Staffing Standards for Kindergarten Teaching Staff and Children in 2013, which formulated the staffing standards and ratio of kindergarten teaching staff and children, and clearly stated that "in full-time service kindergartens, the ratio of teaching staff to children should be 1:5–1:7, and the ratio of teaching staff to children should be 1:7–1:9". The teacher-child ratio of 1:8 is used to estimate the demand for preschool education teaching and administrative staff. From 2015 to 2050, the demand for preschool teaching staff in China will gradually decrease, and by 2050, the demand in the low, medium and high scenarios will be 4,648,600, 5,796,800 and 6,828,700, respectively. Currently, China's teaching staff is far from enough to meet the demand for preschool education brought by the two-child policy. And no matter which standard the entrance rate refers to, the financial investment in preschool education in the future is increasing.

"Compulsory education Law of the People's Republic of China" stipulates that "Compulsory education is the education that all school-age children and adolescents must receive, and it is a public welfare undertaking that the state must guarantee". China implements a nine-year compulsory education system, including primary school and junior high school. According to the law, the enrollment rate is set at 100%. The forecast shows that from 2015 to 2050, the demand for primary school and junior high school seats will shrink year by year. By 2050, the demand for primary school seats in low, middle and high scenarios will be 58.15 million, 69.96 million and 81.26 million, respectively, while the demand for junior high school seats will drop to 32.1138 million, 38.804 million and 43.8524 million, respectively. The State Commission Office of Public Sectors Reform, the Ministry of Education and the Ministry of Finance on Unifying the Staffing Standards for Urban and Rural Primary and Middle Schools sets 1:19 and 1:13.5 as the standards for the ratio of teachers to students in primary and junior middle schools. By 2050, the demand for primary school teachers is between 3,065,000 and 4,276,700, and for junior middle school teachers between 2,378,800 and 3,248,300. According to the calculation, the average education expenditure index of primary school and junior high school is 21% and 29%, respectively. Compared with the financial input of preschool education, primary school education has greatly increased. By 2050, the investment under the low, middle and high scenarios will be 3,761.442 billion yuan, 4,5253.17 billion yuan and 5,256.87 billion yuan, respectively. The investment in junior middle school education is much less than that in primary school. By 2050, the financial investment under the low, middle and high scenarios will be 2,866.34 billion yuan, 3,394.473 billion yuan and 3,917.16 billion yuan, respectively.

Education is the most important public service, and the effective implementation of the strategy of strengthening the country with talents needs to rely on good education quality and environment. After the implementation of the two-child policy, the change of population structure has a direct impact on the education structure, and the existing education scale can no longer adapt to the changing population structure. Under the new demographic situation, the challenges of population change on education in the next 35 years will be volatile. Whether it is preschool education or compulsory education, the demand for seats and teachers will first increase, then decrease, then increase and then decrease, but the timing and pattern of the demand of preschool, primary school and junior high school education are different. From the perspective of seats demand, China will basically need more than 10 million childcare demand every year in the future, and the demand of preschool, primary school and junior high school seats will peak in 2017, 2020 and 2026, respectively, then gradually being surplus. Looking at the demand of teachers, there is a great shortage of teachers for children aged 0–3 in China, while full-time preschool teachers aged 3–6 have been in shortage. The maximum shortage of primary school teachers is more than 400,000 before 2023, but there will be a surplus since then. The surplus number is close to 2 million in the later period, while there will be more periods of insufficient demand for junior middle school teachers than surplus periods.

The two-child policy is an important adjustment of China's family planning policy. The increment of births brought by this policy is superimposed on the existing population stock, which brings great challenge and pressure to the education system. In order to adapt to the new situation of population change, it is necessary to make overall planning and rational distribution, integrate population forecast, urban development and public services, meet the needs for higher quality and more diversified education and strive to achieve more equitable and sustainable development.

Policy Implications

Although the two-child policy has greatly increased the second-child fertility rate, it is mainly due to the sudden release of the long-suppressed desire of older women to have a second child under the original policy, rather than the increase of the second-child fertility rate of young women. So the effect will be short-lived. The decline in women's first marriages in recent years has led to a decline in the birth rate of the first child. If this trend continues, then even if the desire to have a second child is high, it will not actually increase the birth rate of the second child. Moreover, according to the fertility intention survey in some provinces in 2016 and 2017, the proportion of women who have one-child planning to have a second child is less than 30%. The combination of these trends will keep China's fertility rate low in the future, with a high risk of falling into the lowest-low fertility. Therefore, it is necessary to build a strong marriage and childbearing friendly family policy system, in order to achieve a moderate low fertility rate and promote the long-term balanced development of population. Thus, this study proposes the following policy recommendations:

Formulate and Strengthen Marriage Promotion Policies

In the face of the increasing delay in the age of first marriage and the declining rate of first marriage, formulate and implement marriage promotion policies as soon as possible. On the one hand, although the age of first marriage in countries around the world is constantly delayed, the legal age of marriage for women in many countries is under 20, and the legal age of marriage for Chinese women can also be appropriately lowered to meet the needs of more independent and diversified needs for marriage and childbirth. On the other hand, organizations such as the Communist Youth League, Labor Union, Women's Federation and other government and social forces should be strengthened to play a role in helping young people get together, fall in love and get married through various effective forms. At the same time, the state should also formulate policies to reduce the cost of marriage in terms of subsidies for marriage expenses, marriage housing purchase preferences or subsidies, applying for low-rent housing for marriage and extending marriage leave, so as to promote young people to get married. And in the new era and under the new conditions, the state can also carry out new activities and campaigns aimed at promoting marriage and childbearing. In addition, there is a weak relationship between marriage and childbearing in Western countries, while the relationship is strong in China. In Western countries, births of cohabitants or non-marital births have become an important and even a major part of the overall births, which is largely due to the recognition and protection of non-marital cohabitations and out-of-wedlock births, and attempts to institutionalize it like legal marriage. It is suggested that China also consider giving legal protection to stable cohabiting relationships or de facto marriages to help them have children.

Fully Lift the Fertility Policy As Soon As Possible to Promote the Increase of the Number of Births

Although the two-child policy has achieved some results, due to the influence of some factors such as the age structure of women of childbearing age and the delay of childbearing, the number of births has not achieved the expected effect on the whole. Compared with 2016, the number of births in 2017 showed a decrease, and the decrease was even greater in 2018. Low fertility intention is becoming a common phenomenon. In order to improve the implementation effect of the fertility policy and maintain the stable development of population, it is necessary to fully lift the fertility policy as soon as possible, meet the fertility intention of qualified families who are willing to have more children and make up for the decrease in births caused by the decrease in the number of first births and the lack of willingness to have the second children, so as to maintain the stable and healthy development of population on the whole.

Establish a Government-Led, Community-Based and Society-Supplemented Public Childcare System for Infants Aged 0–3

(1) At present, most families still rely on the traditional model of "self-reliance" of parents and women for childcare. Without the guarantee of perfect market childcare services, it is difficult for couples, especially women, to balance career and family at the same time. The opportunity cost of childbearing is high, leading to low fertility intention. Our survey also showed that more than half of women said that providing proper childcare would motivate them to have two children. Under the background of the two-child policy, the establishment of infant care service system has become a top priority. (2) Based on the communities, integrate community resources, construct and improve the community childcare or trusteeship mechanism, carry out family support projects, establish nearby childcare places, reduce operating costs and lower the burden and pressure on families. (3) In terms of the provision mode of childcare services, the concept of pluralism and co-governance can be introduced, social capital can be encouraged to enter, and management techniques and resources of the private sector can be utilized to build high-quality public-private partnership and private childcare institutions. (4) Encourage work units, especially qualified enterprises, to assume social responsibilities, set up childcare institutions and give corresponding preferential policies (such as tax, loan, etc.); enterprises with insufficient conditions are encouraged to cooperate with neighboring communities to provide childcare services for employees

and reduce the burden of picking up and seeing off employees; encourage work units to give mothers proper time for breastfeeding and visiting.

Standardize and Institutionalize Maternity and Paternity Leave Policies and Promote Statutory Parental Leave to Help Achieve Work-Family Balance

(1) Many units still have discriminatory policies for the second-child maternity leave, and the number of days for the second-child maternity leave is shorter than that for the first-child maternity leave. Government departments should regulate the behavior of enterprises and public institutions and urge them to earnestly implement policies to protect the rights and interests of family reproduction. (2) Studies in developed countries show that parental leave can improve the willingness to have a second child. We can learn from their experiences and promote paid and unpaid parental leave. In order to ensure the production efficiency of enterprises, reduce the loss of enterprises and ensure the competitiveness of enterprises, the public finance should subsidize the corresponding expenditure.

Establish a Family Supporting Policy System to Improve Family Welfare and Enhance Family Development Ability

Survey results suggest childbearing subsidies would encourage more than 70% of the women to have two children, and nearly a third of them did not have a second child because of financial pressure. We should learn from the experience of other countries and improve social security policies for childbearing, parenting, child development and education. We will ease the economic pressure on families to have and raise children through birth subsidies, tax incentives, child allowances, family subsidies and housing security. At present, the high housing price brings heavy economic burden to young families. Cities should give priority to two-child families in terms of housing preferential policies.

Family Policies Should Incorporate a Gender Equality Perspective and the Public Sector Should Create a Policy Environment That Promotes Gender Equality

(1) A comprehensive review of the relationship between fertility and family policies in European countries shows that in countries with low gender equality, the role of family policies to encourage fertility will be greatly reduced. Therefore, work-family balance is not just for women, but should be a shared responsibility of couples. (2) Survey results show that more than 40% of women could be motivated to have two children if policies protect their employment from childbearing. In fact, women face all kinds of explicit and implicit discriminations in the labor market, and their career development is negatively affected. The problem of work-family balance is mainly borne by women. (3) In addition to special legislation to protect women from discrimination, it is also necessary to attach importance to husbands' family responsibilities, establish and improve the systems of parental

leave and paternity leave for husbands, promote husbands to participate more in the division of housework and child care and help wives to ease the contradiction between the role of mothers and the role of professional women. A flexible maternity leave transfer system could be implemented to encourage women to flexibly transfer part of their maternity leave to their husbands (when needed) and encourage their husbands to take paternity leave.

Establish a Permanent Government Department to Coordinate Family Policies

Family policies involve multiple functional departments, so it is necessary to innovate the management model. Special agencies should be set up to coordinate family policies, integrate the functions and resources of health, family planning, education, civil affairs, tax and other departments and implement family welfare policies. Before the establishment of a specialized agency, the relevant departments of the Commission of Health can assume this function during the transitional period, coordinate the resources of other departments and study, formulate and coordinate family policies.

References

Yin Wenyao, Yao Yinmei, and Li Fen. 2013. Assessment of Fertility Levels and Adjustment of Fertility Policies: An Analysis bases on China's Provincial Fertility Patterns. *Social Sciences in China* 6: 109–130.

Yuan Xin. 2014. Family Planning Policy Reorientation after the Demographic Transition in China. *Exploration and Free Views* 4: 45–49.

Index

Note: **Bold** page numbers refer to tables; *Italic* page numbers refer to figures and page numbers followed by "n" denote endnotes.

abortion index 111–113, 115; abortion information 123; abortion statistics, poor quality of 115; contraceptive prevalence 115; equations and variables **117, 118**; postpartum infecundability 115
administrative mechanism 14
advocacy-based fertility policy 129
age: births, distribution 34, **35**; distribution data 44, 49; fading population inertia 17; fertility pattern 87–88; for late marriage 15; lower age group 16; at marriage/childbirth 89–90
age-parity-interval-specific total fertility rate 63
age–sex distribution data 46
age-specific abortion rates 115, 119
age-specific cumulative fertility rate 40
age-specific fertility rates 25, 34, **36**, 39, 46, 49, 70, 119, 160; age-specific abortion rates 115; and mortality rates 50; number of births 25; reproductive age structure 44; and total fertility rates **36**, 118; women of childbearing age 25
age-specific mortality rates 46, 49
age-specific population growth rates 47
age structure 14; postpartum infecundability index 116; socioeconomic impact of 171
aging population 177; advanced aging population trend 204–205; centenarians, growing trend of 205–207; elderly population and aging 203–204; elderly population, heterogeneity of 207–208; fertility transition process 202; increasing heterogeneity 208–215; irreversible aging population 193–201; research methods and data 192–193; wavy development of 202
Akash, K. 112
annual population growth 10, 13
annual population surveys 25, 34, 141, 142, 202
average age at first marriage 72–74, *73*
average birth interval ratio 115
average fertility rate 52, 72; data and methodology 43–46; estimation of fertility rates 46–53
average inter-birth interval 89
average life expectancy 10

bed density: obstetric medical service demand 224, **225**; pediatric medical service demand 226, **227**
Beijing's Three-year Action Plan (2011–2013) 241
births: absence of 116; age distribution of 34, **35**; age-specific number of 48; age structure of 49; annual number of 16; China's population censuses 24; control and relax 11, 13; to each age, survival ratios from *31*; estimated average number of 72; 2000-2010 estimated fertility rates 31–32; estimates of annual number **32**; fertility rates 37; information 57; interval 24, 89–90, 93, 104; 1949 to 2017 *12*; policy 142; population changes 23; rates 10, *11*,

Index

13, 16, 45, 48; sample surveys 24; and sampling ratio 23
Blake, J. 116, 124
Bongaarts, J. 58, 93, 112, 115, 116, 123, 124, 145; estimate fertility rate 123; fertility model 111–112, **114**; low fertility model 144
Brass logit transformation 25, 33, 44
Brass, William 39, 45
breastfeeding 4, 115–116, 120, 122, 125, 296, 308

Cai Yong 24, 49, 52
celibacy, fertility-inhibiting effect of 112
censuses: 2000 and 2010 census data, regression analysis *29*; census data quality 23; 1990 census, dramatic decline in 16; characteristics of 23; fertility rates 24; hukou data and 2000 census data *30*; lower-age cohorts 38; 2005 mini-census 40; 2015 mini-census 71, 208; population censuses 69; and population sample surveys 293; Sixth Censuses 24; time reference point of 27–28; *see also* 2000 Census; 2010 Census
Chen Ning 160
childbirth/childbearing: childbearing age 88, 163, 173; and childrearing costs 282; direct and indirect costs 282–284; motherhood penalty 285; postpartum breastfeeding 116; postponement of 97; tempo effects of 14
childcare allowance policy 277
childcare service policies 58, 278–279, 282; education-related demands 235–237, **236**; enrollment seats 235, **236**; Germany 282; Japan 282; public education system 235; teacher-child ratio **236**, 237
child dependency ratio (CDR) 171, *172, 174*, 176
childlessness, lifetime rate of 87
child population (ages 0–14) 162
children born per woman 39, 40, **41**, 41–42
child's information 24
China Health Statistical Yearbook 2018 218
China Maternal and Child Health Development Report 2019 218
China's Education Statistics 2018 250
China's fertility transition 290–291; Stage I (1970–1979) 94–95; Stage II (1980–1989) 94, 95; Stage III (1990–2003) 94; Stage IV (from 2004 onwards) 94
China's low fertility: evolutionary characteristics 69, 72–80; fertility transition 290–291; institutional factors 296–298; other observations 77–80; period 2008–2012 72; structural characteristics 294–296; TFR for first births 72–74; TFR for second and multiple births 74–77; total fertility rate 292–293; trends and evolution of 69–72; ultra-low fertility risk 80–82
China statistical yearbooks 3
China's total population 161–165, **162**, *163*
Chinese Longitudinal Healthy Longevity Study 208
Chinese Model 1, 19
Chinese women: average age at childbirth 89, *90*; of childbearing age 94; marital fertility of 9; marriage postponement 107
Coale, A. J. 43, 44
Coale–Trussell fertility model 40, 54
cohort analysis 25, **26**
cohort-component method 159, 302
cohort fertility rates 39, 65–66
cohort-specific lifetime fertility rates 93
Communist Youth League 14
Compulsory Education Law of the People's Republic of China (Article 11) 233
compulsory education system 261, 272
Confucian culture 136
contraception index 112, 113, 124; calculation of 119; equations and variables **117, 118**
contraceptive effectiveness 120
contraceptive methods 58, **121**
contraceptive prevalence 114, 115, 119–120
counterfactual fertility trends: data and methodology 128–132; east model, results based on 129, 132–138; HDI-related fertility research 127–128; 1971 through 2100 under the east model **137**; 1971–2100 under the world model *133*; world model, results based on 128, 132
CPC Central Committee 14, 15, 17, 18, 129
Cui Hongyan 23
cultural mechanisms 14

Cultural Revolution 13
cumulative fertility rate 39, 40
current family planning policy 17

data: data quality 16, 23; discrepancies 94; labor supply 179–180
Davis, K. 116, 124
death probability 209, *210,* 214
death rate 10, *11*
decision marks 18
Decision on Comprehensively Strengthening the Population and Family Planning Work to Solve the Population Problem 18
Decision on Implementing the Universal Two-Child Policy to Reform and Improve the Family Planning 18
Decision on Strengthening Family Planning Program 15
Decision on Strengthening Population and Family Planning Work to Stabilize the Low Fertility 17
de-familialization 282
Demographic and Health Surveys (DHS) 112
demographic data 38
demographic effects, two-child policy: labor force and labor participation rate 300–302; population size 298–300; structural effects 298–300
demographic influence 187
demographic structure 93
demographic theory 1
demographic transition 15, 144–145, 194; child population 299; "Chinese model" of 1, 19; conventional theory of 1; elderly population 299; working-age population 299
demographic trends: China's total population 161–165, **162,** *163*; data and methods 159–161; dependency ratio 171–175; elderly population 168–171; working-age population 165–168
dependency ratio 171–175
developed countries 87; childbearing ages 88; family planning policy 127
disability rate *209*
discrete-time logit model 141–142, 151
doctor density: obstetric medical service demand 224, **225**; pediatric medical service demand 226–229, **227, 228, 229, 230**

domestic standard 170

East Asian countries: Chinese Cultural Zone 296; TFR trends in 134, *135*; traditional family pattern 135; ultra-low fertility 280; weak family support policies 138
east model, counterfactual fertility trends 129, 132–138
economic reforms 2, 9, 14, 107
education-related demands: child-care services 235–237, **236**; junior high school education 266–270; preschool education 237–261; primary school education 261–266
Education Statistics Yearbook 244, 258, 263, 269, 273
education system 23, 24, 25, 38; compulsory education system 261; educational level 155; education data, regression analysis *30*; education development 181
effective labor supply 185–186, 302
elderly population 168–171; aging population 208–215; with different education **212**; family and kinship structure of 192; heterogeneity of 207–208; increasing heterogeneity 208–215
enrollment seats: child-care services 235, **236**; junior high school education 266, **266, 267**; preschool education 239–244, **240, 242, 243**; primary school education 261, **262**
estimated fertility rates: average fertility rate estimation 43–53; 2010, estimated fertility rates 38–43; male populations, in period 2000–2010 **49**; National Bureau of Statistics **50**; in period 2000–2010 **51**; 1982 through 2010 censuses **52**; 2000 to 2010 period 22–37
Ethiopia, fertility rates in 112
ethnic group 154, 155
European countries: dual fertility patterns 279–280; low-fertility trap 280
European women, marital fertility 9
evaluation: obstetric and gynecological medical services 221–222; pediatric medical service 224
explicit pro-natalist policies **281,** *282,* 282–286, **283**; child allowance 282; childcare service policies

282; direct costs 283; fertility cost-utility theory 283; four-dimensional connotations 283, *283*; indirect costs 283; maternity allowance 282; opportunity costs 283; parental leave policies 282

extramarital sex 113

familism 282

family planning policy 1, 2, 9, 11, 13, 14, 15, 18, 71, 81, 89, 90, 107, 122, 127, 132, 155, 194, 219, 294, 295, 296; absence of 129; advocacy-based fertility policy 129; as basic national policy 17; effects of 129; implementation of 16, 127; importance of 15; of "later-longer-fewer" 14; long-term effects of 2, 129; long-time influence of 21; population growth control 13; population problem 18; reduce fertility 13; in 1950s and 1960s 13; on World Model 2

family structure **214**; economic production 14; family values 136; fertility choice 145; heterogeneity of 214; kinship structure 214; supporting policy system 308

fecundity adjustment factor 113

Feeney, G. 58, 93

female employment 237

Female Worker Labor Protection 235

fertility: accumulative effect 163; age pattern of 87–88; 1990 census, dramatic decline in 16; control 13; decline stage 2, 94, 127, 195; fluctuation of 14, 15; heterogeneity 213; indicators 58; intentions 58; parameters 160; parity structure of 86–87; patterns and determinants 144–156; postponement 93; sex structure of 90; transition process of 2

fertility behaviors 58, 93, 111; influencing factors of 144–145; macro perspective 145; structure of 98

fertility level: quantum effect 295–296; tempo effect 295–296

fertility patterns 2, 98, 142–144; for first births 94; long-lasting impact 127

fertility policy 1, 59, 80, 111, 275, 307; adjustment of 57, 60, 159; advocacy-based fertility policy

129; birth numbers 163; low fertility pattern 5; marriage and childbearing patterns 58; population development strategy 22; and population inertia 59; and pro-natalist social policies 275; second-child fertility 143; social environment 37; two-child policy acts 145; and zodiac preferences 72; *see also* two-child policy

fertility rates 2, 24, 34–37, 71, 78, 93, 127, 128, 193, 198, **213**; age pattern of 88; changes in 111; parity structure of 87; for second births 98; in Stage IV 98

fertility transition 1, 2, 3, 14, 86; evolution characteristics of 3; family planning policy 127; first fertility transition 13–14; fluctuation in 14–15; high fertility regime 9–13; persistent low fertility 17–18; process of 19; replacement level zone 15; second fertility transition 15–17; structural details on 98; with tempo effect 107; three stages of 98

fertility trends, 2006 to 2017: cohort fertility rates 65–66; intrinsic TFR 63–65; progression-based TFR 60–63; total fertility rate 59–60

Fifth Census 23, 24, 94

Fifth Plenary Session of the 18th CPC Central Committee 123

financial incentive policies: childcare allowance 277; maternity allowance 275, 277; special families, allowance 277; tax incentives 277

first births 94; accumulation of 96; first birth rate *80,* 81; proportion of 87

first-child fertility 142, 144

first marriage rate *80,* 81, 82, 141; "tempo effect" adjustment 144; women's average age at 107

formulate and coordinate family policies 309

formulate and implement marriage promotion policies 306–307

France, work-life balance policies 286

Gauthier, Anne H. 275

gender equality 134, 139n4, 286, 308–309

generalized stable population model 46, 71

Germany: childcare services 282; paternity leave and parental leave 282; TFR

Index 315

rose 280; work-life balance policies 286
"gerontological transition" concept 207
Ge Yanxia 23
Global Gender Gap (GGG) 136, 139n4
globalization 196
global population development 9
government, "later-longer-fewer" policy 13
Great Leap Forward 11
gross reproductive rate (GRR) 46
growth rate 204, *205, 206*
Gu Hejun 160
Guo Zhigang 22, 24, 93, 94, 97

Hao Juan 22
Hatzius, Jan 275
HDI-related fertility research 127–128
heterogeneity: aging population 208–215; of elderly population 207–208
higher-age groups 38
higher birth rate 17
high fertility regime 10
high fertility scenario **188**
household income 156
household utility 149–150
Hukou system 23, 24, 25, 26, 27, *30*, 38, 52–53, 76
human capital 178, 184
human capital forecast 183–185
human capital index 184, *184*
human development index (HDI) 2, 127–128; components of **129**; definition 128; HDI scores 130; "inverse J-shaped" pattern 130; measurement method for 131; 2010–2018 model for 131; quadratic functions of 128; regression models **132**
Human Development Reports (UNDP) 127, 129
Human Fertility Database 87
hypothetical cohort 39

implicit pro-natalist policies 286
India, fertility transition 112
indirect estimation methods 43, 57, 142
individual age groups 23
individual women 142
industrialization 274
institutional density: obstetric medical service demand 222–223, **223**
Integrated System for Demographic Estimation 44

inter-birth interval 93
intermediate fertility variables: abortion index 113; contraception index 111, 113; contraceptive prevalence 114; data and methodology 116–122; far-famed model of 111; fecundity adjustment factor 113; fertility estimates 116; 2017 Fertility Survey 111; marriage index 113; postpartum infecundability index 113; proportion married 111; results and analysis 122–124; unmarried women, childbearing age 113
international classification standard 170
"intra-system" data 38
intrinsic fertility rate 58, 59
intrinsic TFRs 63–65; for second births *65*; for third-plus births *65*
intrinsic total fertility rate (ITFR) 93, 94
"inverted J-shaped" pattern 128, 130
irreversible aging population: China's irreversible aging population 197–201; demographic transition 193–196; universal population aging 196–197

Japan 87; childcare services 282; encourage childbirth 135; fertility transition in 15; labor participation rate 181; tax policy and social security policy 286; work-life balance policies 286
Jinying Wang 160
job-protected leave 278; *see also* maternity leave; paternity leave
junior high school-age population 234, 266
junior high school education: enrollment seats 266, **266, 267**; fiscal investment 268–270, **270**; teacher-child ratio 266–268, **268, 269**

Kahn Alfred 282
Kindergarten Work Regulations 304
Kippen, R. 58, 93
Krishna, M. P. 112

labor force 168; adult citizens 285; human capital 190; labor-intensive industries 168; negative impact 191; structure and quality of 5, 185, 301; two-child policy on 7, 191; working-age population *193*
labor force forecast 180–181
labor force participation rate 7, 178

labor force participation rate forecast 181–183
labor participation decomposition 186
labor participation rate 181
labor supply 7; concept definition 177–178; data 179–180; effective labor supply 185–186; human capital forecast 183–185; influences decomposition 186–189; labor force forecast 180–181; labor force participation rate forecast 181–183; older population group **182**; research methods 178–179; sustainable economic development 177; younger age group **181**
large-scale nationwide family planning 13
"later-longer-fewer" policy 13, 14
Law on Population and Family Planning 17
leave-related childcare policies 277–278
legal adult population 177
Leibenstein, H. 6, 275, 283
Leibenstein's cost-utility theory 275
Leitner, Sigrid 282
lifetime fertility rate 39, 58, 65, 93
Li Ling 240
linear regression fitting method 32, 47
Li Qing 160
logit transformation 45
low-and middle-income countries 208
low birth rate 16
low death rate 16
lower-age groups 38
lower-age populations 25, 32, 35, 37, 39, 70
low fertility: definition of 139n3; evolution characteristics 2; levels 144; process 2; rates 22; tend 146
low-fertility countries 2
low fertility trap theory 2, 22, 127, 139n1, 292
low growth rate 16
Lv Wu 240

macropopulation simulation method 192
Ma Jiantang 35
male populations, in period 2000–2010 **49**
marital fertility 9
marriage index 112, 113, 119, 123, 124, 125; birth control 13; China's fertility policy 58; equations and variables **117, 118**; marriage patterns 9, 72; marriage postponement 107; postponement of 97; tempo effects of 14

Marriage Law 15, 95–96, 107
married women, average fertility of 9–10
maternal and child health services: births size and structure 218–220, *219, 220*; data and methods 218; obstetric and gynecological medical resources 221–229, **223, 225, 227, 228, 229, 230**
maternity allowance 275, 277; Russia's financial generosity 277; tax-free allowance 277
maternity leave policies 278; maternity leave 278; OECD countries 282; paid and unpaid leave 281; parental leave 278; paternity leave 278
Ma Yingtong 58
McDonald, P. 58, 93
Medium- and Long-term Education Reform and Development (2010–2020) 235, 257
medium fertility rate 186, **187**
meso-level (family) factors 156
microeconomic theory 144–145
migrant population 21, 161
Ministry of Public Security 58, 69, 83, 142
mortality parameters 76, 160
mortality rate 193, 194, *209*
mortality/survival probabilities 45
mother–children match 24
mother's information 24

National Bureau of Statistics (NBS) 16, 17, 22, 30–31, 32, 33, 35, 37, 39, 48, 52, 66, 69, 70, 72, 80, 83, 141, 177; annual population surveys 141; census data 38; estimated fertility rates **50**; national newborn population 141; sample survey data 38
national economy 13
national educational system 237
national fertility rate 58, 141
national fertility survey 57, 141
National Health and Family Planning Commission of China 57, 69, 70, 116, 141, 293
national newborn population 141
National One-per Thousand Sample Survey on Population Changes 94
National People's Congress 14
National Population and Family Planning Commission 16, 17, 38
National Population Development Planning 2, 19

National Population Development
    Strategy 19
National Program for Medium- and
    Long-term Education Reform and
    Development (2010–2020) 235,
    239
National Two-per Thousand Fertility
    Survey 94
nationwide family planning 13
natural population growth rate 10, *11,* 16,
    17, 127
net reproduction rate *(NRR)* 46, 48, 49, **51**
1988 Fertility Survey 94
1992 Fertility Survey 21
Ninth National People's Congress 17
non-demographic factors 177, 179, 186
non-demographic influence 188
non-manual female workers 148
non-manual occupations 155
nurse density: obstetric medical service
    demand 224, **225**; pediatric medical
    service demand 226–229, **227, 228,
    229, 230**

obstetric medical resources: bed density
    222; doctor density 222; evaluation
    221–222; institutional density
    221–222; medical service demand
    222–224, **223, 225**; nurse density
    222; supply and demand 222
obstetric medical service demand 222–
    224, **223, 225**; maternity beds
    224, **225**; obstetricians and nurses
    224, **225**; obstetric institutions
    222–223, **223**
old-age dependency ratio (ODR) 171, 174
older-age populations 38, 40
2008 Olympic Games 142
one-and-a-half-child policy 15
one-child policy 1, 14, 15, 67, 144;
    consequence of 97; implementation
    of 161
one-per-thousand fertility survey 10

Pang Lijuan 240
parental leave 278
parity-age-duration total fertility rate 93
Parity Progression-based Fertility Rate 58
parity progression ratio 59
parity-specific fertility rates 59, **60,** 86;
    changes in overall fertility rate 108;
    from 1964 to 2017 *87*
parity-specific intrinsic TFR: in period
    2007–2016 **64**

parity-specific progression-based TFR: in
    period 2006–2017 **61**
parity-specific TFRs: in period 2006–2017
    60
paternity leave 278, 281
pay packages: teaching and administrative
    staff 262, 267, 273n25, 273n28
pediatric medical service: evaluation 224;
    medical service demand 226–229,
    227, 228, 229, 230; supply and
    demand 224–225
pediatric medical service demand: facilities
    and bed 226, **227**; pediatricians
    and nurses 226–229, **227, 228, 229,
    230**
period fertility rate 39; intrinsic TFR
    63–65; P/F ratio 39; progression-
    based TFR 60–63; total fertility rate
    59–60
P/F ratio method 39, 40, **42,** 42–43,
    53–54, 293
policy implications: community-based
    and society-supplemented public
    childcare system 307–308; family
    supporting policy system 308;
    fertility policy 307; formulate and
    implement marriage promotion
    policies 306–307; multiple
    functional departments 309;
    promotes gender equality 308–309;
    work-family balance 308
political movement 13
population 1; age distribution of 49; at ages
    0–10 **28**; censuses 3, 22, 23, 69, 70,
    142; changes 23; child 299; control
    11; development strategies 17, 18;
    elderly 299; estimation method 24,
    43; forecasting methods 24; growth
    rate of 24, 44; inertia 57, 59; long-
    term balanced development 18;
    policy 11; problem 18; quality 17;
    reproduction 10, 16, 17, 18; sample
    surveys 16, 159; socio-economic
    impact 300; transition 193;
    working-age 299
population projections, parameters for:
    fertility parameters 160; migration
    161; mortality parameters 160;
    sex ratio at birth 161; starting
    population 159–160
population pyramid 193, 198
Population Reference Bureau 3, 17
post-demographic transition phase 193
post-enumeration survey 57

postpartum infecundability index 111, 112, 113, 115–116, 120; age structure 116; calculation of 120; cultural environment 116; equations and variables **117, 118**; postpartum breastfeeding duration 116
potential support ratios 201
pregnancy 58, 59, 60–63, 70, 119
preschool-age population 234, 238, **238**, 239
preschool education: Beijing's Three-year Action Plan (2011–2013) 241; enrollment seats 239–244, **240, 242, 243**; financial investment 257–261, **259, 260**; institutions 244–245, **245, 246, 247, 248**; national educational system 237; Scheme I 244, **245**; Scheme II 244, **246**; Scheme III 244, **247**; Scheme V 244, **248**; teacher–child ratio 246–257, **249, 251, 252, 253, 254, 255, 256**; three-year action plan 273n9
Preston, S. H. 43, 44
primary school-age population 234, 261, **262**
primary school education: autumn enrollment 233; enrollment seats 261, **262**; fiscal expenditure 263–266, **265**; teacher–child ratio 261–263, **263, 264**
primary school students 17, 38
probability theory 58
progression-based TFRs: for first births *62*; for second births *63, 65*; for third-plus births *63, 65*
pro-natalist family policies: childcare service policies 278–279; conservative regime 280; cross-country comparisons 280; employment prospects and financial independence 287; European and American countries 279; explicit policies **281,** *282,* 282–286, **283**; Fertility Policies Worldwide (1976–2015) 275, **276**; financial incentive policies 275, 277; fiscal support for **281**, 281–282; full-fledged system 275; implicit policies 286; maternity leave policies 277–278; other policies 279; paid and unpaid leave 281; proactive intervention 287; reproductive activities 287;

social democratic regimes 280; Southern European countries 279; United Kingdom and the United States 279
public childcare system 307–308
public education system 235

Qiu Changrong 22
quantity effect 7
quantum effect 107; China's fertility transition *106*; fertility behaviors 98–105; of fertility change 106; fertility transition 106–107; low fertility *106*; period fertility rate 94–98, 106

Rallu, J. L. 58, 93
rapid population growth 11
replacement level 17, 21
"Report on Properly Carrying out the Work of Family Planning" 129
reproductive behavior 113
reproductive health industry 17
"reverse J-shaped" pattern 130
rural areas: economic reforms 107; Marriage Law 107

sample surveys 22, 23, 70, 78
school-age population: admission 233; autumn enrollment 233; compulsory education 234; junior high school-age population 234, 266; preschool-age population 234, 238, **238**, 239; primary school-age population 234, 261, **262**; regulations and systems, China 234; universal two-child policy 234
Scientific Outlook on Development 18
second births 94, 95; age-specific patterns of 98, *99–100*; contributes 74–75; fertility rate for 86, 98, 105; interval-specific patterns of 98, *99–101*; ITFR–TFR difference for 98; postponement of 95, 97; proportion of 86; women, average age 96
second-child fertility: age in China, 2006–2017 *146*; educational level in China *148*; factors affecting 151–156, **152–153**; fertility accumulation 143; heavy financial burdens 150; influencing factors of 142; lowest educational level 147; low fertility 143; meso-level

(family) factors 156; non-manual occupation 147; patterns and determinants 144–145; "tempo effect" adjustment 144; two-child policy 150; in urban and rural areas 146, *147*; women socio-demographic profile 145–151
second-child fertility rates 144; income in China, 2006–2017 *149*
second family planning program 11
second fertility transition 16, 86
Sedgh, G. 115
Seifadin, A. S. 112
17th CPC National Congress 17
sex ratio at birth 90–91, 161
sex structure, lower age group 16
sexual intercourse 113
Sheila, Kamerman 282
Shi Wenxiu 240
shooting method 22, 24
Singapore 78; encourage childbirth 135; fertility transition in 15
16th Five-Year Plan 240
Sixth National Census 23, 24, 38, 69, 90, 160, 181, 198
social and economic effects, two-child policy: maternal and child health services 302–303; school-age population 303–306; teacher-child ratio 303–306
social environment 145
socialism 18
socialist market economy 16
social security system 192
social system 14
social transformation 14
socioeconomic development 21, 57, 58, 59, 127
socioeconomic factors 111
South Korea: encourage childbirth 135; fertility transition in 15
special families allowance 277
stable population age structure equation 44
stable population model 192
stable population theory 43
Stage I (1970–1979), China's fertility 94–95
Stage II (1980–1989), China's fertility 94
Stage III (1990–2003), China's fertility 94, 97
Stage IV (from 2004 onwards), China's fertility 94
"standard" life table 47

Starting Well: Benchmarking Early Education Across the World 253
State Council 17, 18; Decision on Strengthening Family Planning Program 15; nationwide family planning 13; one-child policy 14; Strictly Controlling Population Growth 15
State Family Planning Commission 17
Strictly Controlling Population Growth 15
structural shifts in fertility rate: age at marriage/childbirth 89–90; age pattern of fertility 87–88; birth interval 89–90; fertility, parity structure of 86–87; sex ratio at birth 90–91
Sun Mingzhe 160
supply and demand: obstetric and gynecological medical services 222; pediatric medical service 224–225
survival-based estimation 25
survival probability functions 45
sustainable development 163
sustainable economic development 177
Sweden: generous fertility policies 283; liberal leave policy 282; Parental Leave Act 278; TFR rose 280; work-life balance policies 286
Symposium on Population and Family Planning 15

Taiwan Province of China 87
Tao Tao 128
tax incentives 277
teacher-child ratio: social and economic effects 303–306
teacher-student ratio: child-care services **236**, 237; junior high school education 266–268, **268, 269**; preschool education 246–257, **249, 251, 252, 253, 254, 255, 256**; primary school education 261–263, **263, 264**
teaching and administrative staff: pay packages 262, 267, 273n25, 273n28; standards and ratio 249, 250
tempo-adjusted TFR (TFR') indicator 58, 61, 93
tempo effect of fertility 7, 62; China's fertility transition *106*; fertility behaviors 98–105; fertility decline

107; fertility transition 106–107; low fertility levels *106,* 144; parity progression fertility model 144; period fertility rate 94–98; ultra-low fertility 93
temporal disturbances 98
third births 94
Third Plenary Session of the 18th CPC Central Committee 122
"Three Combinations" 16
"Three Priorities" 16
three-stage PPS sampling method 116
13th Five-Year Plan 239, 241
Tianjin's Medium- and long-term Education Reform and Development Plan (2010–2020) 241
time gap 193
"torturous, heroic and glorious" moments 127
total child population 165
total dependency ratio (TDR) 171, 174
total fecundity rate 122
total fertility rates (TFRs) 1, 9, *12,* 21, **36**, *37,* 58, 69, 86, 93, 112, 194, 280, 292–293; assumptions of 160; China's low fertility evolution 292–293; denmark and sweden 280; drawbacks of 58; fertility trends, 2006 to 2017 59–60; for first births 72–74, *74*; Germany and France 280; "inverse J-shaped" pattern 128, 130; Japan 281; as lifetime fertility rate 58; net reproductive rate 48; in period 1982–1990 50; in period 1990–2000 49; in period 2000–2010 48–49; population censuses 69; quadratic functions of 128; sample surveys 69; for second and multiple births 74–77, *75, 76*; South Korea and Japan 280; "tempo effect" on 63; from 2000 to 2017 *71*; variable-r method 50
Toulemon, L. 58, 93
2000–2010 estimated fertility rates: age-specific fertility rates **36**; 2000 and 2010 census data, regression analysis *29*; births 31–32; birth to each age, survival ratios from *31*; data and methodology 25; education data, regression analysis *30*; fertility rate 34–37;

hukou data and 2000 census data *30*; population at ages 0–10 **28**; populations, estimation of 26; survival ratios *29*; total fertility rates **36**, *37*; women of childbearing age 32–34
true cohort fertility 58
two-child policy 2, 18, 19, 60, 66, 81–82, 86, 98, 107, 146; age-specific second-child fertility rates 145; China's transition to 141; cohort component method 302; demographic effects 298–302; economic effects of 1; fertility patterns 142–144; implementation effect of 3; implementation of 150, 159, 231–232; inconsistent effects of 79; inter-censual fertility rate 293; national fertility rate 141; policy implications 306–309; population-resources density method 230; preschool-age population 234, 238, **238,** 239; recent trends 142–144; roll-out of 22, 88, 92; second-child fertility 141, 144–156; social and economic effects 302–306; socio-demographic differentials 141; women's fertility behavior 144; *see also* demographic trends
"two exemptions and one subsidy" policy 24
2000 Census 16, 22, 25, 26; age distribution data 46; aged 10–20 years 28; 0–10 age groups 26; age–sex distribution data 46; childbearing, postponement of 97; Leslie matrix 23; lower age group 16, 54
2010 estimated fertility rates: China's TFR, estimation of 40–43; data and methodology 38–40
2017 Fertility Survey 7, 8, 57, 59, 65, 66, 69–70, 71, 72, 73, 76, 77, 81, 83, 94, 123, 145; abortion index 123; average age at first marriage 74; fertility rate for first births 73; fertility rates for second births 74; intermediate fertility variables 111; intermediate variables effects 116; marriage index 119; two-child policy 79; women's average age at first marriage 89

Index 321

2010 Census 71; aged 1–4 years 32; aged 10–20 years 35; lower-age populations 32, 35; 1- to 4-year-old populations 37; women of childbearing age 32
2015 mini-census 71, 87, 208
2005 mini-census 40

U graph-shape 115
ultra-low fertility risk 80–82, 93
UN Development Programme 127
UNESCO's Sustainable Development Goals database 240
United Nations 9, 200, 204, 207, 211
United Nations population data 2
United Nations Population Division 3, 192
United Nations World Population Prospects 2019 209
universal two-child policy 1, 2, 69, 79, 80, 81, 98, 123, 142, 180, 187; implementation of 188
unmarried women, childbearing age 113
urban and rural TFRs in 2016 **124**
urban areas: family planning in 11; fertility, impact on 13; nationwide family planning 13
urbanization 19, 67, 72, 193, 274

variable-r method 43, 44, 46, 49, 50, 52
voluntariness of married couples 129

Wang Honglei 240
Wang Jinying 23
wavy development of aging: elderly population and aging 203–204; fertility transition process 202
Westoff, C. 115
women: age at first childbirth 77, *78*; age at first marriage 77, *78*; agespecific proportions of 115; age-specific survival ratios of 34, **34**; average age at first childbirth 60, *61*, 89; average age at first marriage 60, *61*, 72–74, *73*, 89; average age, second birth 96; childbearing age 88; of childbearing age 23, 25, 32–34,
98; fertility control 13; fertility history of 70; fertility, probabilities for 104; lifetime fertility rate 65; pregnancy history 58, 70; prime reproductive years 96; sociodemographic characteristics of 151; younger age groups 40
women of childbearing age: age-specific number of 48; parity structure in 58–59
work-family balance: policy implications 308
working-age population 165–168, 175, 177, 180, 181, 191, 197, 198
work-life balance policies: France 286; Germany 286; Japan 286; Sweden 286
World Breastfeeding Trends Initiative (WBTi) 120, 125n1
World Development Indicators (World Bank, 2020) 129
World Economic Cooperation and Development (OECD) 235
world model, counterfactual fertility trends 128, 132
world population datasets 3
World Population Data Tables 17

Yang Fan 23
Yang Ge 160
Yang Juhua 283
Yang Shunguang 240
Yanxia Ge 160
younger age groups 23, 40
younger marriage 15
Yuan Xin 24
Yu, J. 58

Zhai Zhenwu 54
Zhang Guangyu 24
Zhao Menghan 23, 49
Zhao Mengzheng 52
Zhou Changhong 128
Zhu Qin 22
zodiac preferences 77, 78, 79, 80, 107, 122